WHEN RABBIS
BLESS
CONGRESS

The Great American Story of Jewish Prayers on Capitol Hill

Cherry
Orchard
Books

WHEN RABBIS
BLESS
CONGRESS

The Great American Story of Jewish Prayers
on Capitol Hill

BY HOWARD MORTMAN

BOSTON
2020

On the cover:

Top row, left to right: Bruce Lustig, Mara Nathan, Gary Zola, Laszlo Berkowitz

Second row, left to right: Arnold Resnicoff, Abraham De Sola, Harold Robinson, Levi Shemtov

Third row, left to right: Gil Steinlauf, Ellen Wolintz-Fields, Steven Rein, Amy Rader

Bottom row, left to right: Mark Getman, Hannah Spiro, Gershon Avtzon, Romi Cohn

Library of Congress Cataloging-in-Publication Data

Names: Mortman, Howard, 1967- author.
Title: When rabbis bless Congress : the great American story of Jewish
    prayers on Capitol Hill / Howard Mortman.
Description: Boston : Cherry Orchard Books, October 2020.
Identifiers: LCCN 2020019048 (print) | LCCN 2020019049 (ebook) | ISBN
    9781644693438 (hardback) | ISBN 9781644693445 (paperback) | ISBN
    9781644693452 (adobe pdf)
Subjects: LCSH: Legislative bodies--Chaplains' prayers. | United States.
    Congress--Chaplains. | Rabbis--United States. | Jews--United
    States--Politics and government. | Capitol Hill (Washington,
    D.C.)--Religious life and customs. | United States--Ethnic relations.
Classification: LCC BV280 .M77 2020 + (print) | LCC BV280 (ebook) | DDC
    296.4/509753--dc23
LC record available at https://lccn.loc.gov/2020019048
LC ebook record available at https://lccn.loc.gov/2020019049

ISBN 9781644693438 (hardback); ISBN 9781644693445 (paperback);
ISBN 9781644693452 (adobe pdf); ISBN 9781644693469 (ePub)

Book design by Lapiz Digital Services. Cover design by Kate Connolly.

Published by Cherry Orchard Books, an imprint of Academic Studies Press
1577 Beacon Street
Brookline, MA 02446, USA
press@academicstudiespress.com | www.academicstudiespress.com

Contents

Acknowledgements

Special thanks to the following benefactors, whose generous support helped make the publication of this book possible:

—A. Mark Neuman

Mentor, teacher and friend of my family dating back 35 years. Mark had the honor of signing my ketubah (Jewish marriage contract) as a witness at my wedding in May 2001. No person has been a more valued career and life adviser to me over the past four decades.

—The Soll Family Foundation

Bruce and Joy Soll have known me throughout my adult life. Bruce was one of my bosses in my first job. I am grateful for their friendship over many, many years.

—Washington Hebrew Congregation

Washington Hebrew is the oldest and largest Jewish congregation in the nation's capital, founded in 1852. Chartered by an act of Congress in 1856, Washington Hebrew is proud of the fact that every senior rabbi of the congregation has delivered an opening prayer before a session of congress since the first rabbi guest chaplain in 1860. As Washington Hebrew's current senior rabbi Bruce Lustig reminds his congregation, "we can't know where we are going unless we know from whence we came."

Deep gratitude for the cover art to Kate Connolly of Kate Connolly Studio. Her creativity and artistic interpretation of history brings this book's vision to life.

An immeasurable number of thank you's to the many, many friends who fortified me with spiritual guidance and practical advice throughout this book's journey. Great appreciation to my publisher for embracing the project from the beginning. And dedicated to my beautiful family and my brother and in honor of my parents, may their memories be a blessing.

"Wherever My name is called upon in prayer there will I come and bless thee."
—Rabbi Abram Simon of Washington Hebrew Congregation, citing Exodus 20:24, House of Representatives opening prayer, February 10, 1910

"As I touched the Wailing Wall which is a living symbol of Jerusalem, so I touch this lectern as a symbol of the power with which Thou hast endowed this body."
—Rabbi Mordechai Elefant, Israel Torah Research Institute, House of Representatives opening prayer, December 12, 1974

"Prayer points in two directions. It is a reaching outward and a searching inward at one and the same time. It is a questing and a questioning."
—Rabbi Melvin Goldstine, Temple Aliyah, Woodland Hills, California, House of Representatives opening prayer, October 24, 1979

"The walls of this very Senate hall in which we invoke Your blessing is engraved in bold letters 'In God We Trust.'"
—Rabbi Moshe Feller, Upper Midwest Merkos-Lubavitch House, St. Paul, Minnesota, Senate opening prayer, June 11, 2013

"When the Chaplain offers prayer at each day's opening of this House he invokes upon its Members the benedictions of a Hebrew God and the intercessions of a Hebrew Savior."
—Rep. Walter Chandler (R-NY), June 3, 1922

"The Congressional Record is filled with prayers offered by Jewish rabbis."
—Sen. Marco Rubio (R-FL), amicus brief to the U.S. Supreme Court, July 9, 2013

Introduction

Need more prayer in your life?

Simple solution: Just turn on your television and watch Congress.

The unlikely congregation is the backdrop for a taxpayer-funded ritual dating back to our country's creation. Every session of both legislative bodies—the U.S. House of Representatives and the U.S. Senate—opens with a prayer. The Divine gets his due even before the flag gets a pledge.

This tradition might bother some. You may not like the idea of Congress incorporating religion into its official proceedings. You may not want the *Congressional Record* reading like a prayer book. You may seek policy debate on your TV or internet stream and instead get two minutes of unsolicited religious teachings. Or perhaps you think it's all fine, nothing wrong, no problem with prayer in a public forum. Of all the things Congress does day in and day out, praying to the Almighty ranks among the least offensive. Either way, the fact is: Prayer happens. It's part of Congress, its past, present, and likely future. Just like floor debates and votes. And it's a tradition upheld by the Supreme Court which, despite Moses the prophet's prominence outside on its building—depicted on top, in front, in center on the East Pediment—inside does not open in prayer.

From the Founding Fathers to contemporary times, Congress prayers have fans in high places. Consider what Richard Nixon wrote during the Eisenhower days when he was vice president and president of the Senate: "In the usual order of business of the United States Senate," Nixon wrote in a 1957 collection of prayers offered by the U.S. Senate chaplain, "the invocation is often the best speech of the day. As a matter of fact, in the prayers of the Chaplain, rather than in the hectic day-to-day clashes of debate, we can see the greatness of America, because in the invocations the faith is expressed which brings us all together, whereas the debates often tear us apart."

The greatness of America, Nixon said. Congress' embrace of religion from the beginning might strike some as ironic, perhaps counterintuitive, given a long history of scandal and sin. Sen. John McCain (R-AZ) once jokingly called Washington, DC "a city of Satan." He said it during a Senate session opened by chaplain Barry Black praying to "Almighty God, the prince of peace." Indeed, amid its controversies, Congress carves out a prominent place for the Lord.

On January 13, 2012, the *New York Times* religion columnist profiled the House and Senate chaplains. "At a time when Congress is stunningly unpopular, with approval ratings in various recent polls around 12 percent," Samuel Freedman wrote, "Father [Patrick] Conroy and Dr. Black serve as pastors to what must be one of the most reviled congregations in the country" (page A19).

If Congress is "one of the most reviled congregations," what's worse? For what it's worth, House chaplain Conroy also served as a chaplain in San Quentin State Prison.

Nearly every prayer invokes God. Many are in Jesus' name. And some are Jewish.

Hundreds, actually. As of February 2020, 441 rabbis from over 400 synagogues have opened Congress—increasing at an average rate of 7.5 Jewish prayers per year since World War II (9 in 2018 and 11 in 2019). Jews make up 2.2 percent of the American population, according to an October 1, 2013 *New York Times* report (page A11). It's a higher percentage for rabbis praying in Congress. Of the 527 guest chaplains appearing in the House of Representatives during the ten-year period from September 2006 through September 2016, 35 were rabbis. Six percent. In 2019, the House of Representatives met in session 170 days. Guest chaplains opened those sessions in prayer 83 times. Eleven were rabbis. Thirteen percent.

The participation of rabbis in the tradition of delivering congressional prayers reached a symbolic milestone in the spring of 2018. That's when the total number of rabbi prayers reached 613. It's the same number as commandments—*mitzvot*—in the Torah, according to the Talmud. It's a number that's significant for understanding why Jews are called the chosen people, as Rep. Ed Koch (D-NY) told his House colleagues on September 27, 1971. "It means," intoned the future New York City mayor, "that we have taken on greater obligations than are required of others in pursuing the adoration of God. To Jews this means that a non-Jew who fulfills the seven laws of Noah will find his place in heaven while Jews are required to carry out the 613 commandments."

And from those first 613 rabbi prayers and subsequent ones emerges a narrative of both America's Congress and America's Jews. American political history meets the legacy of the Jew in America to form one American narrative.

This is the story of rabbis who have led Congress in prayer. Who they are and what they say. Their connection to America's politics and policy and history.

This is no argument for or against Congress having prayers, nor the larger, timeless and often acrimonious church-state debate. There are ample loud advocates in both camps. Instead, it's a straight-forward study of a tradition cemented in Congressional history, of which there are abundant stories needing to be told. For Jews, it's a narrower yet no less profound discussion. Rabbis themselves hardly ever raise church-state considerations in their prayers. One rare exception occurred during the beginning of the twentieth century. With seemingly unintended irony, a rabbi praying in the House of Representatives begged the Lord to give government leaders "the spirit of wisdom" to keep "church and state in their fortunate separation." If that wisdom were followed, the next several hundred rabbi prayers might not have been heard. Once, after a rabbi was guest chaplain, Sen. Robert Byrd (D-WV), said, "Prayer and reflection upon the great old teachings of the Scriptures can give us the strength, the resourcefulness, the courage and the vision to see our way. I thank the Rabbi."

Polls show Americans are moving away from believing in God—and just a third of American Jews say they believe in God as described in the Bible. But Congress remains steadfast in its daily embrace of the Lord. Congress showcases prayers from a diversity of voices coming from a range of backgrounds and experiences in a public setting. And that, as the saying goes, is good for the Jews.

To be sure, the directive to pray daily was not issued first by the U.S. Congress. Maimonides got there earlier. The revered twelfth-century Spanish Jewish philosopher cited Torah (Exodus 23:25) in asserting, according to Rabbi Avi Weiss around 800 years later, "It is an affirmative commandment to pray every day as it says, 'and you shall serve the Lord your God.'" You can see Maimonides now inside the U.S. House of Representatives, where his image is among nearly two dozen marble relief portraits over the chamber's gallery door.

Christians have been praying in Congress since the Revolutionary War ended. Jews, since right before the Civil War began. And along the way, some great history, lofty inspiration, notable quirks, plus idiosyncrasies and even cringeworthy moments, language, and personalities, which might have seemed correct at the time but hold up poorly against today's standards. Few of the prayers are dry. There's character and narrative behind most of the rabbis. Although not a traditional academic study, with well over 613 data points to draw upon (prayer primary sourcing via the Congressional Record, the C-SPAN Video Library, and newspaper reports), this unprecedented examination hopefully will aid—even inspire—scholarly research as much as raise general awareness. Among the highlights:

- Of the first rabbi guest chaplain, in 1860, a member of Congress said: "I was pleased with his appearance. I should like to see our Chaplain officiate in costume." The *New York Times* noted the "learned Rabbi, who appears in full canonicals."
- That first rabbi made history only because the first choice didn't speak English.
- Nearly a third of the rabbis are, as you might expect, New Yorkers. But they've also represented many states without many Jews. Like Alaska.
- The first female rabbi—Sally Priesand—didn't make an appearance in Congress until over 100 years after the first male rabbi. The *Congressional Record* got her name wrong. Despite coming from a New York City synagogue and being sponsored by a New York City congresswoman, her glass-shattering early Seventies prayer was ignored by the *New York Times*, which reported extensively the first male rabbi prayer 113 years earlier.
- However, the 613th Jewish prayer in Congress—as mentioned, a number significant in Jewish tradition because it is the number of commandments in the Torah—was delivered by a woman rabbi.
- Rabbis reflect immigration patterns, the American story. They come from 24 countries other than America. In the early days they were part of the well-documented immigration from European countries. Now immigrant rabbis have Latin American roots. The first Latin America-born rabbi to open Congress in prayer did so a year after becoming a U.S. citizen.

- For any fear of Jews overwhelming Capitol Hill and forcing America to prop up Israel, rabbis rarely mention the Jewish state in their prayers. Six percent of Jewish prayers have made implicit or explicit mention of Israel. And those were mostly ceremonial. Virtually none advocated policy. Two rabbis gave prayers during Israel's Six-Day War—and never mentioned it. And before Israel was created in 1948, several rabbi guest chaplains were anti-Zionist.
- Six rabbis who survived Auschwitz have opened Congress in prayer—and 13 post-Holocaust guest chaplain rabbis were born in Germany. A Dachau survivor prayed in Congress while President Reagan was visiting Germany's Bitburg Cemetery, where Waffen SS troops were buried. The first prayer with a Holocaust reference was given by a guest chaplain in the midst of World War II—and he wasn't Jewish.
- A president once invited a rabbi to open the House in prayer in order to prevent war with Britain. A rabbi prayer less than a week before Pearl Harbor warned of "dark forces of tyranny and oppression" and "encircling gloom." The day before D-Day, another rabbi asked God to be "with our armed forces on land, on sea, and in the air." There was a surge of rabbis praying in Congress during the Vietnam War—a golden age for Jewish guest chaplains. The language of their prayers turned against the war just like popular American opinion.
- The record for the greatest number of prayers given by a single rabbi is held by a Navy chaplain.
- During the heart of the Cold War, a rabbi guest chaplain was identified as executive director of the American Jewish League Against Communism. Inc., He never mentioned Communism. But really no need to after citing "the whip of the oppressor" in his prayer. A news account called the rabbi's prayer "unusual." Perhaps more unusual: The rabbi's prayer was offered the same year Sen. Joseph McCarthy (R-WI) nominated him for "the high priesthood of the Ancient Trojan Order of Laocoon and His Descendants."
- Isaiah is the big winner in rabbi prayers: Over one out of every ten rabbi prayers cites him. Three rabbis didn't mention God. The American historical figure mentioned most in a rabbi prayer? George Washington. The most mentioned American Jewish historical figure? The Lubavitcher Rebbe, Menachem Mendel Schneerson.

It is also a vital time for understanding religion and national politics, where there is renewed interest in reporting how the two come together.

After the 2016 presidential election, *New York Times* executive editor Dean Baquet told National Public Radio (December 8, 2016): "I think that the New York-based—and Washington-based too, probably—media powerhouses don't quite get religion. We have a fabulous religion writer, but she's all alone. We don't get religion. We don't get the role of religion in people's lives. And I think we can do much, much better." Doing better might take a while. The *Wall Street Journal* ran this March 28, 2018, correction: "An earlier version of this article incorrectly stated Benjamin Netanyahu said Moses brought water from Iraq. He said the water was brought from a rock."

The Trump era is an appropriate time for a closer examination of prayer and government. Like the Supreme Court, there's no White House chaplain. But prayers and prayer advocacy are part of White House language.

Spokesperson Sarah Sanders was asked by a reporter on July 12, 2017, why President Trump met with his Faith Advisory Board. "The idea that somebody would only pray when they're in crisis I think makes you miss the entire point of what prayer is about. You should do that every day," Sanders said, "I think you can do that in the best of times and the worst of times."

The December 2017 day that the Republican Congress and President Trump celebrated passage of tax reform, Housing and Urban Development Secretary Ben Carson offered a Cabinet meeting a prayer "in the name of the Father, the Son, and the Holy Spirit." Secretary of State Mike Pompeo began an August 16, 2018, Cabinet meeting with a prayer.

During the coronavirus pandemic in 2020, Vice President Mike Pence held regular task force meetings in the Situation Room to coordinate the federal response. Each meeting, according to the April 12, 2020, *Washington Post*, "often begins with a prayer." President Trump himself said during a May 22, 2020, press briefing on reopening houses of worship, "In America, we need more prayer, not less."

On the other side of the aisle, when House Democratic leader Nancy Pelosi gave marathon-length, filibuster-like remarks on immigration on February 7, 2018, she brought a Bible. "I thought when I came to the floor," Pelosi said, "I would be like reading the Bible, because the Bible is so fraught with so many passages that take us to a higher place to have a conversation about human beings, all of God's children, at a higher place."

To be sure, citing Scripture can be tricky for political leaders. Consider Jimmy Carter. He continued teaching Sunday Bible class after winning the presidency. Shortly after his inauguration he offered Bible study at the First Baptist Church of Washington, less than a mile from the White House. On April 22, 1977, the *Associated Press* reported that Carter's lesson "revolved around Christ's driving the money-lenders out of the temple." Carter told his church class, according to the *AP*: "That was a turning point in Christ's life. He had directly challenged in a fatal way the existing church, and there was no possible way for the Jewish leaders to avoid the challenge. So they decided to kill Jesus."

Two-and-a half-miles from the White House, and less than a mile from the Capitol, you'll find the Museum of the Bible. It opened during Trump's first year in office. Inside is a flight simulator called "Washington Revelations." The *Washington Post* on December 20, 2017, called the simulator the museum's "potential Space Mountain hit . . . a thrill ride that revisits much of the scripture and biblical references" on Capitol Hill and Washington's top sites. References include Moses on top of the Supreme Court.

Moses is outside on the Supreme Court building, but he's inside the House chamber. Like Maimonides, Moses' marble likeness is above a gallery door. But Moses' portrait is the most prominent, looking straight down on the House speaker. Benjamin Netanyahu recognized the prophet and lawgiver during his March 3, 2015, address to a joint session of Congress. "Facing me, right up there in the gallery, overlooking all of us, in this august chamber, is the image of Moses," the Israeli Prime Minister said. During his December 11, 2018, farewell speech, Rep. Ted Poe (R-TX) pointed to "the great lawgiver Moses on the far wall looking down directly on the Speaker." (The Museum of the Bible also notes about Moses: "In 1776, Benjamin Franklin, John Adams, and Thomas Jefferson proposed a seal of the United States depicting the Israelites escaping Egypt, from the book of Exodus. From John Adam's description, 'Dr. Franklin proposes . . . Moses lifting up his Wand, and dividing the Red Sea, and Pharaoh, in his Chariot overwhelmed with the Waters.'")

No such vibe in Israel's legislative body. After Pence addressed the Knesset, Rabbi Meir Soloveichik wrote in the *Wall Street Journal* on January 23, 2018, that the Vice President "threaded his remarks with references to Scripture, a rhetorical technique Knesset audiences have rarely heard from a political leader since Menachem Begin resigned as prime minister in 1983."

So, want to hear rabbis cite Moses and Scripture and Torah and Talmud and Mishnah to legislators and the public? Don't turn to Jerusalem—the Knesset does not open with prayer (although, arguably, who in the Knesset isn't a rabbi?). Instead tune into Washington, where Israel's chief rabbis can and have served as guest chaplains in Congress, just like hundreds of others.

You'll find in the center of the nation's capital, on a hill, at the front of each chamber of Congress, a story of Jewish contribution to American democracy that's been well over a century and a half in the making but only now being told.

Part One

Who They Are

In the beginning Congress created the Chaplain.

Article I, Section 1, of the U.S. Constitution gives powers to Congress. And one of Congress' first acts was to empower a chaplain. That was two-and-a-half centuries ago. Congress saw that it was good—and the legislative branch has been praying ever since. An average of 170 prayers a year, House and Senate combined.

The prayer is routinely offered by the official chaplain or a designated guest chaplain. Congress does not dictate their denominations. Both chambers elect chaplains as individuals and not as representatives of any religious body. The first speaker of the House, though, also was a Lutheran minister.

Jews were added to the mix just before the Civil War. The first rabbi, and subsequent ones, were quite a shock to the system. To the Congress and to the media covering Congress.

Hundreds of rabbis later, the novelty of seeing one leading Congress in prayer and wearing a yarmulke has worn off. But their stories build on an important legacy.

Some guest chaplain rabbis entered Congress' chambers already with notable biographies, names deserving a place on any historical who's-who of famous American Jews. Example: In late 1910, 22 notable Jewish scholars met in New York City to write a new English translation of the Hebrew scriptures. It was the first modern attempt to translate the Bible by a body of scholars, rather than by individuals. Four of the participants in this massive undertaking had already given six prayers in Congress:

- David Philipson (Senate, Feb. 2, 1904) translated Numbers.
- Henry Mendes (Senate, April 24, 1888) handled Amos.
- Jacob Voorsanger (House, May 13, 1882; Senate, June 30, 1898) took on Obadiah and Jonah.
- Marcus Jastrow (in the House 1869 and 1871) tackled Job.

(The *New York Times Magazine* on December 11, 1910 [page 13], identified another participant, responsible for Exodus and Leviticus: "Dr. L. N. Dembitz, Louisville, Ky." Lewis Naphtali Dembitz wasn't a guest chaplain, but his nephew became a luminary in another branch of the U.S. government: Supreme Court Justice Louis Dembitz Brandeis.)

Other guest chaplain rabbis weren't that famous. But their equally compelling stories are intertwined with Jewish history, Congress, and America.

Setting the Scene: A Congress at Pray

1: The First Rabbi in Congress

"My house shall be called a house of prayer for all peoples."
—Isaiah 56:7

"The initial recognition by the House of Representatives of the equal status of Judaism, with Christianity, as an American faith."
—American historian and rabbi Bertram Korn's description of Rabbi Morris Raphall's 1860 prayer

On March 8, 1860, the U.S. House of Representatives engaged in a boisterous exercise that seems antiquated by contemporary sensibilities—and perhaps was a bit odd to audiences back then, too.

It conducted a rollicking, noisy election for House chaplain.

A sampling of the congressmen's comments, as captured and transcribed by the *Congressional Globe*, the predecessor to today's *Congressional Record*:

> Mr. Martin, of Virginia, nominated Rev. Reuben Steele, of Lee County, Virginia, as one who had devoted thirty-six years of his life to the preaching of the gospel, and who would come as near praying away the sins of the House as any clergyman.
>
> Mr. Hughes nominated Rev. Mr. Morsell, of Washington city, as an able, pious, and eloquent divine.

Mr. Branch. I put in nomination the whole clergy of the District of Columbia.

The Speaker. That nomination is too extensive. It covers too much ground.

M. Jenkins. I nominate Parson Brownlow, of Tennessee. [Laughter.]

After the laughter that day, 22 clergymen would be nominated and voted on.

One other man of the cloth got mentioned but didn't make the cut for the vote. A rabbi.

Rep. George Briggs, a Republican from New York, rose. "I wish to nominate the Jewish Rabbi who officiated here the day the speaker was elected," Briggs said. "I understand his name is Raphall. I was pleased with his appearance. I should like to see our Chaplain officiate in costume. I do not know that I shall vote for him, though."

Morris Raphall. The rabbi with the pleasing appearance. Recognized for his rabbinical costume then but known now for a more significant achievement. Born in Sweden, he was the first rabbi to deliver a prayer in Congress, a month earlier, February 1, 1860. James Buchanan was president. Thirteen years before the *Congressional Record* began publishing.

"The proceedings were opened with prayer by Rabbi RAPHALL," reported the *New York Times* on its February 2, 1860, front page "It abounded with fervently expressed patriotic and religious sentiment. He implored Divine blessing to direct the House in the election of a Speaker who may preside without favor and fear, and that the members might speak and act for the glory and happiness of their common country. The prayer was listened to with marked attention."

"For the first time in all the years since sessions of Congress had been opened with prayer by a clergyman, a rabbi performed that religious office," wrote historian Bertram Korn in *Rabbis, Prayers, and Legislatures: The First Jewish Prayer in Congress.*[1] "In more than a theoretical sense, therefore this was the initial recognition by the House of Representatives of the equal status of Judaism, with Christianity, as an American faith. Presidents and other public officials had long since issued statements and written letters which took cognizance of the existence of Judaism, but except for an implied, unspecified inclusion of Judaism in the general category of a religion, as

---

1   Hebrew Union College, 1950.

for instance in the Bill of Rights, Congress had never heretofore given its official sanction to the faith of Israel."

Raphall was the lead story in February 9, 1860, *Alexandria Gazette*. Front page, top left headline: "Prayer by a Hebrew Rabbi." The newspaper ran the full prayer and called it "an eloquent and appropriate invocation."

Other observers offered descriptions of a different sort.

Writing on February 17, 2010, in the Jewish publication *The Forward*, Brandeis University Professor Jonathan Sarna reported this reaction to Raphall's prayer: "The Churchman, unofficial organ of the Episcopal Church, responded 'with extreme sorrow, and almost disgust' to the rabbi's prayer. It described his appearance in Congress as 'no less than the official rejection of Christianity by the Legislature of the country.'"

A reporter for the Philadelphia *Press* sounded a "sarcastic note," according to Korn: "beautiful as the prayer was, he said, it was long enough to be a sermon!"

Another *New York Times* account (February 4, 1860, page 1) noted:

> The Christian religion having failed to produce an organization, resort is now had to a learned Rabbi, who appears in full canonicals, and delivers a very excellent prayer. . . . Some think that the Rabbi has been produced by Secretary COBB to insure favorable discount for certain Treasury Notes, while others give the affair apolitical signification, and suspect that Mr. LEVY, of this city, is laying pipes for a ticket to consist of Senators BENJAMIN and YULEE, as the President and Vice of a Southern Jerusalem. At any rate the Rabbi makes an excellent prayer—the crumbling despotisms of Asia figuring largely in the foreground of his invocation."

"One can well understand why every political wit felt he had to add his pun or wise-crack," Korn wrote. "Never before had this phenomenon occurred." Korn, a rabbi who was the first guest Senate chaplain to speak Hebrew during his own opening prayer (July 15, 1955), recounted comments a New York *Herald* reporter heard in the House gallery:

- "The old chap in his regalia. Beautiful white embroidered scarf over his shoulders. Velvet cap on his head. . . ."
- "Going to pray for ten per cent. A month. . . ."
- "A Jew praying for the American House of Representatives! The next thing we shall have will be Shaking Quaker dancing a reel. . . ."

- "Yes, or Brigham Young, surrounded by his harem, threatening to send the administration to hell. . . ."
- "Or a pawn shop in the basement. . . ."
- "But he is a Jew. . . ."
- "Yes, the real genuine original Jacobs—the high priest of the tribe of Levi in New York. . . ."
- "Well, after that I am ready for a black [radical] republican speaker."

(Jews looking like Jews seemed to fascinate certain nineteenth-century congressmen. Here's Rep. Martin Townsend, a Republican from New York, on January 28, 1879: "The Jewish people all through the ages dressed differently from their Christian neighbors. They had a different face. They lived by themselves and had a different faith. Some of their race centuries before had participated in the crucifixion of the Saviour of mankind." Lucky for the Jews, they actually got off easy compared to what Townsend suggested next: "It is said these Chinese are wicked; yes, they are wicked. I have no doubt they are wicked." To be fair, Townsend had company in the 1870s. Rep. John White [R-KY] on March 24, 1876: "It reminds me very much of a Jew merchant that I once heard of." And Rep. James Garfield on December 15, 1873: "Whatever Jews and others may think, we all desire to have a Government that has a good credit." Seven years later, Garfield was elected President.)

Turns out February 1, 1860, was also the date that the House elected the first Republican Speaker of the House. William Pennington of New Jersey was chosen on the 44th ballot. It was "a remarkable coincidence," noted Korn.

Raphall noted the Speaker election in his prayer:

Supreme Ruler of the Universe, many days and many weeks have gone by since Thy servants, our Representatives, first met in this Congress; but not yet have they been able to organize their House. Thou who makest peace In Thy high heavens, direct their minds this day that they may. With one consent, choose the man who, without fear and without favor is to preside over their assembly. To this intent endow them. Father most gracious, with Thy Spirit—'the spirit of wisdom and understanding, the spirit of counsel and might, the spirit of knowledge and of the fear of the Lord.' Let Thy grace guide them, so that amidst the din of conflicting Interests and opinions, they may each of them and all of them hold that even tenor of their way—the way of moderation and of equity. . . .

A 1905 history of Washington Hebrew Congregation contributed this gem to the Raphall story. Turns out, Raphall was the second choice for that landmark day. The problem with the first choice, Washington Hebrew Congregation Rabbi Solomon Lansburgh? He wasn't fluent in English. He spoke German. Disqualified.

"An incident which has grown in interest concerns itself with national events of this period and is related to the local congregation merely because of its being situated in this District," according to Rabbi Abram Simon's 1905 book, *A History of The Congregation in Commemoration of Its Jubilee.*[2] "Because of the slavery agitation when party spirit ran high and furious, and party lines were most sharply defined, a deadlock lasting two months prevented the election of a Speaker of the House Representatives. In desperation, or with the thought that prayer availeth yet in Israel, the Speaker then approached the president of this congregation immediately after the Sabbath morning services, asking if he would not permit the congregation's minister to offer prayer. Owing to Mr. Lansburgh's lack of fluency in English, Mr. A. S. Solomons secured the services of the Rev. Dr. Raphall of New York who, appearing in dignified mien with becoming Tallith and cap, inspired the confidence of all the lawmakers present. His simple prayer for wisdom and harmony was followed immediately by the breaking of the deadlock and the successful election of a Speaker."

Thus, even though Raphall was not Washington Hebrew Congregation's rabbi, the synagogue played a role in securing the first rabbi to give an opening prayer. Washington Hebrew Congregation rabbis for whom German was the primary language wasn't limited to nineteenth-century Lansburgh. Rabbi Joshua Haberman, a more contemporary and frequent guest chaplain from that synagogue, was born in Austria. German was his first language, too. An invitation by the Hebrew Union College in Cincinnati, Ohio, enabled Haberman to come to the United States where he completed his studies and received ordination in 1945, according to a Washington Hebrew Congregation memorial.

More historical color but slightly different historical context from author Robert V. Friedenberg. In *"Hear O Israel": The History of American Jewish Preaching, 1654-1970*, Friedenberg noted Raphall's "reputation as one of the foremost pulpit orators in American Judaism." His "mastery of English provided him with a background analogous to those of the

---

2   Lippman Printing Company, page 16.

outstanding Christian preachers of the day." Raphall "was probably the American rabbi best known in the Jewish community." Friedenberg suggests Raphall's "reputation as an outstanding orator was one of the principal reasons"[3] he was chosen for the first Jewish clergyman prayer in Congress.

And Sarna noted in the *Forward* that Raphall "was once described as the first 'glamour-rabbi' in American Jewish history. Like 'glamour-rabbis' after him, he knew how to attract media attention." Such an ideal qualification to go first!

By 1858, when Congress "decided to rotate among all the local clergy the honor of opening its session, there was a functioning synagogue in the nation's capital": Washington Hebrew Congregation. Although he was a "scholar of Judaism" from the close-by synagogue, Landsberg, a newly arrived immigrant, was "unable to present any type of discourse without speaking in an extremely heavy accent."

Hence, according to Friedenberg, when Washington Hebrew Congregation was requested to send the first rabbi to Congress on February 1, 1860, Jonas Levy, the congregation's lay leader[4] contacted three rabbis contacted three rabbis—Isaac Leeser, Samuel Isaacs, and Raphall—from someplace else.

Friedenberg:

> It is impossible to image to imagine that Levy and his congregation had denied the honor to their own rabbi and those of nearby Baltimore and, instead, invited a rabbi from Philadelphia and two from New York, unless he felt that these men would be much more polished representatives of Judaism to the nation's leaders assembled in Congress. Evidently, Raphall was the first to respond affirmatively to Levy. Consequently, the honor was his.

Other historians agree on Raphall's qualifications—both comfort with Judaism and comfort with the spotlight. "One of the most distinguished leaders of the age," Korn called him. "A man noted both for eloquence and for learning."[5] Sarna noted in *Lincoln and the Jews: A History*,[6] Raphall was

---

3   University of Alabama Press, 1989, pages 42-43.
4   Also brother of Uriah Levy, the first Jewish Commodore of the U.S. Navy and third owner of Monticello after Thomas Jefferson's death.
5   "Rabbis, Prayers, and Legislatures," *Hebrew Union College Annual*, Vol. 23, No. 2, Hebrew Union College Seventy-fifth Anniversary Publication 1875-1950 (1950-1951), page 96.
6   Edited with Benjamin Shapell, Thomas Dunne Books, 2015, page 66.

one of four rabbis to have face-to-face meetings with the 16th President and he was "once described as the first celebrity rabbi in American Jewish history."

Based on that description, one can only imagine how pleased Raphall would have been with what Congress did 100 years later. On February 1, 1960, the House marked the century since the first rabbi prayer with a special appearance by the spiritual leader of the same synagogue as Raphall: B'nai Jeshurun in New York City. Rabbi Israel Goldstein delivered the invocation to mark the century anniversary. Just like Raphall, Goldstein wore a Jewish prayer shawl, a *talis*, and a "velvet cap in the orthodox tradition . . . for historic sentimental reasons."

Goldstein prayed:

> We joyfully mark the 100th anniversary of a prayer Intoned within this Legislative Hall for the first time by a teacher of the Jewish faith. Rabbi Morris Jacob Raphall. It was a day as meaningful for America as for the household of Jacob, tokening not only religious freedom and equality but interreligious fellowship. One hundred years ago our Nation was riven by strife on the threshold of a tragic Civil War. We thank Thee that today our Nation stands before the world one and indivisible.

Voice of America and Radio Free Europe broadcast Goldstein's prayer live to an international audience.

During a luncheon in the Speaker's dining room after he gave the prayer, Goldstein said Raphall's prayer during the 30th Congress "reflected the tension of the times." It was during the administration of President Buchanan, Goldstein noted. And it was shortly following the Harpers Ferry incident with John Brown. In the Senate there was a Democratic majority; in the House, the Republicans had an uncertain majority. "The House was unable to organize itself because It was unable to elect a Speaker. There was turmoil In that kind of atmosphere," Goldstein continued. "Dr. Morris J. Raphall came to deliver his invocation. Styles in prayers have changed. One of the audience [members] who attended the original prayer was overheard to say that although it was beautiful, it was long enough to be a sermon. Chaplain Braskamp impressed upon me this morning that brevity is the soul of prayer."

The next day, House members gave commemorative floor speeches:

- Rep. Joseph Karth (D-MN): "Rabbi Raphall's fame as preacher and scholar became quickly established in America too. not only among the Jewry but also among the Christian clergy so that when the invitation to open a session of the House of Representatives with a prayer came to him, he had long been acclaimed for his erudition and his oratory."

- Rep. Roman Pucinski (D-IL): "By paying tribute to the 100th anniversary in this Congress, this Congress provided a fitting reply to those who today would attempt again a revival of bigotry by desecrating religious shrines throughout the world."
- Rep. Sid Yates (D-IL): "Yesterday, 100 years later, it is most fitting and proper that the event should be noted and celebrated by a repetition of the ceremony by one who bears the same relationship to Congregation B'nai Jeshurun as Rabbi Raphall did a century ago."

Two years later, that centennial was still being marked—by a Christian. Chaplain Rev. Bernard Braskamp opened the House on February 1, 1962, by quoting from the Hebrew book of Malachi 2:10: "Have not all one Father? Hath not one God created us?" Followed by:

We rejoice that in the annals of our national of our national history we have the record of the sincere and simple prayer offered unto Thee in this historic Chamber on this day, 102 years ago, by a beloved and devout spiritual leader of the Jewish faith, who daily poured out his soul in a great passion for righteousness and brotherhood and earnestly prayed that the minds and hearts of our chosen Representatives and of all our citizens might be made the sanctuaries of Thy truth and Thy love.

Pucinski immediately followed Braskamp: "Although members of the Jewish faith had served in Congress prior to 1860, we remember humbly today that this legislative body was in existence for 70 years, opening its daily sessions with prayer, without once listening to a representative of that faith from which so much of our Christian doctrine and worship is derived."

Six years later, during the dark depth of the Vietnam War, Goldstein returned. He opened the House in prayer again on October 3, 1968, a staggeringly bloody day for U.S. soldiers in Vietnam with 48 killed. And again, there was a Raphall mention. This time from Goldstein's sponsor Rep. William Ryan (D-NY), who said, "One hundred years ago Rabbi Raphall's prayer was delivered at a time of grave national crisis when the Nation was on the threshold of the Civil War. Today, this Nation faces a crisis unmatched since that time. If Congress had heeded the prayer of

Dr. Goldstein 8 years ago, the convulsive conflicts and deep divisions of this hour might well have been avoided."

Ryan's words demonstrated that a century after it was offered, Raphall's pioneering prayer continued to inspire. Just like in the immediate days after he stood in the House chamber, celebrated by the February 3, 1860, *Chicago Tribune* (page 2):

> It seemed not a little strange to us to learn, by telegraph, that a Jewish Rabbi made the prayer at the opening of the session of the House of Representatives on Wednesday. We apprehend that many devout Christian hearts will feel almost or quite grieved at this excess of tolerance of what they deem gross error and blindness in matters of religion. We confess to a somewhat different feeling. . . . [W]e cannot but feel, that an example of religious tolerance, like that which occurred on Wednesday at Washington, is most impressive, especially when exhibited by the representatives of one of the great nations of the earth, in the midst of the intense excitement of a heated political conflict. . . . Let timid religionists learn that freedom is more than safe for truth and right. It is the very atmosphere in which they live and flourish.

Today, to some, rabbis praying at the rostrum may still seem "a little strange." But their presence in the literal center of our democracy is an enduring testament to America's place among the great nations—greatness, even in times of hot-take politics. "Rabbis have frequently been among those who have joined the succession" of guest chaplains begun by Raphall, wrote Bertram Korn. "In this regard, certainly, the American principle of religious equality has been faithfully upheld."

And a postscript to the description of Raphall as "a chaplain in costume" for wearing, among other identifiably Jewish items, a yarmulke.

Skullcaps don't shock anymore. In the modern TV era, 218 rabbi prayers in Congress can be seen on video. Of those, the rabbi—male and female—wears a yarmulke 83% (180) of the time. How about a prayer shawl? Just one rabbi has worn a *tallis* in the video era: Mark Getman of Temple Emanu-El of Canarsie, New York. In case you missed his House prayer on July 24, 2019, you might have seen Getman's work elsewhere on TV. Getman has played a rabbi in *The Marvelous Mrs. Maisel*. That makes Getman the first rabbi to appear on both C-SPAN and Amazon Prime Video.

And what was the result of that March 1860 vote for chaplain of the House of the 36th Congress, the one that earned a facetious nomination for Rabbi Raphall? In a nail-biter, Rev. Thomas Stockton, a Methodist, got the win with 59% of votes cast.

It took two rounds of balloting to decide.

2: Why Does Congress Have Chaplains?

"The custom of opening sessions of the Senate and House with prayer is a very old one."
—Sen. Robert Byrd (D-WV), 1980

"This tradition of opening the Senate with a prayer has been with us since the Senate began and the Senate has had a Chaplain before the First Amendment to our Constitution was adopted."
—Sen. Lamar Alexander (R-TN), 2016

A basic timeline of the chaplain history shows that, in Lamar Alexander's words, "this tradition is an essential part of the American character." Starting with the Continental Congress.

September 7, 1774—As the first session of the Continental Congress is meeting, Reverend Jacob Duché, a Rector of Christ Church in Philadelphia, opens the proceedings with a prayer. He is recruited by Samuel Adams. Rev. Duché reads the 35th Psalm and concludes, "All this we ask in the name and through the merits of Jesus Christ."

July 9, 1776—Duché is appointed chaplain to Congress: "Resolved that Rev. Mr. DUCHE be appointed Chaplain to Congress, and that he be desired to attend every morning, at 9 o'clock."

June 28, 1787—During the Constitutional Convention, Benjamin Franklin advocates opening legislative sessions with a prayer. He asks for "prayers imploring the assistance of Heaven, and its blessings on our deliberations, be held in this Assembly every morning before we proceed to business, and that one or more of the Clergy of this City be requested to officiate in that Service."

April 6, 1789—Among its first orders of business upon convening in New York City, the newly minted U.S. Senate appoints a committee "to take under consideration the manner of electing Chaplains."

April 9, 1789—The equally young House of Representatives appoints a similar committee.

April 25, 1789—The Senate elects its first chaplain, the Right Reverend Samuel Provoost, Episcopal Bishop of New York.

May 1, 1789—In one of *its* first acts—and also meeting in New York City—the House elects the Reverend William Linn, a Presbyterian minister from Philadelphia, as the official Chaplain of the House.

September 22, 1789—Congress agrees to authorize the payment of Chaplains, $500 annually. This happens three days before Congress passes the Bill of Rights.

Thus, from the earliest days chaplains and prayers were baked into America's legislative tradition. Today they remain an institutional part of Congress. Byrd said in his 1980 remarks on prayer: "There are those who would attempt to deprive the Senate of this spiritual strength, but I have faith that the Senate will continue in the path that was blazed by others greater than I."

As for the chaplain to the First Continental Congress and Congress' first chaplain—how is Rev. Duché remembered in the contemporary era?

Consider Senate chaplain Lloyd Ogilvie's prayer on September 10, 2001:

> Gratefully we remember the historic event which made possible one of America's most enduring traditions. On September 7, 1774, the first prayer in Congress was prayed when the Continental Congress convened. We praise You that this declaration of dependence on You led to the Declaration of Independence twenty-two months later. We reflect on the many times throughout our Nation's history that prayer broke deadlocks, opened the way to great unity, and brought light in our darkest times.

"*Darkest times.*" The day after Ogilvie's prayer Al-Qaeda attacked the United States. Praying in the Senate on September 12, 2001, Ogilvie urged God "to help us to help us confront and battle the forces of evil manifested in infamous, illusive, cowardly acts of terrorism."

Or consider a different September 11, in 1974, as America was recovering from dark times. The 93rd Congress returned after a summer of Watergate drama: Richard Nixon had resigned from the presidency and was subsequently pardoned by President Gerald Ford. On that first day back, House chaplain Rev. Edward Latch began the session with a recitation of the same prayer Rev. Duché read in Philadelphia to the First Continental

Congress on September 7, 1774. Latch began: "It has been called the First Prayer in Congress. In spirit let us make it our prayer this morning." He ended in Duché's words:

> Preserve the health of their bodies and vigor of their minds; shower down on them and the millions they here represent, such temporal blessings as Thou seest expedient for them in this world and crown them with everlasting glory in the world to come. All this we ask in the name and through the merits of Jesus Christ, Thy Son and our Saviour. Amen.

A 300-word prayer. Speaker Carl Albert, according to the *New York Times* account of that day's House proceedings (September 12, 1974, page 1), called it "the longest prayer."

Two hundred years earlier, though, his prayer earned a review more substantial than a note about its length. He had impressed at least one representative to the Continental Congress. On September 16, 1774, Massachusetts delegate John Adams wrote his wife Abigail: "Mr. Duché, unexpected to every Body struck out into an extemporary Prayer, which filled the Bosom of every Man present. I must confess I never heard a better Prayer or one, so well pronounced."

The infatuation with Duché—and his with America—did not last long. In an October 8, 1777, letter to George Washington, Duché called the Declaration of Independence "hasty & ill-advised" and the battle against the British a "fruitless . . . expense of Blood." Two weeks later John Adams wrote again to Abigail about the chaplain. This time the future president had a different perspective: "Mr. Duché I am sorry to inform you has turned out an Apostate and a Traytor. Poor Man! I pity his Weakness, and detest his Wickedness."

3: Why does Congress Have Guest Chaplains?

> "...[C]ontrary impulses signify two great American themes: Americans should have the freedom to practice any religion they want, but Americans also believe that this Nation was founded under God to fulfill a greater mission. The House Chaplain must reflect both traditions."
>
> —House Speaker Dennis Hastert, March 23, 2000

When in session, Congress is the only American government institution that puts a daily faith-based prayer in a public setting on national television.

Some basics. Prayers are codified in the rules governing how Congress opens each legislative day:

Senate rule: "The Presiding Officer having taken the chair, following the prayer by the Chaplain, and after the Presiding Officer, or a Senator designated by the Presiding Officer, leads the Senate from the dais in reciting the Pledge of Allegiance to the Flag of the United States. . . ."

House rule: "The Chaplain shall offer a prayer at the commencement of each day's sitting of the House."

Both the House and Senate elect their chaplains. At the beginning of each Congress, according to the Congressional Research Service, the House chaplain is elected to a two-year term; the Senate chaplain, like other officers of the Senate in that ongoing body, does not have to be re-elected at the beginning of a new Congress.

More than rules, though: chaplains and prayers are woven into the language you hear from members on the floors of Congress. A sample:

- Rep. Samuel Friedel (D-MD), May 29, 1969: "From the very start of the settlements in the New World, as the American continent was then called, the people who came here declared their dependence upon Almighty God. Before this Congress was established by the present Constitution, the American Colonies established the Continental Congress and it is a matter of historical record that the Journal of that Congress, for September 6, 1774, carries an entry that a chaplain was in attendance and opened the session with a prayer. Thus, from the earliest times to the present, every session of this great lawmaking body began with an invocation. I am pleased to note that the Rules of the House of Representatives, rule VII, so provide."
- Sen. Frank Lautenberg (D-NJ), June 11, 2003: "Since 1789, every session of the Senate has been opened with prayer."
- Rep. Gil Gutknecht (R-MN), July 12, 2005: "I often tell students when they come to visit the Capitol that the first official act of the United States Congress was to appoint a chaplain. The second

thing they did was they prayed, and it was not a perfunctory prayer. They prayed for 1 ½ hours. We have long understood the importance of faith in our society."

- Rep. John Hall (D-NY), June 16, 2010: "House chaplains are a long, proud tradition in the House of Representatives, dating back to the time of our Founding Fathers."

These four elected representatives had something in common. They were all offering remarks about a guest chaplain they had sponsored. And each guest chaplain was a rabbi.

The legislative branch's chaplains have not escaped the notice of the executive branch, which has no paid chaplain.[7]

On several occasions, President Ronald Reagan cited prayers in Congress. "If the Congress can begin each day with a moment of prayer and meditation, so then can our sons and daughters," he told secondary school principals in Las Vegas on February 7, 1984. "I'll try hard now not to be tempted to tell the story of the father and son in the gallery of the Congress one day, and the son asked who that was. And it was the chaplain. And the father explained. And the boy said, 'He's praying for the Congress?' And he said, 'No, he's praying for the people.'"

Two weeks later, in a radio address on prayer in schools, Reagan noted that Benjamin Franklin asked the Constitutional Convention "to begin its daily deliberations by asking for the assistance of Almighty God." In a June 23, 1986, Oval Office interview with *Los Angeles Times* reporters, Reagan repeated that history: "It was Benjamin Franklin that uttered the statement in the Constitutional Convention that finally got them to open the meetings with prayer. And the Continental Congress, before there was the present Congress and the Constitution, always opened with prayer. And to this day the Congress opens with prayer."

Today, nearly eight in ten Americans (77%) support allowing public officials to open meetings, such as town hall meetings, with a prayer. According to a June 6, 2014 Public Religion Research Institute survey on

---

7   A few months into the first Nixon administration, *New York Times* religion editor Edward Fiske called the Rev. Billy Graham "the closest thing we have to a White House chaplain" (*New York Time Magazine*, June 8, 1969). Mind you, according to audio tapes made public by the National Archives, would-be White House chaplain Graham told Nixon in a 1972 Oval Office conversation the Jewish "stranglehold has got to be broken or the country's going down the drain" (reported in the March 17, 2002, *New York Times*, Section 1, page 29.)

Religion & Politics, a majority (58%) of religiously unaffiliated Americans support allowing public officials to open meetings with a prayer.

The third branch of the U.S. government lacks its own chaplain. But it too has involved itself with legislative prayers.

The U.S. Supreme Court decided in *Marsh v. Chambers* (1983) that, "in light of the unambiguous and unbroken history of more than 200 years, there can be no doubt that the practice of opening legislative sessions with prayer has become part of the fabric of our society. To invoke Divine guidance on a public body entrusted with making the laws is not, in these circumstances, an 'establishment' of religion or a step toward establishment; it is simply a tolerable acknowledgment of beliefs widely held among the people of this country."

And the Court said in *Town of Greece v. Galloway* (2014) that "the framers considered legislative prayer a benign acknowledgment of religion's role in society. . . . As a practice that has long endured, legislative prayer has become part of our heritage and tradition, part of our expressive idiom, similar to the Pledge of Allegiance, inaugural prayer, or the recitation of 'God save the United States and this honorable Court' at the opening of this Court's sessions."

Justice Brett Kavanaugh noted both cases during February 27, 2019, oral argument in *American Legion v. American Humanist Association.* "Our cases have upheld religious displays and religious words in cases like *Marsh,*" Kavanaugh said, "the chaplain in Congress, and the prayer cases like *Van Orden*, the Ten Commandments, cases like *Town of Greece*, legislative prayer before a meeting."

In an amicus brief filed in the Supreme Court regarding *Greece,* Sen. Marco Rubio (R-FL) noted, "The Congressional Record is filled with prayers offered by Jewish rabbis." On the opposing site, Rabbi Joshua Davidson of Temple Emanu-El in New York City wrote about the *Greece* decision in the July 30, 2014, *Huffington Post.* He called it "upsetting" and noted that on June 16, 2010, "I was invited to deliver an invocation on the floor of the House of Representatives. But the instructions given me were clear—that my words should recognize the diversity present in the chamber. And that is what is disappointing about this ruling: Not its support of legislative prayer, but the low bar it establishes for a prayer's permissibility."

Davidson was referring to Congress' additional custom, the guest chaplain: A clergyman invited by members of the House and Senate to offer an opening prayer, coordinated by the elected Chaplain. This tradition has roots in the 1850s when, according to the Congressional Research Service (CRS), numerous petitions requested abolishment of the chaplain office, considering "the employment of chaplains in Congress and the military as a breach of the separation of church and state."

For a short period in the late 1850s, the House and Senate did not elect chaplains. Instead, according to the CRS, "local clergy were invited to serve voluntarily as chaplains. However, the difficulty in obtaining volunteer chaplains resulted in Congress returning to the practice of selecting official House and Senate chaplains."

A March 1907 House of Representatives document detailing its procedures provided this decades-old history:

> On January 23, 1856, before the election of a Speaker or the adoption of rules, [Rep.] James F. Dowdell, of Alabama, offered a preamble and resolution reciting the propriety of the House showing their reverence for God, and resolving that the daily sessions be opened with prayer, and providing that the ministers of the gospel in the city be requested to attend and perform the duty alternately.

Thus, both traditions continued: The elected chaplain reappeared—and the guest chaplain remained. We've had guest chaplains ever since. According to the Freedom from Religion Foundation, guest chaplains delivered 39% of the House invocations between 2000 and 2015 (857 of the 2,198 total).

House rules do not require guest chaplains. But they remain a sought-after plum assignment for members of Congress and clergy alike. And it doesn't matter which party is in charge, rare common ground for a Congress driven by majority partisan rules. Inviting guest chaplains is one of the few power members of the House minority party have. A pretty slight power, admittedly, but it's something. Upholding prayer in Congress on October 11, 2017, U.S. District Judge Rosemary Collyer recognized in *Barker v. Conroy*, "It is surely an honor to serve as guest chaplain and open a session of the House with prayer."

Legendary DC observer Drew Pearson wrote in his July 28, 1957, "Washington Merry-Go-Round" column:

> Many a home-town preacher, priest or rabbi visiting Washington on a summer's vacation has confided to his Senator how dearly he would love to deliver the daily invocation in the United States Senate. The Senator then

speaks to the Chaplain of the Senate, and obliging Rev. Frederick Brown Harris always agrees. In fact, he has even prepared a handsome certificate which he gives to visiting clergymen as a souvenir of their experience.

Pearson also reported this wonderful, timeless anecdote:

Recently Rev. Harris confided to Senate majority leader Lyndon Johnson that he was getting concerned about the increasing number of guest ministers. He pointed out that in recent weeks he had been done out of his job in the Senate chamber no fewer than 17 times. "Now look here," consoled Senator Johnson, "if you ever want me to call a halt to this sort of thing, you let me know and we'll just restrict the number of visiting preachers." The Rev. Harris nodded appreciatively. He did not remind Johnson that at that very moment he had two requests from Senator Johnson's office asking special permission for two Texas ministers to preach.

Over 60 years later, the practice remains politically valuable. On February 19, 2019, Paul Bedard wrote in his *Washington Examiner* "Washington Secrets" column: "While it doesn't get much public and media notice amid the increasingly nasty fights on the floors of the House and Senate, prayers from the official and guest chaplains remain an important element of Washington political life."

Listen to these two members of Congress welcoming guest chaplains:

- "We are all aware of the limited opportunities for guest chaplains in the course of the legislative year."—Rep. James Burke (D-MA), May 17, 1971.
- "The opportunity for having visiting chaplain guests is very special as it allows religious leaders from different faiths to begin our day of legislative duty."—Rep. Jim Saxton (R-NJ), July 12, 2007.

The guest chaplains both members were welcoming? Again, rabbis.

To be sure, the very idea of a Congressional chaplain has had detractors.

For a September 17, 2016, *Christian Science Monitor* article on private prayer gatherings and fellowships among members of Congress, reporter Francine Kiefer interviewed Donald Ritchie. "When he was the Senate historian," Kiefer wrote, "Ritchie says he often had to answer queries from outraged citizens and visitors who viewed the chaplaincy and opening prayers as a violation of the separation of church and state. But Article 1 of the

Constitution allows the chambers to 'chuse' their officers, and the chaplains have always been officers, the historian says."

Syndicated columnist Les Kinsolving wrote about chaplain salaries on July 15, 1974 when the two chaplains cost $40,000 per annum. (The Senate chaplain office had a 2016 budget of $436,886; the House Chaplain, $345,000.) Kinsolving suggested of chaplain prayers: "these mini-devotions may well constitute the most expensive liturgy in ecclesiastical history." One newspaper, Virginia's Fredericksburg *Free Lance-Star*, headlined his column: "History's most expensive prayers."

Exactly 100 years before Kinsolving, another question about paying the chaplain. "Why, sir, the Chaplain of the Senate, in 1860, the man who pays so fruitlessly to God in that body, cannot do it for the former salary of $750, but must be increased to $900?" asked Rep. Samuel Cox (D-NY) on March 17, 1874. "I suppose that we get better prayers."

Money was also a concern of Rep. William Howard (D-GA) on September 2, 1916, when the House debated printing 50,000 pamphlets containing the opening prayers offered during the 63rd Congress by chaplain Henry Couden. The cost to taxpayers: $2,126. Howard didn't see the value. With early twentieth-century sarcasm, he wondered whether "the preachers of this country did not have any originality . . . and could not pray to God themselves but had to have a pattern cut out by the Chaplain of the House to pray by." Howard also noted, "I have got real preachers in my district who know how to pray; they are consecrated men, and while the prayers of the Chaplain may be of some value here. I do not think they are of any value to send out: I have no demand in my district for these documents. . . . It is a useless expenditure of money."

Aside from money, there's the issue of the U.S. Constitution. Fourth president and Constitution crafter James Madison called the chaplain position a "violation of equal rights, as well as of Constitutional principles: The tenets of the chaplains elected [by the majority] shut the door of worship agst the members whose creeds & consciences forbid a participation in that of the majority."

House chaplain Patrick Conroy was interviewed in the January 2017 issue of *America*, a Jesuit review. He was asked about the constitutional principle of separation of church and state. Conroy's response:

> Establishing a chaplain was one of the very first acts of Congress, so a
> constitutional challenge to a chaplain would have to go back to the intent

of the founders. When you talk about constitutional separation of church and state, well, the same people that wrote that were praying and hiring a chaplain to pray.

In a February 22, 2019, column, George Will noted that the Supreme Court has held "that any policy or practice by a public entity that touches religion, however marginally, violates the establishment clause unless (a) it has a secular purpose and (b) its primary effect neither advances nor inhibits religion and (c) it does not foster excessive government entanglement with religion. In 1983, the court held, rudely but prudently, that Nebraska's legislature could continue being prayed over by its paid chaplain, thereby implying that the chaplain negligibly advanced religion." Will noted, "The First Congress hired a chaplain, but James Madison, principal progenitor of the First Amendment, later said tersely that this 'was not with my approbation.'"

Madison opposed the hiring of chaplains in Congress because paying them from the national treasury was in violation of the First Amendment's Establishment Clause. As a practical matter Madison also wondered "are not the daily devotions conducted by these legal Ecclesiastics, already degenerating into a scanty attendance, and a tiresome formality?"

Scanty attendance? Sure, that passes the test of time. Sparse attendance when prayers are offered is the reality in Congress today. But a tiresome formality? With all due respect, as they say in Congress, this story of rabbis and their prayers prove Madison wrong.

SECTION II

Who Are These Rabbis?

4: Immigrants and "the New Canaan"

Hundreds of rabbis praying in Congress means there's an abundance of biographical story lines to pursue. Where to start? Best to follow the storyline of Jews coming to America. Like a ship bound for Ellis Island, a good entry point is immigration. First stop: David Philipson.

As an independent Jewish state become a reality in the first half of the twentieth century, many American Jews celebrated the realization of centuries of Zionist dreaming. Many, but not all. Among the dissenters: a loud Jewish anti-Zionist camp. That's where you could find Philipson. The Midwestern-raised son of German immigrants was, according to the *American Jewish Archives*, "throughout his life an opponent of Jewish nationalism of any sort, particularly Zionism."

The Reform rabbi died a year after Israel won independence in 1948. He opened the Senate in prayer decades earlier with this intriguing reference: "We thank Thee above all for this dear fatherland of ours, the promised land of these latter days, the new Canaan."

Not the Canaan of the Hebrew Bible.[8] No, the "fatherland" of Philipson's February 2, 1904, prayer—*his* Canaan—was a different promised land: America. Home to a million Jews.

"The new Canaan," Philipson said, "where modern prophets have preached truths no less inspiring than those spoken by Thy chosen

---

8   God says in Genesis 17:8: "And I will give unto thee, and to thy seed after thee, the land of thy sojournings, all the land of Canaan, for an everlasting possession." In other words, Israel.

messengers of old, where ideals have been set that point to the era of universal brotherhood and peace, the hope of all the great spirits of the race."
He continued:

> May those who guide the helm of our ship of state be constantly mindful of the high mission of this American people among the nations of the earth to stand as the exemplar of justice, the protector of the weak, the foe of all unrighteousness, the scorner of all wrongdoing, the lover of peace. So, imbue all with these ideals that our dear land may stand to the very end as the refuge of all those oppressed elsewhere, the sanctuary of liberty, the haven of peace.

The *Washington Times* put Philipson's picture on its front page, above the fold. The all-capital-letter headline: "RABBI OFFERS PRAYER IN THE U.S. SENATE." The *Times* described the rabbi's "Hebrew eloquence." An eloquence that included describing America as the Biblical promised land, the new Canaan, "the refuge of all those oppressed elsewhere."

Philipson later testified against a 1922 House resolution urging "the establishment in Palestine of a national home for the Jewish people." He told the House Foreign Affairs Committee: "There are those of us who feel that Jewish nationalism does not express the true interpretation of Judaism. We feel that Judaism is a religion and that we are nationals of the country in which we are born and in which we live." During the committee hearing Philipson read a resolution of the Union of American Hebrew Congregations (UAHC), the organizing body of Reform Jews. "We are unalterably opposed to political Zionism," the UAHC said. "The Jews are not a nation but a religious community. Zion was a precious possession of the past, the early home of our faith, where our prophets uttered their world-subduing thoughts, and our psalmists sang their world-enchanting hymns. As such it is a holy memory, but it is not our hope of the future. America is our Zion." Rep. Walter Chandler (R-NY), a Presbyterian, responded: "This is all splendid and inspiring sentiment, and when the [UAHC] proclaimed America their Zion we are compelled to applaud their patriotism. But the Zionist movement is not intended primarily for American Jews, who are happy in the possession of American citizenship and in comparative freedom from religious persecution. It is intended primarily for the wretched Jews of Russia, Rumania, and Poland who are practically shut out from this American Zion by foolishly rigid immigration laws."

Writing in a 1905 essay called "Zionism," Max Nordau, a Zionist leader, noted "a singular doctrine, according to which the Zion promised to the Jews was to be understood only in a spiritual sense. . . . An American rabbi reduced this conception to the striking formula, 'Our Zion is in Washington.'"

As Jews fled from Europe to America, among other places, refuge became a regular theme for rabbis praying in Congress. Over the century specific words changed, as have the typical biographies. But an America portrayed as a new Canaan remained constant.

Rhetorical parallels to ancient Jewish history—the days of Canaan and earlier—can be found in at least one early American landmark event: the Lewis and Clark expedition. In *Undaunted Courage: Meriwether Lewis, Thomas Jefferson, and the Opening of the American West*, Stephen Ambrose offers terms and imagery familiar to anyone with a fundamental under-standing of the Hebrew Bible. "Jefferson and Lewis," he writes, "speculated that the lost tribe of Israel could be out there on the Plains." And, "In the Garden of Eden, man had but to reach out for his food. So too on the Great Plains."[9] Plus, this construct consistent with the urging in Isaiah 2:4 to beat swords into plowshares, and spears into pruning hooks:

> Lewis's objectives, as given to him by Jefferson, were to establish American sovereignty, peace, and a trading empire in which the warriors would put down their weapons and take up traps.

Russia, Poland, Moravia, Bratislava Germany, Hungary—these coun-tries produced early guest chaplain rabbis. A data point illustrating this early twentieth-century ingathering: The 1920 census looked at foreign lan-guage U.S. daily newspapers, average circulation per issue. Yiddish held the top spot, one-fourth of the total daily circulation. The raw number for aver-age combined circulation per issue in Yiddish in 1919, 670,145, was even down from a high of 762,910 (1914). The Jewish population in America had grown to around 3.5 million.

Maurice Harris, president of the Reform Central Conference of American Rabbis, said at Rabbi Isaac Mayer Wise's March 1919 funeral that World War I "wiped out many European theological seminaries that trained rabbis in the past from which issued many of the elder teachers in American Israel." Quoted in the *New York Times* account of Wise's funeral,

---

9   Simon & Schuster, 1997, page 90.

Harris said rabbis "are turning now to America for the building up of seminaries for the training of the Jewish ministry, as Europe just now has turned to America for so many of its material needs."

The immigration theme continued well after the Statue of Liberty welcomed huddled masses yearning to breathe free. Consider Rabbi Leo Heim of Congregation B'nai Zion in El Paso. He gave the June 1, 1967, House prayer. In his sponsoring remarks, Rep. Richard Crawford White (D-TX) noted Heim's prayer "celebrates a significant anniversary. Just 18 years ago today, he entered the United States from Czechoslovakia to become one of our finest citizens."

Which country (other than America) produced the most rabbi congressional prayers? Poland. 26 prayers offered by 19 rabbis born there.[10] Next highest: Germany, with 24 prayers from 16 rabbis native to that country. Austria is third—18 prayers from four rabbis (plus two prayers from an Austro-Hungarian rabbi). And fourth is Russia. 11 prayers from 10 rabbis. The 10th Russia-born rabbi is recent: Lubavitch Yosef Greenberg in the Senate on February 3, 2016. Greenberg represented a state close to Russia: Alaska.

For these rabbis—like for many American Jews—immigration connects the Jewish catastrophe in Europe with the aftermath blessing of America. No better example than Holocaust survivor Arthur Schneier.

Born in Austria, Schneier has been nominated for the Congressional Gold Medal several times. He repeatedly marked the anniversary of his coming to America during his seven prayers in Congress.

In his first—in the House on May 10, 1956—Schneier said, "Almighty God, who hast delivered me from the hands of the Nazi and Communist tyrants and hast brought me to these blessed shores, I lead Thy children in prayer for our land, the haven for the homeless, the refuge for the oppressed. the beacon of hope and faith for all the enslaved in the world."

A year later, on May 9, 1957, he opened the Senate: "On the 10th anniversary of my arrival on these blessed shores, after years of Nazi and Communist persecution, I lead Thy children in prayer for our country, these United States of America, the land dedicated to the sanctity of man, the invigorating spring of liberty where the oppressed may quench their thirst, the beacon of hope and faith of the enslaved in the world."

---

10   In 1933, before German World War II slaughter of Europe's Jews began, 9.5% of Poland's total population was Jewish.

Still giving congressional prayers decades later, on May 8, 1990, Schneier opened the House: "You have saved me from the Holocaust and, 43 years ago today, on May 8, 1947, You brought me to the land of freedom and opportunity, the Nation of immigrants."

You can find a similar theme in the prayers of Rabbi Isaac Neuman.

When Neuman passed away in 2014, his obituary in the Champaign, Illinois, *News-Gazette* noted, "He twice delivered the opening prayer in the U.S. House of Representatives, expressing his gratitude for the refuge he'd been given here." Indeed, Neuman told the House on May 5, 1970: "Humbly a survivor of Auschwitz stands in Thy presence amid the chosen servants of a great people, a generous people, who opened their gates to homeless victims of totalitarianism. All of us here assembled thank Thee for this blessed land dressed in the garments of spring. We raise our voices in gratitude to Thee that on this day 25 years ago, the prisoners were freed from Nazi concentration camps. Grateful are we that this Nation has fought valiantly against the forces of tyranny and brought the torch of liberty to millions of slaves under the Nazi yoke. May this our land remain the fortress of liberty forever."

In his sponsoring remarks, Rep. John Culver (D-IA) noted that when Neuman was liberated by the American troops from the concentration camp at Ebensee, Austria, "he was 22 years old and suffering from typhoid fever, tuberculosis, two bullet wounds received in an escape attempt, and malnutrition after 4 years at Auschwitz and required almost 3 years of hospitalization for recovery. Now, as a U.S. citizen, Rabbi Neuman today has expressed his gratitude before the U.S. House of Representatives both for the successful efforts of the American Armed Forces during World War II and for the subsequent attitude of the American people who opened the doors of their country to the homeless refugees of that war. At a time when there is increasing and almost incessant criticism of both our country and its institutions, Rabbi Neuman reminds us that, as Americans, we, indeed, have much for which to be grateful and proud."

In his second House prayer (April 11, 1983) Neuman again raised "raise my voice in gratitude to Thee because on this day, 33 years ago, I first set foot on these blessed shores. May our country hold true to its traditions, and remain a refuge for the homeless and oppressed, as it has been for us and for all our forefathers." In his sponsoring remarks, Rep. Dan Crane (R-IL) said Neuman "truly knows the difference between a slave state and a free state."

Note that Schneier and Neuman both cited tyranny of others in their prayers celebrating America. You'll find that contrast in other rabbis' prayers, too.

Samuel Soskin in the House on March 1, 1951: "Pioneers and workers with spirits seared by tyranny have come here for refuge and safety. In gratitude for that refuge they have cemented even more strongly the free institutions of our beloved Nation."

Israel Poleyeff in the House on March 3, 1994: "For more than two centuries our blessed and beloved country has been the haven for those fleeing tyranny and oppression. They came to these shores seeking a new life in the land of freedom and opportunity. Our Nation to this day remains a beacon of light to all people and an example to the nations of the world that life, liberty and the pursuit of happiness are indeed the inalienable rights of all human beings."

Poleyeff again, in the Senate on April 5, 1995: "For more than a century, millions of immigrants, my father's family amongst them, came to these shores seeking freedom from tyranny and oppression. To this very day our beloved country still stands as a shining example of individual liberty and limitless opportunity."

For some immigrant rabbis, earning the specific honor of guest chaplain was an additional reason to celebrate America. And Congress.

Sidney Harcsztark, a descendant of a prominent rabbinic family in pre-war Poland, opened the House on March 18, 1965. Rep. Eugene Keogh (D-NY) noted: "Our guest chaplain today is a distinguished Brooklynite, and the following release issued by him is quite interesting: A refugee from Dachau had his dream come true today when he stood before the opening of the U.S. House of Representatives delivering his invocation as a clergyman of the Jewish faith."[11]

According to *An American Jewish Odyssey* by Cipora Schwartz, Max Raisin, who was House guest chaplain on January 30, 1947, wrote in his memoirs: "Nothing so reveals the greatness and the true spirit of America as the sight of a one-time immigrant boy from far-away Poland uttering words of prayer before the men and women who legislate for the noblest and mightiest country in the world."[12]

---

11   Keogh's description of Harcsztark was one of the earliest, if not *the* first, use by a member of Congress of the description "guest chaplain."

12   Ktav Publishing 2007, pages 54-55.

Bertram Korn said in the Senate on July 13, 1955, when there were around 5 million Jews in America: "Thou hast permitted me, the grandson of humble immigrants, who came to these shores in search of the freedom and opportunity which were denied to them in their native lands, I thank Thee that Thou hast permitted me to sing Thy praise in this great legislative forum of the most blessed land in human history."

Korn invoked his immigrant grandparents. Poleyeff cited his parents. Here are others who've done similar:

"Like millions of others in this exceptional land," New York rabbi Jacob Schacter said in the House on April 13, 2000, "all four of my grandparents came to these blessed shores from countries far away to create a better life for themselves and their families. Like millions of others, my father served in the armed forces of this wonderful country and fought to make the world safe for democracy and human freedom."

Rabbi Efrem Goldberg of Boca Raton opening the House April 5, 2011: "As a grandchild of immigrants who fled the Nazis and came to this country 72 years ago this month to find refuge, freedom, and opportunity, I join this House in a prayer of profound gratitude and deep appreciation for the blessings we, the people of the United States of America, are privileged to enjoy." (That appearance in Congress seems to have had a profound impact on Goldberg. In a blog post timed for *Simchat Torah*, a holiday for celebrating and dancing with the Torah, he later reflected: "Imagine the following scene playing out on C-SPAN: On a specific day of the year, the Supreme Court justices together with the member of Congress take copies of the United States Constitution and dance around the floor of the House of Representatives while singing, clapping and lifting the law books high in the air. With each circuit of those carrying the Constitution, the others lean in to affectionately kiss the books before they pass by. This entire scenario seems impossible and the very suggestion of this scene is ludicrous. And yet, this is exactly what we do on Simchas Torah in Shuls around the world.")

Virginia Beach Rabbi Israel Zoberman was born in Kazakhstan in 1945 to Polish Holocaust survivors. He was raised in Israel, moved to America in 1966—and has been guest chaplain four times. Opening the Senate on December 11, 2014, he recalled "my early childhood in a Displaced Persons Camp in Germany's American Zone, and on my 40th anniversary in the rabbinic ministry in the most ecumenical Nation under Heaven."

Philadelphia's Alex Pollack opened the Senate on May 3, 1978. Sen. John Heinz (R-PA) said, "The only one of five children to be born of Russian immigrant parents in the United States, Rabbi Pollack shares a special sense of the 'melting pot' aspects of our national heritage, and one of which I know he is, as we are, extremely proud."

"Proud" of the melting pot now. Some legislators were not as proud just before World War II began, when doomed European Jews really could use that and a whole lot more. In 1939 Congress failed to pass the Wagner-Rogers Bill. It would have admitted 20,000 refugee children—presumably Jewish—into the United States from Nazi Germany. The United States Holocaust Memorial Museum notes on its website: "Roosevelt took no action, and after several months of debate, the bill died in the Senate Immigration Committee during the first week of July 1939." The *Historical Dictionary of the Holocaust* further notes, "A bill that allowed in thousands of children from Great Britain, non-Jewish victims of the 1940 blitz, was enthusiastically endorsed by Congress."

Still, rabbis persist in their appreciation of America.

Russian-born Leon Fram in the House on March 25, 1935, when the Jewish population in America was 4.6 million: "Our forefathers came to this New World and proceeded to establish a new society. Strengthened by their faith in Thee, they resisted the intolerance of the Old World and established a new society based upon mutual understanding."

Austrian-born Joshua Haberman of Washington Hebrew Congregation in the Senate on November 25, 1970: "To these shores Thy children have come from many climes seeking liberty and a new hope in life. All have been pilgrims to this land of promise. Here they found renewed purpose, increased strength and the opportunity to outgrow old fears and suspicions."[13] There were nearly six million Jews in America in 1970.

More pilgrims via Ari Korenblit in the House on November 19, 2003: "For our country which has provided welcoming portals of refuge, sanctuary and opportunity, both material and spiritual. For our country which has been enriched by the prayers and talents from the early pilgrims to our recent citizens. In these troubled times, let us especially remember the early pilgrims who came to these shores with their faith, dreams and hope in God. This is the secret of our endurance, prosperity and success."

---

13 Haberman participated in the National Prayer Service at the National Cathedral three days after the September 11, 2001, terrorist attacks. He read from Lamentations.

Barry Tabachnikoff of Miami Congregation Bet Breira offered this tribute to America in the House on April 24, 1990, a few months before that body passed an immigration Act: "Here our ancestors built a land of freedom, a beacon for the oppressed in every generation and here the poor and homeless came, from every land, from every faith. And here they found acceptance, in a land of pluralism and plenty, a land of opportunity and acceptance. May this, our great country, continue to strive to sustain our noble heritage."

And Gary Zola of Cincinnati's American Jewish Archives summed up the Jewish experience in America when he opened the House on September 21, 2004: "In this year marking the 350th anniversary of Jewish life in this great land, may we all acknowledge our debt to America, to the courageous immigrants who gave us this national inheritance, and to the Source of All for endowing us with the benefit of our patriot's dream—a nation pledged to uphold the conviction that liberty and justice are for all."

Immigrants indeed: The 441 rabbis who have prayed in Congress come from, in addition to America, 27 countries.

None of those countries are Asian. But Asia has produced one prominent immigrant American who one day might get booked for Congress. Angela Warnick Buchdahl is senior rabbi at New York City's prestigious Central Synagogue. She was, according to *The Forward*, the first woman to be ordained as both a cantor and a rabbi and the first Asian-American to obtain either post. Buchdahl hasn't prayed in Congress. But she has prayed in the White House. She led the blessing at President Obama's December 17, 2014, Hanukkah reception. The Founding Fathers, she said, "could not have imagined that in 2014 that there would be a female Asian-American rabbi lighting the menorah at the White House for an African-American president." And on January 3, 2018, Buchdahl gave the invocation preceding New York Gov. Andrew Cuomo's State of the State address. "I was born in South Korea. I was raised in Tacoma, Washington," she said. "But New York is the home that I chose. Because New York is the gateway to America for millions of immigrants, including my family."

In Congress, the timeliest and perhaps most pinpoint use of Jewish experience with immigration came coincidentally when America wrestled with specific anguished news from the southern U.S. border. Intense television news images of migrant children separated in 2018 from their parents inspired a double barrel of Jewish-themed prayers—from a Jew and from a gentile. Chaplain Barry Black opened the Senate on June 18. Leviticus

19:18 and Hebrew Bible prophet Amos (5:24) drove his strong response. "Through the power of your Spirit," Black said to the Lord, "use our Senators to cause justice to roll down like waters and righteousness like a mighty stream. As children are being separated from their parents, remind us to love our neighbors as ourselves and to protect the most vulnerable in our world." Two days later, with the pictures of children still dominating American political conversation, it was a rabbi's turn to open Congress with a prayer. Speaking to the Iowa Democratic Party on October 6, 2018, Sen. Cory Booker (D-NJ) recounted a trip to Dulles Airport. "When Muslim families came off that plane out of detention and walked through," Booker said, "the crowd erupted and cheered them. There were guys in yarmulkes and *tzitzits* cheering Muslim families coming into our country." Booker ended with an Amos crescendo: "If we love each other like brothers and sisters, then justice will roll down like water, and righteousness like a mighty stream!"

And Mark Schiftan of Nashville's The Temple: Congregation Ohabai Shalom was equally relevant with an immigration message grounded in American and Jewish history amid swirling controversy over the Trump administration's detention policies near the U.S.-Mexico border. In the House on June 20, 2018, he called America a "haven for the huddled masses yearning to breathe free"—the Emma Lazarus poem found on the Statue of Liberty. "We and you who lead us are a nation of immigrants," Schiftan said. "Each of us, all of us, are here because of the individually and mutually inspired hopes and dreams of those who came before us, those who often fled persecution to find safe haven on this Nation's shores for them and for future generations that follow them, including each and every one of us . . . Help us, O God, to fulfill the promise of America."[14]

The Hebrew Bible essentially ends in failure: the Jews are in exile. But there's celebration again further along the Jewish timeline. In 1904 Rabbi Philipson hoped "our dear land may stand to the very end as the refuge of all those oppressed elsewhere, the sanctuary of liberty, the haven of peace."

---

14 That theme carried over into the next month. Imam Seyed Ali Ghazvini, Islamic Cultural Center of Fresno was House guest chaplain July 24. "Bismillahir Rahmanir Rahim, in the name of God," he said. "I thank You for having led me to this great Nation, whose history of welcoming immigrants makes it possible for me to give today's prayer." He asked Congress "that no one seeking refuge from war is banned from stepping on our soil based on faith affiliation or race, so that desperate families seeking refuge are not separated."

Over a century later, similar language and vision from Schiftan—even if "new Canaan" is no longer found in the Congressional prayer book.

5: And Now, Latin America

American demographics changed in the early years of the twenty-first century. So did the profiles of rabbis delivering opening prayers in Congress. If immigrant rabbis giving prayers in the prior century came from Poland or Germany or Russia, by 2008 they came from Western Hemisphere locales with longstanding Jewish populations: Latin America.

Mexico. Cuba. Two from Argentina. Modern-day rabbis from those countries had different life stories. But they shared immigrant love for America and appreciation to Congress.[15]

Their story is the story of America, too. Serving in the military. Educated in universities. Representing many political stripes and denominations.

Felipe Goodman was the first Latin American-born rabbi to open Congress in prayer. Born in Mexico City, he was rabbi of Las Vegas' Temple Beth Sholom when he prayed in the House on June 3, 2008. A year later he became a U.S. citizen. "Let us remember," Goodman said, "where we came from so that we may never forget the destination of our journey as a Nation. Let us be always mindful that we are all children of immigrants."

Jacob Luski of St. Petersburg's Congregation B'nai Israel gave the House prayer on October 28, 2009. Rep. Bill Young (R-FL) noted "something very interesting" about Luski: "He was born in Havana, Cuba, on November 2, 1949, which makes him, in just a couple of days, 60 years old. But he left Cuba 50 years ago at the age of 10 and came to the United States with his family." On June 23, 2014, the *Jewish Telegraphic Agency* reported: "In 2010, near the 50th anniversary of his family's coming to America, Luski recalls U.S. Rep. Bill Young of Florida inviting him to deliver the opening prayer before the House of Representatives. 'What a Jewish journey,' the rabbi exclaims."

The July 11, 2012, House guest chaplain was Argentina-born David Algaze. He founded Havurat Yisrael Synagogue in Forest Hills, Queens. Algaze called America "a land where even a humble bicycle messenger can soar to serve in this Hall, where every man has dignity and the capacity

---

15 According to American Jewish Committee data reported in the April 11, 2016, *Jerusalem Post*, estimates of the number of Latino Jews in the U.S. range from 200,100 (3%) to 227,700 (5%) of the 6.7 million Jews in America.

to prosper, where the ignorant can reach knowledge and the persecuted sanctuary."

Also native of Argentina: Claudio Kogan. As rabbi of Temple Emanuel in McAllen, Texas, he gave the House prayer on June 10, 2015. "As an immigrant who came to this country 16 years ago and became an American citizen just 2 years ago," Kogan said, "I join this House in a prayer of profound gratitude and deep appreciation for the blessings we, the people of the United States of America, are privileged to enjoy." Kogan's sponsor was Rep. Ruben Hinojosa (D-TX) whose Latino-majority 15th Congressional District touched the U.S.-Mexico border. Kogan returned to the House on March 12, 2019. He had a new position: Director of the Institute for Bioethics and Social Justice, University of Texas Rio Grande Valley School of Medicine. A new Latino sponsor: Rep. Vicente Gonzalez (D-TX), who replaced Hinojosa. The numbers were updated: "As an immigrant who came to this country 20 years ago and became an American citizen just 7 years ago." But the sentiment remained the same: "I join this House in a prayer of profound gratitude and deep appreciation for the blessings we, the people of the United States of America, are privileged to enjoy."

Finally—and staying with a Texas rabbi—consider Jimmy Kessler of Congregation B'nai Israel in Galveston. His April 4, 2001, House prayer blended many aspirational themes—and several names: "When my grandparents Sol Aron, Pincus Kessler, Fred Nussenblatt, and Ralph Hoffman fled inhuman treatment in Europe, I wonder what their prayers would be this day. Surely, standing in this hallowed place inspires my deepest gratitude for their courage and faith and for the freedom and strength of our great Nation. Moreover, though it may be routine for some of you in this room today, it is truly an awesome moment for me to realize those who have stood here before me and to be privileged to occupy that same space."

In the context of immigration, it's notable that a rabbi from Galveston served as House guest chaplain. In the early part of the twentieth century, the Galveston Movement was a program to divert Jewish immigrants fleeing Eastern Europe and Russia away from crowded east coast U.S. cities, particularly New York, to Galveston docks where they would settle instead. Rabbi Mara Nathan of San Antonio was a House guest chaplain in January 2018. Her synagogue, Temple Beth-El, gives this history: "While Ellis Island accepted the lion's share of Eastern European immigrants during the late 1800s, Galveston, Texas, less than 250 miles from San Antonio, became the nation's second largest port of entry for Jewish refugees. Many of these pioneers made their way to San Antonio, developing a community of merchants, bankers and cattlemen." Nathan's sponsor: Rep. Joaquin Castro (D-TX), a second generation Mexican American.

In a delightful quirk of guest chaplain history, a Galveston rabbi beat Kessler to the House rostrum by over a century—and even preceded the Galveston Movement. Coming from the same synagogue as Kessler—Congregation B'nai Israel—Abraham Blum gave the House prayer on April 26, 1888. Kessler was born in Houston, Texas. Blum in Alsace, France.

6: Rabbis from Big States, Rabbis from Little States

Let's stay in Texas to meet more rabbis. Galveston is an island city on the Gulf Coast of Texas, near the eastern border with Louisiana. Eight hundred miles across Texas, on the far western corner of the Lonestar State near New Mexico in a different time zone: El Paso.

Galveston and El Paso: two Texas cities the length of Texas from each other. And both far away from Washington, DC. But both mid-size towns can claim rabbis who have prayed in Congress.

When Stephen Leon of Congregation B'nai Zion gave the House prayer on July 22, 2009, he celebrated: "How fortunate I feel to live in this blessed country of America where a Rabbi from El Paso, Texas is given the opportunity to offer a prayer before this historic assembly which represents the highest ideals of democracy." Rep. Silvestre Reyes (D-TX) shared the hometown pride: "I know that back in my district, back in El Paso, people have gotten up extra early to see the rabbi give our opening prayer."

An El Paso rabbi in Congress—in fact, any rabbi from the Mountain Time Zone—certainly is an eye-opener. And if America could have watched the House of Representatives on television on February 9, 1967, the people of Beaumont, Texas, might have gotten up earlier, too—even if they do live in the more reasonable Central Time Zone. On that date, Newton Friedman of Congregation Temple Emanuel gave the House prayer.

Mara Nathan of San Antonio delivered the House prayer over five decades later, January 19, 2018. "As far as I know, this is the first time that a San Antonio synagogue temple is going to be represented," she told local KENS-TV news the day before. "Just having the opportunity, as a rabbi representing the Jewish community, representing San Antonio, you know, it's exciting." Nathan was right: 136 years after the first rabbi guest chaplain showed up from Texas, San Antonio became the eighth Lone Star city represented.

Breaking down the rabbis by geography leads to colorful and sometimes unusual home city and state stories.

Which states do these 441 rabbis come from?[16] No surprise: The top producing state is New York. Nearly three in ten rabbi guest chaplain prayers (184 prayers from 136 different rabbis, tops in both categories) via the Empire State. The first male rabbi guest chaplain (Morris Raphall) and the first female (Sally Priesand): Both New Yorkers.

And talk about a concentration of prayer power: Three-quarters of all rabbi prayers have been delivered by rabbis from just nine states. Adding to New York: Pennsylvania (45 prayers from 38 rabbis), Maryland (37 prayers from 29 rabbis), New Jersey (34 prayers from 32 rabbis), Florida (33 prayers from 23 rabbis), California (29 prayers from 22 rabbis), Illinois (20 prayers from 17 rabbis), Minnesota (19 prayers from nine rabbis), Virginia (19 prayers from 13 rabbis). Plus, Washington, DC: 58 prayers from 22 rabbis.

That's 478 prayers from 341 rabbis—77% of the total number of rabbis and 76% of the total prayers. Just from those nine states plus DC.

Almost half of the DC prayers were offered by Washington Hebrew Congregation rabbis. And Washington Hebrew Congregation has produced the greatest number of rabbi guest chaplains of any synagogue in America, eight. Those eight have given a total of 24 prayers, first place among all synagogues. When he sponsored Rabbi Bruce Lustig on May 16, 2019, Rep. Jamie Raskin (D-MD) noted, "Since the Washington Hebrew Congregation was created in 1862, every single one of its senior rabbis has delivered an opening prayer before the U.S. Congress."

Second place goes to B'nai Jeshurun in New York, with eight prayers. Third place: Adas Israel in Washington, DC, with seven prayers. Sitting five miles from the U.S. Capitol pays off. In fact, during the latter part of the nineteenth century, Congress published an annual list called "Places of Divine Worship." Washington Hebrew Congregation—then even closer to Congress, at 8th Street between H and I, NW—always made the cut. It was later joined by Adas Israel.

It is a group of states you would expect to represent the American Jewish population.

---

16 As determined by location of the pulpit or military posting with which they identified as guest chaplain.

Likewise, most of the 11 states which have never been represented by a rabbi giving a prayer in Congress are the ones you would intuitively expect to see on a "no" list: Hawaii, Idaho, Kansas, Montana, Mississippi, North Dakota, Oklahoma, South Carolina, South Dakota, Utah, and Wyoming.[17] (A Wyoming rabbi has been in the House chamber, however. Rabbi Zalman Mendelsohn of the Chabad Jewish Center of Wyoming accompanied Republican Rep. Liz Cheney to the 2019 State of the Union address as her guest.)

If there's one surprise on that not-yet list, it's South Carolina. The Palmetto State has a rich Jewish history. One of the earliest Jewish settlements in the United States, according to an interview with author Sue Eisenfeld in the April 2, 2020, *Jewish Insider* online publication, "was a thriving Sephardi community established in Charleston, South Carolina, in 1695." That community, Eisenfeld wrote in her book *Wandering Dixie: Dispatches from the Lost Jewish South,*[18] "became the largest Jewish community in North America through the 1830s with about five hundred Jewish people, compared to only about four hundred in New York."

In 1800, according to the *Jewish Virtual Library*, Charleston was home to the largest Jewish community in America. One-fifth of all Jews lived there. Charleston congregation Kahal Kadosh Beth Elohim was established in 1749. It is the fourth oldest Jewish congregation in the United States. Its sanctuary is the second oldest synagogue building and the oldest in continuous use.[19]

The others make sense. Like the two Dakotas. No wonder: In the 2010 Census they were the only states in the nation with fewer than a thousand Jews. The *Washington Post* reported on November 28, 2016, that South Dakota went from 1982 to 2016 without a full-time rabbi. Profiling on September 23, 2017, a Lubavitch rabbi headed to South Dakota, the Minneapolis *Star-Tribune* reported there are fewer than 400 Jews living in South Dakota, a state of 865,000.

If Montana ever merited a rabbi guest chaplain, one candidate might be Francine Green Roston. The rabbi of Glacier Jewish Community in northwest Montana, Roston earned national recognition for resisting white supremacists in the state. Roston told the Anti-Defamation League on May

---

17   As of February 2020.
18   Mad Creek Books, 2020.
19   There *has* been a Charleston, West Virginia rabbi in Congress, but not one from Charleston, South Carolina.

8, 2017, "If you move to Northwest Montana, you're not necessarily looking for institutional Judaism. We don't even have a building. It's hard for the bad guys to find us."

Oklahoma, too, is on the not-yet list for rabbi guest chaplains. But in a twist, a rabbi guest chaplain has mentioned Oklahoma in a prayer. An intense, destructive, and deadly tornado struck Oklahoma on May 20, 2013. Three days later, Delaware rabbi Michael Beals opened the Senate. "We send our first prayer to the residents of Moore, Oklahoma," Beals said. "May be Your will that those who are missing be found alive and be cared for. Send comfort to those who have suffered loss, and with the help of those gathered here, send the resources required to rebuild."

Meantime, the list of 39 states plus DC which have produced rabbi guest chaplains includes some surprises.

There's Vermont. Other than Bernie Sanders, Vermont isn't known for Jews and Congress, right? Consider Max Wall. Rabbi of Ohavi Zedek in Burlington for 41 years, Wall was the first—and still only—Vermont Jewish guest chaplain. He opened the Senate in prayer on June 21, 1984. (Wall was born in Poland, as was Bernie Sanders' father.) Vermont's Jewish population, according to a September 28, 2016, *Philadelphia Exponent* article, is estimated to "be between 18,000 on the low end and 25,000 on the high . . . a significant percentage of Vermont's overall population of around 625,000. In fact, it would mean Jews make up a larger percentage of Vermont's population than they do of Pennsylvania's." Yet Vermont's sole rabbi prayer lags far behind—proportionally—the 44 from Pennsylvania. Perhaps it is no surprise, then, that a "small" theme made its way into Wall's prayer: "From the smallest of Your planets 'you took some dust, touched it with four spirit and called it Adam.'"

Smaller states might not get as much attention as the larger ones for their Jewish tradition. But their rabbis in Congress nevertheless spark colorful anecdotes. They make us aware of snippets of Jewish—and American—history that might otherwise go forgotten.

Father Jim Trainor of Wilmington gave the Senate prayer on January 25, 2001. Sen. Joe Biden (D-DE) said, "I only know of a total of three other Delawareans since I have been here who have ever been guest Chaplain. . . Rabbi Kenneth S. Cohen from Congregation Beth Shalom was a guest Chaplain in 1982, and Father Robert Balducelli from St. Anthony's Parish."

Three years later, on May 20, another Delawarean gave the Senate prayer: Rabbi Ellen Bernhardt of the Albert Einstein Academy in Wilmington.

Biden returned to the Senate floor: "Delaware is a small state and everyone seems to know everyone else. We know just about everyone in the State. You can't go to the grocery store, church, synagogue, or mosque without running into people you know. We go to each other's events. It is a little like Alaska—small. Alaska is gigantic, but the population is small."

Bernhardt's presence in the Senate chamber that day enabled Biden to expand his Delaware roll call of clergy. "In my 31st year in the Senate," Biden said, "Rabbi Bernhardt is only the fifth guest Chaplain I have invited from Delaware, following in the footsteps of Father Jim Trainor from St. Patrick's Church, Rabbi Kenneth S. Cohen from Congregation Beth Shalom, and Father Robert Balducelli from St. Anthony's Parish."

Three Delaware rabbis have prayed in Congress, all in the Senate. Regarding Biden's suggestion that Delaware is like Alaska, small in population, how about a rabbi guest chaplain from Alaska?

Prayer answered. Yosef Greenberg of the Lubavitch Jewish Center of Alaska in Anchorage opened the Senate on February 3, 2016. Headline on the website *Chabad.org* on February 10, 2016: "A First in the U.S. Senate: Rabbi From 'The Last Frontier' Delivers Morning Prayer." Sen. Lisa Murkowski (R-AK) marked the occasion: "Today there is a little bit of history being made. It is the first time we have had a rabbi from the State of Alaska who has been willing and able to provide the morning prayer before the Senate."

New Mexico might seem thin on Jewish history. But here's something and someone unusual the Land of Enchantment can boast. Gerald Kane of Temple Beth-El in Las Cruces performed a rare feat among rabbis in Congress. He delivered prayers on consecutive days in both chambers. He opened the Senate on October 1, 2002. Then Kane opened the House the very next day. "Las Cruces is the second largest city in my home State of New Mexico, a very vibrant, growing metropolitan area. It is one of only five communities in New Mexico that has a synagogue. It has the third synagogue that was built in our State," Senate sponsor Jeff Bingaman (D-NM) said. "In talking with him this morning, we were at a loss to think when we last had a clergyman from New Mexico as our guest Chaplain in the Senate." And House sponsor Joe Skeen (R-NM) said, "Jewish pioneers have played an important role in the development of New Mexico for almost 200 years. Since the establishment of the first synagogue in 1883, New Mexico has benefited from the wisdom of many learned Jewish leaders."

Skeen showed a good grasp of New Mexico's Jewish heritage. A November 6, 2018, *New York Times* article (page A12) looked at descendants of Sephardic Jews expelled from Spain in 1492, "many of whom converted to Catholicism but secretly adhered to Jewish traditions as they settled in New Mexico and other frontiers of the Spanish Empire." The *Times* quoted a professional genealogist in Albuquerque: "We know that various people who came to New Mexico in the earliest phases of Spanish colonization had Sephardic backgrounds."

What Kane pulled off—back-to-back rabbi prayers in both chambers on consecutive days—has been accomplished just one other time. And it was the very next year. Milton Balkany gave the Senate prayer on June 25, 2003, and the House prayer on June 26, 2003. To borrow a phrase Chicago Cubs baseball hall-of-fame Ernie Banks made famous: Let's pray two! Of course, Balkany is from New York. Leave it to a sufficiently celebrated big state to muscle in on New Mexico's rare opportunity for Jewish glory.

More consecutive Jewish prayers from surprising states: Minnesota rabbis gave back-to-back prayers (that is, no other rabbi in between) in two different eras. The first time was in the early '60s. Gerald Kaplan of Agudath Achim Synagogue in Hibbing gave the House prayer on April 30, 1962. And Bernard Raskas of Temple of Aaron in St. Paul gave the Senate prayer a week and a half later, on May 10.[20] It happened a second time in the late '80s. Stephen Pinsky of Temple Israel in Minneapolis on June 13, 1989, and Moshe Feller on July 14, 1989—both times in the Senate, and both times sponsored by Sen. Rudy Boschwitz (R-MN). Boschwitz sponsored four rabbis from Minnesota during his two-term Senate career.

One synagogue in Arkansas has produced two Senate rabbis—nearly a century apart. Emanuel Jack of Little Rock's Congregation B'nai Israel gave the prayer on December 14, 1925. Barry Block was guest chaplain on January 31, 2017. Block later became the 65th rabbi to pray in both chambers of Congress, opening the House on January 10, 2020. He was the first

---

20   Raskas was a friend of fellow Minnesotan Pauline Friedman Phillips. Under the name of Abigail Van Buren, she wrote the long-running 'Dear Abby' advice column. Her July 16, 1987, column asked, "Do you have a friend or relative who is anxiously waiting for some tests to come back from his/her physician?" Abby then passed along a prayer Raskas wrote: "God, please give me patience. The doctors do not yet know what is causing my distress. They are making many tests. Over and again, the have taken samples of my blood. They have probed me, listened to my heart, X-rayed me, injected me. And I wait—and wait—and wait!"

House guest chaplain of the new decade. (A rabbi was the last guest chaplain of the prior decade: Arnold Resnicoff on December 30, 2019.)

Another state not typically associated with Jews has been represented three times by rabbis in Congress: Alabama. Twice from Mobile, in the House in 1911 and 1939, both times by Alfred Moses of Congregation Shaarai Shomayim. This early Alabama representation is notably congruent with other Alabama-Jewish history. According to an April 16, 2013, proclamation by Alabama Gov. Robert Bentley (R), "in 1943, in the midst of World War II, at a time of war against the Axis powers and their effort to exterminate the Jews of Europe through mass murder, Alabama led the nation as the first state in America to officially call for the establishment of a Jewish homeland . . . five years prior to the official establishment of the modern State of Israel."

In 1939 Moses bestowed tribute upon a fellow Alabaman, Speaker William Bankhead. His June 16 prayer might make today's House leaders nostalgic if not downright envious: "Bless the President and Vice President of these United States, our beloved Speaker, upon whose able shoulders rests the Elijahlike mantle of a beloved, honored father."

"Beloved, honored" and "Elijahlike." A soaring comparison. All politics is local. Apparently, prayers can be, too.

7: Rabbis from Big Cities, Rabbis from Little Cities

Know the bigger cities. But don't ignore smaller ones. Cities not commonly associated to Jewish tradition also share flavorful history of Jewish life in America.

New York City rabbis gave five of the first 20 Jewish prayers in Congress. But four of the first 20 Jewish prayers came from Cincinnati rabbis.

Why Cincinnati? It has the oldest American Jewish community west of the Alleghenies, according to the *Jewish Virtual Library*. Cincinnati was mid-nineteenth-century America's third largest Jewish community. And as the site for the first campus of Hebrew Union College (HUC), it is also the historic and institutional center of American Reform Judaism. In fact, the three Ohio rabbis who gave those four early prayers—Isaac Mayer Wise, Max Lilienthal, and David Philipson—are part of HUC's institutional history.

Philadelphia rabbi J. Leonard Levy opened the Senate in prayer on January 21, 1895. He was later affiliated with Pittsburgh's Congregation

Rodeph Shalom. According to *Jewish Pittsburgh* by Barbara Burstin, "in 1905 the *Pittsburgh Post* listed Levy as one of the 12 Pittsburghers who had attained a national and international reputation along with the likes of Andrew Carnegie and George Westinghouse."[21]

Alexandria, Virginia, was the home city of Rabbi Sheldon Elster of Agudas Achim Congregation, the July 31, 1973, Senate guest chaplain. Two months after, the very next guest chaplain in Congress also was an Alexandria rabbi: Arnold Fink of Beth El Hebrew Congregation. He opened the House on September 11. And how about back-to-back Springfield rabbi—from different states. Both a year earlier, in 1972, and both in the House. Meyer Abramowitz of Temple B'rith Shalom in Springfield, Illinois, on June 30, followed on September 14 by Barry Schectman of Congregation Ner Tamid in Springfield, Pennsylvania.

(Another rarity: rabbis praying in both chambers on the same day. It happened 12 times between 1892 and 1994. Four times both rabbis were from the same state. Three of those four times that same state was, no surprise, New York. Twice in 1958 and once in 1967. The fourth time was a year later, Pennsylvania. The May 2, 1968, Senate guest chaplain was Morris Landes of Pittsburgh's Congregation Adath Jeshurun. The same day the House guest chaplain was Saul Wisemon of the Delaware County Jewish Community Center, located—here it is again—in Springfield.)

Nashville: another city with a richer Jewish history than you might imagine. According to *Nashville's Jewish Community* by Lee Dorman[22] the earliest Jewish settlers began arriving in the mid-nineteenth century. Rabbi Mark Schiftan of Nashville's The Temple: Congregation Ohabai Shalom gave the House prayer on June 20, 2018. Sponsor Rep. Jim Cooper (D-TN) noted Schiftan's Reform synagogue is the oldest and largest Jewish congregation in middle Tennessee. "The congregation dates back to 1851," Cooper said, "when the Vine Street Temple began worship services in downtown Nashville, even before the Civil War." The Vine Street Temple, dedicated in 1876, produced four rabbi prayers in Congress before America entered World War II. All were in the House—two from Isidore Lewinthal (July 1,

---

21 Arcadia Publishing, 2015, page 85. Levy was also big in Salt Lake. According to the *San Francisco Call* newspaper on June 14, 1898, he was invited to conduct services in the Mormon Tabernacle. It was "the first time in the history of Mormonism that a Jew or a Gentile has been given such invitation."

22 Arcadia Publishing, 2010, page 71.

1912, and January 17, 1917), then two from Julius Mark (January 16, 1931 and December 1, 1941).

Nashville is 70 miles from Pulaski, Tennessee, the birthplace of the KKK. In 1958, Nashville Jews found themselves part of the story of the Southern civil rights struggle. The reason: domestic terrorism. On March 16, a bomb exploded at the Nashville Jewish Community Center. Also, according to *The Temple Bombing* by Melissa Fay Greene the "Confederate Underground" called a rabbi with the Temple in Nashville warning him that his synagogue would be bombed, people who "love" African-Americans (using the N-word) would be shot and a federal judge "would be murdered for enforcing integration decisions."[23]

Eight years after the bombing, on August 11, 1966, Randall Falk of The Temple opened the House. "In a world of crisis and confusion, draw us ever closer unto Thee," the Nashville rabbi urged of God. Falk died on January 19, 2014, the same weekend that Martin Luther King's legacy is celebrated.

Charles Rubel of Congregation Sha'arey Israel in Macon, Georgia, gave the Senate prayer April 21, 1958. Six months later, 50 stacks of dynamite destroyed the interior of the Hebrew Benevolent Congregation, the oldest and most prominent synagogue in Atlanta.

The South produced the first American-born rabbi who opened the House in prayer. Edward Calisch (April 6, 1892, prayer) had deep connections to the region. His pulpit: Congregation Beth Ahabah in Richmond, a Virginia city which just 27 years earlier was the Confederacy capital. Calisch was a Richmond rabbi for 54 years. He died in 1946 in the city's Hotel Jefferson. But his views reflected a different place (he was born in Toledo, Ohio) and a different time. Quoted in *New York Times* articles, he offered a modern appeal to young people. "The youth of today has its right to help create its own philosophy of life, to break away from obsolete conceptions, to go pioneering on new paths" (February 15, 1929). And on June 30, 1922, in the *Times*, he supported admitting women to the rabbinate: "Everyone within the sound of my voice would be glad to welcome women to the sacred service."

America wouldn't have its first woman rabbi until half a century later (actually, 50 years later to the month: June 1972). But once that glass ceiling was broken, women rabbis quickly showed up in Congress.

---

23   Fawcett Columbine, 1997, page 227.

8: Women Break the Glass Pulpit

The first male rabbi to lead Congress in prayer did so in 1860.

The first female rabbi? 113 years later.

On October 23, 1973, Sally Priesand of the Reform Steven Wise Free Synagogue prayed in the House of Representatives.

New York rabbi Morris Raphall's ground-breaking 1860 prayer was reported by the *New York Times*. Priesand's glass-shattering prayer was not. Even though her synagogue was in New York City. And despite being sponsored by a congresswoman representing Manhattan's West Side.

To be fair to the *New York Times* assignment desk and editorial judgment at the time, there was abundant other pressing news going on. The next day's paper had two huge banner headlines on top: "NIXON AGREES TO GIVE TAPES TO SIRICA IN COMPLIANCE WITH ORDERS OF COURT." And "Egypt and Israel Accept New Cease-Fire Call; U.N. Agrees to send Observers to Suez Front."

That day was notable for another reason. In the House of Representatives itself, as the *Jewish Woman's Archive* points out, it was the day the first resolution to impeach President Nixon was offered.

Even if you were listening to Priesand's words, you still might not have been aware of their significance. Here's her entire prayer:

> Once again, we consecrate ourselves to the task of building a better world. Those who sit here have been granted positions of authority by their fellow citizens. May they use their power wisely and for the good of all, and may their decisions ever reflect a true sensitivity toward human needs. May they uphold the law of righteousness in America and courageously defend the democratic system wherever its survival is threatened. Proud of our achievements, yet aware of our shortcomings, may all our citizens unite in the spirit of concord and compassion to solve the problems of contemporary life and to create a world in which all people might at last live together in peace and in unity with none to make them afraid.

Nothing in there noting a greater accomplishment for women. But if Priesand's language did not lay down a history marker, her sponsor's remarks left no doubt what was happening:

This is indeed a historic occasion for more reasons than one. One is because Rabbi Preisand is the first woman rabbi in America[24] and the first to offer the morning prayer to the House of Representatives. . . . Her accomplishments have been recognized by many all over the country. As we learn from her words today, so can we learn from her life; to help others, to give leadership and to be open to change within the institutions of our society must be our goal, as it is hers.

Priesand's sponsor: Democratic Rep. Bella Abzug. "The tough-talking feminist from New York," as the *Associated Press* described her during that era (December 24, 1972).

Abzug wrote in the *The American Jewish Woman: A Documentary History* by Jacob Rader Marcus:[25]

For me, the new consciousness in the Jewish community and throughout the country was perfectly expressed the day I arranged for Rabbi Sally Priesand to deliver the opening prayer at the House of Representatives.

She was the first Jewish woman to do so.

She was the first *woman* to do so.

At that moment, I felt that two movements for social progress had merged and come of age. And I really felt at home in Washington.

Abzug's sponsoring remarks were unique because they brought attention to Priesand's gender. Except for one early exception none of the later sponsors would make mention of the sex of a female rabbi guest chaplain.[26] In fact, it would turn out likewise none of the subsequent woman rabbis who opened Congress would say anything in their prayers specifically acknowledging their gender.

Priesand's House prayer came just over one year after she was ordained as a rabbi—June 1972 from Hebrew Union College in Cincinnati. It was among the shortest waiting periods for any Congress rabbi guest chaplain. (A year before Priesand was ordained, Hilda Abrevaya became the first

---

24 Berlin-born Regina Jonas was the first woman ordained as a rabbi. She was killed in Auschwitz in October 1944.

25 Ktav Publishing, 1981, page 882.

26 The one exception: Rep. James Olin (D-VA) on October 24, 1985—almost exactly 12 years after Abzug. When Rabbi Lynne Landsberg of Staunton, Virginia, gave the House prayer that day, Olin noted Landsberg "was among the first 30 women ordained as rabbis in the United States. She came to the Shenandoah Valley of Virginia last year to serve a seven-county area. She is the valley's only rabbi and first woman in that position."

American woman cantor retained by a synagogue, Temple Beth Shalom in Flushing, Queens. The *New York Times* marked this feminist achievement by reporting on May 30, 1971, that Abrevaya was "a brunette of medium height.")

For clergywomen it was a fast-moving early '70s in Congress. Particularly in the Senate, by design not known for fast-moving anything. The first woman Senate guest chaplain appeared two years before Priesand in the House: Presbyterian Rev. Wilmina Rowland Smith, July 8, 1971

The first Roman Catholic Nun, Sister Joan Keleher Doyle of the Sisters of Charity of the Blessed Virgin Mary, offered the Senate prayer on July 17, 1974. Credit to the Watergate-era Senate. It wasn't until much later for a similar Catholic occurrence in the House. Here's the *Newark Star-Ledger* on September 13, 2000 (page 3): "Sister Catherine Moran of the Newark Archdiocese gingerly stepped to the podium of the House of Representatives yesterday afternoon and offered the invocation—making history as the first Roman Catholic nun and the first non-ordained woman to serve as the chamber's guest chaplain." A third woman guest Senate chaplain was the Methodist Rev. Judith Coleman on October 2, 1974. Then in July 1977 Rev. Margaret Muncie of New York became the first ordained woman Episcopal priest to give the prayer in the House of Representatives. She was ordained three months earlier.[27]

But then, for Jews, things slowed down. Two hundred and eighty-nine prayers by male rabbis preceded Priesand. After Priesand, the next prayer by a woman rabbi wasn't for another 12 years—October 24, 1985, in the House. That's 111 more male prayers later. The Senate waited two decades after Priesand for its first female rabbi. On April 20, 1994, Sen. Russ Feingold (D-WI) introduced to the Senate his sister, Dena Feingold. Rabbi Feingold told the Wisconsin Jewish Chronicle she hadn't thought about a rabbinical

---

27　Adding to the identity-fueled "firsts" of this era: The '70s also featured the first Native American holy man to give a Senate prayer. Frank Fools Crow was part of the Sioux delegation that helped end the 1973 American Indian insurrection at Wounded Knee. On September 5, 1975, at the invitation of South Dakota senators James Abourezk and George McGovern and with his peace pipe at hand, Fools Crow said: "I make my prayer for all people, the children, the women and the men. I pray that no harm will come to them." *People* magazine reported Fools Crow's prayer the next year (October 25, 1976): "As a young man he traveled with Buffalo Bill's Wild West shows, learning to be at ease before audiences. He performed in September 1975 in front of an impressive one, opening the U.S. Senate with a prayer in his native Lakota language." The first Native American prayer in the House was many decades later, November 13, 2019.

career until she learned about Priesand. "Because there was somebody out there doing it, it made it possible for me to think about doing it" (March 31, 2008). Rabbi Feingold comes from Janesville, Wisconsin—as does former House Speaker Paul Ryan. In fact, the same floor of the Janesville building where Ryan's father practiced law, according to *Milwaukee Magazine* in November 2007, also housed the law office of Russ and Dena's father, Leon Feingold.

Fifteen Congress prayers (twelve in the House, three in the Senate) have been delivered by fourteen female rabbis. The thirteenth prayer was offered by Mara Nathan of San Antonio's Temple Beth-El, the first woman to serve as senior rabbi at a congregation in Texas. In the House on January 19, 2018, Nathan wore a yarmulke and recognized "the women and men of our Congress." The last time a female rabbi had given the House prayer was over a decade prior.

Some data for perspective. The *New York Times* reported on May 20, 2006, that 829 women had been ordained among the three denominations—Reform, Reconstructionist and Conservative—that accept women into the rabbinate. The *Daily Beast* reported on March 21, 2013 that women "still make up a relatively small percentage of rabbis in Judaism's largest liberal streams—35 percent of Reform rabbis and 17.5 percent of Conservative rabbis." And Debra Nussbaum Cohen reported in the May 31, 2016, *Jewish Telegraphic Agency* that more than 700 female Reform rabbis have been ordained since 1973.[28] Of the 97 Reform rabbi prayers in Congress starting with Priesand in 1973 up to January 2020, nine were delivered by women—eight in the House, one in the Senate. There have also been been three prayers delievered by Conservative women rabbis and two prayers by one Reconstructionist woman rabbi.

It is unlikely a woman Orthodox rabbi will be added to the mix any time soon. According to the November 2, 2015, *Forward*, the Orthodox Rabbinical Council of America "formally adopted a policy prohibiting the ordination or hiring of women rabbis." Jewish law, *halacha*, contains no particular section on the qualifications of a congregational rabbi, according to Avi Shafran, an Orthodox rabbi and director of public affairs for Agudath Israel of America. But Shafran told *Moment* magazine in October 2018 "the acceptance of female clergy is at least partly motivated by non-Jewish

---

28   The *JTA* also reported that female Reform rabbis make between 80 and 90 cents for every dollar male Reform rabbis earn for comparable work.

societal values and not inherently Jewish ones. That is a major part of why the idea of female clergy has been rejected by the Haredi and traditional Orthodox communities."

More facts about the 14 women rabbis:

- Since 1871, 98 male rabbis made repeat appearances as a guest chaplain before the first female rabbi returned to Congress for a second prayer—Hannah Spiro in 2018.

- Of the 12 for whom there is video of their appearances, six wore yarmulkes.

- The first Conservative female rabbi was September 14, 2006: Amy Rader of Boca Raton's B'nai Torah Congregation. The September 17, 2006, *Boca Raton News* ran her picture with sponsor Rep. Clay Shaw (R-FL) and noted "she became Florida's first female Rabbi to give the opening prayer" in the House. (She is married to Kevin Rader, a Democratic member of the Florida House of Representatives.)

- The first rabbi guest chaplain after Republicans took control of the House in 1995 was a woman, Rachel Mikva. She was the first woman rabbi to serve as House guest chaplain in ten years. Mikva is the daughter of the late Rep. Abner Mikva (D-IL) who was White House counsel in the Clinton administration and a federal judge for 15 years.

- When Delaware rabbi Ellen Bernhardt offered a prayer on May 20, 2004, she became the first—and so far, only—woman rabbi to be introduced to the Senate by a woman presiding in the chair, Lisa Murkowski (R-AK). (In 2016 Sen. Murkowski would sponsor the first rabbi guest chaplain from Alaska, Yosef Greenberg, a Lubavitcher.)

- Rabbi Joui Hessel of Washington Hebrew Congregation gave the House prayer on June 4, 2004, two weeks after Bernhardt gave the Senate prayer. Two years later Hessel was named to *Washingtonian* magazine's list of 20 Fabulous Singles: "They're smart, funny, successful, and available—for now." Hessel married in 2014.

- The first American woman ever to be ordained as a rabbi, Priesand is believed to be the second woman rabbi ever anywhere. The first woman Conservative rabbi, Amy Eilberg, hasn't been a guest chaplain. But she's still connected to Congress. Her father was Rep.

Joshua Eilberg (D-PA). He sponsored guest chaplain Rabbi Leo Landman on October 17, 1967, and Rabbi Harold Romirowsky on March 13, 1969.

And since there have been male guest chaplains from Israel, how about a female guest chaplain from Israel? Actually, yes. One. A month into Newt Gingrich's speakership, February 14, 1995, the House prayer was offered by a woman guest chaplain from Jerusalem. But she wasn't Jewish. The Reverend Ruth Ward Heflin was a Pentecostalist.

A more exclusive men's club than rabbis who pray in Congress is the collection of historical figures whom they mention in their prayers. Rabbis have cited Abraham, Isaac, Jacob, Moses, Aaron, Akiva, Hillel, Amos, David, Solomon—even Jesus. But the first name of a Jewish woman was not uttered until the 611th time a rabbi was guest chaplain. Seth Frisch of Philadelphia's Historic Congregation Kesher Israel marked Purim, on February 27, 2018. "It was Queen Esther who became frightened when the plan revealing a plot to erase the sacred remnants of her people, along with the fundamental teachings of her faith, came to light," Frisch said in his third stint as guest chaplain. "And yet, it was Esther who when confronted by the impending darkness, was able to bring the plot to an end, allowing her people to emerge from the shadow of this horror and live freely, without fear, celebrating life itself, in the light of their new-found freedom."

Here's how men rabbis included women in their remarks before Esther showed up:

- Abram Simon of Washington Hebrew Congregation urged the Senate on January 16, 1905, to "recognize in the great Republic of a united humanity but one citizenship, that of a consecrated manhood and womanhood."
- Samuel Soskin in the House on March 1, 1951: "From of old our country builded by men and women of invincible will has served as eloquent symbol of that liberty so desperately sought by mankind."
- Bertram Korn in the Senate, July 13, 1955: "I thank Thee, lord of all souls, that my daughter and the child yet in the womb of my wife will be privileged to grow in an atmosphere of law and order."
- Bernard Raskas, October 28, 1981: "God of our fathers and mothers, God of us all, we ask Your inspiration and guidance as the Members of the U.S. senate begin their deliberations. . . ."

- Theodore Levy in the Senate on March 8, 1984: "There is only one woman on Earth and her name is All Women."
- Arnold Resnicoff in the House in 2017: "On this date, August 18, we made progress in the past. We ratified the 19th Amendment, tearing down the wall that blocked a woman's right to vote; did what we do best when we are at our best; made a moral right a legal right, enshrining liberty in law."

Tucson rabbi Thomas Louchheim in the House on May 17, 2017, offered this acknowledgment of congressional demographics: "Loving God, each day raise up these good women and men who are serving our country with honor."

Louchheim was sponsored by Rep. Martha McSally (R-AZ). How often does a female member of Congress sponsor a rabbi guest chaplain of either sex? Returning to the '70s, during one stretch of 1975 three straight rabbis were sponsored by women House members. Rep. Marjorie Holt (R-MD) sponsored Rabbi Barry Rosen on September 11. Rep. Elizabeth Holtzman (D-NY) sponsored Rabbi Abraham Feldbin on September 30. And Rep. Gladys Spellman (D-MD) sponsored Rabbi Mendel Abrams on November 3.[29]

Abzug sponsored the first female rabbi (and no other rabbi). But she was not the first female member of Congress to sponsor a rabbi guest chaplain. Republican Rep. Margaret Heckler of Massachusetts was. Heckler sponsored four rabbis during her congressional career, two of whom were before Abzug: Baruch Korff on July 29, 1969, and Norbert Weinberg on June 30, 1970. Heckler also sponsored the first guest prayer by the chief rabbi of Israel: Shlomo Goren on June 24, 1974.

Heckler's four sponsorships from 1969 to 1982 ties her for second place for most rabbi sponsorships by a representative or senator (Democratic Florida Rep. William Lehman holds the title with five between 1975 and 1990). Heckler also ties for first place among Republican sponsors with another woman, Rep. Ileana Ros-Lehtinen (R-FL), and Sen. Rudy Boschwitz (R-MN). From Heckler in 1969 through Rep. Kathleen Rice (D-NY) in July 2019, 27 women senators and representatives (19 Democrats, 8 Republicans) sponsored 36 rabbis.

---

29 Quite a year, 1975. On September 14, Pope Paul VI conferred upon Elizabeth Ann Seton the rites of canonization. She became the first American-born saint of the Roman Catholic Church.

Two footnotes to the Sally Priesand story. She became a guest chaplain in less than a year and a half after becoming a rabbi. That's fast. An even shorter period between ordination and Congress prayer for another woman: Hannah Spiro. She graduated from Reconstructionist Rabbinical College in June 2017. On May 29, 2018, she opened the House. It was Spiro's 28th birthday (for political junkies: it was also John F. Kennedy's 101st birthday.) And it was 613th time a rabbi prayed in Congress—matching the number of commandments in the Torah.

But a government error stains Priesand's place in the history books. The official *Congressional Record* got her name wrong. For her prayer and Abzug's subsequent sponsor remarks, the *Record* spells Priesand as *Preisand*. Which, amid possible greater symbolism and even humiliation and indignity, as a practical matter makes Priesand's prayer tough—aggravating, even—to find if searching for the official account of that 1973 day. Hers is the only name among all the rabbi guest chaplains the *Congressional Record* misspells. The sponsoring member typically submits the guest chaplain's name and prayer for publishing in the *Record*. Abzug's name is spelled correctly.

9: Jewish Military Chaplains Are Congress Chaplains, Too

Here's one common characteristic of a special group of rabbis who have opened Congress: As military soldiers they fought for their country in combat uniform.

Among them:

- Emanuel Jack of Little Rock's Congregation B'nai Israel gave the December 14, 1925, Senate prayer. Jack was a World War I veteran, a Veteran of Foreign Wars commander, and chairman of the American Legion's Americanization Committee, according to Tom Dillard in *Statesmen, Scoundrels, and Eccentrics: A Gallery of Amazing Arkansans.*[30]
- William Berkowitz of New York Congregation B'nai Jeshurun—the same synagogue that produced the first rabbi guest chaplain, Morris Raphall—gave the April 16, 1964, Senate prayer. He was a naval officer during World War II.

---

30   University of Arkansas Press, 2010, page 233.

- Louis Kaplan of Congregation Ohev Shalom in Pennsylvania was House guest chaplain on June 3, 1969. He served in the Army for 21 months, including a year in Korea. He was honorably discharged with the rank of staff sergeant.

Six Jewish soldiers even wore service dress uniforms *while* they prayed in Congress. Two of them:

- Army Chaplain Martin Applebaum in the Senate on February 20, 1992: "Of the treacherous paths upon which evil rides with wild abandon, where fanaticism is camouflaged, as righteous zealotry."
- Navy chaplain Maurice Kaprow in the House on May 5, 2004: "Remember the many members of our Armed Forces, especially those serving far from home in the midst of danger, at the tip of the spear, bringing the hope of democracy where tyranny once ruled."

Applebaum and Kaprow belong to another unique group of rabbis who have opened Congress in prayer: chaplains in the United States Armed Forces. Fifty-five Jewish military chaplains have done so, from all five branches. An impressive, colorful, and patriotic slice of American history.

Some background. During the earliest days of the Civil War, Rabbi Arnold Fischel of New York's Congregation Shearith Israel applied for certification as a military chaplain. Consistent with U.S. law that limited military chaplaincy to Christians, Secretary of War Simon Cameron rejected his application.

"The publicity surrounding the rejection of Rabbi Fischel galvanized the Jewish community," writes Albert Slomovitz in *Fighting Rabbis: Jewish Military Chaplains and American History*.[31] "Individuals and groups determined that this chaplaincy requirement must be changed."

Writing in *We Called Him Rabbi Abraham: Lincoln and American Jewry, a Documentary History*, Rabbi Gary Zola—himself twice a guest chaplain in Congress—notes Fischel "was determined to bring this matter to the personal attention of President Lincoln,"[32] He went to Washington "armed with letters of introduction and reference." Zola provides this December 15, 1861, letter from President Lincoln to Fischel:

---

31   New York University Press, 1998, page 16.
32   Southern Illinois University Press, 2014, page 76.

I find there are several particulars in which the present law in regard to chaplains is supposed to be deficient, all which I now design presenting the appropriate Committee of Congress, I shall try to have a new law broad enough to cover what is desired by you in behalf of the Israelites.

On the floor of Congress a few days later—Christmas Eve 1861—Rep. William Holman (D-IN) said, "My motive in calling the attention of the House and of the Military Committee to this subject is this: it seems that under the legislation of last session a Jewish rabbi is excluded from the right of being appointed a chaplain; and there being a large number of Hebrews in our Army, it is certainly proper, whether they be appointed or not, that they should not be excluded by law."

Outside official DC, the issue was getting attention via the secular press. On January 18, 1862, the *New York Times* reported from the Civil War front line in Louisville, Kentucky:

The Jews of this city are signing a petition to Congress, that as one or more regiments in the United States service are composed of citizens of the United States who are Jews, it is gross injustice to compel them to select a Christian minister as Chaplain. . . . And that the acts of Congress enacting that there can be no chaplain to any regiment except a regularly ordained Christian minister, are unconstitutional, and ought to be repealed.

And, according to Slomovitz, the editor of the *Baltimore Clipper* "reminded his readers that Congress itself had a rabbi open a legislative session with prayer: 'How was it that the same body could deny Jewish soldiers the right to share the prayers of the same clergyman.'"

Mentioning Jewish soldiers was more than a rhetorical device. In *Grant*, Ron Chernow quantifies how many American Jews fought in the Civil War—for both sides. "American Jews were highly patriotic," Chernow writes. "In a population of 150,000, ten thousand served the North or South in the war."[33]

The public pressure campaign succeeded. In 1862, Congress added a clarification to the chaplaincy provision. Slomovitz points out "this additional provision reinterpreted the prior requirement of 'some Christian denomination' to read, 'That no person shall be appointed a chaplain in the United States Army who is not a regularly ordained minister of some religious denomination.'"

---

33 Penguin Press, 2017, page 236.

Lincoln's July 17, 1862, signature enabled rabbis for the first time to serve as chaplains in the U.S. Army. Thus, a providential alignment of two milestone American Jewish breakthroughs in the early 1860s. The first rabbi guest chaplain in Congress, Morris Raphall, 1860.[34] And the first rabbi chaplain in the military, Jacob Frankel of Congregation Rodeph Shalom in Philadelphia in September 1862. (Frankel also was the first Jewish military chaplain of any nation.) And less than a year later the first Jewish military chaplain to serve with troops also became the first Jewish casualty in American military history: In July 1863 Rabbi Ferdinand Sarner of the 54th New York Volunteers was wounded at Gettysburg.

Three decades later, these two types of Jewish chaplains met as one rabbi: J. Leonard Levy. He opened the Senate in prayer on January 21, 1895. Three years later he was an Army chaplain during the Spanish-American War. The leader of Keegan's Brigade of Pennsylvania Volunteers sent Levy a letter on May 25, 1898, saying they were without a chaplain.[35] Noting the "patriotic sentiments you have uttered from time to time," C. M. Keegan asked Levy to accept the post. "The men have banded themselves together for the protection of the Fatherland," Keegan wrote, "and will feel pleased if they can receive spiritual ministrations at your hands in the broad and liberal spirit for which you have become known in this community and throughout the country." Over 2,500 American Jews fought in the Spanish-American war; 8,257 Jews participated in America's wars up to 1865, according to May 4, 1917, remarks by Rep. Frederick Hicks (R-NY).

(Five years later Keegan hardly fit the category of volunteer. He became the third-highest salaried rabbi in America on March 29, 1903 when his synagogue, Rodef Shalom in Pittsburgh, approved $10,000 a year, according to the next day's *New York Times*.)

Jewish participation in the Spanish-American War did not escape the notice of Theodore Roosevelt. On May 25, 1900, the Hebrew Union Veterans' Association and the Hebrew Veterans of the Spanish-American war held memorial services at New York City's Temple Emanuel-El, which

---

34 Rabbi Raphall wasn't in the military. But his son was. He fought in the Civil War. When London-born Major Alfred Raphall died, 35 years after his father, the Washington, DC *Evening Star* noted in its October 15, 1903, obituary: "He served with distinction throughout the war for the Union. He was the first adjutant of the 40th New York Infantry, and served as aid-de-camp on Gen. Ward's staff, and lost his right arm at the Battle of Gettysburg."

35 Cited in the 1898 B'nai B'rith magazine *The Menorah*, Menorah Publishing Company, page 60.

had already produced two rabbi guest chaplains in Congress. According to the *New York Times* the following day there were 96 Civil War veterans and 80 Spanish-American war veterans present.

Roosevelt, New York governor and future president, told the gathering "he had great faith in the Maccabee type," according to the *Times* account. "He hoped that everyone had read the book of the Bible which told of the splendid fighting qualities of the Maccabees." Roosevelt said that in the San Juan attack "he had lost thirteen officers and he cast about to find five men of the very best intelligence and character for five positions which needed good men. He picked them out and found afterward that there were two Protestants, two Catholics, and one Jew. He was very glad to find the Jew among them." Why? "He had observed that the Jews in his regiment showed great ability."

William Franklin Rosenblum opened the House in prayer on April 30, 1928. He, too, was both a guest Congress chaplain and a military chaplain. According to his February 10, 1968, *New York Times* obituary, during World War I Rosenblum fought in the U.S. Navy. From 1928 to 1933 he was a chaplain in the U.S. Army Reserve. And in spring 1967 Rosenblum "conducted Passover Seder services for United States armed forces in Saigon, South Vietnam." (At least one other rabbi guest chaplain held a Seder in Saigon: Alan Greenspan. Not the future Federal Reserve chairman, but an Army chaplain. He led Seder for troops April 4, 1966, and wrote an account in 2004, *With a Siddur & A Salami or S.O.S.—Send over Salamis*. On June 8, 1967, Greenspan was in front of the House of Representatives.)

With a career spanning multiple American conflicts from the Great War to Vietnam, Levy became a model pioneer for the 54 who followed. Since Levy, 12% of the 441 rabbis who have been a guest chaplain in Congress also served as a U.S. military chaplain. Likewise, 13% (81) of the 610 prayers delivered in Congress by a rabbi since Levy were given by a military chaplain (50 in the House and 31 in Senate).[36] Separate calculations for rabbis and prayers are needed to account for guest chaplains who made multiple appearances.

What do these military rabbis say in front of Congress? Their prayers aren't particularly military-themed. The language of most is indistinguishable from that offered by civilian chaplains. A few mentions of Armed Forces

---

36   Meantime, the number of Jews who serve in the U.S. military has declined, according to the *Washington Jewish Week*. From half a million Jewish soldiers during World War II, to one percent of the military now.

here, a few quotes of Isaiah 2:4 ("nation shall not lift up sword against nation") there. Standard stuff. Rather, it is the chaplains' biographies which provide compelling—in many cases, remarkable—history. At least two are buried in Arlington National Cemetery.

Take Karl Applbaum, who gave the House prayer three times (1952, 1963, 1970). Born in Hungary, Applbaum served as a chaplain during World War II and a major in the U.S. Army Reserve. He also was national chaplain to the Reserve Officers Association of the United States. When Applbaum gave his February 26, 1970, prayer, Rep. Seymour Halpern (R-NY) noted, "The rabbi also has a son. Capt. Joseph Applbaum serving in the Army in Italy who also has devoted himself to God. Joseph, the third generation of Applbaums serving in the rabbinate, is Jewish chaplain of the Southern European Task Force. Which brings me to another unique family honor. Karl and Joseph Applbaum are the only father and son rabbis serving the Armed Forces, and only one of two such father-son combinations presently serving as military chaplains."

Korean War veteran Reuven Siegel was another rabbi with the blood of military chaplaincy running through family veins. Representing Temple Adath Israel in the Bronx, he gave the August 12, 1965, House prayer. Rep. James Scheuer (D-NY) noted Siegel "served his country as an assistant force chaplain in the U.S. Navy. He is on the executive board of the Branch of Military Chaplains Association of New York." Siegel's brothers also were military chaplains. According to the April 7, 1958, Seattle *Jewish Transcript*, Army Reserve Chaplain Norman Siegel served as senior chaplain on the staff of the commanding general, U.S. Army Forces in Central Pacific. Rabbi Paul Siegel was an Air Force Reserve chaplain. Noting the three brothers serving as chaplains, the Indianapolis *Jewish Post* suggested on July 17, 1953: "If the record books are checked, it will probably be found that the Siegel family of Baltimore, Md., has set a mark in the American rabbinate and armed forces chaplaincy." The paper noted that Chaplain Norman Siegel held a Bronze Star for service in World War II and Chaplain Reuven Siegel served with the First Marine Division in Korea.

Perhaps the Jewish military clergyman with the most varied background is Arnold Resnicoff, who went to Vietnam after graduating from Dartmouth College as a member of Dartmouth's Naval Reserve Officers Training Corps. During the Vietnam War, he was a naval officer in the rivers of The Mekong Delta. After Vietnam, he served as a Naval Intelligence officer in Europe and then began rabbinical school. Sponsoring his prayer on February 6, 2019, Rep. Don Beyer (D-VA) noted Resnicoff "served in Vietnam and in Europe before attending rabbinical school, and then went on to serve as a U.S. Navy chaplain for almost 25 years. He promoted the creation of the Vietnam Veterans Memorial and delivered the closing prayer in its 1982 dedication."

Military chaplains like Resnicoff who served in combat roles before their studies in the seminary and ordination have a unique perspective. They can better relate to the rank and file service-members.

Resnicoff was in Beirut when, on October 23, 1983, a suicide truck bomb killed 241 Americans. He was among the first to reach the tragic scene. He put down in writing the experiences of that day. President Reagan read his report at the April 13, 1984, Baptist Fundamentalism Convention. "These were the words of Lieutenant Commander Resnicoff," Reagan concluded his speech. "Let us strive to live up to the vision of faith that Chaplain Resnicoff saw that day and let us never stop praying and working for peace."

As if that weren't enough—*Dayenu!*—Resnicoff has this distinction: the most appearances by any Jewish guest chaplain in Congress, military or nonmilitary. Sixteen times as of February 2020, eight each in the Senate and House. His eight in the Senate were all during the first six months of 2003. (In one twist of military history, for his May 19, 2003, prayer, he was introduced to the body by future Obama administration Defense Secretary Chuck Hagel, then a Republican senator from Nebraska.) Seven of his House prayers came during pro forma sessions, another record (the Senate does not have a prayer or pledge of allegiance opening its pro forma sessions) and a benefit of living close to the U.S. Capitol. His first House prayer was July 23, 2016, the same day as the Republican National Convention.

Some rabbis wore their military uniforms to the rostrum. Like Applebaum of the 201st Expeditionary Military Intelligence Bridge in Fort Lewis, Washington. According to the April 26, 2013, *Dayton Jewish Observer*, he served in the U.S. Army for 20 years as a chaplain and retired as a lieutenant colonel. He served as the military liaison to the U.S. Holocaust Memorial Council.

Also from the Army and wearing his uniform: Kenneth Leinwand, installation chaplain for Ft. Meade. He gave the February 16, 2006, House prayer. Rep. Ben Cardin (D-MD): "Colonel Leinwand is the highest-ranking active duty Jewish chaplain in the United States military. The Colonel has been an active duty Army chaplain since 1977. He has served in Iraq, Desert Storm, Bosnia and Kosovo. From 2002 to 2004 he also served as the command chaplain for all U.S. Army ground forces in Europe." Cardin noted Leinwand has been awarded the Legion of Merit, the Bronze Star, the Meritorious Service Medal with four oak leaf clusters, and the Army Commendation Medal with one oak leaf cluster.

In the book *I Am Jewish: Personal Reflections Inspired by the Last Words of Daniel Pearl* Leinwand wrote:

> As the command chaplain on a four-star battle staff planning for major military operations, or in my role as the technical supervisor of 200 chaplains of every major denomination, God has granted me the privilege to serve a congregation of 62,000 soldiers and 130,000 family members throughout U.S. Army Europe. [37]

Kaprow wore his uniform twice. First for his May 5, 2004, House prayer when he was Rabbi Commander of the U.S. Naval Reserve Chaplain Corps in Norfolk. And four years later for his September 25, 2008, Senate prayer when he was with the Center for Information Dominance in Pensacola.

According to a March 6, 2010, *Time* magazine piece by Mark Thompson, Kaprow had a 20-year career in the Navy and visited some 200 ships. An April 4, 2003 profile in *The Jewish News of Northern California* noted that roughly one percent of the Navy was Jewish; Kaprow was the only rabbi with the Mediterranean-based Sixth Fleet. There were only nine rabbis in the entire navy.

In his 2008 Senate prayer, Kaprow said, "our thoughts turn to those brave Americans—young men and women from every part of our country—who volunteer to serve in our Armed Forces. They are soldiers, Marines, sailors, airmen, and coast guardsmen." Similar sentiments a year earlier—January 18, 2007—from another uniformed rabbi military chaplain. Wearing his Navy Service Dress Blues, Rear Admiral Harold Robinson prayed in the Senate "for those who serve us in harm's way: sailors, soldiers, Marines, airmen, and coast guardsmen who willingly sacrifice the protection and comfort of home and family to defend our safety and our security."

Those three rabbis—Robinson, Kaprow, Leinwand—wore military uniforms from 2004–2008, a period coinciding with the height of America's involvement with the Iraq War.[38] Perhaps Jewish military chaplains wore their uniforms at the rostrum during earlier wars, but know definitively

---

37   Edited by Judea and Ruth Pearl, Jewish Lights, 2005, page 157.
38   In 2008, according to the *Jerusalem Post* (April 24, 2008) four Jewish chaplains were serving full-time in Iraq. 311 served in World War II.

for the most recent few decades. Recorded visual images of the prayers go back to 1979, when television coverage of the U.S. House began. Senate TV began in 1986.

Jonathan Panitz of the Navy prayed in the House on October 16, 1991. He is the earliest visible example of a rabbi in military uniform praying in Congress. At the time, Panitz was head of the policy branch in the Office of the Chief of Chaplains at the Pentagon. According to the June 17, 2012, Baltimore *Sun*, Panitz was senior Jewish chaplain of the Sixth Fleet. He was also chaplain for the National Naval Medical Center in Bethesda. And he was half of a rare father/son duo: Jonathan Panitz's father David was Senate guest chaplain on April 27, 1960. David Panitz died nine months before Jonathan's 1991 House prayer.

Grouping the rabbis by which branch of the military they served, the U.S. Army tops the list. Over half—62% (34) Jewish military chaplains—are Army. These rabbis have given 41 total prayers in Congress (28 in the House, 13 in the Senate). Today, there are less than a dozen rabbis on active duty in the Army.

Two who appeared during the Vietnam War had strong West Point connections.

Abraham Chill of Providence gave the June 23, 1965, Senate prayer. He served in the Army during World War II. According to the April 10, 1936, *Wisconsin Jewish Chronicle* (page 14), Chill was the first Jewish chaplain at the United States Military Academy in West Point. He cared "for the spiritual needs of the 15 Jewish cadets."

A year later, on March 21, Avraham Soltes of Temple Emanuel in Great Neck gave the House prayer. He was Jewish chaplain at West Point for 20 years and was buried there. Sponsor Rep. Lester Wolff (D-NY) said that after the prayer Soltes "met with Lt. Gen. J. B. Lampert, Deputy Assistant Secretary of Defense for Manpower and me at the Capitol. General Lampert, former Superintendent at the Military Academy, worked closely with Rabbi Soltes during his assignment to West Point and had high praise for the rabbi's contributions to the spiritual life of the Academy." When President Ford attended the June 4, 1975, West Point graduation ceremony, Soltes gave the benediction. A year before his 1983 death, Soltes told the *New York Times* (May 4, 1982), that half of West Point's "first graduation class in 1802 was Jewish—a distinction, the rabbi noted, owed entirely to Simon Levy, a Revolutionary War veteran who was one of the two graduates that year."

Other notable rabbi guest chaplains from the Army:

- Edward Sandrow was House guest chaplain twice, 1936 and 1966. That 30-year gap between prayers is the fourth-longest for any rabbi with two or more Congress appearances.[39] He was a World War II chaplain. According to his 1966 sponsor Rep. Herbert Tenzer (D-NY), Sandrow rose from rank of lieutenant to major. He served in the Aleutian Islands for a year and a half and received the Army Commendation Medal. And, according to the December 30, 1969, *Jewish Telegraphic Agency*, he became vice-president of the Association of Jewish Chaplains of the Armed Forces of the United States.

- A month after Germany invaded Poland in 1939 starting World War II, Russian-born Isaac Landman gave the House prayer. His September 5, 1946, *New York Times* obituary noted, "When the Army was mobilized on the Mexican border in 1916 he became a chaplain and was said to have been the first Jewish chaplain in the American Army to serve on foreign soil."

- Seymour Essrog, Beth Israel Synagogue in Randallstown, Maryland, gave the April 20, 1982, House prayer. According to his October 19, 2002, *Baltimore Sun* obituary, after his 1959 ordination Essrog joined the Army for two years of active duty as a chaplain and 28 years in the reserves. He retired as a lieutenant colonel.

Two Army chaplains had connections to the early days of the State of Israel.

Irving Block of Congregation Beth Achim in New York served in the U.S. Army in World War II. Then he fought with the Jewish paramilitary Haganah in Israel's 1948 War of Independence. When he gave the House prayer on June 2, 1983, Rep. Bill Green (R-NY) said, "As a member of the Jewish War Veterans, I am proud of the fact that Rabbi Block is the Department of New York State chaplain, Jewish War Veterans and in 1982 was appointed national chaplain of the Jewish War Veterans of the United States."

Morris Margolies of Beth Shalom Congregation in Kansas City, Missouri, gave the House prayer on February 25, 1986. He was born in

---

39   The greatest number of years between guest chaplaincies for a single rabbi is 38. Washington Hebrew Congregation's Louis Stern opened the Senate on August 11, 1876, and the House on June 10, 1914.

Jerusalem, Palestine, before Israel was an independent nation. (Before 1948, "Palestine" could imply Jewish land or people. Thus explaining, for example, this December 4, 1945, *New York Times* story whose construct might look odd now: "Arabs to Boycott Palestinian Goods. . . . The Arab League announced today that its seven-member States would boycott all Jewish-produced goods from Palestine." And the pro-Zionist "Jewish Palestine Pavilion" at the 1939 New York World's Fair.) According to his November 11, 2012—Veterans Day!—obituary in the *Kansas City Star,* Margolies was a chaplain in the U.S. Army from 1951 to 1952, serving much of that time in Korea during the war.

And Maurice Lamm of Floral Park Jewish Center, New York, was remembered for an accomplishment in addition to his March 7, 1963, House prayer. According to the *Jewish Press*, Lamm "was a first lieutenant in the U.S. army, stationed at Fort Benning, Georgia. He built a synagogue in a chapel on the base. The Jewish soldiers would come Friday night to eat a Shabbos meal." In a July 6, 2016, obituary, the *Jewish Press* noted that, around 1966, "the Jewish Welfare Board asked Rabbi Lamm to become its field director of military chaplains with the civilian equivalent of major general. He started traveling to meet, bring aid, and comfort and teach U.S. chaplains in countries such as Vietnam and the Philippines."

Lamm wrote a tribute to a Jewish chaplain killed in Vietnam in December 1968. Two months later, Sen. Jacob Javits (R-NY) entered the tribute into the *Congressional Record*:

The Night They Buried the Chaplain: Midnight on Jerusalem's Mountain or Rest (By Rabbi Maurice Lamm). Morton Singer, an Orthodox Rabbi from Flushing and the East Side of New York, arrived in Chu Lai in October 1968 to begin his work as an Army chaplain In the I Corps area of Vietnam. Six weeks later, on December 17th, with Hanukkah candles in his pack, the rabbi fell to a flaming death in his transport plane which crashed into the underbrush of Vietnam. He was 32. Morton Singer was an unusual man. He volunteered for military chaplaincy service. He volunteered for non-combatant duty in the Six-Day War in Israel. He volunteered for paratroop school. He volunteered for Jungle school In Panama. He volunteered to serve in Vietnam. He wanted to live on the highest level of excitement. He died a shattering death on a pyre with 13 American soldiers, and he was buried on

January 1, in the middle of the night on the Mountain of Best, a hilltop that borders Jerusalem, the city of his love.[40]

Navy chaplains account for 15 of the guest rabbis, offering 35 total prayers (19 in the House, 16 in Senate). Why over twice as many Navy prayers as Navy rabbis? Resnicoff alone has given 16 prayers.

Two Jewish Navy chaplains stand out.

Bertram Korn gave the July 13, 1955, Senate prayer. He was a leading Jewish historian and author—particularly the history of the Jews in the Civil War—and had an accomplished military career. In 1944 Korn enlisted in the Navy as a lieutenant in the Chaplain's Corps, according to the *American Jewish Archives*, where he was assigned to China with the 1st and 6th Marine Divisions. In 1975, he was promoted to Rear Admiral in the Chaplains Corps, U.S. Naval Reserve, the first Jewish chaplain to receive flag rank in any of the United States armed forces. According to his December 17, 1979, obituary in the *Jewish Telegraphic Agency*, Korn was a president of the Association of Jewish Chaplains of the Armed Forces. He was also a national chaplain of the Jewish War Veterans of America. Korn is buried in Arlington National Cemetery. In a September 26, 1997, floor tribute Rep. Jon Fox (R-PA) called Korn "a trailblazer, patriot, and military leader."

Alvin Berkun of Tree of Life in Pittsburgh—the congregation where 11 Jews were murdered on October 27, 2018—was a House guest chaplain in 1983 and Senate guest chaplain in 1991. He was a U.S. Navy lieutenant in the Chaplain Corps, serving as a Navy chaplain during the Vietnam era. Assigned to San Francisco in the mid-1960s, Berkun gave farewell sermons for troops bound for Vietnam. He told the *Pittsburgh Press* on January 2, 1991, "I'd go aboard ship and make an announcement that went something like, 'Attention all Jewish personnel. Rabbi Berkun is on board and would like to meet with you.' I gave them Bibles, prayer books, and even kosher

---

40   Rabbi Singer belongs to a tragic subset of Jewish chaplains, those who gave their lives in combat. According to the Jewish War Veterans National Memorial Museum—reported in the *Pittsburgh Press* in 1991—23 Jewish military chaplains served in World War I, all but one in the Army. And in World War II 311 rabbis served in the armed forces—267 in the Army, 43 in the Navy, and one in the merchant marine (1,045 rabbis applied for the military chaplaincy during World War II, 50% of all the rabbis in the U.S.). Fourteen Jewish chaplains gave their lives while on active duty in the U.S. Armed Forces in World War II and the Korean and Vietnam wars.

food. I was the representative of the Jewish community who had come to see them off."[41]

Recognizing a few more:

- Jacob Rudin of Temple Beth El, Great Neck, New York, gave the House prayer on April 5, 1967. According to *Encyclopaedia Judaica*,[42] he enlisted in the United States Navy Chaplains' Corps and saw duty in the Pacific and in the Aleutians during World War II. And according to an August 24, 1967, dispatch in the *Jewish Telegraphic Agency*, President Lyndon Johnson named Rudin to a 20-man commission that observed the campaign and elections in South Vietnam.

- Ely Pilchik of Congregation B'nai Jeshurun, Short Hills, New Jersey, gave the House prayer on May 12, 1981. Born in Poland, his January 9, 2003, obituary in the *New Jersey Hills Media* noted he was a Navy chaplain overseas during World War II, 1944 to 1946.

- Morris Rosenblatt gave the House prayer on March 14, 1978. His synagogue, Congregation Kneseth Israel, was in Annapolis. That's where he was also the chaplain for Jewish midshipmen at the Naval Academy.

- Herbert Morris of Beth-Israel-Judea Congregation in San Francisco gave the House prayer on May 20, 1992. According to his November 14, 2003, obituary in the *Jewish News of Northern California*, "he signed on several times as a Jewish chaplain aboard cruise ships. His first position as a new rabbi in 1956 was a two-year stint in Japan as a Navy chaplain." Rep. Tom Lantos (D-CA): "A former Navy chaplain stationed in the Far East, Rabbi Morris was commended by the Navy for outstanding work with naval personnel of all religions."

- David Saltzman of Aventura-Turnberry Jewish Center in Florida gave the House prayer on September 6, 1990—the early days of the Persian Gulf War. Saltzman was Navy chaplain with the Seabee Battalion in Guantanamo Bay, Cuba. Later he was, according to his sponsor Rep. William Lehman (D-FL), chaplain with the Marines during the Vietnam War.

---

41 According to the National Archives, 270 Jewish U.S. soldiers were killed in combat during the Vietnam War.

42 Edited by Fred Skolnik and Michael Berenbaum, Macmillan Reference USA in association with the Keter Publishing House, 2007, page 207.

And Arnold Turetsky of Congregation Ohev Tzedek in Youngstown, Ohio (January 16, 1961, House prayer) had a unique distinction for guest rabbis in addition to his naval career. According to *Norfolk, Virginia: A Jewish History of the 20th Century* by Irwin Berent[43] Turetsky, a graduate from the Naval Chaplain School at Newport, Rhode Island, was chaplain of the fifth Naval District. His paid death notice in the July 24, 2004 *New York Times* noted: "Chaplain U.S. Navy and Marines. Opening prayer for U.S. Congress 1961 introduced Hebrew into the Congressional Record."

Jewish Air Force chaplains may have smaller numbers (six guest chaplains, nine total prayers). But no less noteworthy biographies.

Born in Jerusalem, Tzvi Porath gave Senate and House prayers five times between 1960 and 1994. Introducing him to the House on October 27, 1977, Rep. Newton Steers (R-MD) noted Porath was an Air Force chaplain for four years during World War II, was the first Jewish chaplain at the National Institutes of Health and was chaplain at the Bethesda Naval Hospital. Steers himself served in the U.S. Army Air Corps, the direct predecessor to the U.S. Air Force, during World War II. (Porath's 1977 prayer occurred the same day the House authorized broadcast coverage of its floor proceedings; Steers left office after one term in January 1979—two months before House TV began.) Porath also was co-chairman of President Eisenhower's 1957 inauguration Religious Participation Committee.[44] Porath's non-military father, Israel Porath, was Senate guest chaplain on June 5, 1964.

Korean War veteran Brig. Gen. Simeon Kobrinetz, U.S. Air Force, gave the February 26, 1975, Senate prayer. According to records kept by Arlington Cemetery, where he is buried, Kobrinetz was the first Air Force Jewish chaplain of general officer rank. His October 18, 2011, *Washington Post* obituary noted that he "was director of the VA's Chaplain Service from 1984 to 1988 and helped reestablish the National Chaplain School in Hampton, Va. He delivered invocations before presidents and congressional leaders and at national political conventions." Also: the 1996 Veterans Day Memorial Service at Arlington National Cemetery.

---

43 Norfolk History Publishers, 2003, page 183.

44 Four years earlier, Eisenhower became the only president to begin an inaugural address with prayer: "Before I begin the expression of those thoughts that I deem appropriate to this moment, would you permit me the privilege of uttering a little private prayer of my own. And I ask that you bow your heads. Almighty God. . . ."

On June 14, 2018, two days before Flag Day, Steven Rein, Jewish Chaplain for Arlington National Cemetery, became the first Air Force rabbi to wear a uniform for his prayer. Nothing martial about his message, however. Quite the opposite. He told the House: "The Psalmist proclaims: 'How majestic is Your name upon all the Earth,' and wonders, 'What is humanity that You should be mindful of us?' We stand in awe before the beauty and majesty of Your work."

Of the nearly 60 individual Jewish military chaplains who have opened Congress in prayer, none are female. But female Jewish military chaplains do exist. The web site for the U.S. Air Force chaplains featured on top a picture of a female rabbi leading a prayer service. After 40 years of women serving as military chaplains, Rabbi Sarah Schechter is the first and, according to *Military.com*, only female rabbi to serve as chaplain of the Air Force. Perhaps one day she might also pray in Congress—in uniform?

10: World War II Chaplains

Of the 13 million Americans who served in World War II, according to a November 21, 2007, report in the *Forward* citing the American Jewish Historical Society, over half a million were Jewish men and women. And, "after Pearl Harbor, more than half of the rabbis in the U.S. volunteered for duty."

Contrast that display of patriotism to anti-Semitic conspiracy theories that occasionally found their way into official proceedings in the halls of Congress. Fifteen months before Pearl Harbor, during lengthy August 1, 1940, floor remarks, Rep. Jacob Thorkelson (R-MT) spliced together a string of seemingly anti-Jewish screeds—that Members of the Tribe were at once both communist plotters and greedy arch-capitalists.

"Jews organized the revolution in Russia, which was financed by money that came from Wall Street," Thorkelson said. He complained about "Jewish communistic press and the Jewish-controlled national press." And he claimed, "there are very few Jews in the enlisted personnel of the Army or Navy, and I have never seen anyone as a sailor in the merchant marine."[45]

A month earlier, July 18, 1940, the *Jewish Telegraphic Agency* called Thorkelson "rabidly anti-Semitic." The record supports that

---

45   In 1944, according to congressional data, Jews constituted four percent of America's population and seven percent of the country's armed forces.

description. Discussing Jews hoping for their own country in Palestine in 1940, Thorkelson warned of "efforts Judah is employing to destroy and upset Christian faiths in order to establish their own world state." Even the U.S. House of Representatives' own official history page calls him "an outspoken anti-Semite."

Leaving aside Thorkelson's anguish over Jews controlling Wall Street and the media and probably a host of other American institutions, let's consider specifically his mention of the Navy. Thorkelson would have done well to wait a year and meet Rabbi Julius Mark.

Mark was a guest chaplain four times between 1931 and 1969, spanning post-World War I through the Vietnam War. The 1979 *Year Book of the Central Conference of American Rabbis* noted his prayer on the eve of America's entry into World War II:

> On the Monday preceding the infamous Sunday of December 7, 1941, Julius Mark delivered an inspiring prayer for peace in the United States House of Representatives. But peace was not to be, and Julius Mark went to war.[46]

Went to war, indeed. We pick up Mark's story with a floor tribute delivered by Rep. Emanuel Celler (D-NY) on May 23, 1968:

> When the Japanese attacked Pearl Harbor and the United States found itself at war, Dr. Mark, though nearly 43 years of age at the time, immediately offered his services as a chaplain in the Navy. His application was approved and he served his country in uniform from July 1, 1942, to December 31, 1945. He was overseas during the last 2 years of the war. serving on the staff of Adm. Chester W. Nimitz as Jewish chaplain to the Pacific Fleet.

His September 8, 1977, *New York Times* obituary went further:

Soon after the Japanese attacked Pearl Harbor in 1941, the rabbi offered his services to both the Army and the Navy. He was accepted by both, but decided on the Navy, in which he served as a chaplain for three and a half years.

He served the last two years of World War II in the Far East, becoming Jewish chaplain to the Pacific Fleet and rising to the rank of lieutenant commander on the staff of Fleet Adm. Chester W. Nimitz.

---

46   *Central Conference of American Rabbis*, Volume 88, page 139.

During the war, Rabbi Mark wrote more than 10,000 letters to relatives of servicemen and servicewomen, both Jewish and non-Jewish, whom he had met. reassuring those at home that their loved ones were fine.

Other rabbi guest chaplains had intimate connections to World War II.

Robert Kahn of Houston's Congregation Emanu El gave the House prayer on March 3, 1960. He joined the Army as a chaplain in 1942. According to the book *Voices of My Comrades: America's Reserve Officers Remember World War II* by Carol Adele Kelly,[47] Kahn was "among the first to volunteer for service following 7 December 1941, participated in a number of island invasions, and was considered a 'front-line' chaplain." Kahn served in New Guinea and the Philippines with the 6th Medical Battalion of the 6th Infantry Division and later became national chaplain for the American Legion, according to his November 23, 2002, *Houston Chronicle* obituary.

Abraham Feldbin of Congregation of Shaari Israel in Brooklyn delivered the September 30, 1975, House prayer. He was ordained in 1942 and served as an Army Chaplain during World War II. Rep. Elizabeth Holtzman (D-NY) noted that during the war Feldbin "served in the Pacific as U.S. Army chaplain and holds the rank of lieutenant colonel as a chaplain the Army Reserve."

Chicago Rabbi Morton Berman was House guest chaplain on July 1, 1957. The year earlier, a *Chicago Sun-Times* profile noted that he was lieutenant commander in the Navy Reserve during World War II. "He was assigned as a chaplain to the 6th Marine Division, and earned one of his many titles," the May 21, 1956, *Sun-Times* reported. "He had landed with the troops on Okinawa on April 1, 1945, aged 45—one of the oldest chaplains in the Pacific." He carried the Torah in his jeep along with a kosher salami and gefilte fish—gifts from the National Jewish Welfare Board, reported the *Sun-Times*. Berman "commented that his most enthusiastic recipients of kosher salami and gefilte fish on Okinawa were the non-Jewish men." Berman: "You've no idea how kosher salami boosts morale, whether the boy who eats it is named Kinkelstein or Riley."

There are even Canadian World War II connections. Gilbert Klaperman gave the May 5, 1965, House prayer. According to a March 2, 2011, interview in *Matzav*, Klaperman—from Congregation Beth Sholom, Lawrence, New York—was born in Harlem. But he became the rabbi of a Hillel organization

---

47   Fordham University Press, 2007, page 259.

in Queens University in Canada. "At the university, he met several Jewish soldiers and they asked him to become a chaplain. After getting permission from the State Department, Rabbi Klaperman joined the Canadian army." He was a chaplain in the Canadian Army reserve, 1942–43.

Born in Canada, Morris Kertzer of Riverdale Temple in the Bronx was the August 12, 1969, House guest chaplain. He was an Army chaplain during World War II. His December 31, 1983, *New York Times* obituary noted that Kertzer wrote *With an H on My Dogtag*, a 1947 account of his service as a World War II chaplain. He led religious services for U.S. troops on the Anzio beach, the only Jewish chaplain there. He earned a Bronze Star Medal. He later served troops in southern and central France. Kertzer also served as the national president of the Jewish Military Chaplains Association and was the national chaplain of Amvets.

Reflecting on World War II-era chaplains inevitably leads to the Holocaust. Several rabbis were both military chaplains and Congress chaplains as well as first-hand witnesses to the Jewish catastrophe in Europe.

Judah Nadich gave the House prayer on March 6, 1961. In 1945, according to his September 2, 2007, *New York Times* obituary, "when he was a lieutenant colonel in the Army and its senior Jewish chaplain in Europe, and when the horrors of the Nazi concentration camps were being fully revealed, Rabbi Nadich was named to the new post of Jewish adviser to Eisenhower." In 1953, Nadich wrote of his experience in *Eisenhower and the Jews*.[48]

Philip Bernstein of Rochester gave the April 23, 1958, Senate prayer. During World War II, according to the U.S. Holocaust Memorial Museum, the Jewish Welfare Board appointed Bernstein executive director of the Committee on Army and Navy Religious Activities. He served as the adviser on Jewish affairs to the commander of the U.S. forces in Europe between May 1946 and August 1947. Bernstein's "most notable challenge and achievement" during his tenure as Jewish adviser, the Holocaust Museum informs, was assisting the mass movement of Jewish infiltrates from Eastern Europe into the American zones of occupation and helping to dissuade the U.S. Army from closing the borders during the period of the mass migration of Polish Jews after the Kielce pogrom of July 1946. Bernstein later served as chairman of the leading pro-Israel lobbying organization, the American Israel Public Affairs Committee.

---

48   Twayne Publishers, 1953.

Gunther Plaut offered the December 5, 1950, House prayer. Plaut was born in Germany. The day after he was granted American citizenship in 1943, according to the American Jewish Archives, he enlisted in the Army as a chaplain. He was one of the first Allied soldiers to enter a liberated concentration camp. Additional detail from his February 11, 2012, *New York Times* obituary: "Serving as a chaplain with the 104th Infantry, Rabbi Plaut took part in the liberation of the Dora-Nordhausen concentration camp in Germany. Though the survivors were starving, he recalled, they did not ask for food, but for religious items." On April 18, 1985—the Day of Remembrance—Rep. Bill Green (R-NY) said, "Rabbi Gunther Plaut, attached to the 104th Timberwolf Division, which liberated the camp at Mauthausen on April 11, 1945, stated his belief that until that morning many of our men didn't really fully understand what the war was all about. Reflecting on what he himself had seen on that morning, Rabbi Plaut felt it to have been too enormous a crime against humanity to be the responsibility of man alone."

Max Wall of Ohavi Zedek Synagogue in Burlington, Vermont, delivered the June 21, 1984, Senate prayer. During World War II, the Polish-born Wall enlisted in the Army Chaplain Corps. He served with the Ninth Infantry Division during the Battle of the Bulge and the liberation of the concentration camps. From his May 13, 2009, obituary in the *Burlington Free Press:* "As the Jewish chaplain he was able to help thousands of displaced persons. Captain Wall was instrumental in the revival of Jewish worship in Munich and was the first to conduct a Jewish service there after the war."

Yakov Hilsenrath of Beth Judah Temple in North Wildwood, New Jersey, gave the House prayer in 1956 and the Senate prayer in 1963. His March 12, 2014, obituary in the *Home News Tribune*, which noted his two stints as guest chaplain, reported Rabbi Hilsenrath was born in 1932 in Austria, "immigrated to Brooklyn with his family after miraculously escaping the Nazi horror"—and served as a chaplain for Jewish members of the Coast Guard.

A different connection to World War II: On February 7, 2012, Rep. Todd Platts (R-PA) sponsored Jeffrey Astrachan of Temple Beth Israel of York, Pennsylvania. Platts gave this history lesson:

> Rabbi Astrachan is here today to help honor the sacrifice of the four chaplains who gave their lives during the sinking of the troop ship Dorchester during

World War II. This is especially significant because one of the four chaplains, Lieutenant Alexander D. Goode, was once a rabbi with the same congregation in York, Pennsylvania, my hometown that Rabbi Astrachan now serves.

Along with the rabbi, I am pleased to take this opportunity to recognize the courageous sacrifice made 69 years ago by the four chaplains. The Dorchester was torpedoed off the coast of Greenland. Only 230 of the over-900 men on board survived. The survivors recounted the story of the heroic actions of the four chaplains of different faiths: Lieutenant Goode; Lieutenant John Washington, a Catholic priest; and Lieutenants George Fox and Clark Poling, two protestant ministers.

These four servants of God spent their last 18 minutes in this life helping their fellow passengers to safety. When there were no more life jackets to hand out, the chaplains removed their own and gave them to shipmates. They were last seen on the hull of the ship, arm-in-arm in prayer as the ship sank into the icy waters.

Some rabbis were not personally involved with World War II. But their family members were.

Jacob Schacter of New York included this family history during his April 13, 2000, House prayer: "Like millions of others, my father served in the armed forces of this wonderful country and fought to make the world safe for democracy and human freedom." His father's place in armed forces—and Jewish—history deserves more than that one line. According to the elder Schacter's March 26, 2013, *New York Times* obituary:

The smoke was still rising as Rabbi Herschel Schacter rode through the gates of Buchenwald. . . . It was April 11, 1945, and Gen. George S. Patton's Third Army had liberated the concentration camp scarcely an hour before. Rabbi Schacter, who was attached to the Third Army's VIII Corps, was the first Jewish chaplain to enter in its wake. . . . He would remain at Buchenwald for months, tending to survivors, leading religious services in a former Nazi recreation hall and eventually helping to resettle thousands of Jews.

Delaware rabbi Ellen Bernhardt gave the May 20, 2004, Senate prayer. During remarks that ran over 12 minutes, the state's Democratic Senator Joe Biden provided this family color:

Her father, Herman Gordon, was one of the many heroic members of the Armed Forces who chose to enlist in the Army Air Corps at the outset of World War II. Mr. Gordon served as a waist gunner on the Flying Fortress

B-17 bomber. Based in England, his unit performed missions over France and Germany, clearing the way for our troops to land on the beaches of Normandy. On his 24th mission, his plane was shot down over Germany. As a Jew, he became a prisoner of war in Germany for 9 months. The latter 3 months of his imprisonment was spent marching at gunpoint on the infamous "death march"—a desperate move by the Nazis to relocate their POWs straight into the heart of Germany, out of the hands of the Allied forces which were closing in, which I always thought was a metaphor for the insanity, the lust of Hitler and Nazi Germany. This nightmare all came to an end when Mr. Gordon's camp was liberated by General Patton's army.

That nightmare—including Holocaust imagery and history—is found in rabbi congressional prayers through the years. *Shoah* themes continue to this day. As we'll see later, the first prayer with a Holocaust reference, however, was given by a guest chaplain who wasn't even Jewish.

11: Rabbis with Political Connections and Political Networks

Time to consider Richard Nixon's favorite rabbi.

Baruch Korff, a former pulpit rabbi at congregations in Portsmouth, New Hampshire, and Taunton, Massachusetts, met with President Nixon multiple times. On May 13, 1974, as impeachment proceedings in the Democratic-controlled Congress loomed, the two met in the Oval Office. Nixon's personal diary shows a 90-minute meeting beginning at 4:55pm: "The President met with Rabbi Baruch Korff, General Chairman of the National Citizens Committee for Fairness to the President. Rabbi Korff interviewed the President for a book entitled, *Watergate: The Other Side of the Story.*"

No record exists of a book published with that name. Korff did author *The President and I: Richard Nixon's Rabbi Reveals His Role in the Saga That Traumatized the Nation.*[49]

Korff and Nixon met again in the Oval Office on August 6, 1974— three days before Nixon resigned. The rabbi's loyalty continued after Nixon left office. The *Washington Post* quoted him December 16, 1975, calling Nixon "a friend of mine" with whom he communicated "almost weekly." On August 1, 1995, the *Jewish Telegraphic Agency* ran the headline: "Baruch Korff, 'Nixon's Rabbi' and Jewish Activist, Dies at 81."

---

49   Ktav Publishing, 1995.

But that's getting way ahead of our story. A half year *into* the Nixon presidency, Korff delivered the opening prayer in the House of Representatives. It was July 29, 1969. Less than a week earlier, U.S. astronauts returned to Earth after becoming the first to walk on the moon. Korff covered both bases in his prayer: the heavens and the Congress. He thanked "the Lord, who has called this Nation in righteousness and set it for a light among the planets." And he asked God to "motivate this august body of our Nation's legislators to meet the trials of life and liberty."

At the time Korff was not yet a Nixon booster. In 1967 he gave a speech in support of Democratic President Lyndon Johnson. He reflected "in sorrow on the clay champions of the anti-poverty program, housing and education, who burned Johnson in effigy—a man who did more for the cause of the downtrodden than any President before him. What ingrates!" David Greenberg wrote in *Nixon's Shadow: The History of an Image* that Korff "had opposed Nixon in 1960 and 1968 but switched sides in 1972 after the president took up the cause of oppressed Soviet Jews." [50]

Switching sides paid off with A-plus access.

Bob Woodward and Carl Bernstein recount Nixon-Korff Oval Office meetings in their book *The Final Days*.[51] They quote Korff telling Nixon on December 19, 1973: "I'm just a small-town rabbi." Which is what a July 28, 1974, *New York Times* headline repeated: "Small-Town Rabbi Makes 'Big Time' In Leading Anti-Impeachment Drive."

A small-town rabbi with some big-city political chops.

Korff is but one example of a guest chaplain rabbi with strong political connections. Not just to God, but to the other almighty power: government. And "Nixon's rabbi" wasn't the only rabbi claimed by a politician.

"My rabbi." That's what Gov. Mario Cuomo (D-NY) often called Israel Mowshowitz. The rabbi of Hillcrest Jewish Center in Queens gave the House prayer March 15, 1973. In 1980 he met with President Carter for a photo op in the White House.

Carter met another guest chaplain rabbi. Four days before a White House meeting with Israeli Defense Minister Ezer Weizman, he spent time with Rabbi Stanley Wagner of Denver, a multiple-time guest chaplain. That March 6, 1978, White House conversation included Sen. Floyd

---

50   W. W. Norton & Co., Inc., 2003, page 180.
51   Simon & Schuster, 1976, page 101.

Haskell (D-CO). Haskell sponsored Wagner when he prayed in the Senate two years earlier.

Poland-born Rabbi Chaim Rozwaski was House guest chaplain twice, 1967 and 1976. According to *Contemplating the Holocaust* by Rozwaski and Rabbi Bernhard Rosenberg[52]—himself a guest chaplain several times—Carter invited Rozwaski to the White House for the signing of the Camp David peace accord "and for the establishment of the Holocaust Memorial Center."

Political networking goes back to the earliest days of guest chaplain rabbis. Morris Raphall, the first rabbi to pray in the House, was one of four rabbis who had face-to-face meetings with President Lincoln in the White House. The first rabbi in the Senate was Isaac Mayer Wise (a May 21, 1870, prayer). In terms of presidential facetime, the legendary Reform rabbi more than rivals Korff, he exceeds him. Wise's father was studying in Vienna when Lincoln was shot and told his fellow students: "Someday I hope to be able to live and make my home in the land of Lincoln." His son ended up not only living in America but enjoyed relationships with several presidents. Gary Zola, a historian and deliverer of two prayers in Congress, told C-SPAN that Rabbi Wise "met with Presidents of the United States. He had a personal meeting with President Buchanan. He had a personal meeting with Lincoln. Wise delivers a eulogy about Abraham Lincoln." In his eulogy, Zola noted, "Isaac Wise says that he spoke to the president personally." And on April 4, 2019, the U.S. Senate unanimously passed a resolution commemorating the bicentennial of Wise's birth. The Senate recognized "the outstanding accomplishments of Rabbi Wise, which have had an enduring effect on life, culture, and religion in the United States," and it recognized "the extraordinary role of Rabbi Wise in the history of the United States."

Rabbi J. Leonard Levy was Senate guest chaplain on January 21, 1895. He met with President McKinley on March 25, 1897, to discuss economic assistance for farmers. He met with President Theodore Roosevelt on December 5, 1904. The two veterans of the Spanish-American war discussed the Pittsburgh Peace Society. And according to the online history of his Pittsburgh congregation, "At Rabbi Levy's invitation, President William Howard Taft visited Rodef Shalom on Saturday, May 29, 1909. This was the first time that a sitting United States president spoke from the bimah of a Jewish congregation during regular Sabbath services."

---

52   Jason Aronson Inc., 1999, page 215.

Another early rabbi guest chaplain linked to the presidency: Edward Browne. He offered the Senate prayer twice, May 1884 and August 1918. Plus, a House prayer in December 1917. Browne's claim to political fame: He was a participant in President Ulysses Grant's 1885 funeral. In reporting his second prayer, the August 30, 1918, *Associated Press* used that fact to distinguish him: "Rabbi Edward B. M. Browne of New York, only surviving pallbearer of U. S. Grant, offered the opening prayer today in the Senate."[53] Browne also claimed he once employed President Warren Harding as a private secretary (*Evening Independent*, Massillon, Ohio, March 11, 1925).

St. Louis Rabbi Samuel Thurman gave the Senate prayer on February 26, 1945, less than two months before Harry Truman became president upon the death of Franklin Roosevelt. According to *Zion in the Valley: The Jewish Community of St. Louis* by Walter Ehrlich,[54] Thurman "was a longtime friend" of Truman. Thurman repeatedly traveled to Washington throughout Truman's presidency, particularly in the months leading up to the 1948 establishment of Israel. Thurman, Ehrlich wrote, "was singularly honored when he was invited to deliver the invocation at President Truman's inauguration in January 1949, the first rabbi in American history to participate in a presidential inauguration." Truman served as an honorary pallbearer at Thurman's February 24, 1963 funeral.

For President Eisenhower's 1957 inauguration, Rabbi Tzvi Porath—a five-time guest chaplain—served as co-chairman of the Religious Participation Committee.

Camelot connections, too, for rabbis. Morris Gordon of Greenbelt, Maryland, led the Senate in prayer February 24, 1961. According to his March 29, 2005, *Washington Post* obituary Gordon was a friend of Hubert Humphrey and "in 1961, then-Sen. Humphrey asked Rabbi Gordon to lead the invocation before a joint session of Congress for President John F. Kennedy's inauguration."

Gerald Klein likely will be remembered more for his bit part in the November 1963 President Kennedy assassination than the July 1957 opening prayer he delivered in the Senate. He was rabbi to Jack Ruby, murderer of

---

53 The November 28, 1907, Washington, DC *Evening Star* added this color to Browne serving as a Grant pallbearer: "The funeral occurred on the Jewish Sabbath, on which it is unlawful for orthodox Jews to ride in a carriage, therefore Dr. Browne walked from the City Hall to Riverside. The orthodox Jews gave him a gold medal for thus observing the Sabbath, and the Christian clergy of New York had a number of them accompany the rabbi in turns on his walk-in observance of the Sabbath."

54 University of Missouri, 1997, page 176.

JFK's assassin Lee Harvey Oswald. The 1964 report of Warren Commission hearings investigating Kennedy's assassination cited a witness who said Ruby "is religious and is very proud of his Jewish background and heritage. RUBY attends the Temple Emanuel in Dallas where the Rabbi is GERALD KLEIN and the Temple Shearith Israel, which is located on Douglas Street, Dallas, where the rabbi is HILLEL SILVERMAN. RUBY does not speak Hebrew or Yiddish languages" (page 681). (Unlike Klein, Silverman was not a guest chaplain. But he was one of six people identified in the Warren Commission hearings report on page 29 with this description: "RUBY regards the following persons in Dallas as his closest friends.") The Sixth Floor Museum at Dealey Plaza also notes Klein "attended the Trade Mart luncheon on November 22, 1963 and gave a prayer for the late president [Kennedy] at services that evening. A friend of the Zapruder family, Klein officiated at Abraham Zapruder's funeral in 1970."

Stanley Rabinowitz of Washington's Adas Israel Congregation—which *Washington Post* religion reporter Julie Zauzmer has called "perhaps America's most political synagogue" (September 30, 2016)—was guest chaplain three times. On December 1, 1963, according to next day's *Jewish Telegraphic Agency*, he "delivered the sermon at an interdenominational service for the late President Kennedy at a Methodist Church here which was attended by President Johnson. He was one of two rabbis among the six clergymen participating in the service. The other was Norman Gerstenfeld of Washington Hebrew Congregation." Rabinowitz also presided over the August 1972 wedding of Sen. Abraham Ribicoff (D-CT) held, according to the August 5, 1972, *Associated Press*, at Adas Israel.

That was Ribicoff's second wedding (after his first wife Ruth died). The first was in 1931. According to Kurt Stone's book *The Congressional Minyan: The Jews of Capitol Hill*[55] Morris Silverman, "who had confirmed Ruth, conducted the ceremony" at Hartford's Temple Emanuel. And Silverman offered the Senate prayer on September 23, 1963.

Hyman Schachtel of Houston's Congregation Beth Israel prayed in the Senate on August 7, 1957. On January 20, 1965, he prayed on the inaugural platform at the east front of the Capitol. "As Lyndon Baines Johnson and Hubert Horatio Humphrey each places his hand on the Bible to take his oath of office," he proclaimed, "let them know and let us feel that the hands of all of us join theirs in this symbolic avowal that Thou art supreme and

---

55   Ktav Publishing, 2000, page 168.

Thy Holy Word our eternal challenge." Schachtel's prayer followed Leontyne Price singing "America the Beautiful."

Even America's only unelected president is linked to a guest chaplain rabbi. Ireland-born Theodore Lewis gave the Senate prayer on February 18, 1963. Lewis came from Rhode Island's Touro Synagogue, which dates back to Revolutionary War days. He joined other rabbis in the Oval Office with President Ford on July 12, 1976, for, according to his Daily Diary kept by the Gerald R. Ford Presidential Library, "a meeting with rabbis of six colonial Jewish congregations."

Emil Hirsch of Chicago's Sinai Congregation gave the House prayer March 21, 1892. In 1975, President Ford appointed his grandson Edward Hirsch Levi, president of the University of Chicago, the 71st attorney general of the United States. He was the first Jewish attorney general. During the Trump administration, Levi's portrait hung in U.S. Deputy Attorney General Rod Rosenstein's conference room. Rosenstein told the August 3, 2017, *New York Times* about Levi's portrait: "That right there. That's the post-Watergate A.G."

Other rabbis had connections to presidential contenders and their families.

Morris Silverman, an editor and writer of conservative Jewish prayer books, delivered the Senate prayer on February 19, 1959. Sen. Prescott Bush (R-CT), father and grandfather of conservative presidents, offered floor remarks about the Hartford, Connecticut rabbi. And according to an announcement a week earlier from the Rabbinical Assembly of America, while in the nation's capital the Emanuel Synagogue rabbi "is also representing the State Commission Against Discrimination at a meeting of the President's committee of Government contracts."

Albert Plotkin of Phoenix Temple Beth Israel gave the House prayer on May 17, 1978. On June 3, 1998, he presided over the funeral of Sen. Barry Goldwater (R-AZ). His son, Rep. Barry Goldwater, Jr. (R-CA), sponsored the October 24, 1979, prayer by Melvin Goldstine, Temple Aliyah, Woodland Hills, California.

Morton Berman of Chicago's Temple Isaiah gave the July 1, 1957, House prayer. Among those honoring him: Rep. James Roosevelt (D-CA), son of President Franklin Roosevelt. According to a Jewish Telegraphic Agency story in the January 11, 2011, *Jewish Journal* of Los Angeles, Berman joined a group of 293 Southern Californians who walked with Martin Luther

King Jr. in 1965 across the Pettus Bridge to the state Capitol building in Montgomery.[56]

More from FDR's son. Rabbi Jacob Pressman gave the House prayer on February 9, 1961. Temple Beth Am of Los Angeles notes on its online timeline the prayer was "at the invitation of Congressman James Roosevelt." Roosevelt again sponsored Pressman in the House February 28, 1963.

Pressman, incidentally, gave the closing benediction at the 1984 Democratic National Convention in San Francisco. As for the GOP, Rabbi Isaac Neuman, a two-time House guest chaplain, opened a session of the 1992 Republican National Convention in Houston.

Of course, certain guest chaplain rabbis don't just hang out in White House circles. There's congressional networking, too.

Mark Miller of Temple Bat Yahm in Newport Beach, California, was a guest chaplain twice. Rep. Brad Sherman (D-CA)—his May 12, 1998, sponsor—pointed out that Miller's prayer marked "the first time that a legislative assistant has addressed this body, not as a Member, but as a guest chaplain. I am proud to have introduced to this body my rabbi in my formative years and my family's rabbi, Mark S. Miller, who returns to this Capitol many years after serving as a legislative assistant for Senator Mondale." Miller actually made a much earlier appearance in the Senate, in writing. On December 6, 1973, Sen. Mark Hatfield (R-OR) offered floor remarks about Israel's legendary original prime minister David Ben-Gurion, who died a few days earlier. "In reading the many accounts, both published and unpublished which have appeared concerning Ben-Gurion's life and accomplishments," Hatfield said, "I was particularly impressed with a eulogy written by a talented rabbinical student, Mark S. Miller. Mr. Miller's remarks will speak for themselves and I commend them to the attention of my colleagues."

The Senate rabbi on March 19, 1991—Portland Maine's Seth Frisch—once was a legislative assistant to the Senate Foreign Relations Committee chairman. According to Frisch's bio, the four-time guest chaplain "continues to maintain a current and long-standing fellowship with the Office of the Chaplain of the United States Senate."

The daughter of the next Senate rabbi, Pittsburgh's Alvin Berkun (May 8, 1991), was an intern in the office of his sponsor, Arlen Specter (R-PA).

---

56 An earlier marcher with Martin Luther King was Rabbi Joachim Prinz. He addressed the August 1963 March on Washington. Two years later he was Senate guest chaplain. Also, with Dr. King at Selma and the 1963 March: Rabbi Sidney Guthman. He was a guest chaplain in Congress five times.

Orthodox Union executive vice president Steven Weil hosted Speaker John Boehner for dinner at his New Jersey home during the summer of 2012. Weil was House guest chaplain September 20, 2012. Boehner sponsored him.

Ralph Silverstein of Temple Sinai in Brooklyn gave the House prayer on June 13, 1956. Rep. Victor Anfuso (D-NY) called him "a very dear friend of mine for many years." Anfuso cited a Silverstein profile in the Brooklyn *Jewish Examiner*. The article reported Silverstein's "dynamic oratorical gifts were also in constant demand by the Democratic party and it wasn't long before he was a power in its councils. He was [a] delegate to the Democratic State Convention in 1938 all he was one of the most active members of the party's speakers' bureau. He tirelessly addressed rallies indoors and out, delivering radio talks and helped build party strategy."

Should there be any doubt about the value of local connections for rabbi guest chaplains, consider Joel Levenson. He was a Connecticut rabbi when he gave the July 10, 2012, House prayer. Connecticut Rep. Rosa DeLauro (D) sponsored him. Levenson's bio reads: "Due to his strong bonds in the local community, he was asked to deliver the Opening Prayer for the United States House of Representatives, the 112th Congress, Second Session."

Families extend the Congress connections.

Rabbi Jacob Voorsanger gave the House prayer in 1882 and the Senate prayer in 1898. His great-grandson Eric Voorsanger was an intern for Jewish Oregon Sen. Richard Neuberger (D).

The son of Irving Block—June 2, 1983, House prayer—was a House page.

Arnold Mark Belzer of New Jersey gave the House prayer April 20, 1988. Sponsor Rep. Robert Roe (D-NJ) noted the rabbi's son "is my page here in Congress, has not only been elected president of his page class while maintaining a perfect 4.0 average in his studies, but also has been selected as the Speaker's page."

Milton Weinberg of New Jersey Congregation Beth Chaverim gave the House prayer November 19, 1993. His son Hillel held several staff positions in Congress. He worked for Rep. Ben Gilman (R-NY), Sen. Rudy Boschwitz (R-MN), Sen. David Durenberger (R-MN), the House Foreign Affairs Committee/Committee on International Relations—and in the State Department's Office of Inspector General. Gilman mentioned the connection to the Weinberg son during his floor remarks about the father: "Although Hillel is now employed in the other body by the senior Senator from Minnesota [Mr. Durenberger], I still often call upon him for his insight."

In the Senate on June 14, 1982, Kenneth Cohen, Congregation Beth Shalom, Wilmington, Delaware, gave the prayer. Cohen was the pastor of the president of that year's graduating class of the Capitol Page School. The next rabbi prayer in Congress was June 24, 1982, in the House: Eugene Levy, Congregation Beth El in Tyler, Texas. He was sponsored by Rep. Martin Frost (D-TX), his cousin. Baruch Frydman-Kohl of Toronto gave the Senate prayer on November 29, 2012. He was sponsored by *his* cousin Sen. Herbert Kohl (D-WI).

In at least one instance the politics behind a guest chaplaincy veered into complicated intrigue. Syracuse Rabbi Theodore Levy gave the Senate prayer on March 8, 1984. That day the Senate debated an amendment allowing prayer in school. Levy opposed the amendment. Sen. Orrin Hatch (R-UT) sponsored the amendment. Hatch also sponsored the rabbi. Why? Levy's daughter worked on Hatch's staff.[57]

All of which should answer the question on the minds of ambitious and aspiring clergy everywhere: How exactly does one become a guest chaplain? (Of the 83 total guest chaplains in the House in 2019, half—41— had sponsors. Forty different members; one member sponsored two different chaplains. Many of the others were during pro forma sessions when the House has no legislative business and guest chaplains are picked from houses of worship in the surrounding areas of Washington, DC. Rabbis opened the House in prayer 11 times during 2019. Eight of those prayers had sponsors.)

---

57 Non-Jews with family connections: The April 10, 2018, House guest chaplain Rev. Sam Smucker was sponsored by his brother Rep. Lloyd Smucker (R-PA). Consider, too, Rev. Erin Conaway, pastor of Houston's South Main Baptist Church. He was House guest chaplain on June 28, 2007, sponsored by his father Rep. Mike Conaway (R-TX). From Conaway's floor remarks about his son: "He is a man of deep faith in Jesus Christ as his personal savior. . . . Suzanne and I are always proud of your accomplishments, but today we are particularly proud of seeing you opening this session of Congress." *Roll Call's* David Hawkings reported on February 18, 2015 that Conaway, chairman of the House Agriculture Committee, "decided, without getting clearance from or even informing GOP leadership, that every hearing or markup at his committee will begin with a prayer." The day after an October 31, 2017, terror attack, Conaway opened an Intelligence Committee hearing investigating Russia and the 2016 election with a prayer: "Lord, we have circumstances in New York where families are in deep pain and deep sorrow. . . . We ask now, Lord, that we're worthy of your praise and blessing. . . . We ask in Jesus' name."

There have been far fewer of them, but female rabbis, too, can claim significant political connections.

In April 1994, Dena Feingold of Beth Hillel Temple, Kenosha, Wisconsin, became the first woman rabbi to open the Senate in prayer. She was introduced by her brother Sen. Russ Feingold (D-WI).

In May 2004 Delaware claimed the second woman to be a Senate rabbi guest chaplain: Ellen Bernhardt. Sen. Joe Biden (D-DE) told her to "be very proud of your son sitting behind me who is a relatively new member of my staff. He is already having an impact in the conduct of business around here."

The rabbi who prayed in the House on March 8, 1995, had special significance for several reasons. Rachel Mikva of Congregation Hakafa, Glencoe, Illinois, was the third woman rabbi to open the House in prayer. She was the first female guest chaplain to wear a yarmulke. She was the first woman rabbi guest chaplain under new Republican majority control of the House. And her father was Abner Mikva, a former congressman and holder of other top Washington power jobs. Rep. Mikva beat John Porter for Congress in 1978. John Porter eventually became the congressman when Mikva was appointed to the bench. Rep. Porter sponsored Rabbi Mikva as guest chaplain. In his remarks about Rachel, Porter said about Abner: "We have remained good friends over the years, and it is a pleasure to welcome him here today." The *Jewish Telegraphic Agency* March 9, 1995, report on her prayer added this twist: When House chaplain James Ford "learned that Abner Mikva's daughter was studying to be a rabbi, he suggested that she led the lawmakers in their daily opening prayer. That was about six years ago."

Going outside the Jewish world for a moment with this enlightening behind-the-scenes anecdote. Stephen Rodrick was deputy press secretary to Sen. Alan Dixon (D-IL). He revealed in the *Washington Post* on September 21, 2018: "I ghost-wrote the Senate invocation offered by the onetime Nation of Islam leader Wallace D. Muhammad of Chicago— the first time a Muslim had opened a Senate session." That was February 6, 1992. A *Chicago Tribune* article the next day noted Dixon "hosted a reception for him after the invocation. Muhammad told reporters that he will support Dixon in his re-election bid this year." Broadening, then, an observation attributed to Otto von Bismarck: Prayers are like laws, which are like sausages— best not to see any of them being made.

Count on weddings, too, for rabbis' political bonds:

- Washington Hebrew Congregation's Joshua Haberman gave one of his seven prayers on June 4, 1985. He was sponsored by Rep. Ben Gilman (R-NY) who "reiterate[d] my appreciation for officiating at my recent marriage to Rita Gail."
- Hillel Cohn of San Bernardino gave the House prayer on March 21, 2001. Rep. Jerry Lewis (R-CA) noted that Cohn married off two of his children.
- Harvey Goldman of New Jersey gave the Senate prayer on November 14, 1985, sponsored by Sen. Frank Lautenberg (D-NJ). Goldman, according to the March 19, 1992, *New York Times*, presided over the 1990 wedding of Lautenberg's daughter.
- Joel Goor was Senate guest chaplain in July 1968. In September 1996 the San Diego rabbi presided over the wedding of Dr. Emily Ruth Liman. The September 8, 1996, *New York Times* wedding announcement noted the bride's father "was the chief counsel in 1987 to the Senate committee investigating the Iran-contra affair."

Here's a different *simcha*, happy lifecycle event: Rochester Rabbi Judea Miller gave the House prayer October 2, 1986. Rep. Dan Glickman (D-KS) gave floor remarks welcoming him. Miller officiated when young Glickman became a bar mitzvah.

Even political media connections. The May 13, 1974, House guest chaplain from the Arlington Fairfax Jewish Congregation: Marvin Bash. That might be a familiar last name for political/media junkies. The rabbi was once the father-in-law of CNN chief political correspondent Dana Bash (she and the rabbi's son Jeremy, who has served in top staff positions at the Pentagon, CIA and the House Intelligence Committee, are no longer married.)

Arthur Lelyveld twice gave prayers, in the Senate September 1974 and in the House November 1993. The Cleveland rabbi was the father of Pulitzer Prize-winning former *New York Times* executive editor Joseph Lelyveld. "Lelyveld had once considered a career in journalism himself when he was in college," the rabbi's obituary in the April 16, 1996, Cleveland *Plain Dealer* noted. (Lelyveld showed an appreciation of good writing in his sermon following the Kennedy assassination. "There is much more than superficial, external event to link John F. Kennedy with Abraham Lincoln in our thoughts," Lelyveld told Fairmount Temple on November 29, 1963. "Like

Lincoln, he drew upon the model of Scripture in his writing, though his prose style was unmistakably his own. He spoke and wrote with a simplicity that sprang directly from the Bible.")

Here's a real inside-the-Beltway media *and* wedding connection: Irwin Goldenberg was House guest chaplain November 7, 2007. Five years later the York, Pennsylvania, rabbi officiated, according to the June 10, 2012, *New York Times*, at the wedding of *POLITICO* Vice President Beth Lester.

Life cycle milestones include death. Usher Kirshblum offered the House prayer February 8, 1977. Rep. Benjamin Rosenthal (D-NY) sponsored the New York rabbi. Rosenthal died in January 1983. At the Jewish Center of Kew Gardens Hills in Queens, according to the January 7, 1983, *New York Times*, Kirshblum gave the eulogy. Kirshblum died a month later. New Jersey rabbi Daniel Marc Cohen gave the Senate prayer on July 31, 1997. He was sponsored by Sen. Frank Lautenberg (D-NJ). In 2013 Cohen spoke at Lautenberg's funeral.

Getting too close to politicians can lead to unfortunate consequences. Three examples among the rabbi guest chaplains.

Leib Pinter of Brooklyn opened the House on February 18, 1975. The *United Press International* reported on June 23, 1978, that Pinter "was sentenced to two years in prison and fined $17,000 on charges he paid $5,000 in bribes to Rep. Daniel J. Flood of Pennsylvania." Pinter admitted the prior month "he made five $1,000 payments to Flood between 1974 and 1976 to gain use of his influence in getting anti-poverty funding. At the time Flood was a member of the House Appropriations Committee and chairman of the Appropriations Subcommittee for Labor-Health, Education and Welfare."

At Flood's January 1979 bribery, conspiracy, and perjury trial, according to the *Washington Post* (January 25, 1979) "Pinter said he recalled Flood passing him in the hallway of a House office building, patting him on the back and saying: 'Keep up the good work, Murphy.' Pinter said later in the trial that he did not know why Flood had called him Murphy."

In *Newswalker: A Story for Sweeney*, a memoir about working at the New York *Daily News*, reporter R. Thomas Collins wrote: "Pinter's method was to identify key politicians, give them money and honors and then use those relationships to win government contracts to deliver social services. In early 1973, for example, Pinter paid speaker's agent Harry Walker to have Walker's client, House Minority Leader Gerald Ford, appear at the yeshiva's annual dinner and receive the B'nai Torah Humanitarian Award. By the time of the dinner in October 1973, Ford was vice president. Pinter had friends tell reporters, 'Gerald Ford knows only one rabbi, and his name is Leib Pinter.'"[58]

Milton Balkany was a guest chaplain five times, four in the Senate and one in the House. After a May 20, 1987, Senate prayer, Sen. Alan Simpson (R-WY) called Balkany "a real patriot and a delightful friend." Sponsoring his June 26, 2003, House prayer (which occurred the day after he gave another Senate prayer), Rep. Sue Kelly (R-NY) said Balkany "has worked hard to bring the community together in order to continue traditional religious and cultural values."

Balkany was working hard inside the Beltway, too. In an August 14, 1989, story headlined "Getting a U.S. Grant—How the System Really Works," the *Los Angeles Times* reported, "By his own account, Balkany is so well known in Washington . . . he once even declined an invitation to become the rabbi chaplain of the Senate."

Indeed, among the collections in the Senator H. John Heinz III Archives at the Carnegie Mellon Libraries is a letter about Balkany sent from the Department of Interior to the Pennsylvania Republican. The February 10, 1987, letter was written by Hobart Cawood, Superintendent and Chairman, We The People 200 Committee, A National Celebration in Philadelphia of the United States Constitution:

> Dear Senator Heinz: Thank you for your letter concerning Rabbi Balkany giving an opening prayer before the Joint Session of Congress in Philadelphia on July 16, 1987. I am passing your suggestion on to the Senate and House officials that are working on the agenda for the session. I know they will give this matter every consideration.

A December 2, 1990, *Washington Post* investigation of a fundraiser for Sen. Alan Cranston (D-CA) revealed, "A Jan. 2, 1987, 'confidential' memo that the fund-raiser, Joy Jacobson, wrote to Cranston said the senator's office was helping. . . . Balkany get selected to give the invocation at the bicentennial of the Continental Congress in Philadelphia." Referring to Balkany in the memo, "Jacobson told Cranston, 'Apparently you told him that you would speak to" then-Senate Majority Leader Robert Byrd (D-WV) "re his doing the invocation at the July 17th meeting of the Continental Congress in Philadelphia.' She noted Pennsylvania's two GOP senators had

---

58   Ravensyard Publishing, 2002, page 54.

recommended the rabbi. 'Also, Rabbi Balkany wanted to know what has happened re the Chaplain of the Senate. I told him that you or I would get back to him on both of these matters this week.'"

Balkany never did get that appointment to become Senate chaplain. But he did become a number. Inmate 55427-054 at the Federal Correctional Institution in Miami.

Why imprison Balkany? New York *Daily News* headline February 18, 2011: "Brooklyn rabbi sentenced to four years for extorting $4 million from hedge fund." From the story: "Milton Balkany, 64, who headed a religious day school for girls in Borough Park, faced up to nine years in prison, but Manhattan Federal Court Judge Denise Cote said she took into account the rabbi's good deeds. . . . Balkany, a politically connected rabbi who skirted a federal investigation into bribery, misuse of HUD funds and other charges a decade ago, did not address the November conviction but denied the old bribery charges. 'I never gave a toothpick to a public official in my life,' the rabbi said."

Perhaps the most bizarre—even comical—brush with the law was Edward Browne's 1925 encounter with the Secret Service. The three-time guest chaplain was arrested and "charged with annoying" President Calvin Coolidge. No word what annoyed Coolidge. But, according to the March 11, 1925, *Evening Independent* newspaper, Browne "inflicted . . . an avalanche of letters demanding that he be reimbursed for half of the $25,000 he asserts the American Jewish Seventy Elders spent in campaigning for President Coolidge last fall. Rabbi Browne was arrested by Secret Service agents and arraigned in Yorkville court."

Did a charge of "annoying" deter Browne? Hardly. The article further reports, "Efforts were made to settle the case without court action but it was said that the rabbi would not agree to desist from sending letters to the White House."

Not every powerful connection is political. There's celebrity, too. The March 21, 1966, House guest chaplain was Avraham Soltes of Temple Emanuel Great Neck. He also was an army chaplain at West Point. Bruce Springsteen drummer Max Weinberg told the August 31, 2011, *San Diego Jewish Journal:* "Avraham Soltes was Central Casting's image of a rabbi. My cousin's bar mitzvah was his first in 1952, and mine was his last, in 1964. He became the TV host of 'Lamp Unto My Feet' in the mid-1950s. After he left the rabbinate, he appeared as the rabbi in two movies: 'Goodbye, Columbus' and 'The Goodbye Girl.'"

And Las Vegas rabbi Mel Hecht gave the Senate prayer on September 18, 1997. He presided over the funerals of actor Tony Curtis (2010) and Jerry Lewis' mother (1983).

The most awkward political connection might belong to Henry Okolica of Congregation Tephereth Israel, New Britain, Connecticut—though leavened with a quick quip to deflect tension. He gave the Senate prayer on September 19, 1966. The October 30, 2013, *Connecticut Jewish Ledger* reported this incident: "At a fundraiser for Sen. Joseph Lieberman at the start of his Senate career, Okolica fell into the host's swimming pool—suit, yarmulke, and all, Feigenbaum [an Okolica student] says. 'We pulled him out and someone said, "Rabbi, I thought your people were supposed to walk on water." Without missing a beat, the rabbi said, "We only do salt water.""

12: Lubavitchers

"I have met with the Lubavitcher Rebbe and I do not know anyone in public office in the city of New York who has not sought his spiritual blessing."
—Rep. Ed Koch (D-NY), January 23, 1975

"Sure, I like to do things that get me votes from the folks back home. But once in a while it's good to do something that will get me votes in that final election we're all going to have to stand for some day."
—Idaho Sen. William Borah (R) explaining his motive for helping Lubavitch Rabbi Joseph Schneerson, who was arrested by Stalin in 1927 and sent to a Leningrad prison. When Borah took up Schneerson's cause, there were less than 100 voters in the whole state of Idaho

Quick quiz: Which historic Jewish figure has been cited the greatest number of times by a rabbi opening Congress in prayer? You instinctively say Moses, right? A respectable guess: Prophet. Leader. Lawgiver. Seems about right for the receiver, it not outright author, of the Torah.

Moses already loom large over Congress, physically. His is one of 23 marble relief portraits over the gallery doors of the House chamber. The 11 profiles in the eastern half of the chamber face left. The 11 in the western half face right. The 23rd? Moses. As the Architect of the Capitol describes on its website, "All look towards the full-face relief of Moses in the center of the north wall."

Thus, as he looks straight down on the Speaker's podium, Moses is the only full-face figure among those who ring the top of the House chamber.

That prominence isn't lost on Benjamin Netanyahu. During his March 3, 2015, address to a joint meeting of Congress, the Israeli Prime Minister pointed to the portrait. "Facing me, right up there in the gallery, overlooking all of us, in this august chamber," he said, "is the image of Moses."

(There once was a Moses in the Senate chamber, too: Sen. George Moses, a Republican from New Hampshire. He was in office 1925-1933 and was the president pro tempore. No relation, though, from the contemporary lawmaker to the ancient lawgiver. Or to Rabbi Alfred Moses of Mobile, Alabama, the June 16, 1939 House guest chaplain.)

So, with 15 mentions, it makes sense that Moses should rank first, no? But he doesn't. That winning distinction belongs to Rabbi Menachem Mendel Schneerson. The late Lubavitcher Rebbe—considered, as the July 1, 2014, *New York Times* put it, "one of the most influential Jewish leaders of the twentieth century"—beats Moses by two. Seventeen mentions.[59] Just as Moses has a literal permanent place in the chamber of the House of Representatives, so too is Schneerson figuratively forever linked to Congress.

The Lubavitcher movement—a sect of Hasidic Jews—began in Eastern Europe in the latter part of the eighteenth century. "It has grown in stature and significance over the centuries," Rep. Leo Zeferetti (D-NY) said during a January 1975 special order devoted to Schneerson, "surviving persecution, travail, genocide, and every conceivable form of economic and political prejudice." Rep. Ben Gilman (R-NY) said the movement "has been a vibrant, dynamic spiritual force in Judaism for over 200 years. Their dedication to learning and the reverence of the Lubavitcher Chassidim has permeated throughout all of Judaism and all are the better for it."

Schneerson mentions on the House floor go back to the mid-1950s. "On April 11, 1956, a group of Arabs infiltrated into Israel and murdered in cold blood several children and their teachers while they were in the midst of prayer at Habad village," Rep. Victor Anfuso (D-NY) said two weeks later. "The inhabitants of that village are affiliated with a religious and

---

59   As of April 2020.

philanthropic movement whose spiritual head is Chief Rabbi Menachem Schneerson, a resident of my district."

In 1994, a few months after the Rebbe's passing, Congress posthumously awarded Schneerson the Congressional Gold Medal, recognizing his "outstanding and lasting contributions toward improvements in world education, morality, and acts of charity."

In his book *Rebbe: The Life and Teaching of Menachem M. Schneerson, the most influential Rabbi in Modern History,*[60] Joseph Telushkin noted the medal is "the highest award granted by the American government to a civilian." At the time, Schneerson was "the only rabbi, and only the second clergyman, to have received this honor." Subsequent clergy recipients have included, among others, Mother Teresa, Pope John Paul II, Billy Graham, and the Dalai Lama.

When Israel's chief rabbi Yisrael Meir Lau prayed in the House on June 28, 1995, he highlighted the honor: "Thank you for the declaration and proclamation offering the Congressional Golden Medal and tribute in honor of the Lubavitcher Rebbe, Rabbi Menachem Mendel Schneerson, spiritual leader not only for the Jewish people but for all mankind." (An historic twist to Schneerson's Golden Medal: The legislation awarding it passed Congress on October 8, 1994. That was a Saturday. Surely Lubavitchers and other Orthodox Jews weren't watching it on television, which would have violated the laws of the Sabbath.)

Despite all the congressional honor bestowed on him, Schneerson never delivered a prayer opening Congress. But other Lubavitch rabbis have. Twenty-eight prayers have been given by a Lubavitcher, 4% of all rabbi guest chaplain prayers. Broken down by number of rabbis from each of the primary denominations—some gave multiple prayers—there have been 13 Lubavitchers, or 3% of the rabbi total. The rest of the rabbi guest chaplains break down roughly into thirds of the kosher pie. The Reform movement holds a slight edge with 34%, or 150 total number of rabbis. Non-Lubavitch Orthodox rabbis account for almost one-third, 32% (142). Conservative rabbis number 130, or 30%. And four from the Reconstructionist branch, 1 percent.[61]

---

60   Harper Wave, 2016.

61   How does this compare to the overall U.S. adult Jewish population? An October 1, 2013, Pew Research Center survey found that 35% of all Jews identify with the Reform movement, while 18% identify with Conservative Judaism, 10% with Orthodox Judaism (Pew included the Lubavitch with the Orthodox) and 6% with a variety of smaller groups, such as the Reconstructionist and Jewish Renewal movements.

The first Schneerson mention in an invocation was April 18, 1978. "I offer this prayer on the day which has been proclaimed by the President of the United States and both Houses of Congress as Education Day, U.S.A.," Rabbi Moshe Bomzer of Young Israel of Hollywood, Florida, told the House, "in celebration of the 76th birthday of the illustrious and revered leader of world Jewry—the Lubavitcher Rebbe."

As the Rebbe's health declined, growing concern was reflected in subsequent prayers. "It is particularly fitting that we stand before you, Almighty G-D, in this the day when Members of the United States Congress and Senate join with Representatives of the Lubavitch movement nationwide and here in Washington to celebrate the 92nd birthday of the revered leader of the world Lubavitch movement, Rabbi Menachem Mendel Schneerson," another Floridian, Aron Lieberman, said in the House on March 15, 1994. "The Lubavitch Rebbe has been an inspiration to many hundreds of thousands of people world-wide. Included among them Presidents, Members of Congress, international leaders, and heads of state, who have sought and received his advice and blessings. The Rebbe now needs our prayers as he has suffered recently a second stroke and is in critical condition."

And he was remembered in prayers after he died. Here's Rabbi Levi Shemtov opening the Senate on September 17, 1998: "As we debate the significant issues of the day, let us remember the words of the Lubavitcher Rebbe, Rabbi Menachem M. Schneerson, of blessed memory, who taught, 'the only way to soothe the differences between two sides is to seek how we are ultimately all on the same side.'"

Shemtov, Executive Vice President of American Friends of Lubavitch, is close to many members of Congress. In her book *Lubavitchers as Citizens: A Paradox of Liberal Democracy*, Jan Lynn Feldman wrote that he "determine[s] almost completely . . . the tone and direction of day-to-day Lubavitcher operations in Washington. "Shemtov, Feldman wrote, "measures influence by name recognition. Lubavitch is pretty close to a household name on the Hill, and Shemtov feels that he is an increasingly familiar face, well received in Washington political circles, reflecting recognition of Lubavitch's moral authority."[62]

Shemtov and his father Rabbi Abraham Shemtov have both opened the Senate in prayer. They are one of five father/son guest chaplain rabbinical duos. The elder Shemtov's prayer came four years after the son   the second

---

62   Cornell University Press, 2003, pages 52-53.

time a son preceded his father. The other: son Tzvi Porath opened the Senate on February 4, 1960 (and four more times in the Senate and House after that). Israel Porath, the father, opened the Senate on June 5, 1964.[63]

To be sure, Lubavitch rabbis have done more in their prayers than honor the Rebbe. They have brought to Congress advocacy of the involvement of God in the foundation of our government in addition to Jewish teachings. A central part of that message in opening prayers: the Noahide laws.

In 1980, Telushkin wrote, the Rebbe initiated a campaign "to make known among non-Jews" the Noahide laws, "the ordinances Judaism believes to be the prerequisites for a just society." As a result of the Rebbe's campaign, "the preamble to the 1996 congressional bill commemorating the annual Education Day (starting 1978 and observed each year on the Rebbe's birthday) formally recognizes" the Seven Laws of Noah.

When he opened the House on May 4, 1994, Minnesota rabbi Moshe Feller itemized the Noahide laws—and connected one specifically to Congress' work:

> Members of this august body, the U.S. House of Representatives, convene here to fulfill one of the seven Biblical commandments which You issued to all mankind: that all societies must govern by just laws. At the dawn of civilization, as related in Genesis and its sacred commentaries, You issued seven commandments which came to be known as

> the Seven Noahide Laws:
>> To worship You alone and not to serve idols,
>> Never to blaspheme Your Holy Name,
>> Not to murder,
>> Not to commit adultery,
>> Not to steal,
>> Not to be cruel to any living creature, and

> That every society govern by just laws which are based in the recognition of You.

---

63 The other three rabbinical father/son duos: Panitz, Nelson, and Bomzer. Plus one set of brothers, Applbaum, and one set of cousins, Wohlberg, have been guest chaplains. And for good measure, the fifth rabbi guest chaplain, Abraham de Sola, and the 10th, Henry Mendes, were uncle and nephew.

Nevada rabbi Shea Harlig was none too subtle about connecting the House to the Noahide laws—and God—on March 15, 2007:

> The members of this prestigious body, the U.S. Congress, convene here to fulfill one of the seven Noahide commandments: the commandment to govern by just laws which are based in the recognition of You, God, as the Sovereign Ruler of all people and nations. We, the citizens of this blessed country proudly proclaim this recognition and our commitment to justice in our Pledge of Allegiance "One Nation, Under God, with Liberty and Justice for All."

Feller opened the Senate on June 11, 2013, in similar Noahide fashion:

> In their divinely inspired wisdom, the Founding Fathers of our blessed country, the United States of America, established a policy of separation of church and state. However, it was never their intention to separate our country from You. Hence, both legislative bodies of our blessed country begin their sessions invoking Your divine presence and guidance in their legislation. Hence, in our Pledge of Allegiance we declare "one Nation under God," on our currency is printed "In God We Trust," and on the walls of this very Senate hall in which we invoke Your blessing is engraved in bold letters "In God We Trust." Grant that the Senators realize that in legislating just laws they are fulfilling one of the seven commandments which You issued to Noah.[64]

Ben Zion Schaffran prayed in the House on February 19, 1974. It was a few days before House members voted to authorize the Judiciary Committee to investigate whether grounds existed for the impeachment of President Nixon, formally initiating the impeachment process. Schaffran, one of the earliest Lubavitcher rabbis to offer a Congress prayer, said "every governmental assembly is opened with a prayer and even the currency of this country bespeaks trust in G-d. A nation which is cognizant of its reliance on the Almighty will surely weather the storms which have befallen it." An inference to Watergate turmoil, yes? Just as surely as the sponsoring remarks of Democratic Rep. Elizabeth Holtzman, whose New York district

---

64   Note Feller's mention of church and state. Few rabbi guest chaplains have done so. Another rare time: February 16, 1905, Rabbi Abram Simon of Washington Hebrew Congregation. Apparently unaware and/or unconcerned with any irony in the messaging, Simon prayed in the House for God to give government leaders "the spirit of wisdom" to keep "church and state in their fortunate separation."

was home to Lubavitch worldwide headquarters: "At a time when Congress is confronting such difficult and complicated problems, I hope that his words will provide a source of guidance for us."

Rabbi Schneerson. Noahide Laws. Drawing a straight line from God to the U.S. government. These are all core elements of Lubavitch rabbi presentations to Congress. Several have added one additional common element unique to their prayers: The *pushke*. With a theatrical flair.

"In this spirit I would like to take this opportunity to put a dollar bill, on which the words 'In G-d We Trust' are imprinted, into this pushke—charity box," Shmuel Butman said in the Senate on June 12, 1991. "This charity box reminds us all that we have an obligation not only to ourselves and our families, but also, indeed, to our neighbors and to society in general." Liberman similarly opened his 1994 Senate prayer: "Before we begin, I would like to place a token in the charity box to contribute to the needy."

Butman, opening the Senate again on April 6, 2006, combined charity and Schneerson: "In honor of the Rebbe, I want to do an act of goodness and kindness. I want to put a dollar in a pishky, in the charity box."

Without those explanations, observers unfamiliar with the charity box tradition could be forgiven for wondering whether fundraising was now permissible inside the House and Senate chambers. Not to worry, it is not. Meantime, Lubavitch accountants might be delighted to learn that donations to pushkes have been deliberated by the House Ways & Means Committee. In a July 24, 2007, hearing on tax-exempt charitable organizations, this green-eyeshades point was made to the record: "The congregant who, at the local synagogue's morning minyan, regularly places a dollar bill in the pushke, can do the arithmetic to reach a fairly accurate estimate of his donations for the year."

With nine prayers, Feller is near the top of the list for the number of times a single rabbi has opened Congress.

More Lubavitch metrics. The 1990s saw back-to-back Lubavitch prayers offered several times:

- Liberman on May 13, 1992, and Butman on May 14, 1992, both in the House;
- In 1993, Chaim Bergstein on June 9 and Butman on July 28, both in the Senate;
- In 1994, Feller in the House on May 4 and Liberman in the Senate on May 25; and

- Two straight again in the Senate: Levi Shemtov September 17, 1998, and Feller May 20, 1999.

Senators have been close to the Lubavitcher community. Of the 28 congressional Lubavitch prayers, 17 have been in the Senate. Which brings us back to Schneerson.

The August 13, 1979, *New York* magazine reported on Sen. Rudy Boschwitz (R-MN)—Jewish and born in Germany before World War II—for his "Hasidic Connection." "Bearded men in black suits and fedoras doing the Lubavitcher Rebbe's bidding are no strangers to the halls of Congress," said the article's opening sentence. A year after that story, Boschwitz entered into *Congressional Record* a Schneerson speech on family planning. Boschwitz set it up by calling the Lubavitcher Rebbe "one of the truly saintly people of our age and one of the extraordinary leaders of the Jewish faith" (August 27, 1980).

In the October 18, 2013, *Observer*, Rabbi Shmuley Boteach reported that "in the last throes of the campaign" that month, Sen. Cory Booker (D-NJ) "traveled late at night with a small group of his oldest friends to the gravesite of the Lubavitcher Rebbe, Rabbi Menachem Schneerson, in Queens, to light a candle for his father and pray for his memory." In his book on the Rebbe, Telushkin reported on Joseph Lieberman: "Subsequent to his 1988 election to the Senate from Connecticut, the last stop Lieberman made before flying to Washington for his swearing-in was a visit to the Rebbe, at his residence at 1304 President Street, to receive a blessing."

Rep. John Lewis (D-GA) said in 1995, according to a tribute on the Chabad.org website, "We may no longer see the Rebbe with our eyes, but his spirit lives in our hearts and in our deeds." Sen. Harry Reid (D-NV) called Schneerson "one of the great Jewish leaders of our time" in floor remarks after Nevada's Harlig gave the prayer in June 2009.

Schneerson did catch flak from one Jewish leader for prayers even opening Congress at all. In *Religion and State in American Jewish Experience*, Jonathan Sarna and David Dalin reported that in a 1978 letter to Schneerson, Reform Jewish leader Rabbi Joseph Glaser wrote the U.S. Congress "lamentably begins its sessions with a religious invocation."[65]

Not every Lubavitch rabbi mentioned in the Senate has been Menachem Mendel Schneerson. Also cited: Joseph (Yosef) Schneerson—Rabbi Menachem Mendel's father-in-law and predecessor as sixth Rebbe.

---

65   University of Notre Dame Press, 1997, page 295.

"Your servant, Rabbi Yosef Yitzckok Schneersohn, of blessed memory, the world renowned Lubavitcher Rebbe, fled war-torn Europe for these shores of freedom in 1940," Feller said in the Senate on July 14, 1989, "spending the final decade of his earthly existence as a distinguished citizen of these United States of America, laboring with great self-sacrifice to sanctify Your holy name throughout the world."

And here's Sen. Daniel Patrick Moynihan (D-NY) providing more history after Butman gave the June 12, 1991, prayer: "Many Members of the Senate are familiar with the role that a member of this body played in securing the release of Rabbi Joseph Schneerson from a Soviet prison and the emigration of his entire immediate family, including the current Rebbe, from Stalin's Russia. The intervention of Senator William Borah of Idaho on behalf of this beleaguered Chassidic family stands as a noble example of courageous moral leadership."

Stalin was cited again when another Lubavitch rabbi prayed in the House nearly 30 years later, July 25, 2019. "As a descendant of Chassidic Jews who fled the Stalinist regime that persecuted religious observance," Rabbi Gershon Avtzon of Yeshivas Lubavitch Cincinnati said, "I am especially grateful and blessed to be in America, the nation called the 'country of kindness' by the great spiritual leader of our generation, the Lubavitcher Rebbe Melech HaMoshiach, Rabbi Menachem Mendel Schneerson. We thank you for the freedom we have here to practice our faith, and we pray for those who still suffer persecution around the world."

After Rabbi Avtzon gave the House prayer, he visited Ohio Sen. Rob Portman (R). According to pictures Portman tweeted, Avtzon, the Senator, and a group of Chassidim and children danced in front of the Capitol.

13: Sephardic Influence

"We hold these truths to be self-evident, that all men are created equal, that they are endowed by their Creator with certain unalienable rights, that among these are Life, Liberty, and the pursuit of Happiness." When those words were proclaimed in the Declaration of Independence on July 4, 1776, Congregation Shearith Israel, also known as the Spanish and Portuguese Synagogue in the City of New York, was already 122 years old.

Its founders were primarily Sephardic Jews, those who trace their ancestry to Spain and various parts of North Africa and the Middle East, unlike Ashkenazi Jews who trace roots typically to Eastern Europe.

Rabbi Bernard Raskas of St. Paul, Minnesota, was Senate guest chaplain twice. Marking the 500th anniversary of Christopher Columbus' voyage to the New World, he wrote an article titled, "Columbus' Story Has a Jewish Chapter" (entered into the Congressional Record by Democratic Minnesota Sen. Paul Wellstone on October 23, 1991). Raskas included this anecdote of Sephardic arrival: "When the New World was first sighted, the cry of 'Tierra! (Land!)' came from a lookout on the Pinta whose name was Rodrigo de Triana, a marrano who secretly practiced Judaism. That day was Friday, Oct. 12, 1492. It happened to be a Jewish holiday on which Jews sing praises to God and carry the Torah (Pentateuch) scrolls."

Describing Sephardic Jews, the July 23, 2009, *New York Times* noted they "include Moroccans, Turks, Iranians and Iraqis. But most belong to families that emigrated to the United States from the Middle East, especially Syria, because of anti-Jewish attacks there after the establishment of the state of Israel in 1948." A droller distinction was offered by Joseph Epstein writing in the January 28, 2018, *Weekly Standard*: "All I remember from a novel read decades ago, whose title and author's name are lost to me, is that what separates Sephardic Jews from all others, apart from their extravagant genealogical pretensions, is that no Sephardic Jew can stand gefilte fish."

If one person sums up the experience of immigrants seeking refuge in America it is Emma Lazarus. Her iconic "The New Colossus" sonnet ("Give me your tired, your poor . . .") is mounted on the pedestal of the Statue of Liberty, the Mother of Exiles. Proclaiming Jewish American Heritage Month for May 2010, President Obama said Lazarus' "poignant words still speak to us today, reminding us of our Nation's promise as a beacon to all who are denied freedom and opportunity in their native lands."

Rabbi Solomon Schiff cited the Lazarus poem in his July 12, 2001, Senate prayer: "Thou has created this land as a haven of hope for the tired, the poor, the huddled masses yearning to breathe free." So did Chaplain Barry Black when he blessed Senators on October 30, 2015: "Make them bigger in their thinking, in their praying, and in their outreach to the huddled masses yearning to breathe free."

Lazarus was a Sephardic Jew.[66]

---

66 The middle name of Senate Democratic leader Chuck Schumer's (NY) younger daughter is Emma, for Emma Lazarus. Schumer's middle name is Ellis, for Ellis Island.

So too Supreme Court Justice Benjamin Cardozo. He belonged to Shearith Israel. His great grandfather was head of the Touro Synagogue. He was a descendant of Sephardic rabbi Gershom Mendes Seixas, who participated in George Washington's 1789 presidential inauguration.[67] According to the *Jewish Encyclopedia*[68] at the outbreak of the American Revolution Seixas "at once espoused the Patriot cause, though many of the Christian ministers of the city sympathized with the Tories. It was largely due to his influence that the Jewish congregation closed the doors of its synagogue on the approach of the British, and decided to leave the town rather than continue under British rule."

The first two Jewish U.S. senators were Sephardic. David Levy Yulee, Moroccan-Jewish origin, was elected from Florida in 1845. Originally David Levy, he added the Sephardic surname Yulee in 1846. Judah Benjamin, via St. Croix, was elected from Louisiana in 1853. Both were pro-Confederacy during the Civil War. *Jewish Confederates* by Robert Rosen has a chapter titled "Two Sephardic Senators."[69] It notes that both Yulee and Benjamin "played a prominent role in secession." Benjamin became the first Jew to serve in a President's cabinet, as Secretary of State, War, and Attorney General. The President he served was Jefferson Davis.

Consistent with their representation in early American history, two of the first ten rabbis who prayed in Congress were Sephardic. Abraham de Sola of Montreal's Shearith Israel opened the House on January 9, 1872. His nephew Henry Mendes of New York's Portuguese Synagogue opened the Senate on April 24, 1888. Ten years later Mendes founded the Union of Orthodox Jewish Congregations of America.

Sephardic Jews have been seldom seen since then. Only seven identifiably Sephardic rabbis have prayed in Congress. Among those seven: Meir Felman. The rabbi from the Judea Center Synagogue in Brooklyn prayed twice—in the House on May 28, 1962, and in the Senate on April 28, 1964. The two most recent: Asa Haim of Temple Beth Tikva in Fullerton, California, gave the House prayer on November 13, 1985. He was born in Bulgaria. And David Algaze of Havurat Yisrael Synagogue in Forest Hills, New York. Born in Argentina, he gave the July 11, 2012, House prayer.

---

67 On August 5, 2009, Sen. Al Franken (D-MN) said of Supreme Court justice nominee Sonia Sotomayor: "Like Judge Sotomayor, Cardozo was from an ethnic minority. He was a Sephardic Jew, a descendant of Portuguese immigrants."

68 Funk & Wagnalls Company, page 159.

69 South Carolina Press, 2000, page 55.

The tiny number of Sephardic Jews in front of Congress is consistent with the overall small proportion of Sephardim among the greater Jewish population. The *Associated Press* reported on July 11, 2014, that worldwide an estimated three million Jews are of Spanish origin. Most of the United States' roughly five and a half million Jews are of Central and Eastern European heritage, compared to 300,000 with Sephardic roots.

The American Jewish Committee counted 3,727 synagogues in the United States in 2001. Just over a hundred (3%) identified as Sephardic—all but four of which were Orthodox. And a current count of synagogues listed online by the American Sephardi Federation shows 138—the bulk of which are in the New York City area.

Small in overall numbers—and naturally small numbers in front of Congress. But still noteworthy for their contribution to America, even to contemporary Senate history.

Sephardic Jews earned a plug in Senate chaplain Lloyd Ogilvie's April 23, 2001, prayer. "At the beginning of Jewish Heritage Week, we praise You for the immense contribution Jews have made to America," Ogilvie said. "We remember the first Jewish community in Newport, Rhode Island comprised of Sephardim, persecuted Spanish and Portuguese Jews who arrived in the spring of 1658. This group of refugees began to worship together in private homes or rented buildings until a synagogue building, the Touro Hebrew Congregation, was constructed. . . . We thank You for the ten Jewish Senators and their strong moral and social consciences."[70]

And proof that they can be as susceptible to the political sausage-making (kosher sausage, of course) like any other group: Sephardic Jews have a cameo connection to a Senate money controversy. In 1988 Sen. Daniel Inouye (D-HI) pushed an $8 million earmark for constructing schools in France for Jewish refugees from North Africa. Later, he went on the Senate floor and said, "I have made an error in judgment. I fear that I have embarrassed my colleagues. I intend to correct that error." Why? According to

---

70 After poet Henry Wadsworth Longfellow visited Newport in 1852, he wrote "The Jewish Cemetery at Newport": "How strange it seems! These Hebrews in their graves, Close by the street of this fair seaport town. . . . The very names recorded here are strange, Of foreign accent, and of different climes; Alvares and Rivera interchange With Abraham and Jacob of old times." On August 26, 1962, at an observance marking the 200th anniversary of the Touro Synagogue, Sen. Claiborne Pell (D-RI) said Wadsworth's poem "immortalized the nobility of this very congregation. . . . His words capture the rich legacy of history which is all around us in the inspiring atmosphere of this great sanctuary."

a February 1, 1988, *United Press International* report, because of "sugges-tions that the appropriation was motivated by a $1,000 campaign contribu-tion from the head of Ozar Hatora, a group which supports the interests of Sephardic Jews." On the Senate floor Inouye said the group "has a 40-year history of support for Jewish refugees, particularly those who are Sephardic or eastern Jews."

Perhaps the most important contributor to the Sephardic story in Congress is Rabbi Abraham Hecht. Four times he prayed between 1966 and 1983—twice in the House and twice in the Senate.

His January 7, 2013, obituary published by *Chabad* began: "Rabbi Abraham Hecht, a Chabad-Lubavitch rabbi who served as the spiritual leader of Sephardic congregations in North America for more than 65 years, passed away Saturday night at the age of 90. For many years, he was vice president of the Sephardic Rabbinical Council, president of Rabbinical Council for Syrian Jewry in North America, and president of the Rabbinical Alliance of America. Beloved by his congregants, he built Congregation Shaare Zion in Brooklyn, N.Y., into the largest Sephardic congregation in North America."

The article further noted, "Several times, Hecht delivered brief ben-edictions at the opening sessions of the House of Representatives and the Senate." Rep. Stephen Solarz (D-NY) once wrote to him, "it was really good to have you with us here in Washington a short while ago. I've gotten so many favorable comments from my colleagues on your prayer that I think we could elect you, if you're interested, as the permanent Rabbi of the House when we convene next year."

And after an April 21, 1983, prayer, Sen. Daniel Patrick Moynihan (D-NY) offered this tribute: "The Syrian Sephardic community of America has over 30,000 members and has established an impressive record of com-munity service on both a national and international scale. It is a pleasure to have Rabbi Hecht and other distinguished members of the Syrian Sephardic community join us today."

But here's a twist. Despite his leadership of that community, Hecht was not Sephardic. In fact, he once wrote, "There wasn't a trace of Sephardic ancestry in the roots of my extended family tree."

Which members of Congress *could* be Sephardic?

Rep. Alexandria Ocasio-Cortez (D-NY) said in December 2018: "One of the things that we discovered about ourselves is that a very, very long time ago, generations and generations ago, my family consisted of Sephardic Jews."

And three contemporary Republicans merit genealogical examination.

Former Florida Rep. Ileana Ros-Lehtinen had Jewish grandparents on her mother's side. "She knows that they were Sephardic Jews, originally from Turkey, and that her grandfather was a pillar of the Jewish community in Cuba," *The Forward* reported on October 14, 2005. "When she and her parents left for the United States after Fidel Castro took power, her grandfather stayed behind with his ailing wife. Both grandparents died in Havana."

Several years after he lost re-election to the Senate, George Allen of Virginia spoke to the Faith and Freedom Coalition. "I found out in the summer of 2006 that my grandfather was Jewish, and my mother had hid this all these years," Allen told the Christian group on June 15, 2012. "It was a fear of religious persecution that she was trying to protect her baby by hiding this religious heritage." Allen's grandfather, Felix Lumbroso, was incarcerated by the Nazis when they occupied Tunisia during World War II. Tunisia has a long, strong Sephardic Jewish tradition.

And the third: Would you believe Ted Cruz of Texas? Sure, the Senator was raised an evangelical Christian. And yes, he was born in Canada. But might he have Sephardic blood in his ancestry? Consider his grandfather Raphael Cruz. He was born and raised in the Canary Islands. According to the *Jews and the Canary Islands*, in 1492 the Jews of Spain "were given a choice: convert to Christianity or be expelled from Spain. Many chose to hide themselves as 'New Christians,' or *conversos*, outwardly professing to be Christians while practicing their true faith in secret. In 1504 the Office of the Inquisition was set up in the remote Spanish holdings on the Canary Islands to seek out crypto-Jews, sorcerers, and other heretics." [71] The Port of Santa Cruz in the Canary Islands figures prominently in that story. So, it may have been more than a joke when Sen. Cruz—same name as that port—bonded with the Sephardic Legacy Series in 2013. Cruz told the Sephardim gathered on Capitol Hill, "My life experience mirrors the experience of so many Sephardic Jews, facing oppression and coming here seeking freedom. You know in my family my grandfather actually was born in the Canary Islands and moved when he was one year old to Cuba. So, we may in fact be distant cousins. And my father in turn grew up in Cuba and

---

71   Edited by Lucien Wolf, University of Toronto Press, 2001, back cover.

in 1957 he fled Cuba and came to Texas seeking freedom—55 years ago, just as your ancestors."

The first two Jewish U.S. Senators, Yulee and Benjamin, were Sephardic. There have been 33 Jewish Senators since. None Sephardic. Perhaps one day we'll get confirmation that Ted Cruz of Texas is the third.

14: Clergymen as Congressmen?

"We have built no national temples but the Capitol; we consult no common oracle but the Constitution."
—Representative Rufus Choate (Whig-MA), 1833

It's one thing for a visiting chaplain to theologically and gently suggest Congress pass this or oppose that. But that's as far as he or she can go. They can't engage in floor debate or vote on bills. Being selected as a guest chaplain is an honor. It's not an appointment to a post. Federal courts have asserted "the practice of legislative prayer does not provide meaningful input into legislative decision making." On October 11, 2017, U.S. District Judge Rosemary Collyer stated, "the position of guest chaplain is not an office or position of public trust."

But what if that's not sufficient for a chaplain? What if he or she does want to provide more meaningful input? Have any men or women of the cloth gone beyond voting *for* a member of Congress to actually serving *as* a voting member of Congress?

In *Democracy in America* Frenchman Alexis de Tocqueville reported on his early nineteenth-century visit to America. He examined "the position of American priests in political society. I was surprised to discover that they held no public appointments. There was not a single one in the administration, and I found that they were not even represented in the assemblies. In several states the law, and in all the rest public opinion, excludes them from a career in politics."

That was 1835. But religious leaders have been in Congress since the beginning.

According to the Pew Research Center (January 5, 2015), clergymen accounted for nearly seven percent of the first Congress membership. Manasseh Cutler was a minister of the Congregational Church in Ipswich, Massachusetts, a chaplain in the Revolutionary War—and a member of the House of Representatives. The first speaker of the House, Frederick

Muhlenberg of Pennsylvania, was a Lutheran minister.[72] Oliver Cromwell Comstock was a member of Congress from 1813-1819. Then he left Congress, became a Baptist minister, then returned to Congress—as House chaplain. An early iteration of the revolving door, perhaps—lobbying for God.

There are no laws keeping clergy out of Congress (the U.S. Constitution: "no religious test shall ever be required as a qualification to any office or public trust under the United States"). Here are some Christian clergy who have served in the House and Senate in more recent years whose names might be familiar to contemporary Congress watchers:

- Rep. John Buchanan (R-AL)
- Rep. Emanuel Cleaver (D-MO)
- Sen. John Danforth (R-MO)
- Rep. Bob Edgar (D-PA)
- Del. Walter Fauntroy (D-DC)
- Rep. Tennyson Guyer (R-OH)
- Rep. Jody Hice (R-GA)
- Rep. Adam Clayton Powell (D-NY)
- Rep. Bobby Rush (D-IL)
- Rep. Henry Schadeberg (R-WI)
- Rep. Tim Walberg (R-MI)

Cleaver gave the prayer at the first-day session of the 116th Congress, on January 3, 2019.

And despite the Church discouraging priests holding public office, two Catholic priests have served as voting members of Congress, both in the 1970s: Robert Cornell (D-WI) and Robert Drinan (D-MA). (Drinan left office explicitly because of the Pope's orders that sitting clergy not serve in public office. Barney Frank, a Jewish Democrat, replaced Drinan in the 1980 election.) One more tried to join that group. Before hosting "The McLaughlin Group" talking-heads political television program,

---

72   John Muhlenberg, his brother, also was a Lutheran minister who served in the House of Representatives. In a July 7, 2018, *Washington Post* column, John Kelly wrote that he "is most famous for the dramatic way in which he announced that he had decided to fight the British with more than just scripture. From the pulpit of his church in Woodstock, Va., Muhlenberg ended his final sermon with these words: 'In the language of Holy Writ there is a time for all things ... there is a time to pray and a time to fight ... and that time has now come.'" That's from the Hebrew Bible, Ecclesiastes.

Jesuit priest John McLaughlin ran for the Senate—1970, Rhode Island, as a Republican.[73]

Even House chaplain Patrick Conroy once aspired to the other side of the congressional pulpit—where they can have opinions. "By the time I got to high school, I was very interested in things having to do with law and politics," Conroy said during Rep. John Dingell's (D-MI) funeral on February 14, 2019. He attended Claremont College in California. "We learned, more than we would have ever learned in ninth grade civics, to love and to respect the institutions of government and law in this country." At Claremont, Conroy planned to go on to law school like his father and eventually "enter politics and replace either Warren Magnuson or Scoop Jackson. But then I went to Gonzaga Law School in Spokane, Washington and I ran into the Jesuits. I put on the last suit I would ever wear and became a man in black." Conroy told the service, "I put my imagination of law and politics behind me."

And rabbis?

None has ever served in Congress. But several were candidates. Dr. Samuel Buchler ran in New York in 1922—with a quirky asterisk. According to the August 12, 1922, *New York Times*, Buchler "was seeking both the Democratic and Republican nominations for Congress in the Twelfth Congressional District."

He lost both races. What happened to Buchler? We pick up the rabbi's story 20 years later. From the December 23, 1942, *New York Times*: "Samuel Buchler, who was convicted last month of a series of frauds in his operation of the Jewish Court of Arbitration, received yesterday . . . a suspended sentence on a prison term of twenty-five to fifty years." Buchler "charged fees to his clients at his court of arbitration for his 'influence' in solving domestic and business problems."

At least three more rabbis in recent years have run and lost campaigns for Congress. Two in New Jersey: Dennis Shulman, a Democrat, in the fifth congressional district (CD) in 2008; and Shmuley Boteach as a Republican for the ninth CD in 2012. Robert Barr briefly ran as a Democrat during the 2018 election cycle. He dropped out before the primary. His exit statement put Judaism in the first sentence: "When I began exploring a run to

---

73   McLaughlin also was a supporting actor in Watergate. From William F. Buckley's August 8, 1994 *New York Times* eulogy to President Richard Nixon: "Toward the end, Mr. Nixon brought in a Jesuit priest who, from the White House steps, pronounced the President to be 'the greatest moral leader of the last third of this century.'"

represent Ohio's First District one year ago, I was motivated by the same belief that drew me to become a rabbi—the belief that each of us needs to leave our world better than we found it." And a rabbi who served in Newtown, Connecticut, during the town's deadly 2012 school shooting ran for Congress during the 2018 midterm elections. Shaul Praver's website proclaimed: "I am the Newtown Rabbi. I ran into the fire for you. I've listened to your fears and I am ready to speak out for you in Washington."

Rabbis likely will continue to be candidates for office. To rework the title of John Updike's book: Rabbi, Run.

SECTION III

Media Portrayal

15: Media Report the Earliest Rabbis

"A great deal is being said in relation to the fact that a Jewish Rabbi opened Congress with prayer, upon the day on which a Speaker was elected. Well, every other plan has been tried, and we presume it was thought that if the prayer of a Rabbi could not affect the organization of such a Rabble, nothing could."
—The *White Cloud Kansas Chief* newspaper, February 23, 1860, reporting on Morris Raphall's prayer

Rabbi Raphall's pioneering appearance at the House rostrum attracted abundant news coverage. An irresistible hot take for noisy nineteenth-century media gleefully describing the curiosity.

That first prayer also represented the high point for the quantity of media attention given to one rabbi giving one prayer in one chamber of Congress.

But he was hardly the only rabbi to generate gee whiz attention from the press, some of it cringeworthy against today's norms and sensitivities.

Take Abraham de Sola of Montreal's Spanish and Portuguese Synagogue, Canada's oldest synagogue. He gave the House prayer January 9, 1872.

The January 13, 1872, *New York Herald* reported, "The unusual circumstance of a Jewish Rabbi opening the proceedings of the House of Representatives with a prayer has attracted an unusual amount of attention in political and religious circles." De Sola, the newspaper added, "is a benevolent and intellectual looking old gentleman, with a strongly marked Jewish countenance."

The *Herald* reporter scored an interview with that very gentleman who sported a "strongly marked Jewish countenance":

> *Herald*: "What originated the idea of your offering up prayer?"
>
> "Jewish Rabbi": "Well, it had been all arranged previous to my arriving by some friends of civil and religious liberty, who took an interest in the affair. . ."
>
> *Herald*: "I supposed those of your own persuasion in Washington feel gratified that such a privilege has been granted to you?"
>
> "Jewish Rabbi": "Oh, yes; very much gratified; and I am very much pleased myself. There has been considerable talk over it in the religious circles of Washington, and a number of prominent gentlemen have expressed to me their satisfaction at the toleration displayed by the House of Representatives. It is unusual for a foreigner to officiate in this way in that city, but the fact of a Jew opening a Christian assembly with prayer is altogether without precedent."

Without precedent? Perhaps what de Sola considered unprecedented was the first foreign Jew opening the House. His prayer was the fourth by a rabbi guest chaplain in that chamber.

Well into the next century, de Sola appearing in Congress still sparked fascination. On July 10, 1914, the *Canadian Jewish Chronicle* reported, "The spectacle of a British subject of Jewish faith, offering prayers for those who were not of his creed was unique."

The U.S. House historian's office has a drawing depicting de Sola's prayer. The scene "is shown from an unusual perspective, from behind the Speaker's rostrum, looking out onto the crowded Chamber, with the Members present respectfully bowing their heads."

More Jews were involved in congressional "spectacles". The February 3, 1904, Lewiston, Maine, *Daily Sun* reported on top of its front page:

> At its opening to-day the Senate witnessed the unusual spectacle of a religious service conducted by a Protestant minister and a Jewish rabbi. The daily prayer was delivered by Rabbi David Philipson, a professor in the Hebrew college at Cincinnati who was accompanied to the dais usually occupied by the President pro tempore by Chaplain Hale.

Henry Pereira Mendes gave the April 24, 1888, Senate prayer. The *Chicago Tribune*, adhering to what seems to journalism style and standards back then, reported on the New York rabbi's yarmulke. "According to the Jewish custom," Mendes "wore his hat while engaged in prayer." The April 25, 1888, *Tribune* identified Mendes as "a Hebrew." A "Personal Gossip" column reported he "wore his high hat during his prayer, much to the surprise of the senators, who did not seem to be aware that it is not the custom of rabbis to uncover their heads when offering prayer."[74] A German newspaper in Baltimore, according to historian Bertram Korn, suggested that based on Mendes' prayer "perhaps for a change they will next allow even a Buddhist to pray there, for even this religion has its adherents here." Born in Birmingham, England, Mendes' prayer also earned notice in a London newspaper (the May 18, 1888, *Anglo American Times*). Four years later he made news again. He was shot, according to the March 6, 1982, *New York Times*, "in the abdomen at his home by an importunate Arabian mendicant. . . . Mendes made a fatal mistake in not using violence to prevent the fellow from pushing past him and entering the house." The *Times* identified Mendes as "one of the most eloquent and esteemed Israelites in America."

A rabbi attracted *Chicago Tribune* interest that year. Here's how the newspaper reported a December 7, 1892, prayer: "The rather unusual circumstance of having a Jewish rabbi offer up prayer in the Senate chamber was witnessed today. Dr. Joseph Silverman of the Temple Emanuel of New York was introduced to the Vice-President by Chaplain Butler and invoked the divine benediction."

There were less than half a million Jews in America at the time. Despite a Jewish-sounding name, Vice President Levi Morton was not among them. He was an Episcopalian son of a Congregationalist minister.

The December 8, 1892, Salem, Oregon, *Evening Capital Journal* took interest in something Silverman did *not* do: "He did not follow the custom of the so-called orthodox Jews, by covering the head, but stood bareheaded during the proceedings."

Always with the yarmulke!

Silverman's prayer merited mention as well by the *New York Times*, which offered a more straight-forward angle the same day: "The opening prayers in both houses of Congress were said to-day by rabbis of the Jewish faith, Dr. Joseph Silverman, taking the place of the Chaplain of the

---

74   *Frank Leslie's Illustrated Newspaper*, May 5, 1888, page 183.

Senate, while Dr. Isaac M. Wise of Cincinnati officiated in the House of Representatives."

Credit the *Times* with reporting both prayers. (Also credit the *Times* with a March 28, 1915, report on events surrounding the next day's centenary of Wise's birth. The article featured a Silverman sermon about Wise: "He came to America, and found here a congenial home, a country for the expression of his soul. His intense Americanism knew no bounds. . . . His intense Americanism colored all his thoughts and acts.")

December 7, 1892: a date that lives in guest chaplain infamy. The first-time rabbis said prayers in both chambers. The *Wichita Daily Eagle* observed December 13, 1892, that the "circumstance that Jewish rabbi opened the proceedings of congress with prayer, one officiated in each house, is taken by some as indicative of the subsidence of religious bigotry in this country" (page 4). A pairing of rabbis in the House and Senate on the same day has happened 12 times: 1892, twice in 1958, 1966, twice in 1967, twice in 1968, 1979, 1987, 1991, and 1994.[75]

Midway through the twentieth century, rabbinical accessories remained newsworthy. The May 27, 1942, *Washington Post* reported that in his prayer the day before, Rabbi Bernard Bergman "appeared before the Representatives garbed in the traditional robes of his faith." Nachum David Herman gave the March 7, 1950, House prayer. The next-day's *Milwaukee Sentinel* ran a photo of the Brooklynite chatting with chaplain Bernard Braskamp. Herman wears his *talit*, or prayer shawl. The *Sentinel* caption said the rabbi "is dressed in his robes of office."

The March 1, 1899, *Washington Post* cheered Gustav Hausmann's appearance in Congress. Under the headline "A Rabbi at The House," the *Post* offered this review: "It is very rare that a rabbi of the Jewish faith officiates in the House. Rabbi Hausmann is a young man, but has a high standing in the councils of his church. The prayer was very devout." Hausmann ended his February 28, 1899, prayer asking God "to bless the President of the United States with Thy divine wisdom while he guides the ship of State in these stormy days of our history. We pray all this because we love our country, because we love liberty, because we love humanity." Quite a seasoned flourish for a rabbi whom the Post speculated was "perhaps the youngest minister that ever officiated as Chaplain."

---

75 Even rarer is the same guest chaplain who prays in both the House and Senate on the same day. One example: On December 9, 2017, Father Steven Boes of Boys Town, Nebraska, opened both chambers in prayer. No rabbi has done so.

Amsterdam-born Joseph Voorsanger earned his own *New York Times* mention with a June 30, 1898, prayer—delivered in the midst of the Spanish-American War. [76]According to the July 1, 1898, *Times*, the rabbi of Temple Emanuel-El in San Francisco "pronounced the invocation at the opening of the Senate's session today. He prayed that 'all elements which may come from these sacred walls be extended in the form of God's blessing to all humanity, and that the flag under which we live, that for which our fathers fought, be forever the sacred emblem of liberty until time shall be no more.'"

A good record of the California rabbi's words. No mention of what he looked like or wore. Alas for Voorsanger, the *Times* misspelled his last name as Voorsauger.

Sixteen years earlier, Voorsanger was guest chaplain in the House. The Kentucky newspaper Stanford *Interior Journal* reported on his prayer on May 19, 1882. The paper didn't try to spell his name. But it did offer this unique perspective: "A Jewish rabbi opened Congress with prayer the other day. It was the second time that a Jew was ever so humiliated."

16: Local Media Report Rabbis

"How beautiful on the mountains are the feet of the messenger who brings good news."
—Isaiah 52:7, cited by Capt. Alan Greenspan, Fort Dix, New Jersey, House guest chaplain on June 8, 1967

As more rabbis delivered more opening prayers, the media novelty wore off. The number of major newspaper stories decreased. But not for the century-old *Jewish Telegraphic Agency*. The *JTA*, essentially the wire service

---

76   An interesting sliver of American Jewish history is the role California Jews played in the Spanish-American War. On December 13, 1911, Rep. Julius Kahn (R-CA), a German-born Jewish congressman who represented San Francisco, described to the House "the first great influx of Russian Jews to this country in 1882--83. A large number came to the Pacific coast. . . . They have shown themselves ready, if need be, to die for their country. When President William McKinley issued his call for volunteers at the outbreak of the Spanish-American War there was a ready response from every section of these United States. Among the regiments that were mustered into the volunteer service was the First California Volunteer Infantry. . . . There were 109 Jews on the roster of the regiment, and the first American to lay down his life in defense of Old Glory in the distant Philippines was Sergt. Maurice Justh, of the First California Volunteer Infantry—the son of a Russian Jew."

for Jewish media, has chronicled rabbi guest chaplains for decades. Here are some of the *JTA*'s accounts:

- January 9, 1930: "Rabbi Louis I. Newman, of Temple Emanuel, San Francisco, gave the opening prayer at the session of the House of Representatives, yesterday. Rabbi Newman was invited to deliver the prayer by the Chaplains' Association and the Jewish Institute of Religion."

- February 15, 1948: "Dr. Leo Baeck yesterday became the first non-American rabbi to deliver the prayer opening a session of the House of Representatives when he pronounced the traditional invocation at the Lincoln Day meeting of the House."

- June 12, 1956: "Rabbi Samuel J. Fox, spiritual leader of Congregation Anshai Sfard of Lynn, Massachusetts, opened a session of the United States Senate with a special prayer this week. The rabbi's prayer was printed in the Congressional Record."

- May 10, 1957: "Rabbi Arthur Schneier of Congregation Bnai Jacob, Brooklyn, N.Y., today celebrated the tenth anniversary of his arrival in America as a displaced person by invoking the opening prayer in the United States Senate Chamber. A year ago Rabbi Schneier delivered an opening prayer in the House of Representatives. He is 27 years old."

- April 23, 1958: "Rabbi Charles M. Rubel of Congregation Sherah Israel, Macon, Georgia, delivered the opening prayer when the U.S. Senate met today. Rabbi Rubel was invited by Senator Herman Talmadge of Georgia to pronounce the invocation. Sen. Richard Russell, also of Georgia, joined in introducing the Rabbi."

- January 20, 1961: "Congressional Record Uses Hebrew Characters for First Time . . . Rabbi Arnold S. Turetsky, of Congregation Ohev Tzedek, Youngstown, Ohio, was invited to offer the opening prayer before the House of Representatives."

- May 7, 1965: "On the occasion of Israel's anniversary, the opening prayer in the U.S. Senate today was delivered by Rabbi Joachim Prinz, of Newark. He was invited to deliver the invocation by Senator Clifford Case, Republican of New Jersey."

- April 20, 1967: "Rabbi Jay Kaufman, executive vice-president of B'nai B'rith, offered the opening prayer at the United States Senate yesterday. He quoted passages in Hebrew and English from Isaiah and the Talmud in calling for the wisdom 'to find our way out of the toils of war.'"

- July 13, 1977: "Dr. Israel Goldstein, Rabbi Emeritus of Congregation B'nai Jeshurun, N.Y., has been invited to deliver the opening prayer at the closing session of the House of Representatives Thursday."

- March 9, 1995: "This week, Rabbi Rachel Mikva took to the House floor, where her father, also President Clinton's counsel, once debated as a Democratic representative from Illinois. . . . Mikva said: 'It was an honor to offer the opening prayer, and I feel I received a very warm welcome from my father's colleagues and former colleagues.'"

- September 21, 1998: "Alluding to the Monica Lewinsky scandal and partisan conflicts in Congress, a Lubavitch rabbi has asked senators to 'judge each other at least as favorably as we would like to be judged ourselves.' Rabbi Levi Shemtov, director of the Washington office of the American Friends of Lubavitch, led the Senate in its opening prayer Sept. 17, becoming the second rabbi to lead the Senate in prayer this year."

- July 1, 2009: "Rabbi Shea Harlig, director of Chabad of Southern Nevada, opened up Senate proceedings on June 25th with an invocation to honor the 15th anniversary of the death of the Lubavitcher Rebbe, Rabbi Menachem Mendel Schneerson. The invitation came from Senate Majority Leader Harry Reid."

And, as you might expect, local Jewish media is keenly interested. Two from Pennsylvania, for example:

- The *Jewish Chronicle of Pittsburgh* June 14, 1984: "Today, Rabbi Richard M. E. Marcovitz, spiritual leader of B'nai Israel Synagogue, East End, opens the June 14 session of the United States Congress at the Capitol in Washington, DC, the Rabbi was invited to serve as guest chaplain at the request of Pennsylvania Congressman William Coyne."

- *Philadelphia Jewish Exponent* November 13, 2013: "It was a decidedly different congregation—and bimah—Rabbi Joshua Gruenberg of Congregation Beth El in Yardley addressed on Wednesday as he delivered the daily invocation as guest chaplain before the U.S. House of Representatives in Washington, DC The Bucks County rabbi was invited to do the ritualistic honors by Rep.

Mike Fitzpatrick, who had spoken to Gruenberg's congregation last month on domestic and foreign issues, including Iran."

On September 6, 1974, The *Jewish Post* of Indianapolis celebrated a rabbi not even from Indiana:

It's difficult to believe that any man of the cloth, Jewish or Christian, can resist taking advantage of a once-in-a-lifetime opportunity when delivering the invocation at the opening of a session of the House of Representatives. But here is the invocation of Rabbi Israel Moshowitz, of the Hillcrest (Flushing, N.Y.) Jewish Center delivered on March 15, and it is its brevity which is remarkable, not to mention of course, its message.

And a unique intersection of Jewish media and guest chaplaincy when Chaim Lipschitz came to pray. He gave House and Senate prayers seven times between 1958 and 1977. He also was the editor of the *Jewish Press*, the "largest independent weekly Jewish newspaper in the United States," and is identified that way in the *Congressional Record*. Sponsoring the rabbi on April 28, 1977, Rep. James Scheuer (D-NY) noted Lipschitz "has appeared in several CBS television network programs . . . was an accredited press correspondent at the trial of Adolf Eichmann." Scheuer added, Lipschitz, "in his weekly columns in the *Jewish Press*, consistently articulates the achievements of Jewish leaders as reflected in their concern for the individual. Indeed, Rabbi Lipschitz's weekly *Jewish Press* cameo profiles carry messages of inspiration and encouragement."

But not just the *JTA* and Jewish media remain interested in rabbi guest appearances. Rabbi prayers provide newsy angles for local general interest media—hometown papers reporting on hometown rabbis sponsored by hometown members of Congress.

Back to Pennsylvania, take the *Pittsburgh Post-Gazette*. The newspaper reported April 27, 1968:

Dr. Morris A. Landes, rabbi of Congregation Adath Jeshurun, Squirrel Hill, will deliver the opening prayer at the U.S. Senate on May 2 in observance of Israel's Independence Day. A luncheon will also be held in Rabbi Landes' honor in the Senate Dining Room. The invitation to open the session was issued by Dr. Frederick B. Harris, Senate chaplain, and was initiated by Sen. Joseph Clark. A delegation will accompany Dr. Landes from Pittsburgh.

The *Post-Gazette* reported another one on April 20, 1972: "Rabbi Kenneth I. Segel, assistant at Rodef Shalom Temple, Oakland, gave the invocation yesterday at the convening of the House of Representatives. Rep. William S. Moorhead, Shadyside Democrat, introduced the visiting rabbi to House Speaker Carl Albert."

In Maine, the *Lewiston Daily-Sun* noted in its February 26, 1966, report on Norman Zdanowitz's House prayer that "the rabbi will report on his trip and experiences at the Capital at the 8pm service at the synagogue Friday."

Many more local papers have offered a journalistic version of local kvelling over their homegrown rabbinical heroes:

- The March 5, 1971, Hazelton, Pennsylvania, *Standard-Speaker*: "Rabbi Haim Kemelman, East Brunswick, NJ, whose column 'Lines for Living' appears weekly in the Standard-Speaker, had the honor of delivering the prayer opening the Feb. 25 session of the House of Representatives in Washington."
- *Los Angeles Times* August 23, 1997: "The Office of the Chaplain of the U.S. House of Representatives has invited Rabbi Sidney S. Guthman of Congregation Sholom in Seal Beach to be guest chaplain and give the opening prayer before the House on Sept. 4. He was nominated by Rep. Stephen Horn (R-Long Beach)."
- Schenectady *Daily Gazette*, May 16, 1998: "Rabbi Moshe Bomzer, spiritual leader of Congregation Beth Abraham Jacob, the largest Orthodox Jewish congregation in the Capital Region, will deliver the opening prayer in the U.S. House of Representatives on May 21."
- The *Daily Gazette* again on July 11, 2000: "Rabbi Linda Motzkin of the Temple Sinai in Saratoga Springs is scheduled to offer the opening prayer in the U.S. House of Representatives today in Washington, DC. U.S. Rep. John E. Sweeney, R-Halfmoon, invited Motzkin to say the opening prayer, which will be carried on C-SPAN television at about 10 a.m."
- The *Boca Raton News*, September 16, 2006: "A first from Florida.... Congressman Clay Shaw welcomes Boca Raton Rabbi, Amy Rader, to Washington, DC, Thursday, where she became Florida's first female Rabbi to give the opening prayer on the floor of the U.S. House of Representatives."

- Norwalk, Connecticut, *The Hour*, May 23, 2011: "Westport Rabbi Jeremy Wiederhorn will deliver the opening prayer in the U.S. House of Representatives in Washington, DC, this morning . . . Wiederhorn's prayer comes as Israeli Prime Minister Benjamin Netanyahu prepares to address a joint session of Congress this morning."

- *Republican-American* of Waterbury, Connecticut, June 14, 2014: "He traveled hundreds of miles, from Waterbury's Jewish enclave to the nation's Capitol, to deliver a message of faith, fortitude and morality. On Thursday, Rabbi Doniel Ginsberg of Waterbury's yeshiva community was invited by U.S. Sen. Chris Murphy, D-Conn., to offer the Senate's opening prayer."

Local TV news, too. Here's *News 12* in Westchester, New York, on December 16, 2014: "Rabbi Eytan Hammerman, who is in charge of the Jewish Community Center, couldn't believe when he opened his email and saw an invitation to the White House for a Hanukkah reception. Rabbi Hammerman says he kept checking to make sure the email was real. This is Rabbi Hammerman's second invite this year to Washington, DC. Over the summer he was asked to give the opening prayer at the House of Representatives."

Even the *New York Times* cared about the rabbi guest chaplains—for obituaries.

Edward Calisch was the first rabbi guest chaplain in Congress born in America (Toledo, Ohio). His January 8, 1946, *New York Times* obit included his April 6, 1892, House prayer: "His ability as a speaker was recognized early. A year after he arrived in Richmond he delivered on one occasion the opening prayer in the House of Representatives at Washington. At various times he made the principal address at memorial services at Mount Vernon, and twice spoke at the Tomb of the Unknown Soldier."

The *New York Times* obituary of another rabbi went further, memorializing his serving as guest chaplain right in the headline. On May 12, 1948—two days before the state of Israel was established—the *Times* declared: "Dr. G. N. Hausmann, Wrote on Judaism; Rabbi, Former Guest Chaplain of Congress, Dies—Helped Found Synagogue Here." The story noted, "During the administration of President William Howard Taft, Dr. Hausmann was guest chaplain of both the Senate and House of Representatives. He also served as chaplain of the State Senate of Michigan and the State Senate of New Jersey."

These days, local media do the mournful remembering:

- A July 26, 1998, *Chicago Tribune* obituary of Morris Hershman: "He delivered invocations at both the U.S. Senate and the House of Representatives, and during the first inauguration of former Gov. James Thompson."
- When Augusta, Georgia, rabbi Maynard Hyman died, local TV station WRDW noted on August 27, 2006, "He even took his teachings to Capitol Hill, where he delivered an opening prayer to the US Senate and a session of Congress."
- The November 11, 2014, Champaign-Urbana, Illinois, *News-Gazette* obit for Isaac Neuman: "He twice delivered the opening prayer in the U.S. House of Representatives, expressing his gratitude for the refuge he'd been given here."

And when Theodore Levy died, the Syracuse *Post-Standard* remembered his March 8, 1984, Senate prayer. "That day's agenda," the newspaper reported on November 13, 2004, "included debate about a proposed constitutional amendment allowing organized prayer in public schools. Utah Sen. Orrin Hatch, author of the amendment, invited Levy to lead [the] prayer. Levy . . . publicly opposed the amendment. 'Synagogues and churches, as well as our homes, afford ample opportunity for the development of religious values in American children,' he said in a letter to the editor shortly before his appearance as guest chaplain in the Senate."

Hometown papers also capture rabbis' own giddiness from the experience of being a rabbi at the center of legislative democracy. Where more legislative- and process-focused reporting on Congress might breed editorial cynicism, local coverage of rabbis generates glee.

Daniel Fellman of Anshe Emeth Memorial Temple in New Brunswick told the *New Jersey Jewish News* about opening the Senate on January 29, 2009, "It was incredible when I walked in the chamber. It started to take my breath away." The paper reported Fellman "was given floor privileges for the day, spending three hours listening to debates on a children's health insurance program and creation of governmental oversight on hedge funds."

When Solomon Schiff gave his first of three Senate prayers he told the *Miami News* on March 3, 1977, "The words I'm going to recite will be recorded in the same *Congressional Record* that has recorded the words of all our nation's leaders throughout the years. That's a very humbling fact."

The *Queens Courier* ran this item on July 30, 2008: "The U.S. House of Representatives recently had a special guest as local Queens Rabbi Stuart Berman served as its guest chaplain after an invitation from Congressmember Joseph Crowley. 'It was the greatest,' said Berman, who currently presides over the Woodside Jewish Center. 'I was in the seat of power; it's always good.'"

Michael Lotker of Temple Ner Ami in Camarillo, California, told the June 18, 2014, *Ventura County Star* about his House prayer: "It was awesome. One rabbi said life is filled with moments of awe, and this was for me a moment of incredible awe and gratitude."

After Rabbi Barry Block of Little Rock gave the Senate prayer, he told the February 1, 2017, *Arkansas Democrat-Gazette*: "It was awe-inspiring to be on the floor of the Senate, to stand at a place where some great men and women of our nation have stood before me."

In 2012 Ronald Gerson retired from the only synagogue in Athens, Georgia: Congregation Children of Israel. "A personal high point," Gerson told the June 17, 2012, *Athens Banner-Herald*, "came in 1999 [Oct. 13] when then-Congressman John Linder invited him to Washington, where Gerson delivered the prayer that traditionally opens the daily proceedings of the U.S. House of Representatives. 'That was really exciting,' he said. 'The temple was proud and my family and everyone watched it on C-SPAN and my California family got up early to watch it.'"

Indeed, Linder said in his sponsoring floor remarks: "I have been informed that Rabbi Gerson's mother, who lives in California, is probably watching her son at the early hour of 7 a.m. on the West Coast. Gerson wrote in the August 2, 2016, *Athens Banner-Herald* that delivering the prayer was "one of the greatest honors of my 42-year ministry."

17: Rabbi Prayer Fact-Checking

"Thou shalt not utter a false report."

—Exodus 23:1

One thing is for sure: The first rabbi to open the U.S. Congress in prayer was Morris Raphall, 1860.

Beyond that milestone, beware other claims of firsts.

The November 28, 1907, Washington *Evening Star* asserted that Rabbi Edward Browne "was, after the late Isaac M. Wise (the Jewish pope), the first Jew who opened the United States Senate with prayer." Likewise, the August 30, 1918, *Kingstown Daily Freeman* said Browne "was the first Jew to open a session of the Senate when he prayed in the upper House May 27, 1884."

To both claims: Wrong. Browne was fourth.

On September 13, 2010, the *Legal History Blog* called David Philipson an "1890s leader of the Central Conference of American Rabbis and the first rabbi to deliver a blessing at the U.S. Senate." He was the eighth. But don't blame the *Legal History Blog* for getting it incorrect over a century later. The *New York Globe* got it wrong when it happened. The *Globe*'s account of Philipson's prayer in February 1904 called it "the first time in nearly thirty years that a Jewish rabbi had offered prayer in the Senate." No, it was six years—preceded by Jacob Voorsanger on June 30, 1898. Voorsanger gave the House prayer on May 13, 1882. The May 23, 1882, *South Kentuckian* newspaper reported it as "the third time in the history of the country that a Jewish Rabbi has opened Congress with prayer." Nope. The eighth time— sixth in the House.

The *Syracuse Journal* said on its front page about Abram Simon's February 16, 1905, appearance: "For the first time in some years a Jewish rabbi was invited to offer prayer in the House to-day." *Some* years? Sorry: It was the first time since the prior year.

Do "firsts" matter? Who cares which rabbi prayed first in Congress?

Well, here's one kind of person who cared: a rabbi who prayed in Congress. Gustav Hausmann penned a public letter defending his place in the history books. In a January 21, 1926, missive to the *Philadelphia Jewish Bulletin*, Hausmann wrote:

> Recently you reported in your "Bulletin," and it was repeated in our Jewish press-English and Yiddish papers—that Rabbi Jack, of Little Rock. Ark., was the first Jew who opened the United States Senate with prayer. After this, you published a communication from Rabbi Joseph Silverman, of Temple Emanu-El, that the late Rabbi Isaac M. Wise, president and founder of the Hebrew Union College, was the first rabbi to receive this distinction. Thus, accordingly, there were two rabbis who received ths [sic] honor. May I add that in 1919 I opened the United States Senate with an invocation. While I am not absolutely certain, I believe that I am the only rabbi who

opened with prayer both Houses of Congress: the Senate and the House of Representatives.

Alas, pity Hausmann's own fact-checking chops. His Senate prayer wasn't in 1919. It was 1918 (December 12; his House prayer was February 28, 1899). And other rabbis before him had opened both chambers in prayer: Simon, Wise, and Browne.

Another guest chaplain with a desire to publicly correct the record: Edward Sandrow. The Long Island rabbi wrote a February 20, 1948, letter to the *National Jewish Post*. The letter is more remarkable for its tone than its concern for "historical accuracy." It deserves to be read in its glorious overwrought entirety:

> This is the first letter ever written by me to any editor of any paper. It is because of a deep-seated feeling that most letters accomplish little, even assuming that they are carefully read. But I cannot help writing this note, purely and simply for the sake of historical accuracy. As a former student of Professor Alexander Marx, world renowned historian and librarian of the Jewish Theological Seminary of America, I have a penchant for facts that are exact.
>
> In the issue of February 6, 1948 of The Post, it is stated that Dr. Leo Baeck is scheduled to "deliver the opening prayer Friday, February 13th in the United States House of Representatives," that "Dr. Baeck will give the prayer at the invitation of the House of Representatives' Chaplain," that "he is the first rabbi to be so honored."
>
> We love and respect Dr. Baeck, but your data is inaccurate. I gave the opening prayer in the United States House of Representatives in 1936. I was invited by the chaplain to whom I was introduced by one of the Senators and a congressman from my state.
>
> Mr. Editor, an intuition, developed after years of the study of history, leads me to the conclusion that there must have been rabbis before me, and later—between me and Rabbi Baeck, who delivered prayers in the halls of Congress. Mr. Editor, you make so many errors—you can be forgiven for this one. RABBI EDWARD T. SANDROW Cedarhurst, Long Island.

Sandrow was accurate on both intuitions. There were 43 rabbi prayers before his. And Baeck's was 14 rabbi prayers later (Sandrow made a second appearance in Congress in April 1966). Sandrow's penchant for facts was exact, indeed.

The newspaper—the one Sandrow smacked for making "so many errors"—printed a response as short as the rabbi's letter was long:

Rabbi Sandrow is right. The publicity came from the Union of American Hebrew Congregations, and evidently said "the first non-American Rabbi." In the rush the "non" was lost in the shuffle.

As modern-day fact checkers might say: Four Pinocchio's to the *National Jewish Post*. And Baeck was not even the first non-American rabbi to open Congress in prayer. The first was Canadian. Abraham de Sola in 1872. So, give a Pinocchio to the Union of American Hebrew Congregations, too. But reserve some tsk-tsking for the rabbi's requiring 248 words to make the one point.

Barely two years later, another letter to the editor. This time the need to correct the rabbinical record played out in front of the nation. On March 8, 1950, the *New York Times* ran an *Associated Press* story citing Rep. Louis Heller (D-NY). The story had Heller claiming of Nachum David Herman's prayer the day before: "It was the first time in the history of the House that the opening prayer had been delivered by a Rabbi of the Jewish Orthodox faith."

That claim also was made in the *Jewish Telegraphic Agency*: "Rabbi Nachum David Herman, of Congregation Tifereth Israel of Brooklyn, today pronounced the invocation at the opening of the House of Representatives session, marking the first time in the history of Congress that the invocation was recited by an Orthodox rabbi."

And the reality? He was the fifth—eight years after Bernard Bergman. (More on Bergman fact-checking in a moment.)

This March 14, 1950, letter to the *New York Times* by Rabbi David de Sola Pool set the record straight:

When recently Rabbi Nachum David Herman of Brooklyn opened the session of the House of Representatives with prayer it was generally stated that this was the first that such a prayer had been delivered by an Orthodox rabbi. Let us recall that in the year 1872 our Congress in Washington was opened with a prayer offered by the Orthodox Montreal rabbi, Abraham de Sola.

Herman's place in history was inflated significantly more by the *Milwaukee Sentinel*. On March 8, 1950, the newspaper ran a photo of him with House chaplain Bernard Braskamp. The caption asserted: "It was the first time in history of the House that a rabbi delivered the invocation." Missed it by *that* much: 90 years.

The October 25, 1968, *Montreal Gazette* got it right "On Jan. 9, 1872 the Congress of the United States was opened with prayer. This had been the custom since the first Congress met; it has been the custom ever since. On this January day, however, something very unusual took place. The prayers were said by a rabbi standing in Congress. And this rabbi was not a citizen of the United States."

De Sola's prayer earned this tribute in the January 27, 1872, Washington *Daily Patriot* newspaper:

> A significant incident, in connection with Federal legislation, was the opening of the House of Representatives yesterday by prayer from a Jewish Rabbi, the Rev. Professor Abraham de Sola of Montreal, Canada. The prayer offered was eloquent and beautiful and could have been pronounced with propriety in any place of worship throughout the land. While such evidences of liberality are practiced by Jew and Gentile, there is little danger of zealots interfering successfully with the American idea of religious freedom. "Church and State" must remain, as they should, as far distance from each other as the poles.

And a fact-check footnote: de Sola's Wikipedia article says the prayer was in 1873. Off by a year.

Here's another rabbi caught up in fact checking. Over in the Senate, as reported December 15, 1925, by the *Brooklyn Daily Eagle*, "Veteran Capitol attaches saw a precedent established" with Emanuel Jack's prayer the day before. And the *Sentinel* Jewish newspaper noted on January 1, 1926, that in December 1925 Jack opened the Senate with prayer. "This incident was hailed by the American Jewish press as being very significant, since it was claimed that Rabbi Jack was the first Jewish minister in America to have attained the high honor of offering the opening prayer before so august a body as the United States Senate." (Those "claims" were, of course, wrong.)

The *Sentinel* continued: "Now, however, comes Dr. Joseph Silverman, Rabbi Emeritus of Temple Emanu-El of New York, and maintains that Rabbi Jack did not create history for the American Jew at all, since the distinction of having been the first Jew to pray before the United State Senate goes to none other than to the late Dr. Isaac Mayer Wise of Cincinnati. . . ." Then the *Sentinel* added this fact-checking kicker: "Since Dr. Silverman is interested in establishing the accuracy of a historical fact we should like to bring to light one more bit of information concerning this matter. To the best of our knowledge the title Rabbi has never been conferred upon Dr. Jack at all." Ouch! Zing! More from the *Sentinel*: "Dr. Jack at one time attended the Hebrew Union College, but he never graduated from that institution, nor is he a member of the Central Conference of American Rabbis or of any other Rabbinical body."

More Pinocchio's!

Adding one more fact-checking twist that involves Silverman: The *Western Sentinel* of Winston-Salem, North Carolina, reported on December 15, 1892, "A Jewish Rabbi, Rev. Dr. Joseph Silverman, opened yesterday's Senate with prayer. This is the first time this has ever occurred." Nope. It was the sixth time a rabbi opened the Senate with prayer.

(Incidentally, to modern readers it might seem odd to see a rabbi identified as a reverend, "Rev. Dr. Joseph Silverman." In fact, the Reform Jewish movement's own *Union Prayerbook* published in 1895 by the Central Conference of American Rabbis refers to a congregation's rabbi as Minister. According to *Platforms and Prayer Books* edited by Dana Evan Kaplan,[77] the Jewish *Union Prayer Book* called rabbis ministers until 1940. Early rabbi guest chaplains are often identified in the *Congressional Record* as reverend.)

Returning to Bernard Bergman. The June 12, 1942, Pittsburgh *Jewish Criterion* said Bergman, "in his cutaway and skullcap" was the first Orthodox rabbi to lead the House in prayer. The *New York Times* said the same thing on May 27, 1942, that Bergman was "the first Orthodox Jewish rabbi to officiate in that capacity." He was the third. The second was 70 years prior. (In between the two Orthodox rabbis, 32 prayers in the House were offered by Reform or Conservative rabbis.)

Bergman is distinguished for being first in a different category, however. He was the first rabbi guest chaplain sent to prison.

During a March 1956 dinner of the religious Zionist Hapoel Hamizrachi Council, New York Secretary of State Carmine De Sapio paid tribute to Bergman. The last chief of New York's Tammany Hall political machine—who later served two years in federal prison for bribery—called Bergman "a man whose piousness and dedication have set him before the world as a symbol of character, integrity, and leadership."

That character reference was inoperative by the Seventies. That's when Bergman was "the central figure in New York City's nursing-home

---

77   Rowman & Littlefield, 2002, page 31.

investigation," and, according to his June 22, 1984, *New York Times* obituary, "served a four-month Federal prison sentence and an eight-month state sentence after his convictions for Medicaid fraud and bribery."

On March 12, 1976, the *New York Times* investigated how "Bergman Became Involved in Nursing Homes in '39." The story noted:

> As he built his nursing home business, Mr. Bergman also developed friendships with religious and political leaders. In May 1942, while he was still at the Sons and Daughters of Israel, the 32-year-old rabbi was invited by his Congressman, Arthur G. Klein, to give an invocation before the House of Representatives.

The March 30, 2012, *New York* magazine called Bergman "The Medicaid-Fraud Rabbi." In his 1983 book *The Best Defense*,[78] attorney Alan Dershowitz devoted a chapter to explaining why he represented Bergman, "the bearded, yarmulke-wearing rabbi."

Claims of being the first Orthodox rabbi guest chaplain continued to be made as late as 1960. On March 4 that year the *Jewish Criterion* reported Chaim Lipschitz "was the first orthodox rabbi to conduct the opening prayer at the United States Senate." He was the sixth.

The April 25, 1968, *Jewish Chronicle* reported the Senate prayer by Morris Landes of Congregation Adath Jeshurun was the "second time in the history since the creation of the state of Israel that a Rabbi has been so honored." Actually, in the 20 years between the 1948 birth of Israel and Landes' prayer, 66 prayers had been delivered by rabbis in the Senate.

And the *Jewish Telegraphic Agency* reported on January 20, 1961, about a prayer offered four days earlier:

> A quotation from Isaiah in Hebrew characters was printed in the Congressional Record today, the first known instance of the use of the Hebrew language in this official publication, according to Government printing office authorities. The Hebrew quotation was inserted in Volume 107, Number 10, of the Congressional Record covering the proceedings and debates of the 87th Congress, first session. Rabbi Arnold S. Turetsky, of Congregation Ohev Tzedek, Youngstown, Ohio, was invited to offer the opening prayer before the House of Representatives. He included, in Hebrew, the quotation from Isaiah 11:9," The earth shall be filled with the knowledge of the Lord, as the waters that cover the sea."

---

78 Vintage Books, 1983.

A milestone indeed—but with the asterisk that Hebrew had been *trans-literated* into the *Congressional Record* before. An example: During his July 13, 1955, Senate prayer, Bertram Korn of Keneseth Israel in Philadelphia closed with the Priestly Benediction.

The first-in-Hebrew assertion also is found in Rabbi Jay Kaufman's entry in the *National Cyclopedia of American Biography*: it says his April 17, 1967, prayer "was probably the first time Hebrew was spoken on the Senate floor."[79] At least 13 prayers before his included Hebrew.

More fact-checking:

The webpage remembering Abraham Hecht suggests he "was one of the first rabbis to speak in front of the US Congress as he did this numer-ous times throughout his life and career." Correct on the second part. Numerous, indeed: He offered four prayers. But hardly "one of the first." By the day of Hecht's own first prayer—April 25, 1966, in the Senate—76 rabbis had been there, done that, in the Senate alone.

On April 2, 1984, Rep. Pat Schroeder (D-CO) sponsored Stanley Wagner of Denver's Beth HaMedrosh Hagodol congregation. "Rabbi Wagner is one of the few clergymen in America to have delivered invoca-tions both at the U.S. Senate and House of Representatives," she said. Few? By April 2, 1984, 46 rabbis—and that's just the Jewish clergymen—had delivered prayers in both chambers.

Temple Beth-El in Las Cruces, New Mexico, has a web page remember-ing Gerald Kane. The memorial includes this: "In October 2002 Rabbi Kane was invited by Senator Jeff Bingaman and Representative Joe Skeen to serve as Guest Chaplain at the United States Senate and House of Representatives. He is the only clergyman in the United States to have offered prayers on the floor of the House and Senate on two consecutive days." That was correct as of 2002. But it happened again the next year. Milton Balkany did back-to-back Senate and House prayers on June 25 and 26, 2003. A rabbi hasn't pulled off that feat since.

Rep. Robert Wexler (D-FL) called Amy Rader's September 15, 2006, prayer "the second opening prayer led by a female Rabbi in the history of the House of Representatives." It was the eighth. The "About Rabbi Jacobs" wordpress website of Cheryl Jacobs calls her "the first female rabbi to offer a blessing before the U.S. Senate." She was the third.

---

79   University Microfilms, 1975, page 54.

Joseph Langner, Congregation B'nai Israel, Greensburg, Pennsylvania, was House guest chaplain on August 5, 1963. A quarter-century later, August 3, 1988, the *Fort Lauderdale Sun-Sentinel* published an investigation of Langner: "The Media Rabbi With His Ethnic Festival And Plans For Cable Shows, Rabbi Joseph Langner Dreams Big. Some Of Those Dreams Have Been Costly For Himself And Others." The paper reported Langer "called The Jewish People a tax-exempt organization, listed with the Internal Revenue Service. But he later denied ever having made such a claim, saying he planned to apply for a tax exemption. . . . Other questions arise from a 1986 press release on the Temple Beth Israel letterhead, the closest thing to a Langner resume, which he routinely declines to provide. It cites him as a former chaplain of the U.S. House of Representatives, former president of the Long Island Association for Soviet Jewry, and a former Israeli army lieutenant who was decorated for valor during the 1973 Yom Kippur War. Asked about the items, Langner replied that he said congressional invocations for a week, as do many clergy every year. However, guest chaplains usually say a prayer for only one day in the U.S. House."

On the narrow point about being a guest chaplain multiple times, the newspaper was correct. There's only evidence of Langner giving a single prayer.

For reasons related to a Hasidic Jewish community development proposal for Brooklyn in 1975, the curriculum vitae for Chaim Lipschitz—and other rabbis involved in the project—can be found among President Ford's papers[80]. Lipschitz was a repeat guest chaplain. And he wasn't shy about telling the Ford Administration about it: "first rabbi to open four sessions of the U.S. Senate with a prayer." Really, the first? Sorry. Wrong. Norman Gerstenfeld of Washington Hebrew Congregation gave five Senate prayers between 1942 and 1959. OK, but what about Lipschitz's claim of giving four Senate prayers? Just three can be found in the *Congressional Record* before 1975. (There is record of a fourth Senate prayer, but in 1977). But let's spare the Pinocchio and give the rabbi the benefit of the doubt if only because the very next entry in his curriculum vitae says, "Maintains membership in the following Air Line clubs." The item includes:

Admiral Club. . . American Airline
President's Club. . . Continental Airline

---

80   Box 8, folder "Community Development—Project CHAIM Brooklyn NY (2)" of the John Marsh Files at the Gerald R. Ford Presidential Library.

> Flying Colonel... Delta Airline
> Ambassador Club... TWA Airline
> 100,000 Miles Club... United Airline

Any rabbi who brings transparency to the White House about his frequent flyer loyalties deserves to be believed about the number of times he prayed in Congress.

Can a rabbi's prayer be fact-checked? Let's try. "May we repair this world and fill it with decency, justice, and peace," Joel Levenson of Congregation B'nai Jacob in Woodbridge, Connecticut, said in the House on July 10, 2012, "a world for which the prophet Isaiah prayed centuries ago when he said: Let justice well up as water and righteousness as a mighty stream."

Isaiah? Sorry. That was Amos.

Part Two

What They Say

Imagine the House or Senate as a congregation. The rabbi ascends to the *bimah*, the pulpit, and shuffles papers to begin the sermon.

Like a hurry-up offense in football, rabbis have just two minutes to work with. Two hundred words. What wisdom can he or she possibly tell Congress?

There's so much inspiration and instruction to choose from: The Lord, Torah, the prophets. Politics, policy, perhaps economics. How about war, terror, baseball?

Rabbis have said all that—and a lot more. All the while making it interesting, relevant and approachable to an audience that, unlike their home synagogue, has few Jews and may not even like the Jews they do have.

Tough gig, right? Here's how they've pulled it off, starting with an authority higher than even Congress.

SECTION IV

Religious Awareness

18: Putting the Almighty in His Place

"It is good to give thanks unto the Lord, and to sing praises unto Thy name, O Most High.'—Psalms 92:1"
—Rabbi Samuel Cooper, B'nai Jacob Synagogue, Charleston,
West Virginia, opening the House of Representatives,
March 1, 1971

"And all nations which Thou hast made, shall come before Thee, O L-rd and give honor to Thy name.' Psalms 86:9. Thy name is justice, liberty and righteousness."
—Rabbi Rafael Grossman, Baron Hirsch Synagogue,
Memphis, Tennessee, opening the Senate,
March 16, 1982

Shakespeare's Juliet was onto something when she wondered, "What's in a name?"

Justice, liberty, righteousness. Those are names for God. Opening the Senate on May 8, 1991, Rabbi Alvin Berkun of Pittsburgh's Tree of Life Congregation added another: "To the Jewish sages of old, peace was God's very name. Peace—Shalom—is the ideal toward which we must all strive."

God = peace. There's a name, too.

But wait, there's more. A lot more.

A sample of what rabbis praying in Congress have called Him over the years:

Lord; Heavenly Father; Father of Mankind; Father of All Men; *Avinu Shebashomayim* (Our Father in heaven); *Avinu Malkeinu*, Our Father, our King; Universal Father; *Ribon Ha-Olam*, Father of All; Source of Wisdom; fountainhead of all law; Author of Freedom; Supreme Author of Liberty; author of liberty and equality; Eternal One; great Guardian; Gracious Guardian; great Architect of the Universe; Master Architect of the universe; Architect, Creator, and Ruler of the universe; Sovereign of the Universe; Sovereign Ruler of the Universe; Master of the Universe; Master of Memory; Captain of Providence; divine Healer; Determiner of human history; Supreme Creator; Heavenly Creator; Creator and destiny of all flesh; Source of All.

And—a succinct and suitable summary—"God of everything and everyone."

They may call Him different, grand things. But He's always called something. Nearly every rabbi prayer has included a mention of the Almighty. Ahem, using male gender only, mind you. The God of these Jewish prayers in Congress is a masculine God.[1]

Some Godly citations can get quite elaborate—if not any fairer to the fairer sex.

"Almighty God, Father of us all, in the presence of the manifestations of Thy supreme greatness we humbly bow the head and exclaim, 'Holy, holy, holy, is the Lord of Hosts; full is the whole earth of His glory,'" exclaimed David Philipson of Hebrew Union College in the Senate on February 2, 1904, invoking Isaiah 6:3. "Gracious Heavenly Father. Thou in whose sight a thousand years are but as yesterday when It has passed and as a watch in the night when the morning has come," prayed Eugene Blackschleger, Temple Beth-Or, Montgomery, Alabama, in the Senate on March 13, 1962.

"Father of all men regardless of race, color, or creed," prayed Edward Sandrow of Ahavai Sholom Congregation, Portland, Oregon, in the House on February 3, 1936. A contemporary reader with modern day sensibilities might notice Sandrow's effort toward diversity. He included three demographic groups—just not women. There were eight women in the House of Representatives in 1936. But Sandrow earns credit for mentioning women

---

1 In *Overcoming Life's Disappointments*, Harold Kushner (Alfred A. Knopf, 2006) notes that God, "though the Bible will refer to Him grammatically as male, will just as often display a feminine, nurturing side, bringing forth life, feeding the hungry, comforting the fearful, tending to the sick" (page 10).

later in his prayer: "Give these men and women of the Congress, O Eternal, the strength of character and the sturdiness of will to keep from our free shores the spirit of religious prejudice, of racial animosity, of ill-will and misunderstanding so common in other parts of the world but so alien to America."

(Non-Jews have used the Hebrew word for father, *abba*. House chaplain James Montgomery, January 28, 1935: "Almighty God, conscious that there is a power in the earth which transcends the works of man, we linger here in prayer and breathe 'Abba Father.'" House chaplain Daniel Coughlin, three days after September 11, 2001: "Circumstances such as Tuesday's horror shake us to new awareness and the need to pray, but prayer itself originates in You. . . Weeping and groaning deep within us the spirit cries out Abba." And a minister added the Latin term for "for the sake of form," *pro forma*, to *abba* when serving as House guest chaplain. That minister was a woman. Rev. Alisa Lasater Wailoo of the Capitol Hill United Methodist Church on June 20, 2016: "Almighty and most compassionate God, during this ordinary pro forma session, remind us of Your extraordinary love. . . . Your love for each child in our global family, no matter if they call You Abba, Yahweh, Allah, or do not call on You at all." Hearing "abba" stands out. Also interesting: ". . . *or do not call on You at all.*" For atheists?)

Rabbis have reached for the rhetorical heavens when summoning the Lord:

- "Creator of the universe. Thou who hast arranged the stars in their course in the heavens according to Thy will."—Manfred Rechtschaffen, Congregation Degel Israel, Lancaster, Pennsylvania, August 5, 1957, Senate.
- "O God, author of all that Is, who transcendeth space and time."— Abraham Feldman, Temple Beth Israel, Hartford, Connecticut, January 29, 1958, House.
- "Thy presence floods the world as the sun bursts over the horizon."—Arnold Fink, Beth El Hebrew Congregation, Alexandria, Virginia. June 26, 1968, Senate.
- "You are the ultimate mystery of the universe before whom all our endeavors are as naught."—Fink again, September 11, 1973, House.
- "By Thy will the planets in the universe whisper of Your glory and the amoeba came into being."—Max Wall, Ohavi Zedek Synagogue, Burlington, Vermont, June 21, 1984, Senate.

From amoeba to a human:

- "O God who knows the hidden chambers of the human heart."—Frederick Klein, September 18, 2007, House.
- "Our hope is for a world in which every human being is an image of God. According to the Talmud, that means that every human being has infinite value, is equal, is unique."— Irving Greenberg, June 27, 1985, Senate.
- "Mayest Thou guide us, O Heavenly Father, in our striving to become more like Thee, for Thou hast implanted in each one of us a spark of the divine."—Jacob Max, June 20, 1966, House.
- "Of all Your providential acts of creation none is more wondrous than Your fashioning of the human mind and the human spirit. As an ancient rabbi declared: the greatest gift God bestowed upon man was not only that he was created in the divine image but that he was told of that miracle of creation."—Morris Kertzer, August 12, 1969, House.

Navy chaplain Harold Robinson summed up our relationship to God in his January 18, 2007, Senate prayer: "You are creator of heaven and Earth, yet You have created us in Your own image. Though we are creatures of clay and dust, You have shared Your spirit with us." Gerald Kaplan of Agudath Achim Synagogue in Minnesota went with a poetic flair. He opened the House on April 30, 1962, with Englishman William Blake: "As in the words of the poet: I looked for my God, but my God I could not see. I looked for my soul, but it eluded me. I looked for my brother, then I found all three."[2]

Rabbis leverage God to inspire the legislative branch to governing greatness.

Here's Mark Miller of Temple Bat Yahm in California on October 25, 2001: "The 100 who grace this Chamber today stand on the shoulders of those many Senators whose vision elevated our national life and whose courage enriched humankind. We hear the frozen echoes of their lofty debates. We see them arising to confront the issues of their day. We note them chasing not the 'bubble popularity' but seeking the shield of God's favor."

---

2   The August 23, 1967, House guest chaplain—not Jewish—offered a quite intimidating description of the Lord. The American Medical Association's director of the Department of Medicine and Religion, Rev. Paul McCleave, began his prayer this way: "Almighty God, supreme ruler and governor of all things, and whose power no creature is able to resist."

Shmuel Butman of Lubavitch Youth Organization offered a rosy divinely inspired purpose for the legislative branch on June 12, 1991: "Almighty G-d, in Your infinite wisdom, You have established the Members of the Senate as the custodians of honesty and decency." Butman repeated that rarely heard assessment July 1, 1992: "Almighty G-d, in Your infinite wisdom, You have established the Members of this Senate as the custodians of honesty and decency." (Good thing Butman was talking honest and decency in the Senate, not the House of Representatives. The House banking scandal broke in early 1992. Twenty-two members of the House were singled out by the House ethics committee for overdrawing their House checking accounts.)

Gilbert Klaperman of Long Island's Congregation Beth Sholom also connected God with government. His prayer in the House on May 6, 1965: "Almighty God, fountainhead of law and source of government." And Joel Goor of San Diego's Temple Beth Israel prayed in the Senate on July 17, 1968: "Supreme Judge whose throne is raised above the polling booth and whose reward exceeds office gained or temporal victory achieved."

Arthur Buch of Temple Emanuel, Paterson, New Jersey, opened the House on April 25, 1951, this way: "O Thou who dost grant salvation to kings." No king, but a president: Richard Nixon could have used some salvation granting two decades later. Instead, in the throes of Watergate, Ben Zion Schaffran offered this Febraury 19, 1974, reassurance to everyone else in the country: "Honorable Members of the House of Representatives. A nation which is cognizant of its reliance on the Almighty will surely weather the storms which have befallen it."

Seemingly absent from any prayer in Congress is recognition of Mark 12:17: "Jesus said to them, 'Render to Caesar the things that are Caesar's, and to God the things that are God's.'" That has been the theological basis— Christian, at least—for separating God from politics. Early American history suggests some of the country's founders embraced some separation. Although he was a devout Christian, John Quincy Adams, according to the January 18, 2009, *Los Angeles Times,* took his 1825 presidential oath with his hand not on a Bible but upon a "Volume of Laws of the United States." Why? Because, he wrote in a March 1825 diary entry, it was the Constitution he swore to preserve, protect and defend.

Likewise, Alexander Hamilton's observation about God and government proceedings made at our nation's very beginning—during the Constitutional Convention of 1787. In *Alexander Hamilton,* Ron Chernow notes that when Benjamin Franklin suggested on June 28 "that each session start with a prayer for heavenly help, Hamilton countered that this might foster a public impression that 'embarrassments and dissensions within the convention had suggested this measure.' According to legend, Hamilton also rebutted Franklin with the jest that the convention didn't need 'foreign aid.' The Lord did not seem much in evidence at this point in the convention. One story, perhaps apocryphal, claims that when Hamilton was asked why the framers omitted the word God from the Constitution, he replied, 'We forgot.' One is tempted to reply that Alexander Hamilton never forgot anything important."[3]

Justice William Douglas, on the other hand, reaffirmed on April 28, 1952, in the case *Zorach v. Clauson*: "We are a religious people whose institutions presuppose a Supreme Being."

That's certainly evident in the words of legendary House Speaker Thomas "Tip" O'Neill. A quote of his inscribed on the pedestal of the Gerald Ford statue sitting in the Rotunda of the U.S. Capitol pulls no political or religious punches in suggesting that "God has been good to America, especially during difficult times. At the time of the Civil War, he gave us Abraham Lincoln. And at the time of Watergate, he gave us Gerald Ford—the right man at the right time who was able to put our nation back together again."

Rabbi Arnold Resnicoff, a repeat guest chaplain, wrote "Prayers that Hurt: Public Prayer in Interfaith Settings." The writers of the Declaration of Independence and the Constitution, Resnicoff suggested in the Winter 1987 issue of the Military Chaplains' Review, "were careful to choose words—such as 'the Creator' (e.g., 'endowed by our Creator')—which were inclusive, rather than representing any one religion or faith group. But, we need not begin with the founders of America to understand that there are times—and ways—to speak of God in general terms."

According to the Freedom from Religion Foundation, guest chaplains are permitted to give invocations if they: (1) are sponsored by a member of the House, (2) are ordained, and (3) do not directly address House members and instead address a "higher power." That third stipulation holds up in practice. Researchers from Brandeis and Clemson universities studied 200 prayers offered by chaplains to Congress between 1990 and 2010 (published November 13, 2015). They found the prayers included a petition—or a request for something—to God 96 percent of the time.

---

3   Penguin Press, 2004, pages 229-230.

It does leave us wondering, though, for the remaining four percent: to what or whom were they praying?

We can answer that, at least partially, by looking to rabbis who served as guest chaplains and did not mention, refer to, or acknowledge God. It has happened, though rarely.

The first rabbi who offered a prayer without God's immediate presence was Sally Priesand. "Consecrate ourselves to the task of building a better world," Priesand prayed in the House on October 23, 1973. "Those who sit here have been granted positions of authority by their fellow citizens. . . . May all our citizens unite in the spirit of concord and compassion to solve the problems of contemporary life and to create a world in which all people might at last live together in peace and in unity with none to make them afraid."

Two years later, Barry Rosen of Shaare Tikvah Congregation left God out of his prayer, too—despite coming from a Maryland town who name seems ideal for divine inspiration: Temple Hills. Rosen urged the House on September 11, 1975, to "pause to reflect upon the human message of Yom Kippur. We recognize that we err in our relationships with our fellow human beings, and that all men transgress, either knowingly or unknowingly." Rosen continued, "Let us resolve that, in our future interpersonal dealings, we will be more sensitive to others."

Human messaging, interpersonal dealings, sensitivity to others. No God. Very Seventies, though.

One more exception. Tzvi Porath of Ohr Kodesh Congregation neither mentioned nor alluded to the Lord when he opened the Senate on March 25, 1994. Porath, who was born in Jerusalem and took part in the inaugural parade for President Eisenhower, went with this message: "We pray that we return from our recess invigorated, stimulated, and uplifted by the personal contact with the people from our State. . . . May we all be inspired to translate the message of our holy days to bring the inhabitants of our country, whatever their origin, race of creed, into a bond of true brotherhood."

For every other rabbi, God is present. That might offer relief to those concerned about the dwindling number of Americans—and specifically, Jews—who believe in God. In the 2007 Pew Research Center Religious Landscape Study, 92% said yes when asked if they believe in "God or a universal spirit." Eleven years later, in another Pew Research Center survey, 80% said they believe in God. A slim majority of Americans (56%) said they believe in God "as described in the Bible." In that 2018 survey, Jews were much less likely to say they believe in God as described in the Bible (33%).

But no lack of belief among members of Congress, where The Lord is a pillar. As the country moves away from God, at least in poll, Congress remains steadfast.

The *Washington Examiner*'s Paul Bedard reported on February 19, 2019, that "Congress and the military are pushing back on litigation to let atheists preach by making sure that when official and guest chaplains speak, 'God' or prayer be mentioned." Resnicoff explained to Bedard the "newly changed rules": "Now, you submit your prayer in advance and if you don't mention 'God,' they encourage you to add it because there is a big movement by the atheists and the agnostics to have people to pray who are not ordained and the Senate and House are fighting it. So they want to make sure that this is religious prayer." Resnicoff added, "Our military is fighting it and Congress is fighting it. So as a result of that, when they give you the rules, they want you to make it a religious prayer not a generic prayer."

Many rabbis mention God in the beginning of a prayer, like that offered on November 8, 1993, in the Senate by Arthur Schneier: "God bless America." And Ari Korenblit in the House on November 19, 2003: "God bless America." And Bruce Lustig of Washington Hebrew Congregation on May 16, 2019: "Eternal God, without whom life has no spiritual source, no divine meaning, purpose, or destiny, but with whom there is power for the present and hope for the future, refresh our faith that the strains of life may not break our spirits."

Or at the end of prayer, like Norman Geller in the Senate on April 11, 1989: "G-d blessed, G-d blesses, and collectively may our actions continually assure that G-d will always bless America." And Leo Baeck, a German-born survivor of the Holocaust, in the House on February 12, 1948: "Reverently I pray Thee to bless Congress, its men, and its days. From the bottom of my heart I pray: God bless America."

Baeck was a rabbi in Berlin. "God Bless America," of course, is a patriotic song written during World War I by Irving Berlin, also a Jewish immigrant to America. Berlin's father was a cantor in a synagogue. Berlin wrote "God Bless America" as a prayer. And he served as an appropriate ending for the June 12, 2018, House prayer offered by Rabbi Steven Rein of the U.S. Air Force, two days before Flag Day: "As Irving Berlin did 100 years ago, we pray that God bless America."

19: Isaiah, Isaiah, Isaiah

During House floor debate on asylum rights on February 9, 2005, Rep. Barney Frank (D-MA) turned his considerable wit to the third book of Moses. "We often hear Leviticus quoted on the floor of the House," Frank said. "Leviticus 19, chapters 33 and 34, 'When an alien lives with you in your land, do not mistreat him. The alien living with you must be treated as one of your native-born. Love him as yourself, for you were aliens in Egypt.' Now, that is in Leviticus. I know Leviticus gets turned on and off here like an electric bulb, but it does now seem to me that kind of cafeteria approach to religion is something the majority has adopted."

Several decades earlier, the same Leviticus chapter that Frank mentioned was cited by a guest chaplain in the House. On June 18, 1962, Rabbi Samuel Scolnic of Congregation Beth-El in Bethesda, Maryland, borrowed from Leviticus 19:18: "And from out of the dim past comes Thine inspired word 'v-ahavta l'reacha kamocha'—'thou shalt love thy neighbor as thyself.'"

Leviticus is heard in congressional hearings, too. Josh Protas of MAZON: A Jewish Response to Hunger testified before the House Agriculture Committee on March 28, 2017. He cited Leviticus 23:22: "We are commanded to leave the corners of our fields and the gleanings of our harvest and vineyards for the poor and the stranger." Rep. Jodey Arrington (R-TX) responded by citing 2 Thessalonians 3:10: "If a man will not work he shall not eat. . . . We hear that some among you are idle."

Frank's rhetorical point invites quantitative curiosity: How often is "often" for Leviticus citations? For that matter, which parts of the Bible— and there are 929 chapters in the Hebrew Bible—are used most in prayers delivered by rabbi guest chaplains?

The Bible is "the most quoted book in U.S. history here in both the House and Senate," Rep. Louis Gohmert (R-TX) asserted on May 25, 2016. "There was a time when most legislators felt it was helpful to getting legislation passed if they had a verse of Scripture from the Bible that supported their position." [4]

---

4   In December 1982 *Newsweek* magazine reported historians "are discovering that the Bible, perhaps even more than the Constitution, is our Founding document." The cover story was titled "The Bible In America." To be fair if not balanced, in February 1982 *Newsweek* did run a story titled "The Bible in the Bedroom."

We'll take as gospel Gohmert's claim about the totality of Biblical mentions in the House and Senate. But Frank's assertion that "we often hear Leviticus quoted" is true.

The Torah's third book does indeed get substantial attention. Focusing on rabbis who pray in Congress, mentions of Leviticus or citations of specific passages total 13 going back to 1951.

None, though, for the verse Frank cited. Most rabbi prayers that cite Leviticus do so for Chapter 25. It's the legendary "Proclaim liberty throughout the land unto all the inhabitants thereof" verse, number 10.

That verse often is used to make a broader patriotic point about America. And it is part of the rhetorical arsenal used by congressmen engaging in floor debate. During remarks on legislation concerning sending members of Communist and "subversive organizations" to jail, Rep. Abraham Multer (D-NY) said to the House chaplain: "Reverend, sir, on the day on which we are called to vote upon this bill, take as the text for your prayer the commandment from the book of Leviticus: 'Proclaim liberty throughout all the land.'" Multer, Jewish, said that on May 14, 1948—the day the State of Israel was created. Decades later, Leviticus 25:10 was deployed to address partisan strife. A day after a tumultuous State of the Union address rocked Congress and the same day that President Trump was acquitted by the Senate in his impeachment trial, Rabbi Seth Frisch of New Shul of America in Rydal, Pennsylvania, was a guest chaplain. "The Book of Leviticus teaches us," Frisch told the House on February 5, 2020, in words inscribed upon the Liberty Bell in Philadelphia, "Proclaim liberty throughout the land—to all the inhabitants thereof. Thus uniting one of our nation's highest ideals, 'E Pluribus Unum,'—'Out of the many, one.'"

Leviticus is hardly the only part of the Jewish Bible that gets repeated use by rabbi guest chaplains.

Here are other frequently cited passages.

Amos 5:24—five times. Example: Arnold Goodman of Atlanta's Congregation Ahavath Achim in the House on November 8, 1983: "May our leaders continually hear within their inner beings the call of the Prophet Amos who challenged us to live so that justice would well up as water, and righteousness as a mighty stream."

Isaiah 11:9—five times. Morris Margolies of Beth Shalom Congregation, Kansas City, Missouri, in the House on February 25, 1986: "Help us to banish malice and prejudice from our midst, to view all human beings of all races and creeds as having been created in Your image, to regard Your magnificent Earth as our sacred charge—a gift to nourish and to cherish, to cultivate and to beautify. May the vision of Isaiah be fulfilled in our day: 'They shall not hurt nor destroy in all my Holy Mountain. For the earth shall fill with knowledge of the Lord as the waters cover the sea.'"

Micah 6:8—12 times. Gary Zola of the American Jewish Archives in Cincinnati on May 26, 2005, in the Senate: "May all who labor in this house—and in every house—be inspired anew by the prophet Micah's exhortation, a charge that the father of this nation deeply cherished and repeatedly cited: do justly, love mercy, and walk humbly with thy God."

Psalms 118:24—seven times. Edward Paul Cohn of Temple Sinai in New Orleans in the House on September 13, 1989: "We pray in the words of the Psalmist: *Zeh Hayom Asah Adonal Nagllah V'nlsm'cha Vo!* This is the day which the Lord has made, let us rejoice and be glad in it. Heavenly Father, in these soul-stirring times, when from one comer of the world to the other, the hope of liberty and the hunger for freedom are being proclaimed and celebrated, let us give great thanks for the privilege which is ours to live in this day and age."

Psalms 133:1—12 times. Melvyn May of West End Temple Sinai Congregation in Neponsit, New York, on September 25, 2002: "We pray that the spirit that permeates this room today will enhance and enrich the endeavors of our Congressmen and Congresswomen on behalf of all the citizens of our great country, the United States of America. In the words of the Psalmist: How good and pleasant it is for brethren to dwell together."[5]

In "The Relative Influence of European Writers on Late Eighteenth-Century American Political Thought," Donald Lutz found that among the political writings of the founding fathers (from 1760 to 1805), Deuteronomy "is the most frequently cited book, followed by Montesquieu's *The Spirit of the Laws.*"[6] Different results for guest chaplain rabbis in Congress, though: Deuteronomy has been cited nine times. Montesquieu, zero.[7]

---

5 Psalms 133:1 could also be heard just outside Congress' walls on January 20, 2017. President Trump referred to the verse during his inaugural address: "The Bible tells us how good and pleasant it is when God's people live together in unity."

6 *The American Political Science Review*, March 1984 and cited by Daniel Dreisbach in *Reading the Bible with the Founding Fathers*, Oxford University Press, 2017.

7 Deuteronomy has been called Israel's ancient constitution. In May 5, 2017, remarks to the Hoover Institution, Rabbi Meir Soloveichik of Congregation Shearith Israel, the Spanish and Portuguese Synagogue in New York, said, "Deuteronomy is the most political book in the Pentateuch." In *Reading the Bible with the Founding Fathers*, Daniel Dreisbach

Ian Wolk of Temple Shalom in Chevy Chase, Maryland, connected Deuteronomy 16:20 directly with the senators he was addressing for this November 18, 1975, teachable moment:

> It is written: "Justice, justice you shall pursue." May those who serve You here in this body find the humility, the sacred sense of the trust with which they are empowered, and the direction of the heart that will enable them to work for the betterment of all men and women. May they indeed pursue justice, so that Your blessing may come to rest upon them: the blessing of light, of Your favor, of peace.

Which section of the Jewish Bible do rabbis go to the most?

A runaway winner: Isaiah. The 66-chapter book has been cited in 70 prayers. Over one out of every ten rabbi prayers.

And among Isaiah citations, no passage gets heavier use than Isaiah 2:4: "And they shall beat their swords into plowshares, And their spears into pruning hooks; Nation shall not lift up sword against nation, Neither shall they learn war any more." 45 times.

No surprise: Its use typically has been associated with themes of war and peace.

The first citation was in the House, May 11, 1943. In the dark midst of World War II and the accompanying Holocaust, Raphael Hal Melamed of Temple B'nai Israel, Elizabeth, New Jersey, prayed:

> Bless Thou the Chief Executive of our Nation and all who with him share the responsibilities of leadership in these days of crisis. Endow them with strength and wisdom commensurate with the burdens of war, and grant that under their guidance our Nation shall lead mankind into freedom and security. Help us to establish on earth Thy kingdom and Thy sovereignty so that we may behold in our day the era visioned by our ancient prophets, when "nation shall not lift up sword against nation, neither shall they learn war any more."

Next use was during the Cold War. David de Sola Pool of New York's Spanish and Portuguese Synagogue opened the Senate with it on June 28, 1955.

Other contexts in which rabbis have used Isaiah 2:4:

---

observed, "The book of Deuteronomy describes specific structures, institutions, and processes of governance useful in establishing a new political society."

- Mordecai Brill of Philadelphia's Temple Beth Israel in the House on May 28, 1957: "As we approach Memorial Day, may Its meaning impress Itself upon our hearts and minds so that we make our country, through its elected representatives, a mighty force for justice and righteousness in the assembly of nations bringing closer the words of the Hebrew prophet, 'Nation will no longer lift up sword against nation, neither will they learn war anymore.'"
- Charles Rubel of Congregation Sherah Israel, Macon, Georgia, in the Senate on April 21, 1958: "We pray for the welfare of all the nations of the world and for all mankind, which is now undergoing the pangs of a rebirth, through their own representatives at the United Nations. May our beloved United States always be the torchbearer of true international love and friendship, understanding, and liberty, for all. May the day soon come when the words of the divine prophet will be realized, that nation shall not lift up sword against nation, neither shall they learn war anymore."
- Joachim Prinz of Newark's Temple B'nai Abraham in the Senate on May 6, 1965: "May all the peoples acknowledge Israel's right to be, to work, and to create, knowing that there is room enough for Arabs and Jews to live together in harmony. And they shall beat their swords into plowshares, And their spears into pruning hooks; Nation shall not lift up sword against nation, Neither shall they learn war anymore."
- Seymour Essrog of Beth Israel Synagogue, Randallstown, Maryland, in the House on April 20, 1982: "On this special day of Yom Hashoa—when Jews all over the world collectively commemorate the death of the 6 million at the hands of the Nazis—we pray that the day will soon come when there shall be no violence or desolation on Earth when 'nation shall not lift up sword against nation.'"

And in the Senate on July 28, 1993, Shmuel Butman of Brooklyn's Lubavitch Youth Organization heralded "the disarmament agreement among the great nations of the world, starting the process foretold by Isaiah, the prophet of the messianic era. They shall beat their swords into plows, and nation shall not lift sword against nation and they shall no longer learn war."

Isaiah 2:4 has international application as well. It is inscribed in its entirety on the wall of Ralph Bunche Park across from the United Nations.[8] Israel's chief rabbi, Shlomo Goren cited it when he gave the House prayer on June 24, 1974. And in the House on July 1, 1980, Bennett Hermann of Temple Emanu-El of East Meadow, New York, blessed "our good neighbor, the great nation of Canada, who this day observes Dominion Day. They share our dream for a free and better world, in which every man, woman and child will be able to dwell together in peace, safety and prosperity; secure in the knowledge that nation will not lift up sword against nation, and neither will people learn the skills of war anymore."

Joseph Renov of Kesher Zion Congregation in Reading, Pennsylvania, gave the House prayer on September 14, 1978. It was ten days into the Camp David Summit, a pivotal event in the history of the Arab-Israeli dispute. The historic significance of the moment didn't escape the rabbi's prayer, nor did Isaiah 2:4: "May Camp David under Thy providence, lead to Messiah Ben David, that nation shall not lift up sword against nation, nor men learn war anymore."

Keep Camp David in mind for another citation of Isaiah 2:4 in Washington a year later—in the White House.

Israeli Prime Minister Menachem Begin, Egyptian president Anwar Sadat, and President Jimmy Carter all invoked the passage when they signed the Egypt-Israel Peace Treaty on March 26, 1979. Yes, all three. The *New York Times* reported the Isaiah trifecta this way: "By coincidence, they all referred to the words of the Prophet Isaiah. 'Let us work together until the day comes when they beat their swords into plowshares and their spears into pruning books,' Mr. Sadat said in his paraphrase of the biblical text.'"

For considering the prevalence of Isaiah 2:4, let's broaden from rabbis in Congress to broader American government leaders.

With war in Europe looming less than a year away, President Franklin Roosevelt's December 24, 1938, radio broadcast to the nation ended this way, according to the next day's *New York Times*:

---

8   Prayers outside the UN, but not in. Unlike Congress, UN sessions do not begin with a prayer. In 1949 New York Jewish communal leader Martin Schwaeber offered a $1,000 award to anyone who could create an opening prayer for the United Nations. Schwaeber: "Silent meditation is the easy way out" (*Long Island Star Journal*, October 3, 1949). On June 21, 1950 Rep. Robert Rich (R-PA) said, "I remember when we started the United Nations. I was for the United Nations, but I predicted that the United Nations would fail when they refused to open their session with prayer."

The pledge I have so often given to my own countrymen I renew before all the world on this glad Christmas Eve, that I shall do whatever lies within my own power to hasten the day foretold by Isaiah, when men "shall beat their swords into ploughshares and their spears into pruning hooks."

And Isaiah 2:4 was cited again by a president at Christmas at the end of that war. Here's Harry Truman on December 24, 1945, lighting the National Christmas Tree outside the White House:

With our enemies vanquished we must gird ourselves for the work that lies ahead. Peace has its victories no less hard won than success at arms. We must not fail or falter. We must strive without ceasing to make real the prophecy of Isaiah: "They shall beat their swords into plowshares and their spears into pruning-hooks: nation shall not lift up sword against nation, neither shall they learn war anymore."

In April 1964 President Johnson cited Isaiah 2:4 when he announced the United States was joining the Soviet Union in cutting back on the production of uranium and plutonium for use in nuclear weapons. According to a *United Press International* report in the *Sarasota Journal* on April 21, 1964, Johnson "said he believes the action will help speed the day when 'nation shall not lift up sword against nation.'" LBJ cited it again the next month on the campaign trail at Ohio University in the context of domestic issues. Reporting on the race against Sen. Barry Goldwater (R-AZ), the *Associated Press* noted on May 7, 1964:

Johnson told the Athens crowd, predominantly students, now is the time to eliminate poverty, inequality injustice, disease, illiteracy, bigotry, and: "Above all else help to bring about a day 'when nation shall not lift up sword against nation.'"

President Reagan borrowed Isaiah 2:4 for a different, unconventional rhetorical use on December 12, 1983, before the Congressional Medal of Honor Society. He told the members of Congress and others assembled in New York City that "weakness on the part of those who cherish freedom inevitably brings a threat to that freedom. Tyrants are tempted. With the best intentions, we have tried turning our swords into plowshares, hoping that others will follow. Well, our days of weakness are over. Our military forces are back on their feet and standing tall."

Four years later, Reagan had a change of heart about Isaiah 2:4. He and Soviet General Secretary Mikhail Gorbachev signed the Intermediate-Range

Nuclear Forces treaty on December 4, 1987. The *Economist* magazine reported on December 12, 1987, "To celebrate the signing of the treaty, Mr Reagan gave Mr. Gorbachev a pair of cufflinks that depict Isaiah beating swords into ploughshares."

You can spot Isaiah on the Capitol steps during presidential inauguration ceremonies. The two century-old family Bibles that Richard Nixon used in his two wartime presidential swearings-in were open both times to Isaiah 2:4. The *Associated Press* noted on January 20, 1969, about Nixon's first inauguration: "Perhaps in recognition of the darkest issue dividing the nation, the Vietnam War, Nixon decided to have the two brown leather Bibles open at the second chapter, fourth verse of Isaiah."

Earlier in Nixon's political biography, Bibles were open to Isaiah 2:4—when he was sworn in the second time as Eisenhower's vice president, January 20, 1957. He used the Bibles during his 1953 vice presidential inauguration as well.[9]

The Bibles used by Presidents George W. Bush and Bill Clinton in their second inaugurations and by President Grant in 1873 were open to Isaiah (passages 40:31, 58:12, and 11:1, respectively). And Isaiah 2:4 was cited by Rev. Joseph Lowery during his benediction at President Obama's 2009 inauguration.

President Eisenhower did not quote Isaiah 2:4 in either of his inaugural addresses. He waited until the end of his administration. From his "military-industrial complex" farewell address, January 17, 1961: "Until the latest of our world conflicts, the United States had no armaments industry. American makers of plowshares could, with time and as required, make swords as well." Three days later, Isaiah was back, with a new president. Here's Eisenhower's successor John F. Kennedy in his inaugural address: "Let both sides unite to heed in all corners of the earth the command of Isaiah—to 'undo the heavy burdens. . . . (and) let the oppressed go free.'"

Isaiah might have embraced all this official attention. In *Isaiah* chapter 6, God looks for a prophet: "Whom shall I send, and who will go for us?" Isaiah doesn't hesitate: "Here am I; send me." Few are so quick to volunteer for the punishing position of prophet. Harold Kushner observes in *Overcoming Life's Disappointments*: "Hardly anyone (Isaiah may be the only

---

9   Nixon won reelection in 1972 by defeating a minister's son, Sen. George McGovern (D-SD). At the end of the campaign, November 7, 1972, the *Associated Press* ran an item on the candidates' favorite passages from the Bible. Nixon's? The Sermon on the Mount. McGovern's? "The 'beat their swords into plowshares' verse from the Book of Isaiah."

exception) relishes the challenge of being God's prophet, telling people things they do not like being told."[10]

(A quick note about post-Nixon presidents—and Ecclesiastes. Gerald Ford titled his 1979 autobiography *A Time To Heal*. That's Ecclesiastes 3:3. And on September 15, 1977, before he testified to Congress in an expanding personal financial scandal, Jimmy Carter's Office of Management and Budget director Bert Lance prayed with the president in the Oval Office. Among the four prayers, according to Stuart Eizenstat writing in *President Carter: The White House Years*[11] likewise was Ecclesiastes 3:1-8, "to everything there is a season.")

Back to the rabbis—and Isaiah 2:4. Joseph Silverman gave the Senate prayer on December 7, 1892. He returned to the House on January 12, 1904. Two weeks after his House prayer he made a prediction involving Isaiah 2:4. Here is the February 1, 1904, *New York Times* report headlined: "Rabbi Silverman Thinks the Twentieth Century May See the End of War—Anglo-American Treaty":

> Rabbi Joseph Silverman, in the Temple Emanu-El in Fifth Avenue yesterday, talked of the coming of the millennium as indicated by the efforts making for the settlement of disputes between nations by arbitration. He took his text from Isaiah, Chapter ii, Verse 4: "And he shall judge among the nations and shall rebuke many people; and they shall beat their swords into plowshares and their spears into pruning hooks; nation shall not lift up sword against nation, neither shall they learn war any more." This prediction was made, he said, 1,754 years before the present era, and seems about to be fulfilled. It is likely to be carried out in the twentieth century on account of the establishment of the Hague Tribunal and the various societies that are making for peace.

Well into the twenty-first century, the Hague Tribunal is still around in various forms. So too is war.

20: Stop the Rabbi If You've Heard this Before

At the height of the coronavirus pandemic in the spring of 2020, Yossi Klein Halevi, a senior fellow at the Shalom Hartman Institute, detailed what he would tell his children during the Passover seder. "I am a Jew because I love

---

10   Alfred A. Knopf, 2006, page 19
11   Thomas Dunne Books, 2018, page 130.

a good story," he wrote in the April 6, 2020, *Times of Israel.* "And the Jews are a story we tell ourselves about who we think we are. I am a Jew because stories have a purpose."

Klein was focused on the Passover story—"the Jewish people was founded intentionally, to convey the message that this world isn't random but intentional, a reflection of a purposeful creation." But his larger point about the importance of stories plays out in Jewish prayers in Congress, too.

Rabbi prayers in the House and Senate typically have identical structure. Open with an acknowledgment of the Lord and of Congress, most likely in that order. Then maybe a quote from Isaiah or Micah. A quick word in Hebrew. Then "amen." Then make room for the Pledge of Allegiance.

A tried and true formula.

But rabbis sometimes mix it up by inserting a personal flair. Often, it's a good story.

Like this tale Mendel Abrams of Beth Torah Synagogue, West Hyattsville, Maryland, told the House on November 3, 1975:

> It once happened that a famous mountain climber was being interviewed by a journalist. "Why do you climb mountains?" asked the reporter. "To get to the top," was the reply. "Why do you want to get to the top?" "In order to see other mountains," answered the climber.

A good story. And rabbis, after all, enjoy telling a good story. It reinforces their message when they address their congregations. Torah, after all, is one big story.

So why not tell stories in Congress?[12]

Consider what Rachmiel Liberman of the Rabbinical Board of New England told the House on May 13, 1992. Referring to Exodus 25:8 he said:

> We have recently read in the Weekly Bible Portion read at synagogue services, G-d's command to Moses, 'That they shall make for Me a Sanctuary, and I will dwell within them.' Our sages teach us that the term I will dwell within them, instead of the usual form I will dwell within it, means that G-d will

---

12 This is generally more recording history than stating current practice. House Chaplain Patrick Conroy told the author that the chaplain's role is not to tell stories but to say prayers. After all, the chaplain is not addressing Congress, but God. Only Members speak to Congress—via the Speaker—not one another. He told the author that under his tenure he has tried to move House guest chaplains off messages or stories and stick to prayer.

dwell within the heart of each and every person, when he or she strives to build a sanctuary for G-d.

If Congress itself can serve as a sanctuary, then why not fill it with stories. Jewish and non-Jewish stories. The Jewish tradition, after all, doesn't begin and end with what's written in the Bible itself. It continues after. Jewish education encompasses a journey through centuries of subsequent rabbinic commentary. Right up to rabbis in front of Congress, even.

Liberman cited Moses. Other rabbi stories imparted a leadership lesson or two from the law-giving prophet and other wise men.

Seth Frisch of Temple Beth El in Portland, Maine, in the Senate on March 19, 1991:

> In the Book of Numbers, You give us a most unusual view of Moses, Your servant, who has brought the Israelites out of Egypt. He has demanded of Pharaoh to let his people go. While physically they have been freed, they have yet to become in their own minds free. When they are confronted with the harsh realities of life in the desert, they cry out for their past life in Egypt. In this particular passage in Numbers, it is Moses instead who cries out. He says: 'I am not able to bear all this people myself alone, because it is too heavy for me.' And it is You, God, who answers Your servant with compassion. You say to him: 'Gather unto Me seventy of the elders of Israel, whom thou knowest to be elders of the people, and officers to represent them; and bring them to the tent of meeting that they may stand there with thee. 'They shall bear the burden of the people with you, that thou bear it not thyself alone.' These are powerful words for our ancestors in this ancient world, but for us these words founded this great Nation. These are words upon which this United States is but a cornerstone.

That was Frisch's first time as a guest chaplain in Congress. He made his fourth appearance nearly 30 years later. Having moved to the New Shul of America in Rydal, Pennsylvania, Frisch prayed in the House on February 5, 2020. He spoke at the same rostrum where, the night before, President Trump delivered a raucous State of the Union address that ended with Speaker Nancy Pelosi tearing up her copy of the speech. And he prayed four hours before, in the chamber next door, the Senate acquitted Trump in his impeachment trial.

Frisch seemingly channeled both divisive events for this telling this Bible-based story that drew upon American history, too. "I am reminded of Solomon, king of ancient Israel, who would preside over a most unusual judicial hearing," he said. "One in which two mothers would lay claim to the life of one child, a child they each would insist to be their own. This passage allows us to see Solomon's wisdom as preserving the Nation, as we are sadly reminded, so soon after his death, the Kingdom is split asunder. I too am reminded of Abraham Lincoln, when he spoke with prophetic-like-prescience: 'A House Divided Cannot Stand,' which was soon to become 'a war of brother against brother.' From this we would soon learn that our future lies not in enmity, but in unity."

In Numbers 2:2, God instructed the Israelites fleeing Egypt to "pitch by their fathers' houses; every man with his own standard, according to the ensigns." In his June 6, 2018, House prayer, Aaron Krupnick of Congregation Beth El in New Jersey picked up on that theme for instructing Congress. "On the long road for freedom from Egypt," Krupnick said, "You led 12 diverse tribes, instructing each to march under their own banner. They did not always see eye to eye, but they could, nonetheless, walk shoulder to shoulder. In spite of their disagreements, they had sworn an oath to You to be one nation under God. Dear Lord, help the Members of this Congress to be ever mindful of the fact that the right to disagree is fundamental to our democracy."

Arthur Lelyveld of Fairmount Temple, Beachwood, Ohio, looked to Exodus 18:21 for his November 3, 1999, House prayer:

> Jethro, the Midianite father-in-law of Moses, warned his son-in-law, the Great Lawgiver himself, that he would wear himself out were he to continue to handle the responsibilities of leadership alone. "Hear me," said Jethro, "surround yourself with advisers and aides who are truthworthy, God-fearing persons of truth who hate corruption." Grant us, Lord, a portion of Jethro's wisdom, that we may shape our public life to reflect that and probity to which we have always aspired.

Joel Tessler of Temple Beth Sholom in Potomac, Maryland, borrowed from the Bible for his November 9, 1999, story in the House:

> The Prophet Billim is hired to curse the Jewish people, the chosen people of God. Try as he might, God would not place in him the spirit of condemnation and curse, but enveloped him in true understanding with purity and love. Billim uttered these famous words which were said as a person enters the synagogue: "How goodly are your homes of Jacob, your institutions of

Israel?" Why do we praise our homes when we enter the synagogue? The Lord taught Billim that our institutions are only as strong as our homes. If the American family is under siege, is it any wonder that our schools are becoming battle zones for children and teachers?

Battle zones of a different kind: On October 1, 2002, during "these most challenging times" after the 9/11 terror and before the Iraq war, Gerald Kane of Temple Beth El, Las Cruces, New Mexico, opened the Senate. He told a "parable from Jewish tradition": "A man, wandering lost in a dark forest for several days, finally encounters another. He calls out: 'Brother, show me the way out of here.' The man replies: 'Brother, I too am lost. I can only tell you this: the paths I have tried to get out of this forest have led me nowhere. They have only led me astray. Here, take hold of my hand, and let us search for a way out of this dark place together.' 'And so it is with us,' the author of the parable concludes. 'When we go our separate ways, we may go astray. Let us join hands and look for the path out of the darkness together.' Dear God, inspire those gathered in this historic chamber to walk on the path of freedom, respect, and solidarity together into the light of a sun-filled day."

In his two prayers in Congress, Gary Zola of the American Jewish Archives in Cincinnati drew upon more contemporary Jewish figures, both Americans, for his stories. Opening the House on September 21, 2004:

> As we begin legislative deliberations in this great shrine of democracy, we call to mind the words of an American original—Sam Levenson (1912–1980)— the Spanish teacher turned entertainer whose homespun stories about his immigrant parents delighted our nation. Upon his death, Levenson's children discovered their father's ethical will containing these heartfelt sentiments: "To America, I owe a debt for the opportunity it gave me to be free and to be me. To my parents I owe America. They gave it to me, and I leave it to you. Take good care of it. To the Bible, I owe the belief that the human does not live by bread alone, nor do we live alone at all. This is also the democratic tradition. Preserve it."

And Zola in the Senate on May 26 the next year:

> Let us draw devotional inspiration this morning from the life of Rabbi Isaac Mayer Wise, founder of the Hebrew Union College, who led this Senate in prayer 135 years ago to this very week. May one brief moment from the life of this famed American clergyman renew in us a commitment to the core of righteous living. For we have been taught that once, when this rabbi took

ill amidst a class and was compelled to descend from his teaching platform, a young, eager student jumped up, grabbed his arm, and said: "May I help you down, Doctor?" In response to this question, the rabbi uttered words that remind us anew of what is good and what God does require of us all: "Never help a person down," the rabbi told his student. "Try always to help people up."

In the House on September 13, 1990, Jay Marcus told a story "of an elderly Jewish woman who at the conclusion of the Rosh Hashanah service finds herself all alone with no one to exchange the customary Shana Tova, or good year, blessing. She reflects for a moment, and then steps to the front of the sanctuary and opens the ark. 'I know who to wish a Shana Tova, a good year,' she says. 'I'll wish G-d a good year, but what can I wish Him? He has everything,' and she smiles sweetly, looking at the ark and the Torah. 'G-d, I wish You *nachas*, joy, satisfaction and pleasure from all Your children, from all of mankind.'"

Moshe Feller used a story for this October 16, 1991, instruction:

Grant that the Members of . . . the U.S. Senate, consider every human being as an entire world, as Your servants the Sages of the Talmud have taught `Why did G-d create the world in the beginning with but one single individual, Adam? (He could have with His infinite power just as easily created masses of humans.) He did so to teach mankind that every individual is indeed an entire world.

If you have wondered why we hold elections on Tuesdays, perhaps this next story can offer Talmudic help. In the House on Tuesday, July 17, 2001, Mitchell Wohlberg of Baltimore's Beth Tfiloh Congregation said:

I come from a tradition where Tuesdays are considered most propitious: weddings, moving to a new home, good things are to take place on Tuesday. It goes all the way back to the first week of creation, where we note that, unlike other days of that first week, on the second day, on Monday, the Bible does not tell us "and God saw that it was good," while on the next day, the first Tuesday, two times it says, "and God saw that it was good." According to the Talmud, this is because on the second day of the week the waters were parted. That symbolizes the division. That is no good. On the first Tuesday, the third day of the week, the waters were brought together again, and that symbolizes unity, and that is doubly good.

Gary Klein of Temple Ahavat Shalom in Florida called "the Talmud, a work of Jewish religious literature" when he urged God on June 27, 2017, to "help us and our legislators to also understand the Talmudic concept that reinforces this when it states: If you save a single life, it is as if you saved the entire world."

When Dov Hillel Klein opened his May 5, 2010, prayer with a story, he cited a different kind of storyteller. Bill Cosby.

"In the Jewish tradition, one begins an invocation with words of inspiration. I have received inspiration from many individuals, but the person I am thinking of today is America's number one dad, Bill Cosby," the rabbi from Tannenbaum Chabad House in Evanston Illinois said on May 5, 2010. "Several years ago, Bill Cosby spoke at Northwestern University's commencement. He said he was the first person in his family to attend the university. But he came to realize that just going to college does not necessarily make you all that smart, and just by going to college surely does not mean you have all the answers. He came home after his first day of college and his grandmother asked, 'Billy, what did you study?' Cosby replied that in his philosophy class they debated whether or not a half a cup of water was half empty or half full. His grandmother, who did not have a college education or even a high school diploma, responded immediately, 'That's so simple. If you are drinking, the glass is half empty, but if you are pouring, the glass is half full.'"

"I think this is probably the first time that Bill Cosby has been part of the morning prayer," sponsor Rep. Jan Schakowsky (D-IL) said. "Certainly, it is the first time his grandmother has been part of the prayer."

Not only the first time that Bill Cosby showed up in the opening prayer. It was, quite likely, the last for "America's number one dad." Which is why prayers which stick to God have a longer shelf life.

Finally, how about Congress as a team—just like they have in baseball? And baseball, as any fan knows, is chock full of wonderful stories.

Here's how Jay Karzen of Des Plaines, Illinois, opened the House on May 17, 1979:

Recently during a baseball game a dog ran onto the playing field. He settled on third base and refused to move. From the stands came the cry: Bite the umpire. Get off the base. Run home. All to no avail. The dog would not move. A newscaster commenting on this situation noted that the animal did not heed the advice because there was no dominant voice from the crowd. The voices heard in this prestigious Chamber of the House of Representatives are, indeed, dominant voices that shape the direction of this country and help America move ahead. . . . The Congress of the United States is a team: Team (Together Each Accomplishes More).

And thus, the only time a rabbi has included a baseball story in his or her prayer. But not the only baseball mention surrounding a rabbi guest chaplain. An Illinois congressman went to the ballpark, too, on behalf of a Chicago rabbi (Anshe Emet Synagogue) and the Cubs.

"As the rabbi of the congregation closest to Wrigley Field, for 30 years," Rep. Mike Quigley (D-IL) said on April 30, 2015, "Rabbi [Michael] Siegel's prayers for the Cubs have gone unanswered; however, Michael, again, assures me this is the year."

Divine intervention? A year after Siegel was guest chaplain, his Cubbie prayers were answered. They won the World Series.

A different rabbinical baseball story with a Chicago connection, this time via the other Chicago major league team. Chicago White Sox fan Rabbi Bruce Aft was the September 22, 1993, Senate guest chaplain. When he met fellow White Sox fan President Barack Obama at an April 23, 2012, Holocaust commemoration, he wore a Sox yarmulke. Aft's congregation is Adat Reyim in Springfield, Virginia. He delivered the opening prayer in the Virginia House of Delegates on January 8, 2020, the first day of the new legislative session. "I did have a problem as I was driving up today." he said. "My family and I were arguing over which head covering I should wear. I am a Chicago White Sox fan. We live in Washington, DC now." He showed the legislators both a White Sox yarmulke and a Washington Nationals yarmulke. Loud cheers for the Nationals. "Does that mean I wear the Washington Nationals one based upon that? OK, then." And he put on the yarmulke for the World Series champs.

SECTION V

Policy and Politics

21: The Bully Pulpit: Mixing politics into Prayers

Polonius: "What do you read, my lord?"
Hamlet: "Words, words, words."
> —Act 2, Scene 2, *The Tragedy of Hamlet, Prince of Denmark* by
> William Shakespeare

"Will no one rid me of this turbulent priest?"
> —Outburst attributed to King Henry II of England,
> leading to the death of Thomas Becket,
> the Archbishop of Canterbury, in 1170

Saturday Night Live found an unlikely target to zing in mid-October 2013: U.S. Senate Chaplain Barry Black.

During his prayers that fall, Black repeatedly admonished senators over a legislative stalemate that led to a partial government shutdown and raising the debt ceiling (Oct. 3, 2013: "Save us from the madness. . . . Deliver us from the hypocrisy of attempting to sound reasonable while being unreasonable. Remove the burdens of those who are the collateral damage of this government shutdown.")[13] The *New York Times* pursued the story, its findings headlined on October 6, 2013, "Give Us This Day, Our

---

13   During a partial government shutdown that began on December 22, 2018, chaplain Patrick Conroy was gentler but no less obvious in his message: "There are many Americans who look to the people's House as uncertainty about the future of the economy and their livelihoods hang in the balance." Black was more direct on January 10, 2019: "On this 19th day of the partial government shutdown, illumine our darkness, revive our faith, and heal our wounds. . . . Lord, help our Senators to serve our Nation and world, unsullied by base motives of self-interest."

Daily Senate Scolding; Senate Chaplain Shows His Disapproval During Morning Prayer."

CBS News had noticed something similar two years earlier. An "Early Show" anchor introduced an August 6, 2011, report featuring Black this way: "If you were worried that Congress didn't have a prayer of saving the country from default this week, you may have needed more faith. It turns out among the first acts of Congress in 1789 was the establishment of chaplains for the House and Senate. As we noticed this week, the deadline was growing closer and they were growing increasingly troubled by the inaction on Capitol Hill."

And thus begat parody. On October 12, 2013, *SNL*'s "Weekend Update" served up Chaplain Black comedy. Played by Kenan Thompson, "Chaplain Black" prayed: "Lord, give us strength, but especially to those in Congress, and let them stop being a bunch of blubbering knuckleheads that go onto the television and spout all kinds of nonsense." And, "Lord, bless and forgive these braying jackasses." And, "May they find themselves in a restroom stall devoid of toilet paper."

Thompson singed Black but didn't burn him. Thompson's "Chaplain Black" wore a bow-tie. Just like the real chaplain. He also said, "It's not my job to judge, only to minister to those who need it."

Spoof aside, that's actually a fairly accurate job description. (And *SNL* wasn't the only late-night comedy show to feature a chaplain. Stephen Colbert's Comedy Central series *The Colbert Report* had an "official chaplain," Jesuit priest James Martin.)

As the Senate began floor debate over Neil Gorsuch's nomination to the U.S. Supreme Court in early April 2017, real-life Chaplain Black prayed, "Lord, this week our lawmakers must make critical decisions that may affect this legislative body for years to come. Teach them to be obedient to your commands, doing your will, and following your leading." No judgment from him—but recognizing there would be judgment from others.

Senate rules say the chaplain, in addition to the daily prayer, is "available as an advisor and counselor to senators, senators' families, and congressional employees." That guidance carries over to guest chaplains as well.

The June 7, 2015, *Roll Call* noted that after House guest chaplains are selected they "are sent three points to keep in mind: Keep the prayer short, don't get political and remember that the House constitutes a variety of faiths."

Specifically on that second point: Have chaplains ever crossed over into politics?

Here's an example of one who did—and the senator who noticed.

June 12, 1995. Early in the online era when sexually explicit material on the internet was more shocking, the Senate debated an amendment offered by Sen. James Exon (D-NE). He proposed, as the *Washington Post* reported on December 24, 1995, to "crack down on sexual material on the Internet."

Chaplain Lloyd John Ogilvie was barely three months into the job when he prayed:

> We praise You for the advancements in computerized communications that we enjoy in our time. Sadly, however, there are those who are littering this information superhighway with obscene, indecent, and destructive pornography. Virtual but virtueless reality is projected in the most twisted, sick, misuse of sexuality. Violent people with sexual pathology are able to stalk and harass the innocent. Cyber solicitation of teenagers reveals the dark side of online victimization. We are profoundly concerned about the impact of this on our children. We have learned from careful study how children can become addicted to pornography at an early age. Their understanding and appreciation of Your gift of sexuality can be denigrated and eventually debilitated. Pornography disallowed in print and the mail is now readily available to young children who learn how to use the computer. Oh God, help us care for our children. Give us wisdom to create regulations that will protect the innocent. In times past, You have used the Senate to deal with problems of air and water pollution, and the misuse of our natural resources. Lord, give us courage to balance our reverence for freedom of speech with responsibility for what is said and depicted. Now, guide the Senators as they consider ways of controlling the pollution of computer communications and how to preserve one of our greatest resources: the minds of our children and the future moral strength of our Nation.

Two days later, Exon endorsed Ogilvie's message: "I would like to start out this debate by reading a prayer that was offered by the Chaplain of the Senate on Monday, June 12, that I hope will guide us once again. It was so much on point to what this Senator and the Senator from Indiana and others are attempting to do that I think it is worthy of repetition."

Sen. Patrick Leahy (D-VT) likewise noted the new chaplain's participation in policy discussion, but with a different reaction. "If we are going to get involved," Leahy said, "maybe we should allow the elected members of this body doing it." Leahy pointedly added, "After listening to his prayer, it seemed like he was part of the debate."

He didn't stop there: "Perhaps he should allow us to debate these issues and determine how they come out. Maybe pray for our guidance. Allow us to debate them. He may want to find that he has enough other duties composing prayer each morning for us to keep him busy."

Oy!

A rare rebuke of a chaplain by a senator. Rough start for the rookie. Congressional leadership includes whips, but there's no miracle whip. A dozen years later the lesson repeated itself, with harsher consequences, when the House chaplain veered into the policy lane. On November 6, 2017, as the House was debating a Republican tax bill, Father Conroy prayed:

> As legislation on taxes continues to be debated this week and next, may all Members be mindful that the institutions and structures of our great Nation guarantee the opportunities that have allowed some to achieve great success, while others continue to struggle. May their efforts these days guarantee that there are not winners and losers under new tax laws, but benefits balanced and shared by all Americans.

The result? The tax bill passed. And Conroy lost his job. The first time in history the House chaplain has been forced to step down. NBC News reported on April 26, 2018: "Speaker Paul Ryan has ousted the chaplain of the House of Representatives, according to his resignation letter. . . . There have been concerns about the pastor being too partisan." Conroy told the April 26, 2018, *New York Times* it was "unclear" why he was asked to resign and said about Capitol Hill, "There are Catholics who are Republicans and there are Catholics who are Democrats. I don't know if there is a religious divide; there certainly is a political one."

But Conroy's job loss was temporary. It lasted one week. On May 3 in the *Washington Post*, Paul Kane reported Ryan "reversed course" and agreed to keep Conroy on as House chaplain "after an extraordinary showdown that included the priest alleging anti-Catholic bias by Ryan's chief of staff. Conroy, who was forced to step down by Ryan last month, sent the speaker a letter rescinding his resignation and vowing to remain until the end of the year." (And soon Conroy was citing legislation again. May 23, 2018: "During this week, the National Defense Authorization Act is being debated on the floor of the House. May all Members be imbued with Your wisdom, that the results of their deliberations might redound to the benefit of our Nation.")

On July 18, 2019, Conroy raised his hands over the chamber. "This has been a difficult and contentious week in which darker spirits seem to have been at play in the people's House," he said. "In Your most Holy name, I now cast out all spirits of darkness from this Chamber, spirits not from You." Congress pundits compared the moment to an exorcism.

A guest chaplain can spark controversy, too. Here's how the May 10, 2019, *Jewish Telegraphic Agency* reported the prior day's guest chaplain:

> An imam who has wished for the end of Zionism, called for a third Intifada and likened Israel to Nazi-era Germany delivered the opening prayer for a session of the U.S. House of Representatives on Thursday.
>
> Omar Suleiman, the founder and president of the Dallas-based Yaqeen Institute, an organization that describes itself as a resource about Islam, referred to recent attacks on houses of worship—which has included synagogues in the United States—in his opening remarks.
>
> Let us not be deterred by the hatred that has claimed the lives of innocent worshippers across the world, but emboldened by the love that gathered them together to remember you and gathered us together to remember them," Suleiman said in a short prayer after being introduced by Speaker Nancy Pelosi. . . .
>
> Pelosi's office is looking into how and why Johnson invited Suleiman, an official told The Jewish Telegraphic Agency.
>
> Rep. Lee Zeldin, R-N.Y., who is Jewish, said in a statement that inviting Suleiman to deliver the opening prayer was a "terribly bad call."

Responding to the ensuing furor, Suleiman issued a statement: "After giving the invocation in Congress last week, I have been attacked online and threatened with violence. . . . Never did I expect my prayer on the House floor would be so threatening."

Charged episodes like these can lead a reasonable person to wonder about praying in Congress: Why bother? Mixing religion and politics—two tricky minefields in their own rights—can be less like mixing oil with water and more like nitro with glycerol.

The *Senate.gov* website notes that the chaplain can "be expected to add a reference to the legislative situation during times of frustration and end-of-session turmoil. In 1984, as the session dragged on well beyond the scheduled adjournment date, the chaplain prayed 'Father in heaven, we are here under duress, but we have imposed this upon ourselves.' During the 1999 impeachment trial of President Bill Clinton, the chaplain crafted his opening prayers with particular care." In fact, the 21 prayers that Senate chaplain Ogilvie gave during the Clinton impeachment trial—plus one from a guest chaplain—were turned into a bound collection issued by both the Republican and Democratic leaders. (When chaplain James Ford opened the House in prayer on December 19, 1998—the day Clinton was impeached—he recited the Priestly Blessing from the book of Numbers in the Torah.)

On December 5, 2000, a week before the Supreme Court decided the Florida recount case pitting George W. Bush against Al Gore, Ogilvie referred to the national division and frustration. "We return to You in repentance, confessing our urgent need for Your grace," he said. "We cannot open the Senate today with a business-as-usual attitude. So much has happened in these past weeks in the contested Presidential election and the close Senate races. As tension mounts, patience wears thin, and party spirit threatens to displace the spirit of patriotism in America, we ask for Your healing spirit."

The flip side of the policy equation was a (potentially) unique use of the chaplain's power pulpit during the early days of the Iraq War, 2003-2004. Sharon Waxman served as senior national security advisor to Sen. Ted Kennedy (D-MA). In a May 11, 2009, oral history with the Miller Center Foundation and the Edward M. Kennedy Institute for the United States Senate, Waxman said of Kennedy:

> He tried to get the leadership to put the names of all American soldiers killed in the *Record*, to have the chaplain read the names of those killed every week. On national television they do it. The newspapers do it. He could not get the Democratic leadership to do it. They were worried that it would be perceived as political.

A century earlier, on the eve of war, military policy infused the House chaplain's prayer. Rev. Henry Couden said in November 1913 that "every movement looking to a world-wide disarmament . . . is a reflection on the intelligence and religious life of and people to teach the arts of war on land or sea." Couden told Congress "how infinitely wiser it is to conserve the brain and brawn of armies and navies for the peaceful pursuits of life." Couden was no less opinionated in the aftermath of World War I. On February 25, 1919, he expressed to God "gratitude that the President of the United States

[Woodrow Wilson] has landed safely on the shores of America from over the sea, where he went on a mission to assist in establishing a world-wide peace. We pray that his wisdom may have enlightened the entente powers on the gigantic problems which confronted them; that he may be able to make plain to our people the constitution of the peace league entered into by the wise men who framed it; that it may fulfill its purpose and insure to all the world the peace."

Have any rabbis gone political in their prayers to Congress?

Before demonstrating that the answer is yes, let's first recognize some rabbis who, despite politics swirling around the time of their prayers, did not.

Bernard Raskas of St. Paul, Minnesota, was in the Senate on October 28, 1981. That same day senators voted to permit America's sale of AWACS planes and other air combat equipment to Saudi Arabia. The AWACS vote was a landmark battle for the pro-Israel community, a massive lobbying effort it eventually lost. But no mention of the AWACS sale in Raskas' prayer. Instead, broad hope for Senate harmony: "Let each be steadfast to his or her conviction and yet respectful and mindful of the convictions of others. May there always be harmony and helpfulness in this Chamber."

(Minnesota Senator Rudy Boschwitz, a Jewish Republican who opposed the sale, sponsored Raskas.)

On October 23, 1973, Sally Priesand became the first woman rabbi to open Congress in prayer. That was also the date the first resolution to impeach President Richard Nixon was offered in the House. But no mention in the rabbi's prayer. At least, nothing stronger than, "Those who sit here have been granted positions of authority by their fellow citizens. May they use their power wisely and for the good of all, and may their decisions ever reflect a true sensitivity toward human needs."

September 1998 was a busy month of developments in Congress surrounding Monica Lewinsky's affair with President Clinton. On September 9, Independent Counsel Ken Starr submitted his report and boxes of supporting documents to the House. On September 18, the Judiciary Committee agreed to release Clinton's videotaped grand jury testimony. And the day before, September 17—one month after Clinton went on national television to admit he had an inappropriate relationship with Lewinsky—Rabbi Levi Shemtov gave the prayer in the Senate. The head of the Washington office of American Friends of Lubavitch seemed to recognize the unavoidable story playing out nationally. But he kept to rabbinical wisdom:

As our Nation faces tremendous challenges, we also possess a deep, enormous faith and capacity for healing. The Senate, reflecting the Nation, comprises men and women from various political, cultural, and religious backgrounds. We are thankful for the freedom to bring various views, but as we debate the significant issues of the day, let us remember the words of the Lubavitcher Rebbe, Rabbi Menachem M. Schneerson, of blessed memory, who taught, "the only way to soothe the differences between two sides is to seek how we are ultimately all on the same side."

Holocaust survivor Sidney Harcsztark was House guest chaplain on May 1, 1985. It was the 40th anniversary of his liberation from the Dachau concentration camp. Notably, the prayer was offered during President Ronald Reagan's trip to West Germany. The itinerary included Reagan's divisive and infamous visit to the German war cemetery Bitburg where members of the Nazi Waffen SS were buried. But Harcsztark didn't mention Bitburg in his prayer. Instead, he asked that members of Congress be blessed "in their quest to grant real meaning to the dignity of men, as all men are born in the image of God."

His sponsor, though, did not shy from that divisive topic. Rep. Chuck Schumer (D-NY): "Rabbi Harcsztark has been able to help educate those not yet born about the horrors of the Holocaust." Schumer drove home the point: "In light of the events of the past 10 days, it seems more important than ever that we remain vigilant in our task to make sure that no one is allowed to forget this tragic event."

But other rabbis have mixed advocacy and policy commentary into their prayers. Some direct. Others gentler, wrapped in theological themes and seemingly harmless. But evident nonetheless.

Let's first consider direct appeals for legislation. That would include Louis Kaplan, who said in the House on June 3, 1969: "Spur these leaders, especially to translate The Biblical challenge 'to do righteousness and justice' into legislation enabling more Children and adults, in this Nation and elsewhere, to enjoy their 'unalienable rights' in the human family."

And Steven Dworken who said in the House on June 15, 1972: "May this august body, through its legislation, further the ideals of equality, liberty, and justice for all upon which our beloved country is founded."

On August 19, 1965, amid Congress passing President Lyndon Johnson's Great Society programs, Louis Eliezer Wolfish prayed in the House. He asked for "blessings upon the President and the Vice President of these United States, and upon our legislators. Concretize their aspirations to eradicate poverty and disease from this Nation of plenty." *Reading Eagle* columnist Don Maclean, writing on congressional prayers May 11, 1966, called Wolfish's words "a Madison Avenue approach" to prayer.

Stanley Wagner also cited the Great Society when he prayed in the House on February 21, 1967: "Words, millions and millions of them uttered here, have become as countless emissaries from Thee, inspiring a national commitment to Thine ideals, ideals which promote and advance human welfare and have become the foundation and cornerstone upon which our Great Society is built."

Prayers have focused on public policy toward young people.

The 1960 White House Conference on Children and Youth met March 27–31, 1960. On March 29, Julius Mark of New York's Temple Emanuel gave the Senate prayer: "Gathered In this great Capital City, upon the invitation of the President of our country, are thousands of citizens from every section of our land to deliberate upon how best they can assist our children and youth to assume the responsibilities of citizenship in a nation dedicated to liberty."

More youthful advocacy on April 20, 1966, in the House, from Edward Sandrow. He prayed "for our youth, for their homes and schools so that they may be constantly awakened to the great Ideas of faith and the worthy causes of our American way of life—the pursuit of liberty and human rights."

And Joel Tessler of Temple Beth Sholom in Potomac, Maryland, said this to the House on November 9, 1999: "If the American family is under siege, is it any wonder that our schools are becoming battle zones for children and teachers? Money alone cannot substitute for the foundation and grounding that parents, grandparents, and families provide. Every discussion in these halls must be judged with an eye on how goodly are our homes, the homes we help our citizens create."

Reflecting their times, the issues of equal and civil rights come up in prayers.

In the House on June 8, 1961, Morton Kanter was "confident that equal rights will soon be extended to all our fellow citizens." Equal rights again two decades later when, on April 22, 1982, Sidney Guthman stipulated in the Senate: "'Liberty and justice for all' must mean just that. 'Liberty and justice for all'—town and city, poor and rich, old and young—of every race and background. May the day come speedily when equal rights for all will signify more than a cliché." The Equal Rights Amendment failed to meet a 1982 deadline for ratification.

For civil rights, Saul Wisemon said this in the Senate on August 13, 1964: "Save us from racial prejudice and discrimination which destroy our influence for good around the world." Nine days earlier, the bodies of three civil rights workers—two white and Jewish, one black—were found in an earthen dam in Mississippi. On March 13, 1962, Eugene Blackschleger from Temple Beth-Or in Montgomery—Alabama's state capital and focal point for much of the civil rights movement—opened the Senate. "We pray that America may ever remain the land of the free and the home of the brave," Blackshleger said, "where all men shall have the rights to life, liberty, and the pursuit of happiness."

Four decades after Alabama was front-and-center in the civil rights struggle—on September 14, 2006—Rabbi Amy Rader of B'nai Torah Congregation in Boca Raton opened the House noting, "When the theologian of my tradition, Dr. Abraham Joshua Heschel, marched in Selma, Alabama, with Dr. Martin Luther King, Jr., Rabbi Heschel said: 'My feet were praying.' Esteemed men and women in this Chamber, I ask for God's help to move our prayers from our lips to our feet."[14]

Rabbis have used prayers to advocate foreign and defense policy.

Early in his administration, President Donald Trump signed an executive order titled "Protecting the Nation From Foreign Terrorist Entry Into the United States" (March 6, 2017). During the height of public controversy over that order—opponents considered it a ban on certain refugees and immigrants—the Senate welcomed a rabbi guest chaplain. Sponsored by Arkansas Republican Senator John Boozman, Barry Block of Congregation B'nai Israel in Little Rock prayed on January 31, 2017: "With your word, and our nation's Constitution constantly guiding them to pursue liberty and justice, opportunity and equality, for every man, woman, and children within our borders. For those who would peacefully seek refuge on our shores and for each of your children on earth. Make them ever mindful of your command to remember the heart of the stranger."

According to the February 1, 2017, *Arkansas Democrat-Gazette*, "his short invocation had been shaped, in part, by current events." Block told the newspaper: "I am here today to offer a prayer, not a speech, but certainly I

---

14 In June 2016, according to the *Jewish Telegraphic Agency*, 20 senators urged President Obama to posthumously award Heschel the Presidential Medal of Freedom.

have in mind those refugees who seek freedom here in America and who may currently be held up."

Immigration topped the Senate agenda in 1989. Introduced in February 1989 by Sen. Ted Kennedy (D-MA), what would become the Immigration Act of 1990 allowed 700,000 immigrants to come to the United States in 1992-1994. Plus 675,000 each year after that. With the immigration debate as backdrop, Moshe Feller of the St. Paul, Minnesota, Lubavitch House gave this July 14, 1989, prayer:

> Rabbi Yosef Yitzckok Schneersohn, the world renowned Lubavitcher Rebbe, fled war-torn Europe for these shores of freedom in 1940, spending the final decade of his earthly existence as a distinguished citizen of these United States of America, laboring with great self-sacrifice to sanctify Your holy name throughout the world. May his memory be for a blessing and his merit for a shield to the United States of America and its Government which provided him sanctuary and freedom to do Your sacred bidding.

Feller did not directly advocate a position on the pending legislation. But his sponsor Sen. Rudy Boschwitz (R-MN) did:

> Rabbi Feller spoke about the former Lubavitcher Rebbe who fled from Europe in 1940, much as my family did . . . we left Europe, and arrived in the United States in 1935. And he spoke about the Rebbe, how he arrived here, spent the last 10 years of his life in the United States, and what it meant to him and meant to his followers, just as it has meant so much in my family and all the others who arrived in the late thirties under great stress. So, I look at the prayer that Rabbi Feller gave, and I praise him for it. It comes at a particularly appropriate time as we were yesterday considering the immigration bill, and with that immigration bill our shores will open wider to people who are seeking freedom.

During an earlier time of heightened international fear, the Cold War-era Geneva Summit brought together President Dwight Eisenhower, Soviet Premier Nikolai Bulganin, British Prime Minister Anthony Eden, and French Prime Minister Edgar Faure. In the House on July 20, 1955, two days after the summit started, Selig Auerbach gave the prayer. The Wisconsin rabbi urged legislators "to speak the right words which at this crucial hour will give strength and council to our President and his advisers, assembled in Geneva for the purpose of restoring true peace to a stricken world. Let all those gathered there realize the truth of the words spoken by Thy prophet

[Amos] that two opponents can walk together only if both parties commit themselves to adhere to their agreements in truth."

Five years later the world again anticipated a Cold War summit. This time Eisenhower and Nikita Khrushchev were set to meet in Paris on May 16, 1960. On May 4, Morris Hershman of the Joliet Jewish Congregation prayed in the Senate:

> Be Thou with the President of the United States, as he prepares to confer with the leaders of other lands. Make manifest to all nations that as our leaders represent us, we stand behind them, not as Republicans or Democrats, not as Protestants, Catholics, or Jews, but as Americans all, dedicated to the proposition that in Thine eyes all men are created equal.

Three days earlier, though, the Soviets shot down a CIA spy plane and captured the pilot, Gary Francis Powers. The summit collapsed. In the CIA's telling, "Khrushchev torpedoed the 1960 Paris Summit Conference."[15]

A quarter-century later, another Cold War-era summit earned another rabbi mention. A week before President Ronald Reagan met for the first time with Soviet General Secretary Mikhail Gorbachev in Geneva, Haim Asa gave the House prayer. The Bulgarian-born rabbi said on November 13, 1985, "The eyes of all of Your children are focused upon the forthcoming summit. Our respective religions teach that a summit is a place on top of a mountain. Your presence has often been revealed from the summit mountaintops." Asa urged God: "Be with our President and his advisers at the summit, just as you were with Abraham our patriarch at Mount Moriah, with Moses at Mount Sinai, with Joshua at Mount Nebo, and with Jesus at the Calvary summit of Golgotha. We pray that all who come to the summit would work toward shalom; for the survival of our planet, hopefully without sacrificing our freedom."

More policy advocacy during the Vietnam War. B'nai B'rith executive Jay Kaufman opened the Senate on April 17, 1967. Two days earlier Martin Luther King told a massive New York City war protest: "One of the greatest casualties of the war in Vietnam is the Great Society . . . making the poor white and Negro bear the heaviest burdens both at the front and at home." Kaufman struck a similar tone, urging "enactments to stay the unraveling of our Nation's unity, for statutes and ordinances designed to raise the lowly,

---

15 "The Summit Conference of 1960: An Intellifence Officer's View," posted on CIA website, March 19, 2007.

the scorned seething to break the man-forged manacles binding them to despair."[16]

Early in May 1972, the U.S. and South Vietnam suspended participation in the Paris peace talks. Dworken opened the House a month later. "The conference table is a far better arena for settling differences than the battlefield," he said. "May the day soon come when the vast sums spent on machinery of destruction can be spent on machinery of healing, balm, and peace."[17]

And another precise "ask" of the Lord on September 23, 1963—for a treaty. Morris Silverman, a Connecticut rabbi, opened the Senate: "We pray that the test ban treaty, if accepted by this august body, will mark the first step in world disarmament and will lead to universal peace." It was the right time and the right place for that wish. Senators ratified the nuclear test ban treaty the next day, 80-19.

Finally, one rabbi didn't just comment on current events. He *was* a current event. For that tale we go back to the fifth rabbi prayer ever given in Congress—seven years after the end of the Civil War.

A lingering controversy following the war's conclusion was British support for the Confederacy. Specifically, the *CSS Alabama*. Constructed in a British shipyard, Ron Chernow wrote in *Grant*, the *Alabama* "had been the most lethal Confederate blockade runner preying on Union ships, seizing or demolishing dozens before being destroyed by the USS *Kearsarge* off Cherbourg in June 1864."[18]

The April 18, 1898, *Boston Evening Transcript* provided contemporary history:

By far the most important question which has yet been decided by arbitration is that of the Confederate vessel Alabama. There was much ill-

---

16 Civil Rights Movement Archive.

17 As for Christians, Reverend Ian White-Thomson; dean of Canterbury Cathedral, England, opened the Senate May 8, 1967: "Let us pray for peace, especially in Vietnam." Rev. Thomas Hinson of Arkansas prayed in the House on August 31, 1967: "Bless our servicemen with salvation of body and soul, and bring home safely as many as possible. O Thou Prince of Peace, intervene in world affairs, and bring peace to Vietnam." The last U.S. combat troops had just departed Vietnam when Father Thomas Cawley of Johnstown, Pennsylvania, was guest chaplain. On September 7, 1972, he urged congressmen to "terminate the Vietnam war, on conditions of honor, and with a guarantee to the South Vietnamese of freedom from the danger of attack by enemies outside their borders, and of corruption within."

18 Penguin Press, 2017, page 682.

feeling engendered against Great Britain because during the war of the Rebellion she had permitted cruisers to be equipped in her ports for use against the commerce of the United States. There was war talk in the air then, even though the country had just emerged from a long and bloody struggle. The fact that the shipbuilders of Great Britain had lent material aid to the Confederate States was frequently commented on. Millions of dollars' worth of property had been destroyed by the Alabama and vessels of her class.

"*War talk in the air.*" How would the United States calm things down? Send in a rabbi!

And arm him with a unique diplomatic tool: The opening prayer in the House of Representatives.

It was January 9, 1872. Nearly a century later, the October 25, 1968, *Montreal Gazette* told the story of Abraham de Sola, a Canadian:

> He had been invited to perform this ceremony by President U. S. Grant. And he had been invited for an important reason. Relations between the United States and Great Britain were uneasy and embittered. . . .
>
> It was as a gesture of goodwill that President Grant invited a British subject to say prayers at the opening of Congress. As he stood in Congress that day, Rabbi de Sola was not only a British subject performing a ceremony at the opening of the Congress of the United States; he stood in Congress as a symbol of international reconciliation. This gesture of goodwill from Washington was accepted by the British Government in the spirit in which it was extended. . . . An agreement was reached a few months later. In selecting Rabbi de Sola for this purpose and honor, President Grant was selecting one of the most distinguished religious figures of the British Empire. Dr. de Sola had come to win international respect for the depth of his scholarship and for the range and number of his published writings.

And thus a rabbi prayer in Congress—"Bless, them, both these nations who proclaim the glad tidings of peace to the world; draw them yet nearer and nearer to each other in mutual esteem and mutual confidence"—solved a diplomatic quandary and possibly prevented war. It's a bully pulpit even Kissinger never had.

22: How Much Israel?

Every spring on the modern Jewish calendar Holocaust Remembrance Day is followed quickly by Israel Independence Day. Going from tragedy to celebration was a quick pivot as well for a guest chaplain rabbi and survivor. In February 1948, shortly after World War II ended and just before the Jewish state's War of Independence began, German-born Leo Baeck became the first rabbi in front of Congress to mention or allude to Israel, bridging the two dominating and uniquely twentieth-century Jewish events.

How often does a rabbi praying in Congress use that opportunity to talk about Israel?

It's rare. Those looking to advocate a narrative that Jews have disproportionate influence over U.S. Congress policy toward Israel won't find much supporting evidence among the words of rabbis who've prayed there. Fact is, there have been few pro-Israel or any kind of Israel-focused messages in the prayers. Of the 571 prayers delivered by rabbis between Israel's May 14, 1948, independence and February 5, 2020, 38 (under 7%) included implicit or explicit mention of Israel (or the Middle East). And among those, virtually none advocated policy.

When a prayer has contained words or themes focused on Israel, most likely it was tied to a special, obvious occasion or ceremony. Perhaps marking Israel's birthday. Or noting milestone war or peace breaking out in the Middle East. Or connecting the Holocaust's end with Israel's beginning.

An example of a rabbi linking Jewish past with Israel's present: Laurence Kotok. "We stand this day torn between conflicting emotions, between sorrow and joy. Sorrow as we have just observed Yom HaShoa—the day of memorial for the 6 million Jews and 5 million Christians who were the victims of the holocaust," the Long Island rabbi said in the House on May 2, 1979. "And yet we feel joy as today we celebrate Israel Independence Day, this the 31st anniversary of the Israel reborn out of the ashes and destruction of the holocaust."

Philip Bernstein of Temple B'rith Kodesh in Rochester opened the Senate on April 23, 1958. At the time he was chairman of the American Zionist Committee for Public Affairs. (The next year, AZCPA became the American Israel Public Affairs Committee for which Bernstein served as chairman as well.) Bernstein's 1958 prayer marked Israel's tenth anniversary. It combined Holocaust imagery with appreciation of democracy:

> Standing before Thee at this historic hour in this historic place, our thoughts turn to the ancient people who early found their way to Thee, clinging to Thee with unflagging devotion, bearing witness through the generations to Thy living presence. It was Thy love that sustained them. Thy promise which preserved them through every trial and tribulation, and brought them, creative and faithful, to this momentous hour. Be with them now as, risen from the ashes of persecution and slaughter, they stand erect, strong and free in their ancestral homeland. They that sowed in tears have come home with joy, bearing their sheaves. . . . We are grateful for the kinship of spirit which has linked this bastion of democracy in the New World to that beachhead of freedom in the Old World.

His prayer was previewed by the *Jewish Telegraphic Agency* two days prior: "Members of Congress are expected to pay tribute to Israel in addresses on the floor of Congress on April 23. Rabbi Philip S. Bernstein has been invited by the Senate to recite the opening prayer. Rabbi Bernstein is chairman of the American Zionist Committee for Public Affairs. The House has invited Rabbi Goldstein to offer a similar prayer."

In fact, Goldstein was identified in the *Congressional Record* as chairman of the American Committee for the Celebration of Israel's 10th anniversary. And his prayer indeed was similar in linking Israel's story to America's:

> If a thousand years are but as yesterday in Thy sight, 10 years are but as a moment. Yet there are great moments in the human drama which attest to the divine spark in man and to Thy finger in history. Such was the fashioning of these United States of America into a new society of human freedom and dignity. Such too has been the restoration and rededication of an ancient people to nationhood upon Its ancient soil thrice hallowed by religious inspiration. . . . Our beloved America, reared in the spiritual heritage of ancient Israel's timeless book, helped the modern State of Israel come into being, and strengthened It during Its infant years. And little Israel has given as well as received. It has given an example of how to reclaim the soil and how to redeem human beings, of how to provide homes for the homeless, and boons of freedom and dignity for the underprivileged. . . . Grant, O God. that the bonds which make us feel a sense of spiritual kinship with Israel may grow with the years.

Treasuring America for supporting the Jewish state's continued existence is the most common theme for prayers containing Israel messages.

In the House on May 13, 1965, David Halpern asked God's "blessing upon these Members of our Congress, the spiritual heirs of those who were so instrumental in bestowing upon the seed of Israel the restoration of their homeland. May that sister democracy, together with all the world, know the blessing of peace."

Rabbis praying in Congress on an unfortunate date—April 20, Hitler's birthday—have used the occasion to celebrate the modern state of Israel foundation after the Holocaust. In 1961, Alex Goldman of Philadelphia asked that all the nations "with America at the forefront, lead the effort to bring peace and security, freedom and understanding, to all mankind. May Israel, as she celebrates her 13 years of independence this day, ever cherish the principles upon which democracy is founded." Again on Hitler's birthday, three years later, Milton Richman of Scranton, Pennsylvania, said in the Senate: "I rise as an American before our great leaders, and as an American of the Jewish faith, mindful of my brothers in the new State of Israel on their 16th birthday, and grateful for America's great help."

In the House on April 30, 1952, Hungarian-born Karl Applbaum of Bayside Jewish Center noted, "There are many nations which are thankful to our beloved country for the aid which we have given them in their struggle for freedom. Among them is the nation of Israel whose fourth anniversary is being celebrated today by all freedom-loving peoples of the world. Never will the children of Israel forget that our country was the first to recognize its independence and its right to exist as a free nation."

Applbaum prayed in the House again on April 29, 1963: "The Jewish people, the world over, shall be eternally grateful that at a critical juncture in human history 15 years ago, it was this august body which gave its support and recognition to the reestablishment in Thy Holy Land of an abode for the harrowed and harassed children of Israel." (When Applbaum returned to the House on February 26, 1970, New York Republican Rep. Seymour Halpern noted the rabbi "has been honored to deliver the invocation on three previous occasions in the House of Representatives, each time marking an anniversary of Israel.")

The next day in the Senate, his rabbinical brother Sidney Applbaum of Brooklyn's Congregation Beth Judah offered similar thanks to America for backing Israel in the early days: "It was our beloved country which by its recognition of the State of Israel enabled that ancient yet new land to open its heart and its doors to the oppressed remnants of the Hitler holocaust, holding aloft to the hapless returnees a vision of renewal and rebirth."[19]

And the *next* day in the Senate? On May 1, 1963, another rabbi opened the session with a prayer. An unprecedented three consecutive days. England-born Solomon Freehof of Pittsburgh's Rodeph Shalom Temple said, "On this 15th anniversary of the independence of the State of Israel, we thank Thee especially that among our allies is the small and precious Republic built In the Holy Land where Thou didst first reveal Thyself unto us all. The origins of this new state are much like ours."

As Israel continued to mark more anniversaries of its independence, so too did rabbis continue to remind Congress of Israel's kinship to America. These messages were particularly common in the '60s.

"On this day when my fellow Jews here and in the State of Israel celebrate the 16th year of its establishment," William Berkowitz of New York's Congregation B'nai Jeshurun said in the Senate on April 16, 1964, "we are grateful that the fallen tabernacle of David is risen up again, that Israel's ancient dream has come true with the noble help of these United States."

Again in the Senate a few days later, Richman of Scranton's Madison Avenue Temple gave the prayer. His April 20, 1964, offering—cited above— was one of a string of rabbis in the '60s from Pennsylvania with a similar pro-Israel message.

David Goldstein of Philadelphia's Har Zion Temple in the Senate on May 15, 1967: "We think especially today of the State of Israel, which celebrates the 19th anniversary of its foundation. In it we see a stronghold of democracy and a demonstration of the excellence of our ideals when they are put into practice and become a reality. We pray for Thy protecting care for the United States of America, for the State of Israel."

And Morris Landes of Pittsburgh's Congregation Adath Jeshurun in the Senate on May 2, 1968: "On this day, the 20th anniversary of the State of Israel, we are thankful as well for an ancient prophecy come true, whereby the people of the Bible have returned to the land of the Bible there to found once again a nation promised by Biblical Writ. We are grateful that the dream and the prophecy have joined together in the sympathetic support manifested by our great Nation to the concept of a reborn State of Israel during the decades when that State was aborning, and in the brotherly friendship

---

19 Hitler would not be mentioned again in a rabbi prayer for another five decades. Arnold Resnicoff in the Senate on September 1, 2017: "Today, in 1939, Hitler invades Poland."

that has prevailed in the two decades of Israel's existence between our own glorious and established democracy and the young democratic bastion in the Near East which is the State of Israel."

Nearly half—44% (15)—of the Israel mentions came during the 19 years between Israel's 1948 creation and the 1967 Six-Day War. Israel's strongest military alliance during that period was not with the United States, as it is now. It was with France. Things changed after 1967. France imposed an arms embargo on the Middle East, which mostly hurt Israel. And America became Israel's strongest political and military ally, forging the "special relationship" we now know. But during the period 1948-1967 Israel needed any help from America it could get—even divinely inspired rhetoric from the floor of Congress.

After the 1967 war, the number of mentions diminished. But here's a twist: Two rabbis gave House prayers *during* the Six-Day War. Neither mentioned Israel.

On June 6, 1967—day two of the war—Martin Halpern of Shaare Tefila Congregation in Washington, DC, spoke generally about "this time of crisis and threat to the safety of the world and to the security of all mankind." Nothing specific to Israel. The first congressman to follow Halpern with floor remarks, however, offered a quite pointed perspective on the war. Rep. Emanuel Celler (D-NY): "Israel stands alone. . . . Even the United States, pledged to protect the borders of Israel and to keep the Strait of Tiran open, falters. A State Department spokesman yesterday, despite the strongest, longstanding commitments, had the hardihood to speak of 'our neutrality in action, word, and deed.'"

And two days later, June 8—two-thirds of the way through Israel's quick and decisive victory—Alan Greenspan didn't mention Israel, either. What made his prayer even more intriguing is that he was an army chaplain in Vietnam. The year before he conducted a Passover Seder in Saigon for American troops. Similar to Halpern's offering, in Greenspan's prayer only general mentions of "troubled days" and "awesome problems." The timing of those days and location of those problems went unspecified.

Another rabbi—Joachim Prinz of Newark's Temple B'nai Abraham— placed his gratitude for Israel's creation somewhere else. He spoke of the Holocaust in the Senate on May 6, 1965. But instead of recognizing America for boosting Israel, Prinz credited an international organization which rarely makes the cut for admiration in the pro-Israel community. "The bloodletting of so many millions in the land of persecution and the perseverance of the Jewish people made the dream and prayers of Israel come true," Prinz said. "Seventeen years ago, with the concurrence and approval of the United Nations, the land of Israel was established. . . ." (The November 29, 1947, UN Partition Plan for Palestine recommended the creation of independent Arab and Jewish States. The Jewish Agency for Palestine accepted the Plan; Arab leaders and governments rejected it.)[20]

Interestingly, even surprisingly, it has been decades since a rabbi has opened Congress with a prayer marking Israel's birthday. As of April 2020, the last prayer with this explicit theme was delivered, as quoted above, by Kotok back on May 2, 1979—merely a month and a half after House floor proceedings began to be televised.

The most recent anniversary of any kind having to do with Israel cited in a prayer? May 21, 1998. Moshe Bomzer of Congregation Beth Abraham-Jacob in Albany, New York: "Let us also realize this coming Sunday, May 24th, marks the 31st anniversary of the reunification of the City of Jerusalem, eternal capital of the state of Israel."

And just one mention of the dominant pro-Israel lobbying organization. Not by a rabbi, but by his sponsor. Rep. Gus Bilirakis (R-FL) noted that Gary Klein of Temple Ahavat Shalom (guest chaplain on June 27, 2017) "currently serves on the National Council of AIPAC."

Meantime, several rabbis *from* Israel have made appearances in front of Congress.

The House has hosted two Chief Rabbis of Israel. Both born in Poland. The first was Shlomo Goren, the army rabbi who blew the shofar when Israeli troops captured the Temple Mount in 1967. He said, "With courage and vision the President inaugurated an era of peace and with wisdom and understanding, the lawmakers sustained his foundation of peace." That was June 24, 1974. Six weeks later, facing impeachment by lawmakers who had sustained his foundation of peace, President Nixon resigned.

The second, Yisrael Meir Lau, prayed on June 28, 1995. He offered a very specific message, a "thank you for the declaration and proclamation offering the Congressional Golden Medal and tribute in honor of the Lubavitcher Rebbe, Rabbi Menachem Mendel Schneerson."

Mordechai Elefant of the Israel Torah Research Institute opened the House in prayer on December 12, 1974. "As I touched the Wailing Wall

---

20 A year earlier, during the presidential campaign, Prinz told his congregants at sabbath evening services: "A Jewish vote for Goldwater is a vote for Jewish suicide" (*New York Times,* September 27, 1964).

which is a living symbol of Jerusalem," he said, "so I touch this lectern as a symbol of the power with which Thou hast endowed this body; and as You were with David who laid the cornerstone of Jerusalem and withstood the power of Goliath so shall You be with the men and women of this Chamber whose allegiance to You has passed on from the Torah and the prophets that followed."

You're far more likely, by the way, to see rabbis pray in the chambers of the U.S. Congress than in the chambers of the Knesset, the Israeli legislative body. The Knesset does not open its sessions with prayer.

Several more rabbis were born in Jerusalem in pre-war Israel—Palestine—and ended up with pulpits in America.

Tzvi Porath was rabbi of several synagogues in the Washington DC area. From 1960-1994 he offered four prayers in the Senate and one in the House. He was born in Jerusalem in 1916. His father Israel Porath—the "dean" of Cleveland's Orthodox rabbis for almost five decades, according to the *Encyclopedia of Cleveland History* website—gave the Senate prayer on June 5, 1964 (four years *after* his son gave his first Senate prayer). He too was born in Jerusalem, in 1886.

Others: Abraham Shoulson of Franklin Square Jewish Center in New York gave the House prayer on May 6, 1971. He was born in Jerusalem in 1917. David Shapiro of Temple Sinai in Hollywood, Florida, gave the House prayer on May 13, 1975; born in Jerusalem in 1907. Aaron Segal of B'nai Israel Congregation in Wilmington, North Carolina, gave the House prayer July 25, 1978; born in Jerusalem 1916. And Morris Margolies of Beth Shalom Congregation in Kansas City, Missouri, who gave the House prayer on February 25, 1986, was born in Jerusalem in 1921.

Atlanta Rabbi Harry Epstein, who gave the House prayer on March 16, 1978, was born in Lithuania. He became one of the first students at the Hebron Yeshiva in Palestine in 1924.

A rabbi *moving to* Israel got an official send-off after his July 1, 1957, prayer. The August 16, 1957, *Jewish Telegraphic Agency* reported: "The House of Representatives paid tribute to Rabbi Morton M. Berman of Chicago, Ill., who delivered an opening prayer this week. Members of Congress arose on the House floor to thank Rabbi Berman for delivering the prayer and noted that he is leaving the United States to make his home in Israel." And talk about bon voyage, how's this for the way-life-used-to-be nostalgia via Rep. Barratt O'Hara (D-IL): "Rabbi Berman, who served with great distinction and bravery in World War II . . . is leaving Chicago and his friends there to make his permanent residence in Israel. I understand he is sailing in the next day or two."

Sailing!

Even though he was moving to Israel—making *Aliyah*—Berman still incorporated a gracious patriotic American theme in his prayer: "As we approach the Day of Independence, our hearts are filled with the recollection of the sacred values upon which this Nation rests, upon the concept of equality of all men and of the right of all men to the enjoyment of those rights which God affords us and which our Nation guarantees to all the people."[21]

Two rabbis who gave prayers in Congress died around the time Israel gained independence. Gustav Hausmann was guest chaplain twice, in the House on February 28, 1899 and the Senate December 12, 1918. Hausmann died May 11, 1948, three days before Israel was born. Hausmann died May 11, 1948, three days before Israel was born. A week after Hausmann died, Joshua Liebman gave the first Congress prayer by a rabbi following Israel's creation. In the Senate on May 19, 1948, Liebman urged, "Inspire these lawgivers to make America an ever more beautiful gem of earth where cooperation shall be the dream and equal justice the dynamic goal—America thus the example to all the world. Cause us to realize that now all nations, from the oldest unto the newest, Israel, dwell today on the same street of atomic destiny, and therefore we must live and work together so that our children's children shall have a planet to inherit."

Three weeks later, June 9, 1948, Liebman died. He was 41. The next day, Sen. Leverett Saltonstall (R-Mass.) noted on the Senate floor, "Today the Chaplain in the first line of his prayer in opening the session of the Senate said, 'Every day we are reminded how fragile is the thread of our lives.' On May 19 Dr. Joshua Loth Liebman of Temple Israel, Boston, Mass, acted as Chaplain of the Senate. He was a great America, a fine churchman, and an inspiring orator. In this morning's newspaper we read of his untimely death following a sudden heart attack." Saltonstall continued, "I am deeply sorry to hear of his passing, but proud that I knew a great American and a fine

---

21 A year earlier, a guest chaplain with his own early connection to Israel was Baptist. New Jersey Rev. Dwight Baker was sent to Nazareth in the 1950s to rebuild the Baptist Mission to the Holy Land. In the House on February 1, 1956, he prayed for God "to give divine wisdom and guidance to President Eisenhower and Prime Minister Eden as they confront themselves with the urgent problems of the Middle East and other areas strained by tension." Eisenhower and Eden had wrapped up talks in Washington that day. The Suez Crisis occurred later that year.

churchman." Liebman's June 10, 1948, *New York Times* obituary also noted he left behind an adopted daughter, "a Polish-born refuge, whose parents were killed during the Nazi purges."

Perhaps even more striking than the limited amount of pro-Israel language found in rabbi prayers in Congress is the number of times Zionism has been specifically mentioned: Zero.

In fact, some of the earliest rabbis to offer prayers—before the state of Israel was established—are notable in Jewish American history for being vocal *anti*-Zionists.

The small group of anti-Zionists was a persistent part of the American Jewish community before World War II. For some, creating a Jewish nation-state contradicted the notion of a return to Israel only after the coming of the Messiah. Others on the more secular end of American Judaism saw the U.S. as a true homeland, which had allowed for expansive educational opportunities and with less anti-Semitism compared to European pogroms and discrimination in other parts of the world.

Norman Gerstenfeld of the Reform Washington Hebrew Congregation, who delivered two of his five Senate prayers before Israel gained independence, "spoke ardently against the idea of a Jewish state," according to the *Jewish Virtual Library*. In *Jewish Studies at the Turn of the Twentieth Century*, Marc Lee Raphael includes a chapter titled "Rabbi Norman Gerstenfeld's Crusade Against Zionism, 1935-1948." Raphael writes on Gerstenfeld's radio addresses as a platform for opposing Zionism. Gerstenfeld noted that among his listeners were "every member" of the Senate Foreign Relations Committee.[22]

Another Reform rabbi, Louis Wolsey of Philadelphia Congregation Rodeph Shalom, gave the House prayer on February 8, 1940. Two years later Wolsey founded the American Council for Judaism. Wolsey's Council was, according to *Jews Against Zionism: The American Council for Judaism, 1942-1948* by Thomas Kolsky, "the only American Jewish organization ever created to fight Zionism and the establishment of a Jewish state."[23]

Not just a few rabbis. Some Jewish lay leaders, too, were vocally anti-Zionist. In September 1918, former New York State Attorney General Simon Rosendale—an organizational leader of Reform Jews—wrote a lengthy letter to Rep. Rollin Sanford (R-NY). He called Zionism "pretentious" and

---

22   Brill, 1999, page 354.
23   Temple University Press, 1990, page 1.

compared it to "distasteful, dangerous, and outworn doctrines . . . from the evils of which the world is being more and more saved." Sanford included every single one of Rosendale's 2,394 words in the January 31, 1919, *Congressional Record*.

World War II changed minds. "Before World War II there was great debate in the Jewish world over Zionism. Reform Judaism, for example, was for decades anti-Zionist," Charles Krauthammer wrote in the May 11, 1998, *Weekly Standard*. "The Holocaust resolved that debate."

Indeed, after Israel was established many rabbis like Gerstenfeld and Wolsey who had previously been anti-Zionist switched sides. They became champions of the Jewish state. For Wolsey it was a profound reckoning with world reality. At a New York City Hanukkah ceremony on December 18, 1927, according to the next day's *New York Times*, Wolsey said, "Twenty-five years ago the Jew was so much afraid of the pinpricks of anti-Semitism that he was guilty of an awkward self-consciousness. The ordinary observer of Jewish life must not note that the fever of Jew hatred is passing from the souls of the nations." Four months before Wolsey's remarks, the Nazi Party held its first rally at Nuremberg.

23: Econ 101

"A man who does his prayers in public."
—Mark Twain's definition of Publicans, Jewish tax collectors for
the ancient Romans

"Jewish genius in finance has become proverbial and need not be discussed by me. Suffice it to say that the Rothschilds determined for decades in Europe questions of peace and war. Other great Jewish financiers In Europe are the Bleichröders of Germany. The Schiffs, Seligmans, and Guggenheims are well-known American financiers."
—Rep. Walter Chandler (R-NY), June 30, 1922

In addition to God, spirituality, tradition, and many more faith-based attributes, Judaism is replete with economic guidance. Macro and micro alike. A sample:

- Leviticus 25:29: "Anyone who sells a house in a walled city retains the right of redemption a full year after its sale. During that time the seller may redeem it."

- Amos 8:4-5: "You who trample the needy and do away with the poor of the land, saying, 'When will the New Moon be over that we may sell grain, and the Sabbath be ended that we may market wheat?'—skimping on the measure, boosting the price and cheating with dishonest scales."
- Talmud: "Whoever does not teach his son a trade, it is as though he taught him to commit robbery."
- Talmud: "If one buys and sells on trust, he must not compute the inferior goods on trust and the superior at par, but either both on trust or both at par."
- Proverbs 14:23: "In all labor there is profit."
- Maimonides: "The greatest level [of charity], above which there is no greater, is to support a fellow Jew by endowing him with a gift or loan, or entering into a partnership with him, or finding employment for him, in order to strengthen his hand until he need no longer be dependent upon others."

And more. Enough teachings, it would seem, to round out the curriculum of a first-year business school class.

So why shouldn't rabbis supply their own economic thoughts to Congress?

Indeed, they have.

Rabbi prayers offer an economy of words. From the ways and means of broad theory and concepts . . .

- "As we approach Labor Day, we pray that the representatives of capital and labor will realize that both are vital and indispensable partners in our unparalleled economic order, and that both must plan and labor together in harmony in order to promote a better way of life." (Norman Zdanowitz, King's Park Jewish Center, Long Island, in the House on August 29, 1967.)
- "Bless the President of these United States upon whom rests a heavy burden to satisfy all diverse elements in his constituency. The task which he has undertaken is most demanding. He needs Thy help so that he might steer our ship of state through the turbulent waters of conflict, misunderstanding, war. and inflation." (Karl Applbaum, Avenue "M" Jewish Center, Brooklyn, in the House on February 26, 1970.)

. . . to the practical and consumer-oriented.

- "We come together from the world of committee hearings, meetings with constituents, the morning headlines, and the Dow Jones average." (Sheldon Elster, Agudas Achim Congregation of Northern Virginia, in the Senate on July 31, 1973.)
- "Grant a complete and rapid recovery to our energy crisis so that those who are in discomfort may once again become comfortable." (Barnett Hasden, Beth Israel Synagogue, Bristol, Connecticut, in the House on February 1, 1977. President Carter addressed the nation on energy two months later.)

And even some differing thoughts on the importance of money in our lives.

This:

"Bestow Your blessing upon the Members of this House. Grant them good health, family enrichment, financial security, and the wisdom to decide issues with prudence and compassion." (Edward Davis, Young Israel Temple, Hollywood, Florida, in the House on June 4, 1996.)

Or this:

"Money alone cannot substitute for the foundation and grounding that parents, grandparents, and families provide." (Joel Tessler, Temple Beth Sholom, Potomac, Maryland, in the House on November 9, 1999).

With some contemporary business news headlines thrown in, too.

Missed CNBC the morning of September 13, 1990, a year after the cable business channel launched? No worries. You might have gotten caught up with business headlines by watching the rabbi of Young Israel, Staten Island, open the House. "Yesterday in New York major philanthropists overnight became paupers as the Japanese banks foreclosed on 43 major real estate buildings," Jay Marcus said. "Overnight magnates of real estate have been broken. During these days of awe we realize that man's quest for power, and dominion and acts of aggression are puny, misguided and doomed to failure."

Plus national economic advice from a rabbi from another nation, no less.

During late 2012 anguish over the looming "fiscal cliff," Congress got both a budgetary lesson and a rock-climbing tutorial from the rabbi of Canada's largest synagogue, Beth Tzedec Congregation in Toronto. "Rather than fear falling off a cliff, help our leaders to learn to chimney," Baruch Frydman-Kohl said in the Senate on November 29. "In climbing, chimneying requires pushing off one side of a mountain cleft and then the other to advance higher. The resistance of each face of the rock contributes to the ascent. Help these leaders to appreciate individual initiative and care for the distressed, to value competition and find a path for cooperation, to be mindful of human liberty and be grateful for mutual help, to recognize the occasional need for force and to forcefully pursue peace. Enable them to chimney up the cleft of our differences, to reclaim fiscal integrity and maintain social concern, to be exemplars of responsibility and reasonableness."

Frydman-Kohl had a family connection to the business world and the Senate. Cousin Herbert Kohl (D-WI) sponsored him. Kohl made his fortune as heir to the department store retail chain that bears his family name and presumably sells rock climbing sportswear.

Arnold Resnicoff was the first rabbi guest chaplain in the House after Democrat Nancy Pelosi regained the speakership in 2019. In a prayer shortly after the federal government reopened following a record 35-day partial shutdown—what many political observers called a Pelosi victory over President Trump—his message to all powerful people was unmistakable. "We the people don't give up. Neither should our leaders," he said on February 6. "Let our nation never slumber: no closings, fits and starts; no honest pay denied for honest work; no time out from efforts to improve our lives, achieve our dreams."

In one Senate prayer. a non-Jewish clergyman borrowed from Jewish tradition—and the Bethesda Naval Medical Center—to underscore a president's point on national fiscal matters. On July 13, 1985, doctors removed a tumor from Ronald Reagan's colon. Moments after leaving the operation recovery room, Reagan said he wanted to solve the budget deficit "this week." His urgent fiscal plea apparently was heeded by the Senate chaplain. Richard Halverson cited Isaiah 10:1-2 when he prayed three days later: "Woe to those who make unjust laws, to those who issue oppressive decrees, to deprive the poor of their rights and rob the oppressed people of justice; making widows their prey and robbing the fatherless." Halverson then drew this spiritual and oncological conclusion: "The warning of Isaiah is timely. Like a malignancy, the national deficit permeates and infects every issue that confronts the leadership of our Republic. And it will not go away. Thou knowest the confusion, the pressures, the conflict, that compound the already difficult task of making numbers come out right."

(Senate chaplain Frederick Brown Harris incorporated tragic Jewish history in an economy-themed February 5, 1961, op-ed in the *Washington Star*: "It may take the dread threat of another world holocaust to change the lusty cry, both from those who have much and from those who by comparison have much less, 'give me, give me.' Certainly in the present day demands for a paternalistic Government we have raised a generation who think much more of a bill of rights than they do of a bill of responsibilities.")

Rabbis have had their own background in finance and economics—even lineage.

Ely Rosenzveig of Congregation Anshe Shalom in New Rochelle, New York, gave the House prayer on May 9, 2001. Rep. Nita Lowey (D-NY) pointed out he was "a master of economics and student of Talmud."

John Linder of Temple Solel in Paradise Valley, Arizona, offered the House prayer on March 22, 2016. Rep. Ruben Gallego (D-AZ) noted Linder "spent his early years as a community and labor organizer, and later helped run his family's scrap metal recycling business before entering rabbinic school."

One hundred and forty years earlier—July 13, 1876—Max Lilienthal gave the House prayer. He had his own considerable business family connections. Three years after his House prayer, his son Philip married Belle Seligman, daughter of banker and businessman Joseph Seligman. He had helped refinance the Union's Civil War debt. President Ulysses Grant offered Seligman the top post at the Treasury Department. He declined, sticking with his business career.[24] Seligman would have been the first Jewish treasury secretary. Henry Morgenthau earned that distinction in Franklin Roosevelt's administration.[25]

---

24 *The Universal Jewish Encyclopedia*, 1943, edited by Isaac Landman, page 469.

25 Another Seligman connection to Grant via Joseph's brothers Jesse and Henry. In his 2017 *Grant* biography, Ron Chernow described those two as "Bavarian Jewish brothers who became lifetime friends and later emerged as wealthy bankers and substantial donors to Grant's presidential campaign." Meantime, lest there be any doubt about the Seligman connection to Jewish tradition, consider that among the siblings' names were Genesis-inspired Abraham, Isaac, Jacob, and Joseph. Plus a sister. You guessed it: Sara.)

Today, if you're making money through funds managed by Seligman Investments, you have the descendants of the fifth rabbi to open the House of Representatives in prayer to thank.

One rabbi had an unusual career path which nearly included business. Stephen Baars opened the Senate on May 22, 2008. Sen. Joe Lieberman (D-CT) listed his curriculum vitae:

> Born and raised in London, Rabbi Baars originally envisioned himself working in business or sales until, at age 19, he went on vacation to Israel and became enamored with Judaism. When he finally returned to London 6 months later, he had made up his mind to become a rabbi. . . . After completing his studies, Rabbi Baars moved to Los Angeles to work for Aish HaTorah. It was in L.A. that he tried a second career as a stand-up comedian. On the advice of a friend, Rabbi Baars began taking comedy classes at UCLA and performing standup in clubs. In fact, he is the only rabbi to have performed at the famous L.A. Improv. Eventually, he would stop performing because he found his spiritual work more rewarding. His comedic skills, however, would play a role in his future work, serving as means for him to get his message across to audiences. In 1990, Rabbi Baars moved to the Washington, DC, region and began teaching Jewish studies classes throughout the DC area. Some of his students included Senators, Representatives, and top business leaders.

Those three potential career paths—businessman, rabbi, standup comedian—do share one common trait: Always making the sale.

24: Space, A Rabbi's Final Frontier

"When you look up to the sky and behold the sun and the moon and the stars, the whole heavenly host, you must not be lured into bowing down to them or serving them."

—Deuteronomy 4:19

*"When I behold Thy heavens, the work of Thy fingers,
the moon and the stars, which Thou hast established;
What is man, that Thou art mindful of him?"*

—Psalms 8:4-5

"The heavens are the heavens of the Lord; but the earth hath He given to the children of men"

—Psalms 115:16

"We are now approaching lunar sunrise, and for all the people back on Earth, the crew of Apollo 8 has a message that we would like to send to you. In the beginning God created the heaven and the earth. . . ."

—Astronaut William Enders, December 2, 1968

Space is no final frontier for a rabbi praying in Congress. Rabbis have been zooming to the stars for over 50 years, incorporating America's space program in their messages to the House and Senate.

On February 20, 1962, John Glenn became the first American to orbit the earth. He did so three times. On May 24, 1962, Scott Carpenter also orbited the earth three times. And on June 18, 1962, Samuel Scolnic of Congregation Beth-El in Bethesda, Maryland, ascended to the House rostrum. His prayer was a sobering response—a buzz kill, even—to America's giddiness over the right stuff:

> We have turned our attention to the vast reaches of outer space, but we know all too well the harrowing problems that continue to plague us here on earth. The mysteries of Thy universe beckon to us, but the hard realities of this planet will not leave us. If one crisis follows another, it is because our earth has become a tiny, shrunken, little planet.

Scolnic's prayer seemed rhetorically linked to a landmark speech delivered at the Capitol the year before. "Let both sides seek to invoke the wonders of science instead of its terrors," President John F. Kennedy urged in his January 20, 1961, inaugural address. "Together let us explore the stars, conquer the deserts, eradicate disease, tap the ocean depths and encourage the arts and commerce."[26]

The following year featured a spacecraft with an appropriate name: Faith. And a prayer a bit more celebratory. In the House on May 16, 1963, Rabbi Nathan Taragin prayed for God "to bless Astronaut L. Gordon Cooper's orbital flights to culminate successfully and his space capsule Faith 7 to return safely." Which it did.

The space program continued to capture rabbis' imagination as the years of exploration continued.

---

26   JFK's next line invoked a Jewish prophet: "Let both sides unite to heed in all corners of the earth the command of Isaiah—to 'undo the heavy burdens . . . (and) let the oppressed go free.'"

Unmanned Lunar Orbiter 4 was taking pictures of the moon when Herbert Bomzer of Brooklyn opened the Senate on May 23, 1967: "In this space age, help us to conquer the space we have permitted to develop between ourselves and our fellow men."

Howard Simon of Baltimore gave the House prayer on May 26, 1969— the same day as the splashdown of Apollo 10. He smartly opened by citing I Kings 8:27: "And the heaven of heavens shall not contain Thee." And then suggested, "we stand in admiration of three men who have realized this potential. They are the voice of America, a land of limitless possibilities."

On July 24, 1969, the Apollo 11 astronauts returned to Earth. During the mission, Neil Armstrong and Buzz Aldrin became the first humans on the moon. Michael Collins played the crucial but less-heralded role of running the ship and keeping it safe for the pair's return from the lunar surface. Five days later in the House, Baruch Korff of Congregation Agudath Achim in Taunton, Massachusetts, thanked "the Lord, who has called this Nation in righteousness and set it for a light among the planets." Korff lauded one of the Nixon administration's most notable accomplishments years before becoming identified in public opinion as a defender of the only president to resign, under threat of impeachment by the House and near-certain conviction and removal in the Senate.

Nearly a year earlier, on July 25, 1968, when a successful moon landing by man was no sure thing, Seymour Stauber of Ahavas Sholom in Randallstown, Maryland, prayed in the Senate. "In the past century, we have uncovered the veiled secrets of our universe," he said. "We are conquering outer space."

By 1971 men were on the moon. Psalm 23 assures, "The Lord is my shepherd; I shall not want. He maketh me to lie down in green pastures." But not just lie down—a Shephard can zoom sky high. "On this day in 1971, Alan Shephard hit two golf balls on the moon," Arnold Resnicoff remembered in the House on February 6, 2019. "First human swings beyond the confines of the earth." The citation of Apollo 14 was also the only mention of golf by a guest chaplain rabbi.

But contemporaneously in 1971, one dour rabbi had seen enough of the outer reaches. Perhaps he found no value in lunar golf. On February 25 in the House, Haim Kemelman of the Jewish Center in East Brunswick, New Jersey, opted for buzzkill instead of Buzz Aldrin. Kemelman hoped "we may move forward from our Apollo-moon project to an Apollo-man project: to banish dread disease; to conquer the dark craters of the mind;

to heal bruised hearts; to master the inner, space of man for peace in trust-power, as we have mastered the outer space of the moon with thrust-power; to see a new heartrise of man, as we have seen a new earth-rise from the moon." Kemelman added warily, "It is more important to bring heaven down to earth than to bring man up to heaven."

Likewise, a few weeks after the Apollo 16 manned moon mission, Irving Greenberg advocated more pressing needs on earth. "May our vision exploring the heavens, bringing men back safely," the New York rabbi said in the House on May 16, 1972, "overcome our blindness neglecting earth, abandoning men to suffering."

The rabbis' concerns about prioritizing domestic and other world concerns above space exploration mirrored the public's fading interest in NASA's work. The 1995 movie *Apollo 13* depicted network television executives' reluctance to carry the star-crossed mission live due to declining ratings in space missions. It only became a national story when the three astronauts on board were imperiled by a technical malfunction and their lives endangered—a mission that thankfully ended with the trio's safe ocean splashdown.

And while space missions generally spurred soaring rhetoric by public officials in the JFK mold, some were less enthusiastic. As a senator in the early 1970s, Walter Mondale (D-MN) opposed funding for what would become the Space Shuttle program, saying the billions in public funds it required would be better spent fighting poverty, hunger and other, more tangible earth-bound maladies. Well into the 1990s, Rep. Barney Frank (D-MA) made similar arguments about funding for the international space station.[27]

Despite those scattered concerns, by the early 1980s the Space Shuttle program returned America to aeronautic giddiness. The Challenger had just landed after its third mission when Senate chaplain Richard Halverson prayed on September 13, 1983. Among that Shuttle's crew: Guion Bluford, the first African-American to fly in space. Halverson opened the Senate: "'He's got the whole world in His hands.' Father God, we thank Thee for the profound truth in this simple Negro spiritual." Then Halverson went Jewish, citing the Hebrew Bible, Isaiah 40:15: "We recall our first view of the Earth from space—like a colorful marble—a speck floating in vastness. Isaiah the prophet declared, 'Behold the nations are as a drop in the bucket,

---

27 One bill Frank co-sponsored, H.R. 3687 introduced on November 22, 1993, was titled quite efficiently: "To Cancel The Space Shuttle Program".

and are counted as the small dust of the balance.'" Halverson suggested, "We act as though we are the center of the universe. Help us to see ourselves as Thou dost see us, infinitesimal by comparison to the universe around us."

The Hebrew word for God made an appearance when Senate Chaplain Lloyd John Ogilvie offered a space-themed prayer prayed on July 8, 1997. Ogilvie got quite specific in his enthusiasm: "O Yahweh, our Adonai. . . . Our eyes have been glued to our television sets to witness the awesome achievement of landing Pathfinder on Mars and we have seen the venture of rover Sojourner on Martian rock after a 309-million-mile, 7-month journey from Earth. Guide our space scientists as they gather information about Mars and we are reminded of the reaches of Your Lordship."

Another mention of space travel by a rabbi followed tragedy. The Challenger exploded January 28, 1986. The first Space Shuttle mission after the Challenger, on Discovery, launched September 29, 1988. That same day Jeffrey Wohlberg of Adas Israel Congregation in Washington, DC, was in the Senate. "We add our personal and collective prayers," he said, "for our astronauts. May they ascend in peace and return in peace." Which they did.

A rabbi guest chaplain is connected to the second Space Shuttle tragedy. Columbia broke up on February 1, 2003, killing its seven-member crew. The memorial service was held three days later in Houston. Among the participants was Navy chaplain Harold Robinson. He eulogized Ilan Ramon, the first Israeli astronaut for NASA. "When we view our little planet from out in space, we learn the unity of all humanity here on earth," Robinson said. He served as Senate guest chaplain four years later.

America's swashbuckling Buck Rogers space travel days may be behind us. But one guest chaplain will be enshrined in the stars forever. Thomas Louchheim of Tucson gave the House prayer on May 17, 2017. His influence, though, extends past Arizona. And even beyond Earth. Next time you look up at the heavens, look closely for asteroid 9584 Louchheim. It's the only space object in the universe named after a rabbi. And how fitting that in English, the name of his synagogue, Or Chadash, means "new light."

25: Green Prayers: The Environment

"And out of the ground made the Lord to grow every tree that is pleasant to the sight, and good for food; the tree of life also in the midst of the garden, and the tree of the knowledge of good and evil."
—Genesis 2:9

"She is a tree of life to them that lay hold upon her, and happy is every one that holdest her fast."

—Proverbs 3:18

Meantime, down on terra firma and a third of a mile from the U.S. Botanic Garden: The environment and related earthly wonders have sparked equally soaring language by rabbis offering prayers in the Capitol building.

Milton Balkany of Brooklyn's Congregation Bais Yaakov painted a vivid landscape in the Senate on June 25, 2003. "Let our notes wend their way from the hot Mojave sands to the cool waters of the Great Lakes," he said. "Let our song echo in the footsteps of Lewis and Clark as they courageously unraveled the mysteries of this free land. Let our lyrical prayer soar up the peaks of Mount Hood and Mount McKinley until they reach the summit of Your glory and Your mercy."

Balkany's American geography overview continued the very next day in the House. "The majestic sequoias tower over the Alpine expanses, and yet they continue to stretch upward toward the sun," he rejoiced. "The mighty Colorado River carved the awesome grandeur of the Grand Canyon eons ago, yet it continues to surge ever onward. The thrashing tide of the Atlantic has brought innumerable ships to port, and yet the waves ebb and flow without cease."

Balkany's earthy enthusiasm did not stop there. Back in the Senate on March 22, 2007, he admired that "snowflakes windswept to sky-piercing peaks do more than cloak mountaintops in their fine wintry vestments. Their varied crystalline structures speak of how You, the Master Artist, have sculpted our world to exemplify the beauty of contrast." He queried: "Consider the rent of rock running through the Grand Canyon. It is a break, a fissure, a divide miles deep and, yet, is there a sight more majestic?"

Less grandiose in adjectives but no less sweeping in scope: The prayer Jacob Rudin of Temple Beth El, Great Neck, New York, offered the House. "Our land is fertile," he said on April 5, 1967, "her mountains robed with majesty, her heavens traced with the proud beat of eagles' wings. Everywhere in the outer world, distance; the far horizon, the long reaches to the stars, the deep-sounding seas."

Seasons can dictate environment-themed prayers.

Stuart Weinblatt of Congregation B'nai Tzedek in Potomac, Maryland, informed the Senate on February 6, 1996: "This time of year is referred to on the Jewish calendar as Tu B'Shevat, the New Year of the Trees. Since ancient times, this day, in the dead of winter, serves to remind us of the human responsibility to care for the Earth, affirms the importance of planting trees, and thus asserts the intricate relationship between humanity and the environment in which we live."

Springtime 1978 brought two particularly plant-friendly prayers in the Senate. On May 3, Alex Pollack of Philadelphia's Congregation Emanu-El exclaimed, "After a night of rest, this morning the sun rose to herald a new day. New flowers have bloomed and the plants have borne new fruit. Let us, here in these hallowed Chambers, be inspired and refreshed by the ever-renewing miracles of life and God's laws of the universe."

And on May 18, 1978, Jacob Max of Randallstown, Maryland, said, "You put forth grass and fruit trees on this firmament. Teach us to share Your bounty, each fruit in its season, with those who are hungry." And, "You created every creature that creepeth, every winged fowl and every fish in the sea." After creepeth creatures, he continued, "You created cattle and beasts and man on the same day but not in the same image. Teach us to transcend the animal kingdom by being decent, just, and fair, lest there comes a day when the 'beasts' will run free."

Warren Stone of another Maryland synagogue, Temple Emanuel in Kensington, also went green. "Our time on Earth is short; we are like a flower that will fade," he said in the House on July 11, 1996, "a cloud passing by, like dust floating on the wind, a dream soon forgotten." No wonder Rep. Connie Morella (R-MD) said, "Rabbi Stone is a staunch environmentalist, and often weaves into his sermons messages about the importance of protecting our natural resources and maintaining a safe and healthy environment." Put another way, Stone rocked the House.

During Sukkot Jews celebrate the autumn harvest and dwell in a foliage-covered booth. Hannah Spiro prayed in the House on September 24, 2018—the first day of Sukkot. "God, we thank You for the Jewish festival of Sukkot . . . and for Your commandment to build temporary structures, to eat and sleep in them under the stars, and to welcome in guests," the rabbi of Hill Havurah near Capitol Hill in Washington, DC, said. "May the Sukkot season and the beauty of changing autumn leaves inspire each one of us to welcome, to serve, and, for this brief time we are allotted, to generously live." A year earlier in the House, on October 24, David-Seth Kirshner of Temple Emanu-El in Closter, New Jersey, hoped that America's future generations "can enjoy the blooming flowers and sweet fruits of our labors."

The environment is not just for modern-day worship. Several natural elements were combined in the House on January 7, 1930. Louis Newman of San Francisco prayed, "Make us to know, O Lord, that though the rock be strong and iron-cleaving, that iron be strong and fire melting, that water quench fire, that the clouds gather up the water, that the winds dispel the clouds, that man is stronger than the winds."

The tree of life—*Etz Chaim*, found in Genesis and several places in Proverbs—gets its due, as well. Four synagogues whose names include *Etz* or Tree have sprouted rabbis who sprung prayers:

- Congregation Tree of Life, Valley Stream, New York (Bertram Leff, September 12, 1967, in the House)
- Congregation Etz Jacob in Los Angeles (Mark Brener, July 1, 1968, in the Senate)
- Congregation Etz Chaim, Flossmoor, Illinois (Chaim Rozwaski, June 8, 1976, in the House)
- Tree of Life Congregation, Pittsburgh (Alvin Berkun, twice: May 8, 1991 in the Senate, and October 14, 1993 in the House. The Pittsburgh congregation tragically rose to national prominence in fall 2018 when a white nationalist gunman stormed Shabbat morning services and killed 11 service attendees)

Despite these congregations having eco-friendly names, none of the prayers mentioned anything green.

Perhaps the best soil stewardship came during a World War II-era prayer, drawing contrast with that global struggle. Israel Goldstein of Congregation B'nai Jeshurun borrowed from Micah 4:4 when he opened the House. "May victory crown our hopes, our labors, and our sacrifices," the rabbi said on April 21, 1942, "and bring nearer the day when all men shall dwell in safety, everyone under his vine and under his fig tree, with none to make him afraid."

Goldstein was in good company for using that citation. In *Reading the Bible with the Founding Fathers* Daniel Dreisbach called Micah 4:4's vine and fig tree "George Washington's favorite biblical phrase."[28]

---

28 Oxford University Press, 2017, page 212.

SECTION VI

War, Evil, Terror

26: War!

*"Strife runs rampant in the land, mounting din and discord.
Aberration sweeps the world, escalating madness—war!"*
  —Rabbi Murry Penkower, Congregation Hope of Israel in the
    Bronx, opening the House in prayer September 20, 1967.

War!

In a rabbi's prayer? Yes. Quite often, in fact. And well before the heart
of that very dark war in Vietnam that coincided with Penkower's prayer.

The agonies of battle—in contrast to the aspirations of Isaiah—made
their rhetorical way into rabbi Congress prayers almost 100 years before the
war between North and South Vietnam. They started with the war between
America's own North and South.

The first prayer offered by a rabbi guest chaplain came just over a year
before the Civil War began. The national descent toward disunion was well
underway. With prophetic use of Psalms 133:1, Morris Raphall said in the
House on February 4, 1860:

> Let Thy grace guide them, so that amidst the din of conflicting Interests and
> opinions, they may each of them and all of them hold the even tenor of their
> way—the way of moderation and of equity—that they may speak and act
> and legislate for Thy glory and for the happiness of our country; so that from
> North and from South and from East and West, one feeling of satisfaction
> may attend their labors while all the people of the land joyfully repeat the
> words of Thy Psalmist: "Lo! how good and how pleasant it is for brethren to
> dwell together in unity."

Fourteen months after Raphall suggested Americans be joyful and brethren dwell together in unity, the Civil War began. Don't tell the Psalmist.

During the smoldering aftermath of that brutal war, London-born Canadian Abraham de Sola became the fifth rabbi guest chaplain in Congress. He opened the House on January 9, 1872, with a celebration seemingly grounded in Reconstruction:

> Thou permittest us, even now, to witness a victory of peace infinitely greater than any victory achieved in war, at any time, and by any people, in that this nation and its parent nation are settling their differences, not by might, not by power, but by Thy spirit . . . as aforetime and among other peoples many a vindictive and bloody struggle, destroying both the material resources and oral sense of those engaged, has originated in much less important considerations, we have special cause to thank Thee that this evil was averted.

De Sola also suggested, "in all their deliberations for the public weal, let not personal or partisan hostility find place; but suffer harmony, patriotism, truth, and justice to pervade them, so that to bigotry there may be given no sanction, and to persecution no assistance." *Bigotry no sanction.* That's language from President George Washington's August 1790 Letter to the Hebrew Congregations of Newport, Rhode Island (now the historic Touro Synagogue). It was the first of nine times Washington's famous passage would be cited by a rabbi guest chaplain.

A few decades later, shortly before America joined Europe in the Great War, Isidore Lewinthal opened the House. On January 17, 1917, the Nashville rabbi prayed, "We stand upon a shore unshaken, to look out upon the nations of the earth that are rocked and tossed as a ship upon the sea bestormed. We are in peace, while they are in tumult; we are without blood, while they are walking in garments rolled in blood."

Less than three months later, America would be "*with blood.*"

Edward Browne gave two prayers in Congress while America was fighting World War I. Both offered identical descriptions of Woodrow Wilson. In the House on December 13, 1917, the New York City rabbi gave a "special blessing upon the President of the United States, our olive-branch President, who is waging an olive-branch war in order to bring about an olive-branch, genuine peace amongst all the nations of the earth." Likewise, in the Senate on August 30, 1918, Browne gave a "special blessing upon the President of the United States, our 'olive-branch' President, who is waging this 'olive-branch' war to give a genuine 'olive-branch' peace to this blood-flooded world." Browne also prayed for God's "special guidance for our own patriotic boys who are now ready to lay down their lives for the cause of justice and humanity, each of them being a 'lamb of God that taketh away the sins of the world.'"

World War I ended November 11, 1918. A month later another New York City rabbi opened the Senate. On December 12, Gustav Hausmann credited God with the successful Allied outcome: "Thou who didst grant unto us the privilege of being victorious on the side of right against might; Thou who didst choose America to enlighten the nations of the earth; Thou who didst endow us with the gift and spirit of democracy, we beseech Thee to continue to guide and lead us." Planning ahead, he added, "May the deliberations at the peace conference abroad result for the great benefit of humanity and redound to the honor of this Nation."[29]

The wish that liberty be enjoyed by all people of the earth was tested again with the next World War. A few days before Pearl Harbor and America's entry into World War II, Julius Mark of Nashville's Vine Street Temple gave the House prayer. Foreboding language dominated the rabbi's December 1, 1941, offering. Starting with, "In a time when the dark forces of tyranny and oppression compass us. . . ." Continuing with, "amid the encircling gloom." And ending with an eve-of-war flourish: "Suffer not their adversaries to triumph over them, but let the glories of a just, righteous, and God-fearing people increase from age to age. We invoke Thy blessing not because we are better than other men, but because we would be worthy of receiving it by living honorably, courageously, and usefully."

Mark was on the House floor six days before Pearl Harbor. One day before another milestone World War II event, another rabbi gave an opening prayer. He, too, was unaware that in mere hours the wartime world would dramatically change. Nonetheless Solomon Metz of Adas Israel Congregation in Washington, DC, likewise offered words that hinted at impressive (divinely inspired?) military foresight. Here's Rabbi Metz opening the Senate on June 5, 1944 a day before D-Day:

---

29 Some non-Jewish history surrounding Congress-opening prayers from this era. The first prayer delivered by a Senator on the floor was April 5, 1917. The Senate was voting to declare war on Germany. Sen. Reed Smoot (R-UT), a Mormon and ordained LDS apostle, prayed: "God bless and approve the action to be taken by the Senate this day. Oh, Father, preserve our government and hasten the day when liberty will be enjoyed by all the people of the earth." For reasons lost to history, the prayer can be found in a 1922 edition of *The All-American Cook Book: Being A Collection Chiefly of Recipes of the Favorite Dishes of Famous Americans*.

In this hour of crisis in our struggle with the cruel enemy, when the fate of the world trembles in the scales of destiny, we turn to Thee in humility and contrition, praying from the depths: Be Thou with our armed forces on land, on sea, and in the air. Guide them and sustain them. Grant us a speedy and decisive victory.

A "decisive" victory, yes. Eventually. But "speedy"? Not before Samuel Thurman opened the Senate on February 26, 1945: "Our hearts being heavy laden with anxiety and sorrow that the flower of our youth, the strong and the brave, the free sons and daughters of America, must now be offering themselves in fierce and cruel combat against enemies that either do not know Thee or have forgotten Thee and Thy commandments," the St. Louis rabbi said. "They scoff at Thy power and scorn Thy law of justice and right-eousness. Grant speedy victory to our brave fighting forces—a victory that shall bring in a new order of fellowship and faith and lasting justice and peace."

Max Raisin of B'nai Jeshurun in New Jersey wrapped up World War II-themed prayers on January 30, 1947, in the House: "In the grim struggle through which we have just passed Thou hast strengthened our arms and hast finally blest us with victory."

No similar victory lap for Vietnam War-themed prayers.

The messaging started out strong: confident, proud, reflecting good faith. On February 21, 1966, as the number of American troops in Vietnam was still climbing toward an eventual top level of over half a million, Norman Zdanowitz gave the House prayer. "Vouchsafe Thy blessings upon the gallant men of our Armed Forces who have gone forth to arrest the reckless wave of unprovoked aggression and bloodshed on distant shores," the Maine rabbi said. "Crown their efforts with triumph and enable them to achieve the suppression of tyranny and lawlessness. May the United States remain a citadel of freedom and a watchtower from which rays of light and hope shall be beamed to those who are now living in darkness, poverty, and despair."

The first specific mention of Vietnam by name from a rabbi guest chaplain was just over a week later. Opening the Senate on March 1, Louis Wolfish said, "Guard and protect the members of our Armed Forces in Vietnam and throughout the rest of the world." Another specific men-tion of Vietnam a month later. Arthur Buch opened the House on April 1. "Convert the agony of Vietnam into a triumph of the spirit," the New

York rabbi said. "Remove the strange symbols of hawks and doves from our midst, and restore the American eagle in its majestic soaring heavenward as our chief concern and pride."

And in the House on June 26, 1968, Rhode Island rabbi Jacob Handler urged "blessings upon our men and women serving in the Armed Forces in Vietnam under the banner of our beloved country. Watch over them in their hours of danger."

Several rabbis explicitly cited "military might" in their prayers during this era. "We must develop superior military might and diplomatic dexterity," said Morris Teller of Chicago's South Side Hebrew Congregation in the House on August 9, 1954—the same year defeated French forces withdrew from Vietnam and American military special forces began covert operations in the Southeast Asian nation that would culminate in full-scale war that claimed upwards of 58,000 lives. Likewise, Albert Pattashnick, a Baltimore rabbi, noted in the Senate on June 17, 1965, that "while we must develop superior military might and diplomatic acumen, we must also be filled with Thy holy spirit." Back to dexterity two years later when, on September 26, 1967, in the House, Israel Botwinick of Temple Tel-Or, Havertown, Pennsylvania, said, "While we must develop superior military might and diplomatic dexterity, we must also be filled with Thy holy spirit." David Shapiro of Temple Sinai, Hollywood, Florida, added competence to the equation on January 24, 1968, in the House: "While we must develop superior military might and diplomatic competence, we must also be filled with Thy Holy Spirit."

And military might was on the mind of Meyer Leifer of New York's Congregation Emunath Israel when he was House guest chaplain February 11, 1965: "While we must develop superior military might, we must also be filled with Thy Holy Spirit to preserve the superiority of our democratic way of living." Identical to Wolfish in the House half a year later. "While we must develop superior military might," Wolfish said on August 19, 1965, "we must also be filled with Thy Holy Spirit to preserve the superiority of our democratic way of living."

Newton Friedman of Congregation Temple Emanuel in Beaumont, Texas, had similar thoughts in the House on February 9, 1967: "Suffer not our adversaries to triumph over us, but let the glories of a God-fearing people increase from age to age. Enlighten with Thy wisdom and sustain with Thy power our President in these trying days as he leads us in two wars, the war against Communist aggression overseas, and the war on poverty here at home."

America suffered 28,262 fatal casualties in Vietnam in 1967 and 1968, according to the National Archives. That's nearly half of all U.S. deaths during the entire war. Those two years saw a surge in rabbis praying in Congress: 38 times. During the three and a half years America fought in World War II, rabbis prayed in Congress seven times. (Since Pearl Harbor, there have been an average of 7.5 rabbis booked for Congress guest prayers per year.) Two rabbis even spoke on one day: May 23, 1967. Both Orthodox, both opening with a Psalm. Herbert Bomzer in the Senate and William Spigelman in the House.

Over the course of direct U.S. military involvement in the Vietnam War (March 8, 1965, when the first troops landed at Da Nang, through March 29, 1973, when the last troops left the country) rabbis made 106 appearances as guest chaplains. That's 17% of the total number of rabbis between 1860 and 2018. A tumultuous, bloody time in American history. But for rabbis praying in Congress, a golden age.

As public opinion turned against the Vietnam War, with war policy headed in the direction of failure, so too did the tone of their prayers turn ominous.

Consider the two prayers on May 23, 1967. Spigelman of Los Angeles' Congregation Shaarei Tefila: "As the flesh of humanity is now being scarred by the corrosive acids of brutality. we beseech Thee to eradicate false pride that would impede the passionate quest for a just peace, which is the poetry of life. Inspire our leadership to pierce the barriers of callousness, which is submerged beneath the waves of suspicion and inundated by the tides of abject fear. No country has bequeathed profounder love for all mankind. Let us therefore never succumb to the shocks that man is heir to nor acquiesce to the regimen of cruelty which divides and destroys." Bomzer of Young Israel of Ocean Parkway in Brooklyn: "In this era when our sincere desires for lasting peace are frustrated by events in Southeast Asia and the Middle East, when evil has captivated the attention of many of our generation. . . ."

Earlier that month in the Senate (May 9) Jacob Weitzman cited "the agonizing struggle in which we are now engaged, united and strengthened by a common destiny." On August 8, 1967, in the House, Louis Gorod hoped "that the sound of battle and the terror of war for all mankind the world over may soon cease."

Robert Widom spoke in the House on February 17, 1970, of "a world haunted by the skeletons and ghosts of a shattering war past and present, and in the throes of fear of massive destructive forces held back only by a thin leash."

Five years after the fall of Saigon, no mention of Vietnam when Bennett Hermann opened the House on July 1, 1980. The rabbi from Temple Emanu-El, East Meadow, New York, covered several other wars, though: "We are ever conscious of our country's great historical commitment to the laws and traditions of freedom, rooted in our colonial period, sharpened by the American Revolution, tempered by the Civil War, and ennobled by our involvement in the great world wars."

David Saltzman bridged two wars. As a Navy chaplain, he was among the Marines in Vietnam. And he opened the House on September 6, 1990—one month after the start of the U.S. military buildup to repel Iraq from Kuwait, culminating in the the Persian Gulf War months later. "Our prayers are with the members of the Armed Forces," Saltzman said, "who are once again announcing to the world that the United States has learned from our past and is true to our ideals and purposes."

After the combat phase of the Gulf War concluded, Shmuel Butman gave the Senate prayer. "We were witness to a crisis in the Middle East of international proportions and gravest implications," the Lubavitch rabbi said on June 12, 1991. "We thank you, dear G-d, for the miraculously low casualties among the allied forces led by the United States of America, and thank You that our troops have returned home—and are returning home—safely." Miraculously low, indeed: 149 U.S. combat deaths in the Gulf War.

Near the beginning of America's next Iraq war, Barry Black was elected U.S. Senate chaplain. But there were several months before his June 2003 election when a number of guest chaplains opened each session. One was Arnold Resnicoff, Captain of the U.S. Navy Chaplain Corps. He was guest Senate chaplain eight times between January 22, 2003 and June 16, 2003—a period coinciding with the start of Operation Iraqi Freedom. Mentions of the Iraq War in the prayers of this Navy rabbi were unavoidable and frequent.

An example from May 5, 2003, in which Resnicoff opened with Ecclesiastes 3:1:

O Lord who gives to everything a season, and a time for every purpose under heaven: a time for war; a time for peace; a time for life; a time for death; and always time for hope. We take time now, as this week starts, and as—we pray—the fighting in Iraq nears its end, to honor those who serve, who fight, who sacrifice in times of war, so that the time of peace—of real peace—might be. We take time now to offer thanks: for freedoms that are far from free, for they are bought and paid for at the cost of lives cut short, and family dreams that now can never be; and at the cost of lives that will be touched and haunted by memories so painful that most of us give thanks that we will never know, nor ever fully comprehend. . . . We honor in a special way their families, those they love and who love them, for whom the battlefields seem much more close to home.

Resnicoff hoped "the fighting nears its end." That prayer was answered. But much later. The last U.S. troops withdrew from Iraq in December 2011.

Exactly one year later another Navy chaplain, Commander Maurice Kaprow of the U.S. Naval Reserve Chaplain Corps, was a guest chaplain. On May 5, 2004, the Iraq War was central in Kaprow's prayer, too:

As we meet here in the safety of this House of Representatives, let us remember the many members of our Armed Forces, especially those serving far from home in the midst of danger, at the tip of the spear, bringing the hope of democracy where tyranny once ruled, and the specter of peace to those who for years cowered in terror and lived in tumult. We pray for the safe return of those deployed to the four corners of the Earth, sailors and Marines, soldiers, airmen, and Coast Guardsmen.

Other prayers during that period acknowledged the Middle East war. In the House on April 30, 2003, Manny Behar asked God "to grant success to our soldiers in Iraq, Afghanistan, and around the world. May they speedily achieve their mission and return home to the embrace of their families." David Halpern, Jewish chaplain of the 71st Infantry, 42nd Rainbow Division of the New York National Guard, said in the House on June 17, 2003, "that to safeguard our own freedom, we must speak out against oppression, and, where warranted, even take up arms against it. We pray that our President will succeed in his determined mission of building peace with security and of shining the bright light of freedom upon that benighted part of the world."

Solomon Sharfman, Young Israel of Flatbush, included two topical conflicts in his 1983 prayer, one of which foreshadowed the next chapter in America's military history. He opened the House on October 27. Four days earlier two terrorist truck bombs killed 241 U.S. peacekeepers in Beirut barracks. Two days earlier the United States invaded Grenada. And that night President Ronald Reagan addressed the nation on both events. At 10 a.m. that day, Sharfman noted in his prayer "grave crises that beset our country" and "the awful threat of war that darkens the earth."

It would be merely one of many times the war on terror would influence the language of a rabbi guest prayer.

27: The Holocaust

On July 23, 1942, the Nazis began mass deportations from the Warsaw Ghetto. It was a death sentence for hundreds of thousands of Polish Jews. That date coincided with Tisha B'Av, the saddest day in the Jewish calendar, when the many tragedies Jews have encountered are commemorated.

It was also a day a clergyman opened the U.S. House of Representatives with this prayer:

> We would not allow the garden of Israel of God to die out of our grateful memory. Her flowers are of perpetual bloom. We would hear again the voice of Moses and feel the warm, brotherly spirit of Jonathan and David, calling, pleading for tolerance and shaming man's inhumanity toward his brother man. Our Mother of us all, amid the grim ghostly cruelties of the dictator lands, let thy righteous judgment fall and condemn eternally the wreckers of the world's glory, whose dust no epitaph will flatter and no sacred monument call back their deeds of darkness and death.
>
> Do thou hover above the synagogues of our country as thy children breathe again the spirit that once inspired old Judea as they view the far flung lands of a righteous God.

The July 24, 1942, *Jewish Telegraphic Agency* reported those words with this headline: "Sufferings of Europe's Jews Marked in Prayer in House of Representatives."

It was the earliest prayer in Congress directly recognizing the Jewish catastrophe in Europe.

The clergyman delivering the prayer? He wasn't Jewish. House Chaplain James Montgomery was a Methodist.

Three months later, guest chaplain Rev. John Compton Ball of Metropolitan Baptist Church in Washington, DC, opened the House: "We realize this morning as never before the truth of the expression, 'Man's inhumanity to man makes countless thousands mourn.'" Ball included in his October 17, 1942, prayer Psalms 19:14: "May the words of our mouth and the meditations of our heart be acceptable in Thy sight."

The following year, on April 19, German forces entered the Warsaw Ghetto. Their goal: Complete the deportation of Jews and liquidate the Ghetto. But the Jews refused to surrender. They fought back.

The other Methodist chaplain in Congress opened the Senate a few weeks later, also quoting the Jewish Bible. "In this day of desperate danger and crisis," Rev. Frederick Brown Harris said on May 3, 1943, "may the soldiers of freedom have the weapons for complete victory." Harris included Psalms 137:5, a bedrock of Jewish and Zionist tradition: "If I forget thee, O Jerusalem, let my right hand forget its cunning; let my tongue cleave to the roof of my mouth if I prefer not thee above my chief joy."

The Warsaw Ghetto Uprising lasted a month. On May 16, 1943, the Germans burned the Ghetto. They destroyed the Great Synagogue of Warsaw.

A few days earlier, May 11, 1943, Raphael Melamed gave a House prayer that mentioned ghetto walls. "Grant redemption to the victims of the inhumanity of our foes, lingering in concentration camps and behind ghetto walls," the rabbi of Temple B'nai Israel in Elizabeth, New Jersey, said. "Bring them from darkness unto light and from slavery into freedom."

Just under a year after Nazi Germany surrendered to the Allies ending World War II in Europe, Norman Gerstenfeld of Washington Hebrew Congregation opened the Senate. "Make us to understand that we, too, by our own default, were responsible for the weakening of the peace that permitted the bloody holocaust of evil to capture the high places of mankind," he urged God on April 29, 1946.

Nachum David Herman of Congregation Tifereth Israel in Brooklyn opened the House on March 7, 1950. His prayer had a guilt-ridden message and construct similar to Gerstenfeld's: "Make us to understand that we, too, by our own default, were responsible for the infamous carnage that was inflicted on the people of the book."

We, too, by our own default, were responsible. Punishing introspection. Too strong?

Pre-Holocaust, consider what Rep. Walter Chandler (R-NY) revealed in the House during June 30, 1922, floor debate over a resolution favoring the establishment in Palestine of a national home for the Jewish people. "Only yesterday in private conversation with a Member of this House, himself a Jew, while discussing this resolution, I was told that the days of Jewish persecution had practically passed forever, that the age of freedom and enlightenment was at hand, and that Jewish persecution was no longer a valid motive, a rational excuse, for the Zionist movement," Chandler said. "I was astonished to hear him say this." [30]

For the period during the Holocaust, the David S. Wyman Institute for Holocaust Studies website offers this bit of Capitol City history:

> Throughout the Holocaust years, only one rally for rescue was held in the nation's capital: a march by more than 400 rabbis, organized by the Bergson Group and the Orthodox Va'ad ha-Hatzala, three days before Yom Kippur [1943]. Jewish leaders feared the spectacle of rabbis marching through Washington would cause anti-Semitism and embarrass the president, and President Roosevelt's Jewish advisers urged him to refrain from meeting the leaders of the march. The president heeded their advice.

October 7, 1943, *New York Times* coverage added this Congress angle to the event:

> Several hundred rabbis, in patriarchal vestments, stood on the Senate steps of the Capitol today and petitioned Vice President Henry A. Wallace to deliver the "remnants of the people of the Book," from persecution in Europe... The Vice President, standing hatless outside his office, heard the plea intoned in Hebrew.

An asterisk to Herman's 1950 prayer: Like Gerstenfeld, he used the word Holocaust. But the context was not the destruction of Europe's Jews. Herman noted "our responsibility for the weakening of the peace that permitted the bloody holocaust of communism to rise in high places of mankind."[31] He also named one of the most reviled villains in Jewish his-

---

30 In context of the unnamed Jewish member of Congress who astonished Chandler, consider also what the *New York Times* said about Hitler two months after President Harding signed the "Mandate for Palestine." In a November 21, 1922, profile, the *Times* reported that "several reliable, well-informed sources confirmed the idea that Hitler's anti-Semitism was not so genuine or violent as it sounded." The *Times* also said, "Hitler, in addition to his oratorical and organizing abilities, has another positive asset -- he is a man of the 'common people' and hence has the makings of a 'popular hero,' appealing to all classes."

31 *Los Angeles Times* writer Paul Brownfield has pointed out, "the capitalized Holocaust,' to refer exclusively to the Nazi annihilation of European Jewry, didn't gain purchase among the general public until the 1960s and '70s, a gradual evolution that some historians argue began with the 1961 trial of Adolf Eichmann."

tory, whose mere mention sparks disruptive angry noise during the Purim holiday service. "This, the month of Adar on the Hebrew calendar, commemorates the deliverance of the Jews of Persia from the hands of Haman," Herman said. "Let us strengthen our bonds with God and pray that He deliver mankind from the Hamans of our days." No indication in the *Congressional Record* whether congressmen booed and stomped their feet when they heard "Haman."

The first rabbi mention of Nazis was March 10, 1956, in the House. Arthur Schneier, a Holocaust survivor, also included Communists in the mix: "Almighty God, who hast delivered me from the hands of the Nazi and Communist tyrants. . . ."

In the years since, the Holocaust continued to appear in rabbi prayers.

"During this 20th anniversary period marking the end of World War II with its heinous Nazi death camps," said David Halpern of Brooklyn opening the House on May 13, 1965, "the camps that snuffed out 6 million Jewish lives, we pray that man may never again experience such evil." It was Yom HaShoah, Holocaust Remembrance Day. Halpern returned to the House chamber on June 17, 2003, his message older but consistent: "Almost six decades have passed since the age of the Nazi death camps, the places where 6 million Jewish men, women and children had their lives cruelly and brutally ended, their only sin that they were born Jewish." Halpern continued: "The world has watched helplessly as in the last decade hundreds of thousands of different nationalities and ethnic groups have been slaughtered. We pray that the destruction of man by his fellow because of religious beliefs or racial origins will be known no more."

Joel Tessler of Temple Beth Sholom in Potomac, Maryland, noted in his November 9, 1999, House prayer: "Today is the anniversary of Kristallnacht, the night of the broken glass, when darkness descended upon Nazi Germany and thousands of synagogues were set on fire." Arnold Resnicoff marked the anniversary of another milestone Holocaust event. "On this date in 1945," he said in the House on November 20, 2018, "we helped convene a court in Nuremberg, proclaiming some actions so inhuman that they are crimes against humanity itself. We condemned the false belief that any humans are less than human: 'life unworthy of life.'"

Rabbis have contrasted the darkness of Europe during the Holocaust with America's beacon of light:

- "Forged in the furnace of dark strife, we have emitted a flame that lit the path of freedom for all who dared to take it and radiated a warmth for all the needy."—Chaim Rozwaski of Congregation Etz Chaim in Flossmoor, Illinois, opening the House on June 8, 1976.
- "As we today commemorate the suffering of the Holocaust, may we learn to live together in harmony, working to bridge our differences in the laboratory of democracy that protects us all."—Barry Tabachnikoff of Miami Congregation Bet Breira in the House on April 24, 1990.
- "Six million were annihilated for the sole reason of their faith and birth. Millions more have suffered cruelty only because hate reigned. To the children of the martyred and abused, America said we shall help you and you shall have a land and a friend."—Rafael Grossman, Baron Hirsch Congregation, Memphis, in the Senate on March 16, 1982.

Others recognized the role of the U.S. military . . .

- "On this Holocaust Remembrance Day, our nation recalls victims of the Holocaust: a Holocaust brave Americans took up arms to fight, and many gave their lives to end."—Resnicoff in the Senate on April 29, 2003.
- "Today people around the world remember the martyrdom of 6 million Jews who perished in the Holocaust. We also remember the leadership shown in this very Chamber, and the courage of our Armed Forces who brought an end to the Holocaust by defeating the Nazi regime."—Manny Behar in the House on April 30, 2003.

. . . and of righteous gentiles:

- "Yesterday, in these hallowed Halls, the United States Congress posthumously honored Raoul Wallenberg for his humanitarian efforts in saving Jews during the Holocaust. Please, God, enable this body to continue to advocate for decency and be the moral compass of our Nation."—Dovid Cohen of New York's Young Israel of the West Side, in the House on July 10, 2014.

Holocaust mentions have even prompted a reference to fictionalized television. Moshe Bomzer of Fort Lauderdale gave the House prayer on April 18, 1978. His sponsor was Rep. Herbert Burke (R-FL). Burke said:

The TV serial entitled "Holocaust" is being shown this week nationwide. It deals with the problems faced by the Jewish Community in Europe during the late 1930s and early 1940s. It is a harsh reminder of man's inhumanity to man, and of the particular cruelty to which Jews have been subjected because of their faith. Good people, and good leaders know that education and remembering the past are the only keys to preventing future calamities. The work of Rabbi Bomzer in south Florida may seem unrelated to the TV movie, but he is preserving and nurturing the faith that sustained the Jewish people for centuries.

In addition to invoking in general the six million who died in the Holocaust, rabbis have focused on specific communities and individuals. "Sixty years ago this day, the Germans invaded greater Hungary to oust the government and begin deportations of hundreds of thousands of Jews and others," Elie Spitz of Congregation B'nai Israel, Tustin, California, said in the House on March 18, 2004. "Many of those who survived have modeled an affirmation of life and a passion for justice in the shadow of tragic loss."

Spitz's mention of survivors while remembering Hungarian Jews leads to rabbis with their own personal, direct connections to the Holocaust.

Hungarian-born Laszlo Berkowits of Temple Rodef Shalom in Falls Church, Virginia, opened the House on June 14, 1988. Rep. Frank Wolf (R-VA) said in his welcoming remarks: "As a concentration camp prisoner at the end of the war Rabbi Berkowits was moved from Budapest to the infamous Auschwitz camp, then as the allies advanced on Hitler's army he was moved to Ravensburg and finally to Wobbelin where he was liberated by United States 82d Airborne troops."

Also born in Hungary: Henry Kraus of Temple Beth Ami in West Covina, California. He gave the House prayer in 1978. In his sponsoring remarks Rep. Jim Lloyd (D-CA) noted, "It was on this day, April 4, 1944, that he was forced by the Nazis to wear the Yellow Star of David as a sign of degradation. Along with his congregation, he was deported to Auschwitz and later, Buchenwald. The American 3rd Army liberated him in 1945. After the war, he became chief rabbi of Western Hungary." Similarly, Rep. Esteban Torres (D-CA) noted in August 1, 1985, remarks about Kraus, "after the Germans occupied Hungary in March 1944, he was deported with his congregation by the Nazis to Auschwitz and later, Buchenwald. Although he was exempt from the anti-Jewish laws because of his father's extensive military service, he chose to go and be with his congregants. He was liberated from the German concentration camp in 1945 by the American Third Army."

Six rabbis who survived Auschwitz have opened Congress in prayer—all in the House of Representatives.

Here are more rabbis who escaped from other European countries. They survived the Nazis . . . and ended up in front of the U.S. Congress, the literal center of American democracy.

Austrian-born Schneier began his 1990 House prayer this way: "You have saved me from the Holocaust and, 43 years ago today, on May 8, 1947, You brought me to the land of freedom and opportunity."

Washington Hebrew Congregation's Joshua Haberman gave the June 4, 1985, House prayer. Sponsor Rep. Ben Gilman (R-NY) noted Haberman "began his studies at the University of Vienna, but was forced to continue his education following the Nazi invasion in the United States at the University of Cincinnati and the Hebrew College in Cincinnati."

Dov Edelstein of Moses Montefiore Synagogue in Appleton, Wisconsin, opened the House on March 8, 1979.[32] Rep. Toby Roth (R-WI) noted Edelstein "is a native of Romania and was ordained to the rabbinate in Hungary in 1944. He is also a former inmate of the Nazi concentration camp at Auschwitz. Following the war, he was one of the 50,000 Jews interned by the British in camps on Cyprus prior to the establishment of the State of Israel."

Polish-born Rozwaski twice delivered the opening prayer in the House: October 24, 1967, and June 8, 1976 (cited above). During the latter prayer he said of Jews: "Forged in the furnace of dark strife, we have emitted a flame that lit the path of freedom for all who dared to take it, and radiated a warmth for all the needy." According to the bio in his book *Jewish Meditations on the Meaning of Death* "Rabbi Rozwaski survived the Holocaust by hiding, as a child, with an aunt, uncle, and partisans in the forest."[33]

Also native of Poland, Morris Shapiro of Long Island gave the April 8, 1975, House prayer:

> As we commemorate the Holocaust where 6 million of Thy children were sacrificed as burnt offerings on the altar of human bestiality, we pray to Thee to make us cognizant of this awesome reality that Thou hast granted man free will and that every man has the potential to use this power to create an

---

32 Edelstein was the last rabbi to give the House prayer before live TV coverage of the House floor, via C-SPAN, began later that month.

33 Jason Aronson, Inc., 1994, page 215.

Auschwitz. We pray to Thee that this day may serve as a challenge to every Member of this Chamber to question himself—What am I, who represent the most powerful Nation in the world, doing to prevent another holocaust from reoccurring? For anything that has happened once can happen again. The same events that took place in Germany can take place again in the Middle East and in the Soviet Union. O God, help us to face this grave challenge that it is in the hands of these United States of America that the survivors of the ashes of Auschwitz have placed their destiny.

In his sponsoring remarks for Shapiro, Rep. Jerome Ambro (D-NY) noted that it was on that April 8 day, "30 years ago, Allied troops began their liberation of Hitler's concentration camps revealing to the world the horrendous extent of the Nazi holocaust. Unfortunately, Rabbi Shapiro was both a tragic witness to and a refugee from Hitler's terror. Rabbi Shapiro was just 22 years old when the Nazis round up the Jews of his town of Lublin, Poland, for liquidation. He and his sister hid in the attic above Gestapo headquarters for 4 days and then ran off through the woods where they were eventually found by a Christian farmer who, in exchange for money, hid them in a crawlspace cave for 2 years." Shapiro emigrated to the United States in 1948. The April 17, 1975, *Long-Islander* newspaper reported on Ambro's remarks, noting he "concluded by entreating: 'help us to face this grave challenge that is in the hands of these United States of America that the survivors of the ashes of Auschwitz have placed their destiny.'" Rep. Jack Kemp (R-NY) added more thoughts, thanking Shapiro "for his very eloquent plea in behalf of all of mankind on the occasion of the 30th anniversary of the liberation of the Buchenwald concentration camp. It is of great importance that the House pause today to contemplate man's inhumanity to man and to make it clear to generations to come that we could not forget, and would not forget, the Holocaust."

Polish-born survivor Sidney Harcsztark gave the House prayer twice: March 18, 1965, and 20 years later, May 1, 1985. The second appearance was in the midst of controversy over President Reagan's visit to Germany's Bitburg Cemetery, where Waffen SS troops were buried. That prayer merited a story in the May 1, 1985, *Associated Press* headlined: "Holocaust Survivor Delivers Opening Prayer." The *AP* noted Harcsztark's prayer occurred on "the 40th anniversary of his liberation from the Dachau concentration camp." Sponsor Rep. Chuck Schumer (D-NY) said, "In his 40 years since liberation from the Nazi extermination camp, Harcsztark has been able to educate those not yet born about the horrors of the Holocaust." Harcsztark's earlier House prayer was reported in the May 1965 newsletter issued by the Association of Jewish Refugees in Great Britain, which noted the Dachau survivor "delivered the invocation at the opening session of the House of Representatives on Purim."

Another Polish-born survivor, Rabbi Isaac Neuman, also gave House prayers twice. Neuman survived four years in Nazi slave labor and death camps, including Auschwitz and Mauthausen. He was a rare survivor: almost a full four years in the harshest slave labor camps. His May 5, 1970, sponsor was Rep. John Culver (D-IA). Culver noted the day marked Neuman's 25th anniversary of his liberation by the American troops from the concentration camp at Ebensee in Nazi German-occupied Austria. Ebensee was the last camp liberated—the war ended two days after it was freed. The Nazis built the V-2 rocket in Ebensee and, slaves, like Isaac Neuman, were forced to dig a tunnel deep inside a mountain in order to protect the project from Allied bombers. Culver noted that at the time of his liberation, Neuman "was 22 years old and suffering from typhoid fever, tuberculosis, two bullet wounds received in an escape attempt, and malnutrition after 4 years at Auschwitz and required almost 3 years of hospitalization for recovery." Rep. Dan Crane (R-IL) sponsored Neuman on April 11, 1983. He noted, "immediately following the completion of his education in Warsaw, war erupted in Europe, World War II, as we all know it today. We cannot begin to imagine what went through his mind as he spent the war years in the camps of Auschwitz and other Nazi concentration camps. Doubtless he would try to forget, if remembering was not so important to the entire world."

In total since the Holocaust, 19 different rabbis born in Poland have prayed in Congress. Solomon Sharfman was House guest chaplain on October 27, 1983. He was born in 1915 in a Polish city whose name is associated with the depths of Holocaust evil: Treblinka. Fortunately for Sharfman, his family emigrated to the United States in 1920. Two decades later Treblinka became a Nazi killing center.

Perhaps even more satisfying—triumphant, even: 13 post-war guest chaplain rabbis were born in Germany.

Norbert Weinberg of Congregation Adas Israel in Fall River, Massachusetts. He offered the House prayer on June 30, 1970. According to his bio at a later pulpit (Congregation Agudas Achim Anshei Sfard— The Adams Street Shul, in Newton, Massachusetts), "In 1938, his father was arrested by the Nazis and spent six weeks in the Buchenwald concentration camp. After his release, the family was able to leave Germany and fly to England." In her sponsoring remarks, Rep. Margaret Heckler (R-MA) noted, "Himself a fugitive from injustice in Nazi Germany, Rabbi Weinberg has come to our shores much like the Pilgrims in the early seventeenth century, to foster the brotherhood of man under the fatherhood of God."

Henry Okolica delivered the House prayer on October 1, 1964, and the Senate prayer September 19, 1966. The *Connecticut Jewish Ledger* profiled him on December 2, 2011: "It's been a full journey for Rabbi Henry Okolica over his first century—from Kristallnacht and a Gestapo jail cell in his native Germany to refuge and pulpits in New York, Washington, Florida, and, for 50 years, as spiritual leader of Congregation Tephereth Israel in New Britain." In September 13, 1983, floor remarks, Rep. Nancy Johnson (R-CT) recounted how Okolica was recently in Germany to visit his hometown of Aschaffenburg. Johnson said Okolica returned "to his birthplace to see the progress the city government has made in building a documentation center and shrine to commemorate the historic events of the years between 1933 and 1945 during which the entire Jewish community of Aschaffenburg was dispersed or wiped out by the Nazis. Seven hundred years of uninterrupted Jewish community life came abruptly to an end with the advent of Hitler's rise in Germany in 1933. In only 10 years, the entire Jewish community of Aschaffenburg was wiped out; 135 Jewish citizens were known to be deported to Poland's concentration camps, 37 to Theresienstadt, and seven committed suicide before the deportations began."

Israel Kanarek gave the May 1, 1975, House prayer. Rep. Richard Ottinger (D-NY) noted Kanarek "was born in Leipzig, Germany, in 1917. After completing secular studies at the Higher Real Schule in Leipzig, he went to pre-war Lithuanian great Torah Centers of higher learning, where he was ordained. Arriving in the United States in 1941, he was one of the first founders of the Institute of Advanced Studies in Lakewood, N.J."

Hillel Cohn gave the House prayer twice, June 30, 1977, and March 21, 2001. His synagogue: Congregation Emanuel El in San Bernardino. That California city is remembered in contemporary times for being the location of a December 2, 2015, terrorist attack. His Temple bio notes, "native of Germany, he was brought to the United States as an infant by his parents who were refugees from Nazism."

The next rabbi born in prewar Europe to pray in Congress came 19 years after Hillel Cohn—and he was also a Rabbi Cohn. Romi Cohn. Holocaust survivor and a Holocaust fighter as a member of the Jewish underground in his native Czecholovakia. Rabbi Romi Cohn gave the House prayer on January 29, 2020—75 years after Auschwitz was liberated.

"Almighty, open my lips. May the words of my mouth declare Your praise," Cohn began, reciting the Priestly Blessing found in Numbers. "As a young boy of 13 years, I was condemned to be dead, to be murdered along with my entire family, including my 3-year-old little sister, by one evil man, may his name be erased forever. But my life was spared. I was saved by my Father, by You, O Lord, the Father of the Universe, who brought me to the shores of this beautiful country, the United States of America, the land of the free, where I found a safe and new home."

At the age of 90, Cohn was among the oldest—if not the oldest—rabbi guest chaplains. He was in the House almost exactly 160 years after the first on February 1, 1860. Cohn was the second rabbi guest chaplain to mention Donald Trump. "May You, Lord, accept with mercy our prayers for our country," he prayed, "for our President, Donald Trump; our Vice President, Michael Pence; my Congressman, Max Rose; and all his noble colleagues."[34]

Rose noted that Cohn "built a renowned career as a mohel in New York City for over 25 years." He offered additional biographical detail, including fighting Nazis. "Under Nazi rule, he saw the Hitler Youth attack his father in the street," the Democrat from Staten Island and parts of Brooklyn said. "When war broke out, he joined the partisans fighting Nazi tyranny. At 15 years old, Romi was the youngest member of the Czechoslovakian partisan forces. Among other feats, he helped save 56 Jewish families escape the horrors of the Holocaust. He fought with the partisans until the end of the war and then went in search of his own family. Of his parents and six siblings, only his father and two sisters had survived."

Rabbi Cohn died less than two months after his prayer. He survived the Nazis but couldn't survive the coronavirus. The *Times of Israel* reported his passing with this March 24, 2020, headline: "Holocaust survivor rabbi who led US House in prayer dies of coronavirus at 91." Rev. Dan Cummins of Capitol Worship was House guest chaplain on March 27, 2010, the day Congress voted for $2 trillion in coronavirus economic relief. Cummins began his prayer with this tribute: "This morning we pause to remember Your humble servant, 91-year-old Holocaust survivor Rabbi Romi Cohn . . . May his memory be a blessing."

---

34 Pence became the third vice president mentioned by name in a rabbi guest prayer. The others: Richard Nixon (by Rabbi Charles Rubel in the Senate on April 21, 1958) and Lyndon Johnson (by Rabbi Gerard Kaplan in the House on April 30, 1962).

The life of German-born Rabbi Joachim Prinz of Temple B'nai Abraham in Newark took a unique journey through America's history. He addressed the August 28, 1963, March on Washington for Job and Freedom. He was the speaker immediately before Rev. Martin Luther King delivered his "I Have A Dream" speech. Two years later, as the Senate was in the midst of considering the Voting Rights Act of 1965, he gave that chamber's opening prayer. "For 2,000 years, after the Holy Land had passed into foreign hands," Prinz told the Senators on May 6, 1965, "the Jewish people suffered in countries all over the globe. Herded into ghettos, they were subjected to discrimination and degradation, to injury and death. In our own days, 6 million of them lie buried in the mass graves of the concentration camps of Europe. Yet in all these centuries of hatred and bloodshed, they did not abandon their faith in God, nor did they forsake their belief in man's innate goodness and the principles of justice and peace." Sen. Joseph Tydings (D-MD) noted Prinz "was a former rabbi in Berlin, Germany, where his outspoken criticisms of Hitler resulted in his repeated arrests by the Nazis before his expulsion from Germany in 1937." Reporting on the 1963 March on Washington, the August 29, 1963, *New York Times* noted Prinz was expelled by Adolf Eichmann.

Survivor Kurt Metzger opened the House in prayer on June 5, 1968, a few hours after Robert F. Kennedy was shot by a Palestinian/Jordanian immigrant. RFK was still alive at the time of the prayer. The website *JewishGen. org* calls Metzger "Nuremberg's last Rabbi": Born in that infamous German city, he became the pre-war rabbi in Landau. He was arrested in Breslau in November 1938, incarcerated in Buchenwald for several months, and after his release was rabbi of the Congregation of Nuremberg. He arrived in America in October 1940. He became an Army chaplain and wrote *Guidebook for Jewish Chaplains.*

Metzger's journey from Europe inferno to U.S. military chaplain is a path followed by another German-born rabbi who gave a House prayer. Selig Auerbach was born in Hamburg. He escaped the Nazis by moving to Holland and then England in 1940, then to the United States. During World War II he volunteered as a chaplain in the U.S. Army in the South. On July 20, 1955, he gave the House prayer. He was also the Jewish chaplain for the 1980 Lake Placid Winter Olympics. It was the first time in the history of the Olympics, according to the January 31, 1980, *Jewish Telegraphic Agency*, "that religion has been officially recognized."

Two other rabbis affiliated with the U.S. military, both born in America, had connections to the Holocaust.

Judah Nadich of Park East Synagogue gave the House prayer on March 6, 1961. On October 1, 1982, Rep. Stephen Solarz (D-NY) marked the New York synagogue's centennial: "During World War II, Dr. Nadich served as the first military adviser for Jewish affairs to General Eisenhower. In that post he was deeply involved in the efforts to save the lives of tens of thousands of Jews in DP camps, and without his interventions many more would have died." Nadich's September 2, 2007, obituary in the *New York Times* added, "With hundreds of thousands of survivors moved by the victorious armies into so-called D.P. camps set up by the Allies, Rabbi Nadich became appalled at the conditions they faced."

Kenneth Leinwand, an Army chaplain who achieved the rank of Colonel, gave the February 16, 2006, House prayer. Leinwand was the command chaplain for the U.S. Army Europe and the Seventh Army in Heidelberg, Germany. A year earlier he offered the prayer in a Medal of Honor ceremony at the White House. On September 23, 2005, President Bush presented the medal to Tibor Rubin, an American prisoner of war in the Korean War who, when he lived in Hungary during the Nazi era, was rounded up with his family and imprisoned in Mauthausen Camp in Austria.

Another American-born rabbi with a Holocaust connection was Shimshon Sherer. He led the Senate in prayer on June 29, 1999. Six senators took to the floor with tribute to his father, Morris Sherer, who had died the year before. Among them:

> Sen. John Ashcroft (R-MO): "One often cited example of Rabbi Sherer's activism occurred almost immediately after he became a part of the leadership of Agudath Israel. During Hitler's reign of terror, when all too many here and around the world remained silent about the unspeakable atrocities committed against the Jews in Eastern Europe, Rabbi Sherer spoke and insisted that action was necessary. . . . With his still tiny organization, he sent shipments of food to Jews suffering under the terrible injustices of Hitler's regime, and he helped many to escape to gain refuge here in the United States of America."
>
> Sen. Trent Lott (R-MS): "In the worst of times for European Jewry, he put Agudath Israel in the forefront of assisting the persecuted and saving the hunted. And with the defeat of Nazism, his organization pitched in to help refugees and immigrants."

Sen. Daniel Patrick Moynihan (D-NY): "Rabbi Sherer's earliest work on behalf of the Jewish community was the grassroots, and largely illegal, organization and transport of food shipments to starving Jews in Nazi-occupied Eastern Europe in 1941. His efforts also produced affidavits for European Jewish refugees that helped them immigrate to the United States."

Other rabbis have been relatives of or descendants from Holocaust victims and survivors.

Austrian-born Yakov Hilsenrath of Beth Judah Temple in Wildwood gave the House prayer on March 1, 1956. His March 10, 2014, obituary in the *New Jersey Jewish News* noted that his "family fled after Kristallnacht, eventually settling in the United States."

Max Landman opened the Senate on January 2, 1961. Sponsor Sen. Vance Hartke (D-IN) gave this family history: "His brother, Hermann Landman, was a resident of Germany. Rabbi Max M. Landman, who offered the prayer in the Senate this morning, came to the United States at the age of 12. His brother decided to stay in Germany. While he was there he wrote a book entitled 'Gegen Kampf.' He wrote the book in opposition to 'Mein Kampf,' the author of which book was Adolf Hitler, of course. Hermann Landman thought Hitler would be a passing phase in Germany and that he would soon leave the scene. Much to his dismay, that did not occur. The rabbi attempted to flee from Germany but was apprehended at the Czechoslovak border and was sent to a concentration camp, where he was kept for many years. In 1944, Rabbi Hermann Landman's brother was cremated alive under orders of Eichmann."

And opening the House on April 5, 2011, Efrem Goldberg noted he is "a grandchild of immigrants, who fled the Nazis and came to this country 72 years ago this month to find refuge, freedom, and opportunity."

One more guest chaplain was part of the Holocaust story, but he wasn't a rabbi and hardly a victim: Archbishop Valerian Trifa. According to *Citizen 865: The Hunt of Hitler's Hidden Soldiers in America* by Debbie Cenziper, Trifa was "a prominent leader of the Romanian Iron Guard, a violent, fascist, and antisemitic movement whose members greeted each other with the Roman salute—arms extended and palms down."[35]

After the war, Trifa emigrated to the United States. He settled in Michigan and was ordained as a bishop in the Romanian Orthodox church.

---

35   Hachette Books, page 46.

"As head of the Romanian Episcopate in the United States," according to a December 2008 Office of Special Investigations report, "Trifa was a powerful and influential religious figure." The *New York Times* wrote in his 1987 obituary, "Before his past was disclosed, he was an honored prelate. In 1955, Archbishop Trifa gave the opening prayer before the United States Senate." In the Senate on May 11, 1955, he called America a "trustee of priceless human liberty and dignity" and prayed "for the peace of the whole world, for the welfare of mankind, and for the union of all." Journalist Drew Pearson cited Trifa's Senate prayer during his May 30, 1955, radio show *Washington Merry-Go-Round*, according to *Alleged Nazi Collaborators in the United States after World War II* by Christoph Schiessl.[36] Pearson said, "Attention Senators! How did it happen that Viorel Trifa gave the opening prayer before you Senators two weeks ago? Just who, Senators, picks the churchmen who lead you in prayer?" He was sponsored by Richard Nixon.

If anything, the Trifa prayer serves as a reminder to always vet the guest chaplain. If only Nixon had Google.

This chapter opened with the liquidation of the Warsaw Ghetto in April 1943. Salomon Faber's prayer, 40 years later, is a good close. The rabbi from Anshe Sholom Jewish Center, Kew Gardens, New York, was in the House on April 13, 1983—the same day that the American Gathering of Jewish Holocaust Survivors convened in Washington. Faber recognized the history: "At this hour, when thousands of Holocaust survivors gather in this great city to voice their gratitude to America for a new life in freedom and dignity, we implore Thee O G-d: Grant us inspiration, discernment, and courage to help establish the triumph of right over might." Rep. Joseph Addabbo (D-NY) underscored the history: "It is most fitting that Rabbi Salomon Faber open today's session of Congress as the thousands of survivors of the Holocaust gather in Washington this week to commemorate the Warsaw uprising and the sacrifices that millions of Jews had made during World War II."

And a post-script, the post-war appearance in Congress by survivor Leo Baeck, the second foreign-born rabbi to deliver an invocation opening the House. At the time, just after the war, he was a resident of London. During the war, Baeck spent over two years in Theresienstadt, a Nazi concentration camp. Before that he was a leading rabbi in Germany and chairman of the German Rabbinical Conference.

---

36   Lexington Books, 2016, page 100.

In *Days of Sorrow and Pain: Leo Baeck and the Berlin Jews*, Leonard Baker wrote, "Before the war Baeck had criticized the silence of the United States and other nations in the face of the Nazi abuse of Jews. Since that time he had witnessed the massive American effort to defeat Germany to assist refugees." When he stood before the House of Representatives on February 12, 1948, Baker wrote, "it was an appreciative man."[37]

But Baeck's prayer mentioned neither the Holocaust nor Nazis. Not even Europe. Or his own war experience. Its focus was elsewhere: America's 16th president. And its opening was a rhetorical homage to the Gettysburg Address.

> We pray unto Thee on this day on which six score and nineteen years ago was born that man who came to be Thy servant, "the man in whom is the spirit," and who for the sake of this land became witness and testimony of humanity, herald of Thy command and Thy promise, to the everlasting blessing of this country and of mankind. Our Father, day by day Thou sendest forth Thy messengers, Thy angels-our chances to be unselfish and righteous, our opportunities to walk in Thy ways- they are the messengers that come from Thee. We must not miss them nor disregard them. Almighty God, Thou choosest people and selectest nations "to bring them into the place which Thou hast prepared"; Thou changest the times and the seasons; Thou makest history enter the world. Thy servant, Abraham Lincoln, in a message to Congress, said, "We cannot escape history," so help us, O God, that we may not evade history, but may we be granted history. Reverently I pray Thee to bless Congress, its men, and its days. From the bottom of my heart I pray: God bless America.

Baeck offered that prayer on Lincoln's birthday. Tucked within this pro-American aspiration from this non-American speaker was another citation: Exodus 23:20. "Bring them into the place which Thou hast prepared." In fact, God was preparing to do just that. In three months, the Jewish people indeed would be "granted history"—the state of Israel would be born. And Lincoln's words about America in the Gettysburg Address could be equally said about the Jewish state: "this nation, under God, shall have a new birth of freedom."

---

37   Oxford University Press, 1980, page 326.

28: "Godless, Ruthless, and Unprincipled": Communism

"Secure our borders to be free from totalitarian ideologies, pagan philosophies, and the anti-democratic principles."
—Rabbi Israel Goldberg, Ahavas Sholom Agudas Achim Anshe Sphard, Randallstown, Maryland, opening the House on June 4, 1971.

Invoking God at the rostrum hasn't been merely a theological or spiritual exercise. For many rabbis during the Cold War, the mention of God—actually, the absence of God—was a bayonet of rhetorical attack. Where there is no God—just pagans—there is enemy.

Several rabbis used "Godless" in nearly identical descriptions of Communism.

"In these soul-stirring times," said Morris Teller of Chicago's South Side Hebrew Congregation in the House on August 9, 1954, "we seek peace but we must muster all available forces to safeguard life and liberty from possible onslaughts of godless, ruthless, unprincipled aggressors."

"In these serious and soul-stirring times," said Meyer Leifer of New York City's Congregation Emunath Israel in the House on February 11, 1965, "when freedom-loving America which is founded upon liberty and justice for all, is being threatened by the onslaught of godless, ruthless, and unprincipled aggressors."

"We seek peace, but not flinch from the onslaughts of godless, ruthless, and unprincipled aggressors," said Baltimore rabbi Albert Pattashnick in the Senate, June 17, 1965.

"We seek Thy blessing and guidance in these serious and soul-stirring times," said Yonkers rabbi Louis Eliezer Wolfish in the House, August 19, 1965, "when freedom loving America, which is founded upon liberty and justice for all, is being threatened by the onslaught of godless, ruthless, and unprincipled aggressors."

"In these soul-stirring times," prayed Israel Botwinick of Temple Tel-Or, Havertown, Pennsylvania, in the House on September 26, 1967, "we must safeguard life and liberty from possible onslaughts of godless, ruthless, and unprincipled aggressors."

David Shapiro of Temple Sinai in Hollywood, Florida, found soul-stirring times six years apart. "In these soul-stirring times," he said on June 25, 1962, opening the Senate, "we seek peace; but we must safeguard life and liberty from possible onslaughts of godless, ruthless, and unprincipled aggressors." And, "in these soul stirring times," Shapiro said opening the House on January 24, 1968, "we seek peace, but we must safeguard life and liberty from the possible onslaughts by godless, ruthless, and unprincipled aggressors." The times were again stirring Shapiro's soul when he returned the next decade. "Master of the Universe, in these soul-stirring times we need Thy guidance and Thy blessing," he said in the House on May 13, 1975. "We must safeguard life and liberty from the possible onslaught by godless, ruthless, and unprincipled aggressors."

Anything stronger than "godless, ruthless, unprincipled" to stir the soul?

Ratcheting up the threat level, some additional rabbinical characterizations of the red peril:

- "in this hour of menace"—Arthur Buch of Temple Emanuel, Paterson, New Jersey, April 25, 1951, in the House.
- "sinister forces are threatening to undermine the principles upon which this land was established"—Karl Applbaum, Bayside Jewish Center, April 30, 1952, in the House.
- "menacing are the manifold dangers on the horizon today"—Jacob Agus, July 20, 1953, in the Senate.

Could prayers get even tougher still?

Indeed. Brace yourself for a blast from Samuel Rosenblatt on June 11, 1954. "The task confronting them is exceedingly grave because the sinister forces, that have arisen to engulf the world and immolate on the altar of their lust for power the freedom of their fellow men, are becoming daily more threatening," the rabbi from Baltimore's Beth Tfiloh Congregation said in the House. "The menace presented by these enemies of democracy and religion, who are undeterred in their arrogant seizure of the possessions of lands and peoples by either the fear of God or scruples of conscience, has already produced a harvest of hysteria and confusion among the advocates of individual liberty and the champions of the democratic way of life."

To be sure, rabbis weren't the only spiritual leaders using such fiery language during that era. "Either Communism must die, or Christianity must die, because it is actually a battle between Christ and the anti-Christ," wrote evangelist Billy Graham in 1954.[38]

---

38 Marshall Frady, *Billy Graham, A Parable of American Righteousness*, Simon & Schuster, 1979, page 237.

Even the father of al-Qaeda, Sayyid Qutb, went starkly anti-Communist. According to Lawrence Wright in *The Looming Tower: Al Qaeda and the Road to 9/11*, Qutb wrote in 1948, "Either we shall walk the path of Islam or we shall walk the path of Communism."[39]

Putting its Cold War money where the Cold War rhetoric was, the U.S. government fought Communism with prayer. On February 26, 1954, Sen. Alexander Wiley (R-WI) proudly reported to his colleagues about "extensive religious programing beamed behind the Iron Curtain in the fight against godless communism." In 1953, between seven and eight percent of the total broadcasting time on Voice of America (VOA) was devoted to religious programing. That included "statements, interviews, sermons, prayers, religious holiday messages by clergymen which touch to any extent on religion or religious life." Sitting in VOA studios on February 25, 1957, in remarks delivered over the entire radio network of the United States Information Agency, President Eisenhower said Communism's "avowed program is to destroy totally the religion, governments, institutions and traditions of the Christian world, the Buddhist world, the Islamic world, the Judaic world, and the world of every religion and culture."[40]

Two Christian guest chaplains in the House stand out from the era.

In April 1956, Rev. Harold Rigney of Fu Jen Catholic University in Peking, China, asked God "to comfort our fellow Americans, who are suffering unjustly in the cruel prisons of Communist China." Rep. John Kluczynski (D-IL) said, "Although it is not a custom in this House to make any remarks about the Chaplain who delivers the prayer at the opening of the session, we have with us this afternoon a man who has served over four years in a Communist Red China prison camp. I am very happy that Father Harold Rigney is again a free man."

And in February 1976, Rev. A. Reid Jepson took to the podium. He was vice president for Public Ministries, Far East Broadcasting Co., which beams gospel radio messages to countries like the Philippines, Indonesia and South Korea. His bicentennial year prayer: "Among us there may be unbelievers, scoffers, blasphemers, but there are believers in God, servants of Jesus Christ, lovers of mankind." He added, "With millions behind curtains-we evaluate our God-given freedom and turn first to the Lord of the Bible."

---

39 Alfred A. Knopf, 2006, page 13.
40 In the early days of our country the federal government granted land to the "Society of the United Brethren for Propagating the Gospel among the Heathen."

With all their descriptions of godless Communism, how many rabbis actually said the word Communism in their Congress prayers? Just three.

The first was Nachum David Herman. He prayed in the House on March 7, 1950. With the end of World War II less than five years earlier still clearly in mind, Herman anguished, "We come to Thee with burdens on our minds, and hearts saturated with haunting fears of a peace lost and a war hovering about; with deep anxiety over the future of our children in a world trembling on the side of chaos; a world moving rapidly downward into the anarchy of a ghastly morrow that may sweep like a tidal wave out of the impenitent evil of totalitarianism." He continued, "Make us to understand that we, too, by our own default, were responsible for the infamous carnage that was inflicted on the people of the book, and our responsibility for the weakening of the peace that permitted the bloody holocaust of communism to rise in high places of mankind."

Then, on May 10, 1956, in the House, Holocaust survivor Arthur Schneier began the first of seven prayers he delivered in Congress over five decades this way: "Almighty God, who hast delivered me from the hands of the Nazi and Communist tyrants and hast brought me to these blessed shores, I lead Thy children in prayer for our land, the haven for the homeless, the refuge for the oppressed." Schneier opened similarly in the Senate the next year, on May 9: "Heavenly Father, on the 10th anniversary of my arrival on these blessed shores, after years of Nazi and Communist persecution, I lead Thy children in prayer for our country."[41]

When many countries concluded their experiments with Communism, Jay Marcus prayed in the House. "What a remarkably momentous year," he noted on September 13, 1990. "We have witnessed the demise of communism and the budding of democracy in Eastern Europe."

But, oddly, no mention of Communism from Benjamin Schultz. He opened the Senate on June 2, 1955. No synagogue or pulpit listed for him in the *Congressional Record*. Instead, Rabbi Schultz's identification is "executive director. American Jewish League Against Communism. Inc." Of course, when your prayer includes the phrase "whip of the oppressor," even without explicitly saying Red Menace there's little doubt about the reference. Schultz thundered:

---

41 That 1957 Schneier prayer was cited by Sen. Marco Rubio (R-FL) in his 2013 brief to the U.S. Supreme Court supporting "America's tradition of appointing legislative chaplains and solemnizing legislative sessions with prayer."

Preserve us from godless cynicism in the dress of diplomacy. They cry peace, peace, but there is no peace. No peace for us while men cry out under the whip of the oppressor. No calm for mankind while one-third of earth cowers in terror. . . . Help us to realize that facile appeasement, like some cosmic drug, may relieve a tension, but poison a world.

According to a May 9, 1958, *American Mercury* column titled "The Rabbi the Reds Hate Most!" by Victor Lasky, "It was the proudest moment of his life. The prayer was so unusual, it was picked up by the United Press."

Unusual indeed. Schultz's bold language was contrary to the beliefs of some American Jews in that period. According to the online Jewish Women's Archive Encyclopedia, Communist Party historians estimate that "that almost half of the party's membership was Jewish in the 1930s and 1940s, and that approximately 100,000 Jews passed through the party in those decades." (Of course, that's a sliver of all the Jews in America at the time. According to "Statistics of Jews—1929" by the American Jewish Committee, 4,228,000 Jews resided in the United States in 1927).

Schultz's fervent and public anti-Communism fervor earned him a fan in that era's leading domestic communism hunter. Two months earlier the *Chicago Tribune* ran this headline: "M'Carthy Hails Rabbi Schultz' Fight on Reds." The April 21, 1955, article reported from a testimonial dinner in New York City. Sen. Joseph McCarthy (R-WI) called Schultz an "indispensable man" in his fight against communism "and said he had done distinguished service to his faith and his country." Roy Cohn was at the dinner, sharing the dais. In a Senate floor tribute on May 20, 1955, McCarthy said of Schultz: "For these many years, he has been hurling with deadly accuracy and with impetuous force his spear into the flank and belly of this contraption of deceitfulness." McCarthy added, "I am honored to nominate Benjamin Schultz for the high priesthood of the Ancient Trojan Order of Laocoon and His Descendants."

A rabbi as priest! Not since Jewish priests, *kohanim*, made sacrificial offerings at the original temple in Jerusalem over 20 centuries ago. (Before it was destroyed not by Communist menace, but Roman menace.)

When Communism ended, did ruthlessness end, too? A few years after the fall of the Berlin Wall, on November 7, 1991, Milton Balkany suggested these next steps to the Senate: "When G-dless and ruthless regimes crumble, we must exhibit our allegiance and dedication to the principals of our democracy."

And you don't need to be a Communist to be ruthless. You can be a post 9/11 terrorist, too. Here's Dov Hazdan opening the Senate on April 11, 2002: "In these soul-stirring times we need Thy guidance and Thy blessing. Serious is the challenge that free countries and America face. We seek peace, but we must safeguard life and liberty from possible onslaughts of godless, ruthless, and unprincipled aggressors."

Since the modern-day terrorist is many things but godless—devotion to all-merciful and omnipotent God, after all, is the core principle for many contemporary terrorists—perhaps the use of godless in 2002 was merely nostalgic hearkening back to simpler Cold War times?

Adding to the rhetorical complexity: Must one be Communist to be godless? Could America lack God, too? Senate chaplain Richard Halverson looked inward on February 7, 1994: "We have no standards when it comes to morality and ethics. We have no god—not even a Caesar. We have become a godless, relativistic society."

He ended the prayer: "We pray in His name who is Incarnate Truth. Amen."

29: War on Terror

"This is a time of challenge to our interests and our values and it's a time that tests our wisdom and our skills. At this time in Iran, 50 Americans are still held captive, innocent victims of terrorism and anarchy."
—President Jimmy Carter, State of the Union Address delivered before a Joint Session of the U.S. Congress, January 23, 1980

When the Iran hostage crisis dominated the American conversation, guest chaplain rabbis made it a central theme of their prayers as well.

"The 1980's have been born in turmoil, strife, and change," President Carter proclaimed, opening the 1980 State of the Union address. He then discussed at length the "international terrorism" in Iran. A month before Carter was at the House rostrum, Abraham Hecht stood in that same place, praying. On December 4, 1979, 30 days after Iranian students stormed the U.S. embassy in Tehran taking dozens of Americans hostage, Rabbi Hecht lamented, "Our Nation is now facing serious challenges throughout the world. Our magnificent democracy, beacon of light and hope in a world shrouded in the darkness of oppression, hatred, and violence, is under attack."

Half a year later, July 1, Bennett Hermann of Temple Emanu-El, East Meadow, New York, prayed "from the bottom of our hearts for the peace and safety of those hostages in Iran."

Americans were still being held against their will when, on September 9, 1980, Stanley Rabinowitz of Adas Israel Synagogue in Washington, DC, prayed in the Senate. He hoped for "a day when no person shall be hostage for the land of his birth."

With the Americans in Iran lacking freedom, one rabbi connected their plight to a Jewish holiday whose central message is freedom. Solomon Freilich opened his March 18, 1980, House prayer noting:

> Today is the first day of the Hebrew month of Nissan when my people are soon to usher in the glorious Passover Festival of Freedom, commemorating redemption, renewal, and rebirth. At this anxious hour and on this day which has been declared a national day of prayer, our hearts go out in love, in hope, and in prayer for the innocent Americans still being held hostage in a distant land. Oh Lord, Thou who hast, from the heights of Sinai, proclaimed through ancient Israel the eternal law of human freedom, we pray, hasten the day when our 50 fellow Americans speedily return to our shores unharmed in body and spirit, reunited with their families and loved ones.

The Iranian hostage crisis would not be the only time a rabbi guest chaplain would link a Jewish holiday to terror making news. The events of September 11, 2001, provided several more opportunities to do so—and notably via New Yorkers in the House of Representatives.

The first rabbi guest chaplain after the 9/11 attacks was from Rochester. Alan Katz of Temple Sinai on October 4: "Today is the third day of the Jewish Festival of Tabernacles, Succoth, our Feast of Booths. This festival is also called the Time of Our Rejoicing, and begins only five days after Yom Kippur, our most solemn of holy days." Katz continued, "As the Jewish people from ancient days to the present dwelt and survived in Harvest Booths under the protecting wings of God's presence, bless our entire Nation with the shelter of love and peace that helps us to regain our confidence and security. Be with the leaders of our country who, in wisdom and compassion, seek to establish justice and peace in our Nation and in the world." He implored, "Allow us to stand upright and tall in the face of all that comes our way, always champions for freedom and peace."

On December 12, 2001, Peter Rubinstein of midtown Manhattan's Central Synagogue connected 9/11 to the Jewish calendar as well:

> We gather during this festival of Hanukkah when Jews celebrate the blessing of light and rededication and renewal. Long ago, those enemies who would have destroyed us profaned our sacred altars. They wished to rid the world of the fundamental teachings of our faith: that peace is founded upon justice, that all human beings are God's creation deserving of ultimate decency and goodness, and that the loveliness of light will always, in the end, obliterate the suffocating specter of darkness.

The succession of rabbi prayers following 9/11 expressed a wide range of emotions. Grief, hope, anger, spirituality, hope.

The second rabbi after the terror attacks prayed on October 25. Mark Miller of Temple Bat Yahm in Newport, California, said of Senators: "How we need the inspiration of their steadying hand on the tiller as we awaken to war's alarms and deadly pestilence."

Another Californian, Carole Meyers of Temple Sinai of Glendale, said in the House on November 8, 2001: "It takes courage to pray meaningfully in the wake of events shaping our lives. It is not that we do not turn to God, we do. We come with our praise and with our entreaties, but we strain to hear an answer, to sense God's presence radiating back to us, over the abyss that grief and fear have created." Meyers' sponsor was Rep. Adam Schiff (D-CA). After she died in 2007, Schiff said in a floor tribute: "In 2001, shortly after the tragic events of 9/11, Rabbi Meyers had the distinction of delivering the opening prayer in the House of Representatives. In such a sad and somber time Rabbi Meyers' prayer was uplifting and life-affirming. Her words helped console our nation."

Others with post-9/11 prayers:

- Abraham Shemtov in the Senate on March 12, 2002: "This Nation leads the world in the struggle of freedom against tyranny and of good over evil."
- Dov Hazdan in the House on June 6, 2002: "We stand before Thee as the world faces very dangerous and troubling times."
- Milton Balkany in the Senate on June 25, 2003: "Bring us back to the times of fearless skies and unbridled New York nerve, of tranquil school yards and cool back porch nights."

The events of 9/11 informed remarks of members of Congress who sponsored rabbis as well. Rep. Robert Dold (R-IL) said of Aaron Melman on May 31, 2012: "On September 12, 2001, he found a way to get to Ground Zero, and thereafter provided comfort and support to those first responders in need." Rep. Anthony Weiner (D-NY) said of Melvyn May on September 25, 2002: "When he arrived at Neponsit, he arrived at, frankly, a most troubled time in our community. He arrived in October 2001, one month almost to the day after the horrific attack on the World Trade Center that took so many of our neighbors in Rockaway, and he arrived also one month before a terrible plane crash in Belle Harbor, a stone's throw from his congregation's home. During that time, Rabbi May, with dignity and with great understanding, led our community through that most difficult time."

September 11 may be the most infamous of acts of terror in contemporary time. But other significant terror incidents have made their way into rabbi prayers.

TWA Flight 847 was hijacked by members of Hezbollah and Islamic Jihad on June 14, 1985. The two-week ordeal included taking dozens of prisoners hostage and separating passengers with Jewish-sounding names. National Jewish Resource Center president Irving Greenberg gave the Senate prayer on June 27, three days before the crisis ended. He said: "We fully recognize the brokenness—the hostages, the hunger, the sickness, oppression, and human frailty. Faith is our commitment—notwithstanding the obstacles, we commit our lives and our efforts to transform the world."[42]

Later in 1985 Palestinian terrorists hijacked the Achille Lauro cruise ship in the Mediterranean Sea. They shot and killed wheelchair-bound Leon Klinghoffer. Then they then pushed him overboard. Twelve days after the hijacking ended, on October 22, Simcha Freedman of Miami's Adath Yeshurun Synagogue told the House:

> Adlai Stevenson once said, "Man cannot reduce the truth to ashes, he may murder his fellow man with a shot in the back, but he does not murder

---

42 A Flight 847 hostage became a guest chaplain. Father James McLoughlin of St. Peter's Roman Catholic Church in Geneva, Illinois gave the House prayer on April 16, 1991. In his sponsoring remarks, Rep. John Cox (D-IL) noted Father McLoughlin "was held a hostage for 17 days, and through that experience came to understand the difficult problems that we as a country and the world face in the Middle East." Cox added, "During Father Jim's visit here to Washington, he had the opportunity to visit the grave of Robert Stethem, of Maryland, at the Arlington Cemetery. Robert Stethem died as one of the hostages on TWA flight 847."

justice." Dear G-d, we have faith that truth, justice, and peace shall yet prevail despite the fulminations of those who so viciously attempt to prevent it. We believe the dream is real and that it will come to fruition due to those brave peoples who fight against tyranny and terrorism. They are the last best hope of mankind.

(Freedman's Stevenson quote comes from the Illinois governor's first public appearance after losing to Eisenhower in the 1952 presidential election. Stevenson made remarks at an Alton, Illinois dedication ceremony for a memorial to Elijah Parish Lovejoy, an Abolitionist editor and minister killed by a mob there in 1837 [Alton *Telegraph*, December 22, 2017]. Stevenson spoke on November 9, 1952, the same day that Israel's first president Chaim Weizmann died. Weizmann's last words were: "Eisenhower is a very fine fellow.")

In the fall of 1993, Yasser Arafat came to Washington, DC, bringing some hope for peace. The leader of the Palestine Liberation Organization shook hands with Israeli Prime Minister Yitzhak Rabin at the White House on September 13, 1993. A week later, September 22, Bruce Aft of Congregation Adat Reyim in Virginia was Senate guest chaplain. "As we gather together during this historic time, we are grateful for your blessings," Aft said. "Recognizing that the potential for peace and human fulfillment is strong, we accept the awesome responsibility to do our share to realize this potential."

Islamic militants attacked the American diplomatic compound in Benghazi, Libya on September 11, 2012. They killed the U.S. ambassador. Steven Weil of the Orthodox Union gave the House prayer nine days later. Sponsored by Speaker John Boehner, Rabbi Weil said, "Allow the members of Congress to be Your partners in making a more perfect world, and grant them the insight and the vision to always be mindful of the responsibilities they bear. We implore You to guide and strengthen them so that they can do what must be done to save the world from those who wish to perpetrate terrorism and evil."

Dovid Cohen gave the House prayer during the Israel-Hamas battle in Gaza in the summer of 2014. "We live in a world 'on fire,' where there is turmoil throughout the globe; a world that is ravaged by terror and barbarism," Cohen said on July 10, "a world where youthful potential and its rich contributions are instantaneously destroyed."

March 22, 2016, saw the deadliest terrorist event in Belgium's history: three coordinated bombings in Brussels. John Linder of Temple Solel in Paradise Valley, Arizona, prayed in the House that same day: "Give us strength and reason during these perilous times; bring consolation to the bereaved in Belgium."

Acts of domestic terrorism, too, have coincided with a rabbi prayer in Congress. Robert Silvers of Congregation B'nai Israel in Boca Raton gave the House prayer on April 17, 2013—two days after the Boston Marathon bombing:

> Though some seek to disrupt the peace and deprive us of our very lives, as we witnessed in Boston, we pray that their actions be thwarted and that You continue to shelter us with Your canopy of peace. Send healing of body and soul, O God, to the victims of this act of terror, to our Nation, and to all who grieve with them. Keep forever in Your loving embrace the souls of those who lost their lives. We pray that those who do harm be brought to justice.

The manhunt ended two days after the prayer when Dzhokhar Tsarnaev was captured. He was sentenced to death.

Another Florida rabbi gave the House prayer after more domestic terrorism. Gary Klein of Temple Ahavat Shalom in Palm Harbor was guest chaplain on June 27, 2017. Earlier that month a shooter in Virginia attacked Republicans practicing for the congressional baseball game. Klein began his prayer: "We pray first, O God, that you join with medical professionals to help Congressman Scalise and others injured with him experience complete recoveries."

Also in Virginia in 2017, a woman was killed protesting a neo-Nazi white supremacist rally in Charlottesville. Six days later, on August 18, Arnold Resnicoff noted in his House prayer: "This week we mourn the pain and death of neighbors—the clashes in the street, the shouted words of hate—attacks against the very dreams that remind us who and what we yearn to be." Resnicoff was back in the House on September 1: "Neo-Nazis, racists, bigots, would quench the flame of freedom's holy light."

Opening the first House session after 11 Jews were gunned down in Pittsburgh on October 27, 2018, was evangelical Amber Murrell of the United States Air Force. "May they enjoy Your shalom even as they face the ever-present daunting tasks before them," she said of the representatives on October 30, 2018. "Jehovah Rophi, the God who heals, please heal our land." Senate chaplain Barry Black said on November 13, 2018:

"Lord, continue to extend Your mercies to the Members of the Tree of Life Synagogue in Pittsburgh." Resnicoff was the first rabbi in Congress after the Pittsburgh tragedy. His November 20, 2018, House appearance coincided with the 73rd anniversary of the day the post-World War II Nuremberg war trials began. "We condemned the false belief that any humans are less than human: 'life unworthy of life,'" Resnicoff said of the U.S.-convened Nuremberg court. "Such thinking leads to slaughter, even here at home: dead children in their churches, hated for the color of their skin; beatings, killings, lynchings that stained our landscape, and our history, with what poets called the strange and bitter fruit of bodies hanging from the trees; and last month, in a Pittsburgh synagogue, men and women murdered because the shooter thought 'all Jews should die.'"

Five Jews were wounded during a machete attack on a Hanukkah party in Monsey, New York, on December 28, 2019. Resnicoff gave the House prayer two days later. "With this decade's last House prayer, we give thanks for progress, look ahead with hope," Resnicoff said, "but with eyes wide open to prejudice, hatred, terror that remain—fueling violence like the anti-semitic Hanukkah party attack Saturday, the Texas church attack Sunday." It was the first-ever specific mention of anti-Semitism in America in a rabbi prayer. (On September 13, 1990, in the House, Jay Marcus noted "the ugly rise of anti-Semitism in Russia and Eastern Europe.") Resnicoff's timely reaction made world-wide news, including stories in the *Washington Examiner* and on CNN. Showing his remarks on December 30, 2019, the CNN host said, "As 2019 winds down, a prayer this morning on Capitol Hill, from a Rabbi marking the end of the year with a message of hope."

Finally, two rabbis noted earlier gave prescient prayers in the days leading to profound World War II events: Julius Mark just before Pearl Harbor and Solomon Metz just before D-Day. Similarly, less than two months before the 9/11 Al Qaeda attacks on the U.S., Rafael Grossman of Baron Hirsch Synagogue in Memphis gave the House prayer. His words of June 20, 2001, could have been spoken after, as well: "Thy children everywhere look to this hall of democracy for hope and strength, as old and young continue to face the evil hand of terror and exploitation. Give us determination to bring joy and life to victims of terror and might against those who perpetrate it."

30: Weapons and Soldiers

"They say, Whether our lives and our deaths were for peace and a
new hope or for nothing we cannot say: it is you who must say this. . . .
We leave you our deaths: give them their meaning. . . We were young,
they say. We have died. Remember us."
—"The Young Dead Soldiers" by Archibald MacLeish,
cited by frequent guest chaplain Rabbi Arnold Resnicoff
during his May 28, 2018, Memorial Day Prayer at
the Vietnam Veterans Memorial

You might think a prayer would be the last place to find weapons. But depending on the era—and with whom America is warring—arsenals have been abundantly represented in rabbi prayers in Congress. So have the soldiers who use them.

We begin with two rabbis from Massachusetts—and the atom.

Three years after America dropped A-bombs on Japan, the first rabbi guest prayer entered the atomic age. Joshua Liebman of Boston's Temple Israel opened the Senate on May 19, 1948, five days after Israel became an independent nation. "All nations, from the oldest unto the newest, Israel," Liebman said, "dwell today on the same street of atomic destiny." On June 5, 1956, Samuel Fox of Congregation Anshai Sfard in Lynn stated, "Great is our task in this thermonuclear age, when man has assembled such great powers of destruction."

The Cold War era brought vivid imagery surrounding a nuclear blast— and accompanying angst.

In the House on June 11, 1954, Samuel Rosenblatt of Baltimore hoped that "the protean energies of nature released by the discoveries of science will be harnessed in the service of human well-being alone." And in the House on March 12, 1958, Julius Neumann of New York's Congregation Zichron Moshe said, "In these days of tension and tumult, permit us to hear 'the still small voice' above the thundering detonation of A- and H-bombs and behold 'the great light' beyond the blinding flashes of nuclear power."

"Awesome and final fireworks of the nuclear holocaust will be unleashed unless the head instructs the heart to supply the wisdom needed to keep the peace," warned Leon Adler, of Temple Emanuel, Kensington, Maryland, in the Senate on July 10, 1963. In the midst of the early '80s installment of the Cold War, Louis Tuchman had similar thoughts. The rabbi of Peoria's Congregation Agudas Achim said in the House on March 30, 1982, "Today, amidst darkened skies, may the glorious light of Thy countenance shine forth brightly. May we soon witness the day when the ominous clouds of evil and hatred shall no longer flash athwart the skies."

Not just bombs. Rockets, too.

In the Senate on February 19, 1959, Morris Silverman of Hartford's Emanuel Synagogue hoped "that our strength be revealed not only in guided missiles, but in guided leaders." Three years later, again in the Senate and again from a New England rabbi, that hope was repeated. David Berent, Congregation Beth Jacob, Lewiston, Maine, on June 13, 1962: "Give us guided leaders, instead of guided missiles."

Let's stay in the air. In the House on March 7, 1963, Maurice Lamm described "a globe jigsawed with boundaries, separated by Iron and Bamboo Curtains, cut up into airspace, divided by latitude numbers, and fenced with radar screens." Lamm remained airborne in the Senate on March 15, 1966: "Not by the rocket's red glare and the bombs bursting in air, may we have proof that the flag is still there—but by the tranquility of men's souls, the decency of their actions, and the unspoiled quiet of nature's dawn, will we have proof that the stars and stripes are forever."

Not to neglect the action on the ground, of course. That's where soldiers are recognized for their service. Five rabbis have included citation of Memorial Day in their prayers.

Among them, Moshe Bomzer in the House on May 21, 1998, "the last days of the congressional session prior to our national Memorial Day weekend," as he pointed out. "It was exactly 130 years ago almost to the day that Congress resolved that a day be set aside to recognize and memorialize those who had given their lives to defend our country." And Hannah Spiro in the House on May 29, 2018: "On this day after bittersweet Memorial Day . . . remembering those who died in service. . . ."

Samuel Thurman of United Hebrew Temple in St. Louis prayed in the Senate as World War II was ending. On February 26, 1945, he said, "The flower of our youth, the strong and the brave, the free sons and daughters of America, must now be offering themselves in fierce and cruel combat against enemies that either do not know Thee or have forgotten Thee and Thy commandments." Thurman asked God for "speedy victory to our brave fighting forces." Felipe Goodman of Temple Beth Sholom in Las

Vegas prayed in the House June 3, 2008. He wanted to "protect the men and women of our Armed Forces who stand in harm's way so that we may enjoy the blessings of freedom and liberty." Aaron Melman of Congregation Beth Shalom in Northbrook, Illinois, urged the House on May 31, 2012: "Protect our Armed Forces and speed our victory over tyranny." And Doniel Ginsberg of Yeshiva Ateres Shmuel in Waterbury, Connecticut, opened his Senate prayer on June 12, 2014, by blessing "the brave men and women of our Armed Forces who have left their loved ones in defense of freedom.

In the Senate in April 2003, Navy chaplain Arnold Resnicoff remembered "twenty years ago, in a foxhole in Beirut: I looked around at others in the bunker, and had a simple thought. 'We Americans,' I said, 'must have the only "interfaith foxholes" in the whole Mid-East.'" He returned to that theme when he opened the House on July 18, 2016: "I was in a Beirut foxhole, 1983, religious war, but U.S. foxholes were unique: interfaith. . . . I learned that day that if more foxholes, if more people made room for others' faiths, we would need far fewer foxholes and have more cause for faith."

In the House on February 21, 1966, Norman Zdanowltz of Congregation Beth Abraham in Maine recognized "the gallant men of our Armed Forces who have gone forth to arrest the reckless wave of unprovoked aggression and bloodshed on distant shores." Likewise, in the very next prayer in Congress, in the Senate on March 1, 1966, Yonkers rabbi Louis Wolfish asked of God, "Guard and protect the members of our Armed Forces in Vietnam." Adding the Navy, here's Samuel Rosenblatt of Baltimore's Beth Tfiloh Congregation in the House on February 1, 1971: "universal brotherhood is far more effective in resolving international as well as internal conflicts than battleships, tanks, and guns."

In 13 rabbi prayers, Congress was reminded in some specific way of "the process of Messianic fulfillment when swords will be beaten into plowshares and spears into pruning hooks, and nations will then no longer wage war," as Atlanta's Arnold Goodman put it on November 8, 1983. That's 13 swords issued by Isaiah 2:4. In the House on November 5, 1981, Ephraim Sturm supplied sabers to the arsenal: "In a world torn with distrust and confronted with starvation, with the threats of rattling sabers and the realities of hostilities, the United States of America remains as a citadel of moral integrity."

Weapons and Isaiah came together again in the February 2, 1988, Senate prayer:

May your servants find reassurance and encouragement in God's promise through the prophet, Isaiah: "No weapon that is formed against thee shall prosper; and every tongue that shall rise against Thee in judgment thou shalt condemn."—Isaiah 54:17

That prayer was offered by Chaplain Richard Halverson. A Presbyterian. And he was assessing a different yet equally vicious battlefield: "Senators are tempting targets for relentless, voracious attacks on their integrity, performance, personal, and family lives."

SECTION VII

Congress Institutions

31: Prayers Go Inside Congress

"We ask Your blessings for our country, for its Government, for its leaders and advisors, and for all who exercise just and rightful authority. Teach them insights of Your law, that they may administer all affairs of state fairly, that peace and security, happiness and prosperity, justice and freedom may forever abide in our midst."
—"A Prayer for Our Country" written by Talmudic scholar Louis Ginzberg in 1927. Offered by Rabbi Paul Kerbel, Nevey Shalom Congregation, Bowie, Maryland, during his October 23, 1991, House prayer

"When politicians and presidents pray, they're essentially performing a rite of humility and submission to a higher order— if not to God then at least to something greater than themselves. Implicit in this public exercise is a show of faith in scriptures that guided this country's founders."
—*Washington Post* columnist Kathleen Parker, May 4, 2018

"Congressional chaplains are a useful adornment to the American political tradition and opening prayers emphasize the serious nature of congressional labor."
—*Weekly Standard* columnist Philip Terzian, May 11, 2018

Senate chaplain Richard Halverson served up classic Jewish guidance when he began his July 10, 1990, prayer with Psalms 121:8: *"The Lord shall preserve thy going out and thy coming in from this time forth, and even for evermore."*

It's the kind of protection God would offer if She were in the business of travel insurance: Your journey is guaranteed by the Lord. We all could use that dose of emotional stability traveling through airports these days.[43]

In what direction did Halverson head in July 1990 with that guidance? Straight into the heart of the Senate. The institution, the calendar, and all. Picking up:

> We thank Thee for Thy faithfulness to all who serve in this place and their families during this last recess—for safety in travel, for family time together, for strength for the work required, for time with constituents and exposure to the people, for rest, recreation, and renewal. Thank Thee for Thy loving care, provision, and guidance. Grant that the Senators and their staffs will be enabled in these next four weeks to accomplish everything necessary and desirable. Deliver them from trivial and futile activity and guide them in the way of truth and justice.

Halverson showed that prayers don't impart lofty, sweeping inspiration alone. They also cover concrete political reality and legislative schedule.

Soon after the 1992 election Halverson cited gloomy prophet Jeremiah when he told Senators, "Political campaigns arouse the worst in us: negativism, egotism, factionalism, cynicism, anger." He urged, "Prevent critical issues from being pingpong balls batted back and forth on TV." Another TV reference in Halverson's July 14, 1994, prayer: "When the press and the media have finished their tasks, when the talk shows have exhausted their discussions, when the citizens have written all their letters, when the lobbyists have done their work, the 100 men and women who comprise this body are left with the decisions."

Halverson went deep inside Senate personnel with another sorrowful and graphic prayer in 1989. On April 4 (a date already associated with assassination, Martin Luther King's), he paired a Senator's aide—"We remember Sheila Burke in the loss of her father so soon after her mother's death last

---

43 That particular Psalm begins, "I shall raise my eyes to the mountains, from where will my help come?"—a question incorporated into Jewish liturgy; "*Esa Einai*" is one of the most popular prayers in times of trouble. Sen. James Lankford (R-OK) cited the passage on March 25, 2020, during debate over economic relief for the coronavirus pandemic: "of all the things that are going on in Washington, DC, right now, you will hear people repeating over and over: our hope is not in government; our hope is not in how much money we can spend. We understand full well, when we lift up our eyes to the mountain—to this hill. We understand full well where our help comes from, and it is not from all the folks in this room. Our help comes from the Lord."

year"—with a Senator's son—"nothing in the Nation or the world is more important right now than 6-year-old Albert Gore Ill, hit by a car last night, in the hospital with a broken thigh and rib, ruptured spleen, bruised lungs, and concussion." A year earlier Halverson offered medical thoughts about Sen. Joe Biden (D-DE), who was entering the hospital to correct an aneurysm in an artery that supplies blood to the brain. "God of Abraham, Isaac, and Israel," Halverson prayed on April 21, 1988, "We thank You for the excellent reports concerning Senator Biden, and we pray that he will be prepared in body, mind, and spirit for the surgery that remains to be done."

Opening the Senate on another April 4, in 1985, there also was no mention of the anniversary of Dr. King's slaying. Instead, Halverson stuck to the practical—the Senate calendar. "In these closing hours before recess," Halverson said, "help the Senate to accomplish what is needed so that the ghosts of unfinished business will not haunt them during these next 10 days." He ended: "Having just, in this last hour, seen Mohammed Amin's most recent film on the tragedy of Africa, I want to thank You that the Senate passed the African famine relief bill."

House chaplain Patrick Conroy went with the Hebrew Bible to say farewell to a concluding Congress on December 20, 2018. "As the 115th Congress draws near a close, we are reminded by Scripture that for every thing, there is an appointed time: A time to weep, and a time to laugh. A time to be silent, and a time to speak," Rev. Conroy said. "In the people's House there is also a time to win an election and a time to lose; a time to be sworn in and a time to retire. While it may be difficult to go through such transitions, we know, as did the author of Ecclesiastes, that the time does come to say goodbye to those who will be missed dearly for, indeed, in electoral politics, that is just the way it is."

Rabbis provide their own share of down-to-earth, nitty-gritty practical advice to Senators and Representatives doing their day jobs.

"We meet this morning prepared to conclude the agenda of the final days of this session so that we may return to our communities for the scheduled recess." Instructions from the Majority Leader? Nope: it's Tzvi Porath of Ohr Kodesh Congregation, Chevy Chase, Maryland. Sounding less like a clergyman and more like a blue ribbon commission, Porath told the Senate on March 25, 1994, "We trust that our constituents realize that the deliberations in which we have participated, the judgments we have made, and the conclusions we have reached will reflect the directions they would want us to go. We look forward to the coming days to be able to meet with our citizens to get their ideas, their thoughts, their input. We pray that we return from our recess invigorated, stimulated, and uplifted by the personal contact with the people from our State."

"May the efforts expended in worthy aspirations, and the deeds accomplished through exemplary commitment, help bring nigh to You those who look to this House for guidance and direction," remarked Rabbi Robert Rothman of Rye on October 6, 1983. "May the power of principle rather than the principle of power be the measure of this leadership's contribution," he further urged. "Teach them neither to be afraid of espousing good causes nor of cherishing good convictions. Save them and us from that life's outlook which consists of slogans that numb the mind, starve the soul, and stultify progress."

"May we always remember that this [House] Chamber must not become an ivory tower, isolated from the masses we represent. It must stand as a bastion of strength and a beacon of light for a bewildered humanity," instructed Arthur Schneier of Brooklyn's Congregation B'nai Jacob on June 16, 1958.

Prayers (and the following Pledge of Allegiance) are among the few neutral moments in a Congressional session. Evan Hoffman of Congregation Anshe Sholom, New Rochelle, New York, seemed aware of the unifying potential of prayer when he opened the House on October 29, 2019. "In a time of polarization and rancorous dispute," he urged God, "we beseech Thee to help our elected officials maintain decorum, civility, commonality of purpose, and a sense of shared American destiny."

When Arnold Resnicoff was guest chaplain a month later, he took his cues from an emotional and electrifying moment that had just occurred on the House floor. Rep. John Lewis (D-GA) was saying farewell to a former member of the other party retiring for health reasons. Fellow Georgian Sen. Johnny Isakson sat on the Republican side of the chamber. Lewis said, "I will come over to meet you, brother." He walked over. The two old friends hugged. Resnicoff marked the encounter in his prayer. "On this House floor last week Congressman John Lewis walked across the aisle, honoring, embracing, Senator Johnny Isakson with simple but inspiring words: 'I will come over to meet you, brother,'" Resnicoff said on November 29, 2019, the day after Thanksgiving. "When we see another not as other, but instead as brother, sister, neighbor, that is cause for thanks." A few weeks later, a rabbi returned to the aisle theme. "At this time of grave division, inspire these Members of the people's House to reach across every kind of aisle," Barry

Block of Congregation B'nai Israel, Little Rock, asked of God on January 10, 2020. He was the first guest chaplain of the new decade.

Earlier thanks from "self-help" rabbi Joshua Liebman of Boston's Temple Israel, whose mid-twentieth-century therapeutic spiritual prescriptions mirrored in tone those of positive-thinking minister Norman Vincent Peale. He prayed in the Senate on May 19, 1948. "We thank Thee for this great Senate of democracy in this hallowed America," Liebman opened. "Cause us to understand that laws are given that men shall live by them and not die by them."

Reviewing a Peale biography in the *Washington Post* on December 16, 2016, Mitch Horowitz noted Liebman's *Peace of Mind* "dominated bestseller lists in 1946, six years before Peale's 'The Power of Positive Thinking.' (Liebman, a deeply searching and intellectually rigorous man, died at age 41 in 1948. His name faded as Peale's rose.)"

Maybe so. And maybe Peale officiated at the 1968 wedding of Julie Nixon and David Eisenhower. And maybe Peale was President Trump's boyhood pastor. But he never was a guest chaplain in Congress.

Some rabbis play (or pray) to the room, literally.

Jimmy Kessler's April 4, 2001, House prayer was more like a *qvell*. "Though it may be routine for some of you in this room today, it is truly an awesome moment for me to realize those who have stood here before me and to be privileged to occupy that same space," the rabbi from Galveston said.

Likewise, Harold Kravitz of Adath Jeshurun in Minnetonka, Minnesota, told the Senate on June 9, 2015: "It is a privilege to be inside this Capitol Building, richly designed to inspire those who govern to achieve the loftiest goals possible for this Nation."

Sheldon Elster of Agudas Achim Congregation, Alexandria, Virginia, went even deeper inside the Senate on July 31, 1975—to hearing rooms. "We come together from the world of committee hearings, meetings with constituents," he prayed, "to give pause/To praise/To give thanks."

And talk about inside the Beltway: A rabbi from Fairfax, Virginia— mere miles from Capitol Hill—connected Torah to Congress. Melvin Glazer of Congregation Olam Tikvah opened the House on September 26, 1996, noting, "Next week the Jewish people will celebrate the holiday of Simhat Torah, the festival when we will conclude the reading of the Torah." He continued, "As you will soon come to the end of this congressional session, you too will conclude yet another chapter in the glorious Torah of the United States."

Another rabbi played to the Beltway region's favorite professional sports team. The Washington Redskins beat the Miami Dolphins in the Super Bowl on January 30, 1983. Two days later, the Capital City was still celebrating as Morris Hershman of Joliet Jewish Congregation approached the rostrum. The rabbi joined the party—at least rhetorically. "Upon this august and illustrious body representing the people of the United States tackling the weighty matters before it," he said, "we humbly invoke Thy divine benedictions." If 'tackling' wasn't hint enough of where this was headed, the rest of the prayer was unmistakable. "As we meet in this Super Bowl of governmental activity that impinges on the life of every American," he said, "help us to realize that when an issue becomes a political football there can be many fumbles. Penalize not, we pray Thee, our country for our offenses and may our defense ever be honorable and justified. Help us to pass to those who come after us a tradition unsullied and enhanced."

No instant replay required to spot *those* football/Congress metaphors. And that's without mentioning any prayers surrounding a certain fourth-down handoff to the winner of the Super Bowl's Most Valuable Player award, Redskins running back John Riggins.

How about a Most Valuable *Prayer* award? For Congress-speak, it might go to a guest chaplain who wasn't a rabbi but a pastor from New Orleans. Here's how Rev. Elmo Romagosa opened the House on March 2, 1966:

> O Supreme Legislator, make these gentlemen ever distinguished by fidelity to your word. Make seniority in your love ever germane to their conduct. Make them consistently vote yea in the cloakroom of conscience that the expiration of life's term they feel no need to revise and extend. . . When the Congress of life is adjourned and they answer the final quorum call, may the Eternal Committee report out a clean bill on their lives. Finally, by unanimous consent of the Heavenly House, may the Infinite Speaker recognize them on both side of the aisle with this reward: "Well done, good and faithful servants of my people."

As the *Associated Press* described it the next day, Romagosa "showed some of the nation's lawmakers how to pray in the language of the legislator."

(A clergyman keenly aware of legislative life was Senate chaplain Frederick Brown Harris. He addressed educators in Abilene, Texas, on March 15, 1960. With the skill of any Washington insider, Harris brought tribute to the state's legendary legislator, Senate majority leader Lyndon Johnson.

"He is as able a leader of a deliberative body as our country has produced," Harris said of LBJ, as inserted in the March 22, 1960, *Congressional Record*. "In his alert brain there seems to be a built-in diagram of the Senate. With uncanny accuracy he is aware of the probable attitudes and reactions of the Senate Members to pending bills. But all that knowledge is the result of painstaking care and toil.")

The prayer perhaps most valuable in reflecting the reality of Congress life was written by a Jew. But not a rabbi, a Senator. And not for delivery in the chamber, but in a book. Describing the ordeal of fundraising in *Al Franken, Giant of the Senate*,[44] Franken (D-MN) re-imagined Reinhold Neibuhr's "Serenity Prayer," a favorite of Alcoholics Anonymous. Franken offered "The Democratic Senator's Serenity Prayer": "God Grant Me the Serenity to Accept the Things I Cannot Legislate, The Courage to Legislate the Things I Can, The Wisdom to Know the Difference And the Patience to Explain That Difference to My Donors."

32: May Their Memories Be A Blessing/RIP: Rest In Prayer

"We are unspeakably grateful for the wisdom—the insight of King David concerning life beyond this life. Death is but a shadow through which we pass between life here-and-now and life eternal. We do not walk alone through this valley for the Lord, our Shepherd, is with us."
—Senate Chaplain Richard Halverson, April 9, 1991

"Grow old along with me!
The best is yet to be,
The last of life, for which the first was made:
Our times are in His hand . . .
Let age approve of youth, and death complete the same!"
—"Rabbi Ben Ezra" by Robert Browning

A poem cited on the House floor by Rep. Frank Horton (R-NY) during April 23, 1963, eulogy to Rep. Meyer Jacobstein (D-NY), "a poor Jewish boy who had made good." Poem also cited on the House floor by Rep. Carlton Sickles (D-MD) March 1, 1965; Rep. Claude Pepper April 7, 1965 and May 8, 1975 (D-FL); Rep. Charles Wilson (D-TX) February 26, 1973; and Rep.

---

44   Twelve, 2017.

Tip O'Neill (D-MA) September 13, 1979. And on the Senate floor by Sen. Olin Johnston (D-SC) March 13, 1962; Sen. Robert Griffin (R-MI) October 1, 1971; Sen. Hubert Humphrey (D-MN) June 14, 1977; and Sen. Howell Heflin (D-AL) November 12, 1991. And many others.

With over 630 rabbi prayers delivered in Congress so far, likely at least some would coincide with a milestone in American history. Like the death of a political leader. Like a Kennedy.

Rabbi Harold Smith of Chicago's Congregation Agudath Achim of South Shore gave the first House prayer after Congress' ten-day adjournment that followed President Kennedy's assassination. "Immersed though we be in somber thoughtfulness," Smith said on December 4, 1963, "we nevertheless see ample reason for gratitude and consolation in the demonstrated capacity of our great and glorious Republic to carry on, in our saddest and darkest hours, with strength and determination, with peacefulness and orderliness, with respectful relegation of party differences—all characteristic only of free world democracies. We continue to pray, as we always shall, for the soul of our fallen leader, John Fitzgerald Kennedy. We pray also, from the very depths of our being, for the welfare of our newly risen leader, Lyndon B. Johnson."

Smith wrote in the July 1, 1993, *Chicago Tribune* of his appearance in Congress: "Seldom had I seen such a group of grief-stricken, dejected people."

Kurt Metzger of Temple B'nai Israel in Olean, New York, opened the House on June 5, 1968. It was the day after JFK's brother was shot in Los Angeles. Bobby Kennedy was still alive when the House session began. Metzger was the first to offer a prayer for the Senator's recovery: "In this hour of shock over the wounding of Senator Robert F. Kennedy we beseech Thee to bestow upon him complete recovery from his injuries and to restore him to our country and to his family in renewed health and vigor." RFK died the next day.

Rep. Charles Goodell (R-NY) sponsored Metzger. Three months later Goodell resigned. He accepted Governor Nelson Rockefeller's appointment to fill the vacant New York Senate seat caused by Kennedy's assassination.

Not just the most famous members of the legislative branch, like a Kennedy, merit divinely inspired attention. Rabbis have comforted Congress when lesser names have answered the final roll call.

Pro-segregation Sen. Walter George (D-GA) died August 4, 1957, just under a year after he was defeated for re-election. Manfred Rechtschaffen of

Congregation Degel Israel, Lancaster, Pennsylvania, was guest Senate chaplain the next day. In a prayer reported in an August 6, 1957, *Associated Press* story that ran in the *New York Times*, Rechtschaffen eulogized:

> America has suffered the loss of a statesman. Walter Franklin George, of Georgia, is gone. He served his State and this Nation loyally. He was a southern gentleman. He had the respect and confidence of his colleagues in the Senate. His words and deeds Inspired the confidence of nations. "Is it constitutional and wise?" were his criteria for legislation. Party lines fell away before this great American. Father, full of compassion, grant rest beneath the wings of Thy presence among the holy and pure to Walter Franklin George.

Styles Bridges was a Republican Senator from New Hampshire for nearly a quarter-century. He died November 26, 1961. New Hampshire rabbi Jacob Handler was in the Senate two months later. His January 17, 1962, prayer honored "the memory of a man of valor and vision, of great courage and devotion, whose deeds and action, here in the Senate and in his own beloved home State, New Hampshire, represented the highest ideals of noble living and American citizenship. Grant that the soul of the Honorable Styles Bridges, whose memory we cherish, may be bound up in the bond of everlasting life. May the reminiscences of his life stir our finer sensibilities and arouse within us a desire to emulate the splendid example set for us by Styles Bridges as he served Thee and his fellow men with such great sincerity, kindness, loyalty, and devotion."

Rep. Julius Kahn (R-CA), who was Jewish, sponsored the army Selective Service Act of 1917. "Many of the boys who go to the front will be wounded," he said after drawing the first draft number of World War I. "Many of them will be killed. But Jews at all periods of the world's history have always been ready to make the supreme sacrifice whenever the land that gives them shelter demands it." Kahn died on December 18, 1924. The House met on February 22, 1925—rare for them, it was a Sunday—to memorialize Kahn. Abram Simon gave the opening prayer. "We thank Thee for whatever influence Julius Kahn was able to render to his country," the rabbi from Washington Hebrew Congregation said. "We feel that he was always in the line of duty, and upon the altar of his country placed the gift of a rich and endowed soul. We thank Thee for his leadership in the hour of danger, and for the numbers of men who rallied when the call went forth, who were ready to offer all of their best to the country."

House Appropriations Committee chair Martin Madden (R-IL) died April 27, 1928. The *Daily Illini* reported the next day: "One of the Republican leaders in Congress and a power in the House of Representatives, was stricken with an acute heart attack today and died a few minutes later. The end came as he sat in his desk in his capitol office, talking with a colleague. He suddenly placed his hand over his heart and sank down in his chair. He was removed to a couch in the room and despite efforts to revive him he passed away without regaining consciousness." Another Washington Hebrew Congregation rabbi gave the House prayer three days later. For Madden, William Franklin Rosenblum "render[ed] tribute to a colleague and friend who has gone to sit in the assembly on high. His voice will no longer sound in these Halls, his presence no more abide in our midst, who but yesterday was eager and alert in the performance of his duties, even as we are at this hour."

Republican Rep. B. Carroll Reece died in office on March 19, 1961. He served in the House longer than anyone in Tennessee history. Rabbi Israel Gerstein gave the House prayer the next day. "We praise Thee for the services of one of our consecrated colleagues who has been recalled to Thee," Gerstein said. "Send the healing balm of Thy consolation to the members of his family, and may his memory ever inspire us to noble living."

Rep. Arthur Younger (R-CA) died June 20, 1967. Harvey Waxman, Congregation Beth Medrosh Elyon, Monsey, New York, was in the House the next day. "In this hour of sorrow we pray for our beloved companion who has gone into Thy nearer presence," Waxman said. "We thank Thee for him, for the contribution he made to this body and to our country."

A guest rabbi's memorial to a Senator also has been cited. After Harry Truman died in December 1972, Sen. Edmund Muskie (D-ME) offered a floor tribute to the former Senator and resident. Muskie included a Truman eulogy delivered by Rabbi David Berent of Congregation Beth Jacob in Lewiston, Maine: "Harry S. Truman was not only a Senator with a conscience; but pre-eminently the conscience of the Senate." Berent had delivered the Senate prayer on June 13, 1962.

As for House leadership, Speaker William Bankhead (D-AL) was sick and mere months away from death when Louis Wolsey of Philadelphia's Congregation Rodeph Shalom gave the prayer. On February 8, 1940, Wolsey said, "Bless the Speaker of this House and restore him to health and to his responsibility."

In more contemporary history of the Speaker, a rabbi offered a prayer after a House leader suffered a death—a political death. In fact, the rabbi sponsored by Speaker John Boehner's deputy had a unique encounter with political history. Reported by the *Mahopac* (NY) *News,* June 19, 2014:

> It was only fitting that a rabbi would give the opening prayer on the floor of the U.S. House of Representatives on the day after Majority Leader Eric Cantor's historic defeat in the Virginia primary. The defeat of Cantor, who was widely expected to be the first Jewish Speaker of the House, caused a political earthquake on Capitol Hill, and Mahopac Rabbi Eytan Hammerman, who was given this once-in-a-lifetime honor, was in the thick of it.

The *Washington Post*'s Dana Milbank noted Hammerman's prayer in his June 11, 2014, column, the day following Cantor's demise:

> Just before noon, Boehner emerged, but only to begin the day's session on the House floor. There, he listened to the opening prayer from a guest chaplain, a rabbi who asked God to inspire "the many races, colors and ancestries that make up our blessed country."

Milbank also tweeted: "Closest we'll get to Jewish Speaker of House; guest chaplain, Rabbi Eytan Hammerman, gives today's opening prayer."

33: The Congressional Prayer Room

"And let them make Me a sanctuary, that I may dwell among them."
—Exodus 25:8

"When you pray, go into your room, close the door and pray to your Father, who is unseen. Then your Father, who sees what is done in secret, will reward you."
—Matthew 6:6

"Preserve me, O God, for in thee do I put my trust."
—Psalms 16:1. The words surrounding George Washington kneeling in prayer portrayed on a stained glass window in the Congressional Prayer Room.

Need a place to pray?

How about right on the floor of the U.S. House of Representatives.

In the old days you could. Not just chaplains or members of Congress. Anyone. In actual church services. Honest to God.

During May 2017 floor remarks, Sen. James Lankford (R-OK) explained:

> Statuary Hall was once the House of Representatives, where the House gathered. It was also the largest gathering place in Washington, DC, and many churches for years met in Statuary Hall to be able to pray. It was the common meeting place. In fact, for a period of time in the early 1800s, four churches a Sunday used at that time the House of Representatives Chamber— what is now known as Statuary Hall— as their place for worship. Thomas Jefferson worshipped there. In fact, every President from Thomas Jefferson all the way to Abraham Lincoln attended church on Sundays in Statuary Hall.

Indeed, in 1800 Congress approved the use of the just-completed Capitol structure as a church building. Sunday services were alternately administered by the House and Senate chaplains. And in 1853 Congress declared that congressional chaplains have a "to conduct religious services weekly in the Hall of the House of Representatives."

That kind of use for Statuary Hall is, obviously, no more. And the House now meets in larger quarters. It moved into its present chamber in 1857.

But there still is a place to pray. A dedicated room. The Congressional Prayer Room.

And it began its spiritual contribution to Hill life about a century after the Statuary Hall church services ended.

On January 2, 1968, Sen. Everett Dirksen (R-IL) gave ABC News anchor Howard K. Smith a Capitol tour. They stopped near the Rotunda. "Howard is well to take a look at the prayer room," Dirksen narrated, "which was established in 1954 here in the Capitol. The members can come here and get their peace and joy and solitude that the soul so desperately needs in moments like that."

The camera panned the room. Dirksen continued: "You'll notice that stained glass window which shows George Washington in prayer. And then the quotation is from the 16th Psalm: 'Beautiful thing, preserve me, O God, for in Thee do I put my trust.' It is indeed a very inspiring place."

Created during the Cold War, the Congressional Prayer Room surely was meant to be, at least in part, a spiritual response to the Soviet Union. Take that, godless Communists: No similar room inside the Kremlin.

The room's sole purpose, according to the House Chaplain office, "is to provide a quiet place where individual Representatives and Senators may withdraw to seek Divine strength and guidance, both in public affairs and in their own personal lives." The Chaplain's website further notes, "Just as prayer was offered at the constitutional convention and is still offered today at the beginning of each session of Congress . . . so, too, does the prayer room give the men and women who have the gravest decisions to make for America and the world an opportunity to be alone with God."

When the room was established by resolution on May 4, 1954, Joseph Martin[45] of Massachusetts was House Speaker. In his 2003 biography of Martin—*A Compassionate Conservative*—James Kenneally wrote:

> As Speaker of the House, he was once asked by a colleague to order the House Chaplain to shorten his daily prayer. Martin refused, allegedly replying, "this is the only church I have, you know." Maybe this response explains why Martin labored so hard and was so proud of his efforts in getting a prayer room in the House chambers.

Martin was the last Republican House speaker until Newt Gingrich in 1995. He designated Democratic Rep. Brooks Hays of Arkansas chairman of the special Chapel Committee. It had three members. The other two were Republicans. Thus, Hays was uniquely the only Democratic committee chairman in the Republican majority 83rd Congress.[46]

In the House on August 5, 1954, Hays put the room's purpose in this context:

> I believe people might be surprised at the number of times men in these seats have prayed silently for themselves. I know that I have been inspired on occasions by an intimate opening of the mind of a colleague in reverently insisting that prayer is needed. What we want in the prayer room is a place of retreat where encouragement can be given to that attitude of reverence and meditation; where one can find the resources that lie outside himself.

And in an August 12, 1960, statement to the *Arkansas Gazette*, Hays offered a theological perspective on the room's legislative history:

> One of the senators suggested that to provide a place of prayer at the Capitol would violate the Biblical injunction to pray in secret. By pointing out that a

---

45   Lexington Books, 2003, page 4.
46   University of Arkansas University Libraries Digital Collection, Brooks Hays materials.

literal application of this principle would preclude all prayer in churches and synagogues, we convinced the member that it was not a serious objection. Moreover, since the room was to be used not for assembly but was solely for individual use, the prayers thus encouraged really met the standard of secrecy enunciated by Jesus.

One report about the room appeared in the Paris, Texas, *News* on July 24, 1955. It quoted Rep. Richard Poff (R-VA). He said the new prayer room was no "large assembly hall through which demagogues and hypocrites can parade their religion." Rather, it was "a small, simple, sanctified retreat to which the elected representatives of the people may repair for meditation." During debate on the floor of Congress, members may suggest the absence of a quorum. "In the prayer room," Poff said, "a quorum is one—and God."

Showing the room to C-SPAN on November 27, 1994, Rep. J. J. Pickle (D-TX) said, "Members from time to time will come in, sit down—House members, Senate members—and make their own little private prayer about the legislation, or whatever issue facing the country."

One evening in 2011, during partisan brinkmanship over increasing the limit on federal borrowing, South Carolina Republicans "retreated from the speaker's office to the chapel," the *Washington Post*'s Paul Kane remembered on December 20, 2018. "After prayer, they opposed [Speaker John] Boehner's efforts to broker a compromise."

As for the room's design, it "proved something of a challenge," according to Jay Price writing in *Temples for a Modern God: Religious Architecture in Postwar America*. Example: "When the design of the stained glass-window's central medallion initially featured a scroll, some felt it looked too Jewish. The revised medallion replaced the scroll with a picture of George Washington kneeling in prayer."[47]

The prayer room is not on any public Capitol tour. The public is not admitted. House Chaplain James Ford told C-SPAN on January 6, 1994: "We have a prayer room, a meditation room that's available for members and staff to go to. We don't use the word chapel because that implies you have services there. We don't have services."

Actually, at least once it was the site for services. During the mid-Sixties, the 89th Congress, which passed Great Society legislation. For a very Jewish reason.

Here's Rep. Abraham Multer's (D-NY) October 22, 1965, explanation:

---

47   Oxford University Press, 2012, page 49.

This year the Rosh Hashanah holidays—the Jewish New Year—fell on legislative days. Unfortunately, the parliamentary situation was such that it was impossible to extend the courtesy to the Jewish Members—15 of them—of forgoing roll calls on those 2 days. If we attended religious services either in our places of worship in our home districts or in the temples and synagogues which welcomed us in Washington, DC, we could not possibly get to the floor of the House on time each day without violating our traditional practices. With the warmly sincere and hearty cooperation of our distinguished Speaker, John W. McCormack, we were permitted to temporarily convert the non-denominational congressional prayer room in the Capitol to a synagogue for our prayer services. We were then enabled to attend to our religious duties as well as our governmental obligations, serving both and doing violence to neither. While keeping church and state completely separate each gave the other full respect and obeisance.

In a May 18, 2017, C-SPAN interview, LBJ biographer Robert Caro noted "in this incredible burst in 1965, [Johnson] passes the Voting Rights Act, Medicare, Medicaid, 16 separate education bills, everything that whenever poor people get paid to go to college now, it's Lyndon Johnson, passes Head Start. He does this all in a very few months." A busy legislative year—and New Year—indeed. Good thing the Congressional Prayer Room is right off the House floor.

It's also a place for weddings. Future Senate Majority Leader Mitch McConnell married future Labor and Transportation Secretary Elaine Chao in the Congressional Prayer Room on February 6, 1993. Ten years earlier Sen. Pete Wilson (R-CA) married Gayle Graham there.[48]

No rabbi serving as guest chaplain has mentioned the prayer room in his or her floor prayer. But several rabbi guest chaplains are linked to the room's history.

One rabbi with multiple guest chaplain appearances was instrumental in the room's creation. Congress appointed Norman Gerstenfeld of Washington Hebrew Congregation, who gave the Senate prayer five times between 1942 and 1955, to the four-person advisory panel deciding the room's design. The panel's purpose was to "make sure that no part of the furnishings and no symbol used would give offense to members of any church, and at the same time incorporate in the fabric and decoration of

---

48   United Press International, May 29, 1983.

the room the basic unity of belief in God and His Providence that has characterized our history."[49]

David de Sola Pool of New York City's Shearith Israel Synagogue was Senate guest chaplain on June 28, 1955. He provided these thoughts to a 1955 congressional document called *The Capitol in Story and Pictures*:

> In the Capitol, the national building that represents every American, the Prayer Room speaks to the individual heart. All inhabitants of this land, whatsoever their race, creed, or color, enjoy full religious liberty. All are brothers, alike children of the one Divine Father.
>
> The Prayer Room and the daily opening of Congress with prayer, symbolize this unifying brotherhood under God, and the recognition by the Nation as a whole of the need of divine guidance and blessing in the conduct of its affairs. In this sense the Nation has chosen as spiritual motto "In God we trust."

Another rabbi with a similar connection to both the Congressional Prayer Room and prayer in Congress: Saul Wisemon. He was a four-time guest chaplain (three in the House and one in the Senate between 1963 and 1973).

Wisemon spoke Hebrew each time he opened a Congressional session in prayer. Rep. John Monagan (D-CT) recognized that fact when on December 4, 1963, he marked the 100th anniversary of the Capitol's completion. "Exactly at 12 noon on Monday, December 2, standing in the rotunda," Monagan said on the House floor, "Rabbi Saul Israel Wisemon, of the Beth El Synagogue, Torrington, Conn., offered a prayer of meditation to commemorate this historic event. He then went to the Prayer Room, directly off the rotunda, to once again offer this prayer. Rabbi Wisemon, long a student of American history said: *There is no other symbol that signifies to the Nation and the world—the idea and ideals of American democracy*

---

49 Gerstenfeld is connected to more Congress institutional history. He gave a reading at the 1962 laying of the Rayburn House Office Building cornerstone. Also on the platform that May 24 day: President Kennedy. The *Associated Press* reported Gerstenfeld, one of three clergymen, "drew an approving smile from Kennedy when he said: 'Mindful of the experience at your inauguration. I have chosen a brief selection.' His reading lasted about 20 seconds, in marked contrast to the lengthy utterances of clergymen at the inauguration." When Gerstenfeld died on January 27, 1968, he merited editorials in both the Washington *Evening Star* and the *Washington Post*: "the Rabbi enriched the Intellectual life of Washington." Walter Mondale said on the Senate floor: "For many years he had shared in the life of this city as a selfless civic and religious leader."

as does the Capitol. It was also the first time that the 3,500-year-old Priestly Benediction had been recited in the original Hebrew in the rotunda."

(Wisemon earned a different kind of notoriety 20 years later. "Police said a warehouse rented by a rabbi contained more than 10,000 allegedly stolen religious books and microfilms that had disappeared from schools, libraries and synagogues throughout the Northeast," the *Associated Press* reported from Vineland, New Jersey on May 5, 1983. "The discovery was made in an investigation of Rabbi Saul Wisemon. . . . Authorities want to question Wisemon about the disappearance of a Torah—a valuable hand-written scroll of Jewish law—from a Bridgeton temple.")

Hebrew again over a half century later when Eytan Hammerman showed up. The rabbi of Temple Beth Shalom, Mahopac, New York, gave the June 11, 2014, prayer. Afterward, according to extensive front-page *Mahopac News* coverage of Hammerman's appearance on Capitol Hill, his sponsor Rep. Sean Patrick Maloney (D-NY) "gave a personal tour of the Capitol building." He "brought Hammerman and his delegation to the private prayer room used only by members of Congress. In that room, Hammerman gave the Hebrew 'Shehecheyanu' blessing, which thanks God for our life and health and for allowing us to reach the special occasion."

The Congressional Prayer Room isn't the only place to hear a Jewish prayer in the Capitol building.

According to his bio, Rabbi Shmuel Herzfeld of Ohev Shalom Talmud Torah in Washington, DC (who gave the May 23, 2014, House prayer) teaches a "regular class on Judaism at the US Senate."

Jay Marcus was House guest chaplain on September 13, 1990. Four years earlier, on April 26, 1986, the *New York Times* profiled the Talmud classes he taught for members of Congress:

> The Place: H-131, a small lunchroom on the House side of the Capitol. The Attendees: Eight members of Congress, two wives, a handful of assorted aides and friends, two Israeli diplomats and one rabbi. The Purpose: Study of the Torah, the Talmud, Biblical prophets, good, evil and God.

Rep. Gary Ackerman (D-NY) said in his 1990 sponsoring remarks: "For the past seven years, Rabbi Marcus has been the teacher and confidant of a number of our colleagues and their families. Under the sponsorship of the Genesis Foundation, Rabbi Marcus has conducted a semimonthly congressional Bible class. Over the years, about 30 of our current and former colleagues, as well as members of their families have participated in these classes. Rabbi Marcus' class has been a shining light in our busy schedules."

Reflecting on Marcus' long-ago study group, former Ackerman aide Bob Levi reported in the August 10, 2018, *New York Jewish Week* an amusing anecdote. "The importance and centrism of Israel infused many discussions," Levi wrote. "In fact, in 1992, the congressional participants instructed staff to roll a television into the room to view one of Secretary of State Baker's rants against Israel. Ironically, during a subsequent session, on the day in which PLO Chairman Yasser Arafat visited the Capitol, he was steps away from joining the study group in the room. That potential disaster was averted."

Prayers have been part of Congress since its beginning. But some Hill traditions—official and otherwise—do end. Ice bucket delivery to House members, for instance, stopped in 1995. Here's another relic from the past. When the *Associated Press* did a story on the Congressional Prayer Room on February 26, 1971, it reported an interesting lineage to its location: It "used to be a place where page boys—confesses a former one who begs 'don't quote me'—tossed dice when superiors weren't looking."

Which simply means the room now is used for a different set of holy rollers.

SECTION VIII

America the Exceptional

34: An Irish Rabbi Walks into the Senate Chamber

"God, we thank you for giving wisdom to Presidents George W. Bush, Barack Obama, and Donald J. Trump for proclaiming May as Jewish Heritage Month."
> —Rabbi Richard Boruch Rabinowitz, Aish International, May 3, 2017, House guest chaplain

"We remember with fervency all the men who under Thy providence conceived, resolved, and maintained it through all its vicissitudes to the present moment—Washington, Warren, Adams, Jefferson, Lincoln, Grant, Garfield."
> —House chaplain Rev. Henry Couden, May 19, 1900

Looking for a list of names of famous American historical personalities? Look no further than the pantheon of legendary Americans whom rabbis cite in their Congress prayers.

Beginning, like all great American tales do, with George Washington.

The Touro Synagogue in Newport, Rhode Island, is the oldest synagogue building still standing in the United States, dedicated in 1763. In August 1790, President Washington wrote the synagogue with this often-quoted message against intolerance:

> For happily, the government of the United States, which gives to bigotry no sanction, to persecution no assistance, requires only that they who live under its protection should demean themselves as good citizens, in giving it on all occasions their effectual support.

Washington also visited the Touro Synagogue in 1790, a year before the Bill of Rights was ratified.

On February 18, 1963, marking Touro's 200th anniversary, the congregation's own rabbi, Theodore Lewis, gave a prayer in Congress. Lewis said of Senators: "May their actions ever be a reflection of the immortal words that George Washington addressed to the Hebrew Congregation in Newport, Rhode Island, 'To bigotry, no sanction; to persecution, no assistance.'" A rich example of America as melting-pot, Lewis was no native-born American. He came from Dublin. At the time of his prayer, Lewis was the only Irish-born rabbi in the United States and one of the few Irish-born rabbis in the world. As a rabbi in Ireland, he finished sermons in Gaelic.[50]

That direct connection between the first president and a synagogue is a bond still remembered today in the American Jewish community. No wonder George Washington is the most mentioned of American figures: Nine citations by rabbi guest chaplains over the years.

Some are timed for his birthday. Jacob Sable of Riverdale Jewish Center in the House on February 25, 1960: "May the wisdom and courageous spirit of our first President, George Washington, ever serve as a lantern to illumine the steps of the dedicated men and women who serve Thee in the Halls of Congress. May his words, 'to bigotry no sanction, to persecution no assistance,' serve as a powerful citation of democracy."

Some are timed for when he began in the presidency. Michael Siegel of Chicago's Anshe Emet Synagogue in the House on April 30, 2015: "On this day that George Washington was inaugurated as the first President of the United States in 1789, we ask You, God, to bless each and every Member of this august body with the same courage that he exhibited in his time, in order to fulfill the vision and purpose of this great land for us and all who will follow in the future."

Washington is often portrayed as an American Moses. Gustav Gottheil of New York was the third rabbi to open the Senate in prayer, January 16, 1884. Four years later he was back in Washington, presiding over a meeting of the Jewish Ministers' Association. Gottheil told the gathering, according to the May 23, 1888, *New York Times*: "For the first time in the history of our association we meet in the national capital, in the city that bears the name of one on whom the most honorable title was bestowed that can adorn the memory of man, 'Father of his Country.' He is to the American

---

50   David Meyer Hausdorff, *A Book of Jewish Curiousities*, Crown Publishers, 1955, page 52.

people what Moses is to the Jew. Both are types of republicanism, whose illustrious example will remain a source of inspiration for all time to come."

Mount Vernon's website offers more on the connection:

> Washington was heralded as the political savior of the nation for delivering America from the bondage of Great Britain, akin to Moses delivering the children of Israel from the bondage of Egypt. Verses from the final chapter of Deuteronomy that described the death of Moses were frequently used in New England eulogies to illuminate the significance of Washington's passing.

Another early patriot scores a prominent link to Moses: Patrick Henry. It's a connection based on a fundamental timeless value: freedom.

Joseph Liberles of Chicago's Temple Ezra in the House on May 2, 1957:

"From the day when Moses cried out: 'Let my people go,' to the moment when God commanded Israel to 'proclaim liberty throughout the land and to all the inhabitants thereof,' from the hour when Patrick Henry exclaimed, 'Give me liberty or give me death,' to the resounding of the four freedoms, men have never ceased to be free. May our passion for freedom never abate."

Dov Bidnick in the Senate on May 14, 1981: "From that epoch-making day when Moses proclaimed 'Let my people go!,' to the time when Israel was commanded to 'Proclaim liberty throughout the land and unto all the inhabitants thereof' from the historic hour when Patrick Henry exclaimed, 'Give me liberty, or give me death!', to this moment men have never ceased yearning, working, and dying for the inalienable right to be free."

Even during the height of the Vietnam War rabbis stuck to a freedom theme. On July 8, 1965, Herbert Bomzer prayed in the House: "Teach us to ever appreciate the priceless heritage of freedom endowed us by our forefathers. Prom the immortal words of the first emancipator, Moses, 'Let my people go,' to the biblical command, 'Proclaim liberty throughout the land and to all the inhabitants thereof.' from the historic demand of Patrick Henry, 'Give me liberty or give me death,' to the declaration 'that all men are created equal,' to this very day men have never ceased yearning and dying, for liberty."

Apparently that freedom sentiment was so strong it simply had to be repeated. The House heard identical words the next month. Here's Rabbi Louis Wolfish on August 19, 1965: "Teach us, O God, to ever appreciate the priceless heritage of freedom endowed us by our forefathers. From the immortal words of the first emancipator, Moses, 'Let my people go,' to the biblical command, 'Proclaim liberty throughout the land and to all the inhabitants thereof,' from the historic demand of Patrick Henry, 'Give me liberty or give me death,' to the declaration 'that all men are created equal,' to this very day men have never ceased yearning and dying, for liberty."

A double-barrel of Patrick Henry-fueled freedom![51]

A bit less fervent language when another early American was cited in the Senate on September 18, 1997. Las Vegas Rabbi Mel Hecht: "May we approach the turn of our century in the same spirit that our Founding Fathers and mothers approached theirs, by believing in our hearts, as Thomas Paine advised, that we have it in our power to begin the world over again."

Meir Felman of the Judea Center in Brooklyn opened Congress twice. Both times he plugged the founders. May 28, 1962, in the House: "As we enjoy the rewards earned by the labors of our Founding Fathers, may we fully comprehend that the tasks they so nobly advanced are never finished." Similarly, April 28, 1964, in the Senate: "As we enjoy the rewards earned by the labors of our Founding Fathers, may we understand that the tasks they so nobly advanced are never finished."

As might be expected of someone whom historians repeatedly rank first for presidential leadership, Abraham Lincoln merits multiple mentions.

- "As we approach the birthday of Great Emancipator, who gave this country a new birth of freedom, may we ever echo his words 'With malice toward none, with charity toward all.'"—Newton Friedman, Congregation Temple Emanuel, Beaumont, Texas, February 9, 1967, in the House.
- "This month we have commemorated the birthdays of two great American Presidents. They have given our Nation dignity of purpose and the courage to act in times of adversity. Their commitment to the freedom of all men will continue to serve as a shield of honor—a banner of distinction."—Simeon Kobrinetz of the

---

51 Notable that all these Patrick Henry mentions were made before 2004. That's when Ron Chernow published *Alexander Hamilton* (Penguin Press). Chernow describes the states' consideration of the U.S. Constitution in 1788: "As Hamilton tangled with Lansing [in New York], neither knew that Virginia had on June 25 become the tenth state to ratify the Constitution. Like their New York counterparts, antifederalists there posed as plucky populists, even though their ranks included many rich slaveholders. Patrick Henry, the leading antifederalist, warned delegates who supported the Constitution, 'They'll free your niggers.'"

Chaplain Service of the Veterans Administration on February 26, 1975, in the Senate.

- "Thy servant, Abraham Lincoln, in a message to Congress, said, 'We cannot escape history,' so help us, O God, that we may not evade history, but may we be granted history."—Leo Baeck in the House on Lincoln's birthday, February 12, 1948.

- "It was exactly 130 years ago almost to the day that Congress resolved that a day be set aside to recognize and memorialize those who had given their lives to defend our country in times of war and in times of peace. President Abraham Lincoln expressed it best when he stated: 'That we here highly resolve that these dead shall not have died in vain. We can do them no greater honor than to keep alive that which they gave their lives to preserve; love of country, duty, honor and defense of the right as it is given to us to see the right.'"—Moshe Bomzer, Congregation Beth Abraham-Jacob, Albany, New York, May 21, 1998, in the House.

And in the Senate in 2003, Captain of the Chaplain Corps of the U.S. Navy Arnold Resnicoff recalled "words spoken by a Senate nominee—Abe Lincoln—on this day, June 16, in 1858. 'A nation divided against itself cannot stand,' he said, and we 'cannot endure half slave, half free.'" The next Lincoln mention came 14 years later. And it was Resnicoff again, by then retired from the Navy. On September 1, 2017, marking the date Germany invaded Poland in 1939, sparking World War II, Resnicoff said in the House, "Lincoln taught: remember those who fought, gave their all, by continuing their unfinished work with increased devotion to their cause. Then they don't die in vain."

Author Harold Kushner labels Lincoln "America's Moses" and recalls a professor of his who called Lincoln's Second Inaugural Address "the only modern document that could be inserted in the book of Isaiah and not seem out of place."[52] And connecting Lincoln to the Jewish experience is not just for Jews. House chaplain Henry Couden on February 12, 1917, called Lincoln "a Moses leading his people through the Wilderness to the Land of Promise; surely if ever a prophet or seer was inspired of Heaven so was Lincoln inspired of God."

Without raining on the Jewish inaugural parade for Lincoln, it's worth noting he was the last president to include a substantive plug for

---

52 *Overcoming Life's Disappointments*, Random House, 2006, page 33.

Christianity in his inaugural address. "Intelligence, patriotism, Christianity, and a firm reliance on Him who has never yet forsaken this favored land are still competent to adjust in the best way all our present difficulty," Lincoln told "Fellow-Citizens of the United States" on March 4, 1861. (Christianity appeared in Barack Obama's first inaugural address, too, but more to catalogue groups of people: "We are a nation of Christians and Muslims, Jews and Hindus, and non-believers.")

Moving through American history, rabbis have cited a wax museum of presidents.

- ". . . bless our beloved President of the United States, Dwight D. Eisenhower, whom Thou didst endow with Thy heavenly spirit to enable him to save our country from mortal enemies. Give him health and strength, to continue to lead us into the paths of peace and prosperity, justice and righteousness. Send down Thy heavenly blessings, also, upon our beloved Vice President of the United States. Richard M. Nixon, who stands beside our leader at all times, to help him guide our land to its destinies."—Charles Rubel, Congregation Sha'arey Israel, Macon, Georgia, April 21, 1958, in the Senate.
- "We pray for Thy blessing, united together, upon your dedicated servants, John F. Kennedy, the President of these United States; Lyndon B. Johnson, the Vice President; the Speaker of the House of Representatives; and all the Members of Congress."—Gerald Kaplan, Agudath Achim Synagogue, Hibbing, Minnesota, April 30, 1962, in the House.
- "Pour down Your bountiful blessings upon our distinguished and beloved President, Lyndon B. Johnson, his family, and all the peoples of this great democracy, so that peace and prosperity, freedom and tolerance increase and endure throughout the length and breadth of its borders."—Abraham Hecht, president, Rabbinical Alliance of America, Brooklyn, April 25, 1966 in the Senate.
- "We pray for the welfare of our Government, led by our distinguished President, Lyndon B. Johnson."—Hecht, again, in the House on July 29, 1968.

Hecht's presidential name dropping—two LBJ mentions—continued into the Reagan era. He was, in fact, the only guest rabbi to cite Reagan by name. Here he is in the Senate on April 21, 1983, three days after the U.S.

embassy bombing in Beirut: "We ask also for Your blessings for our dear President Ronald Reagan and his family, and for the members of his cabinet, and advisers."

Mordekai Shapiro didn't mention Reagan directly when he gave the House prayer on July 25, 1985. But he did refer to Reagan's cancer surgery that month: "Grant Thee, O Father of Mercy, a full and speedy recovery to our President as we pray for the continued good health of all the leaders of our democracy that they may lead with vigor and strength."

Reagan's White House successor got a similar specific wish for speedy recovery when he was sick with atrial fibrillation due to hyperthyroidism. Rabbi Alvin Berkun of Pittsburgh's Tree of Life Congregation said this in his May 8, 1991, Senate prayer: "During these days of concern for our President, we join in prayer to the Lord our God that our President, George Bush, be blessed with good health and well-being and that he continue to be endowed with vigor of body, mind, and spirit."

The next president got two mentions. On March 15, 1994, Aron Lieberman opened the House asking "for Your blessings for our President Bill Clinton, and for the members of his cabinet." The second a year later, June 20, 1995, in the Senate: "We pray that You protect and guard our President, Bill Clinton, that You shield our President and all elected officials from any illness, injury, and influence." That was George Holland of Beit Hallel in Wilmington, North Carolina—a synagogue that "acknowledge(s) Yeshua (Jesus) as the promised Messiah who lived, died and was resurrected as our King and High Priest."

And that's how it stood for over two decades: the last mention by name of a President in a rabbi prayer in Congress was uttered by a Jew for Jesus. Then on May 3, 2017, in the House, a rabbi from Aish International, a Jewish outreach organization started in Jerusalem, name-checked an unprecedented three presidents in one fell swoop. Richard Boruch Rabinowitz: "God, we thank you for giving wisdom to Presidents George W. Bush, Barack Obama, and Donald J. Trump for proclaiming May as Jewish Heritage Month." It was also, for all three, their first mention in a rabbi prayer. Trump earned another rabbi mention from Holocaust survivor Romi Cohn in the House on January 29, 2020: "May You, Lord, accept with mercy our prayers for our country; for our President, Donald Trump; our Vice President, Michael Pence, my Congressman, Max Rose."

It's mostly famous American men who get the mentions. But two women have been acknowledged.

In the House on June 16, 1939, Alfred Moses referenced Katharine Lee Bates: "May our vision of a greater America be realized in the imperial poem written by a brilliant daughter of our people: Oh, beautiful for patriot dreams That sees beyond the years." Resnicoff quoted Bates in two of his House prayers (August 18, 2017 and December 26, 2019).

The other woman cited in a rabbi prayer? "We pause now, before this Senate session starts," Resnicoff said on May 21, 2003, "to recall that on this day—in 1881—and in this city—Washington, DC—Clara Barton and a group of friends founded the American Red Cross."

Time will tell if another American woman ever will be included in a rabbi's guest prayer.

Meantime, for all these mentions of famous Americans, one legendary American Jew has yet to earn a rabbi mention: baseball player Sandy Koufax.

35: Praying for Iconic American Institutions

Global war was just weeks away from the opening shot when Rabbi Alfred Moses of Mobile led the House of Representatives in prayer. As we just saw, in a rabbinical twist his patriotic, eve-of-war, June 16, 1939, invocation was anchored in words written by a non-Jewish woman. Katharine Lee Bates was more than a songwriter who wrote "Goody Santa Claus on a Sleigh Ride." She also penned a beloved American poem, "America The Beautiful."

That was one of many instances in which an iconic American institution or symbol would be cited by a rabbi in Congressional prayer, often prompted by surrounding American history or events.

Take the Bicentennial. Rabbis gave America's 200th birthday prominent play in the years leading up to the patriotic celebration.

The first reference came as early as the tumultuous decade prior. Joel Goor of San Diego's Temple Beth Israel urged the Senate on July 17, 1968, "to remain sensitive of the age-old dream that for almost 200 years has burned in the breasts of America's legislative leaders, a vision that exists but in the minds of dreamers, the utterances of prophets, and the prayers and practices of men of vision—of a time when liberty will be proclaimed unto all the inhabitants of our land."

Congress heard these Bicentennial-themed messages as July 4, 1976, approached:

- September 12, 1974. Cleveland Rabbi Arthur Lelyveld in the Senate: "Two centuries ago our country's fathers built on the foundation of two strong piers of Biblical conviction: the affirmation of the supreme worth of the individual: the vision of the perfected society."
- July 31, 1975. Lewis Weintraub of Temple Israel, Silver Spring, Maryland, in the House: "As we approach our Nation's Bicentennial we pray Thee to unite all the inhabitants of this land into a bond of true brotherhood promoting the welfare of our country and the happiness of its citizens."
- September 30, 1975. Abraham Feldbin in the House: "In this Bicentennial year, our country's fourth jubilee, we increasingly appreciate the blessing of freedom."

Feldbin continued to cite an American symbol anchored in Torah:

> The Liberty Bell has inscribed upon it from Leviticus: *Proclaim, liberty throughout the land unto all the inhabitants thereof.* From Leviticus, chapter 25, verses 9 and 10, we read: *Thou shalt proclaim with the blast of the shofar— the ram's horn. And ye shall hallow the fiftieth year and proclaim liberty throughout the land unto all the inhabitants thereof; it shall be a jubilee unto you.* The shofar calls to duty and dedication. It is the Biblical Liberty Bell. Today in the fourth jubilee of American Independence, we recall the Shofar and Liberty Bell with the prayer that our beloved land may ever continue true to its destiny and principles.

Feldbin's prayer also was notable for this rare distinction: The *Leviticus* verse he cited was printed in Hebrew in the *Congressional Record.*

Others who rang the Liberty Bell in their prayers:

- Max Landman in the House on March 12, 1962: "May the sound of the Liberty Bell echo to the four corners of the earth calling all men to walk side by side to the mountain of the Lord and there build the temple of love, of faith, and of true peace."
- Aaron Segal, born in Jerusalem, in the House on July 25, 1978: "We feel unshakeable commitment to Your divine decree from the sacred Biblical text of Leviticus: 'Proclaim ye liberty throughout the land, to all the inhabitants thereof.' This message etched upon our Liberty Bell in Philadelphia is the reminder of our country's

unswerving, unyielding ideology, as a guide to America and all mankind.'"

- Sidney Guthman in the Senate on April 22, 1982: "If our Nation is to remain true to its essential character then the Levitical command engraved on our Nation's Liberty Bell should become a reality in our lives! 'Proclaim liberty throughout the land unto all the inhabitants thereof.'"

Opening the House eight years earlier—July 2, 1974—Guthman found inspiration in another American foundation: "Two days hence, we, Thy children, will observe the 198th anniversary of the historic day when the Founding Fathers of this Nation signed the Declaration of Independence." Guthman continued with this patriotic paean: "Built upon these foundations, the young Nation matured, grew in affluence and influence, and became the mightiest defender of freedom and the most dependable bastion of democracy."

The Declaration of Independence has been called American scripture. The Constitution might be American Torah (leaving the Talmud to serve as every Supreme Court decision of the Jewish people). It too has been celebrated by rabbis praying in Congress.

The Constitutional Convention convened in Philadelphia in May 1787.

Two hundred years later to the month, two rabbis on the same day in both chambers marked the landmark event. On May 20, 1987, Malcolm Cohen of Temple B'nai Israel, Dale City, California, opened the House: "As we observe this 200th anniversary of our Federal Constitution this year, let us be imbued with its spirit and inspired by its words." Simultaneously, Milton Balkany thanked Senators who, "with dedication, wisdom and courage enact the manifestations of our celebrated Constitution, thus perpetuating the principles of our Founding Fathers, pronouncing the fervent desire of our far flung population, and fulfilling the word of G-d—which we read in the Bible—'Proclaim liberty throughout the land unto all the inhabitants thereof.'"

Twenty years earlier, April 19, 1967, Gershon Chertoff opened the House with his own tribute to the U.S. Constitution:

The Founding Fathers of these United States made our Government one of laws and not of men; of laws designed to set men free—to think for themselves, govern themselves, pursue happiness for themselves, and so become themselves. The laws of our polity were to reflect our commitment to the divine law of justice and equity. Wherefore we appeal to Thee to kindle a legal conscience in the heart of the Nation. Persuade us of the supremacy of the law as embodied in the Constitution, its authorized interpretations, and the enactments made under its provisions.

Such rich foreshadowing to see Chertoff urging God to "kindle a legal conscience in the heart of the Nation." You might recognize the New Jersey rabbi's last name. His son kindled a legal career in the Nation's heart, Washington, DC. Michael Chertoff served as a judge for U.S. Court of Appeals, a federal prosecutor, assistant U.S. Attorney General, Secretary of Homeland Security, and counsel at the powerful DC law firm Covington & Burling, whose offices are ten streets from the U.S. Capitol.

Martin Applebaum cited another document at the center of American democracy. "Having recently celebrated the 200th anniversary of the Bill of Rights," the chaplain with the 201st Expeditionary Military Intelligence Brigade in Fort Lewis, Washington, said in the Senate on February 20, 1992, "our beloved country's declaration of principle, we pray our resolve be strengthened. . . ."

In the midst of all this Constitutional love, consider an additional America storyline. While rabbis have lovingly celebrated American symbols and canonical documents as they prayed with government leaders, some of America's early government leaders weren't necessarily thrilled to be joined by Jews. At least not at the beginning.

In his book *Jews, Turks and Infidels*, Morton Borden wrote, "As colonies became states, most adopted bills of rights that guaranteed freedom of religion. So did the federal government. At the same time, many Americans defined the United States as a Christian nation. Jews, Turks, and Infidels (or any other exotic group), they believed, could worship as they pleased but had no right to participate in its government."[53]

And Ron Chernow wrote in *Alexander Hamilton*, "For all the high-toned language of The Federalist, Hamilton knew that the New York convention would come down to bare-knuckled politics. A prominent antifederalist had already warned him that 'rather than to adopt the Constitution, I would risk a government of Jew, Turk or infidel.'"[54]

Rabbis offering tribute to America in their prayers have transcended that darker corner of American history.

---

53 University of North Carolina Press, 1984.
54 Penguin Press, 2004.

Instead, we remember the words of Chaim Seiger on March 5, 1969, just as the number of American military personnel in Vietnam peaked: "May we prize highly and protect carefully the gifts of conscience and principle that were handed to us from Sinai through Lexington and Concord," the Tennessee rabbi said in the House. Fifty U.S. soldiers were killed in combat in Vietnam that 1969 day. Among all the over one hundred days in which rabbis prayed in Congress during the Vietnam War era, it was the bloodiest.

And this from Gordon Papert in the House on March 20, 1975, as Americans were still traumatized from Watergate: "Like the Founding Fathers of this great Republic, may we be inspired by the spirit of Israel's prophets to love mercy and to pursue justice for all the citizens of our land."

Several rabbi House prayers have occurred on June 14, inspiring more bonding with Americana: Flag Day.

Bernhard Rosenberg, 1979: "We gather today to give glory and honor to our flag and country. On June 14, 1777, the words of our valiant forefathers rang throughout the corridors of our hearts. Americans, communicate these symbols to your children. White signifies purity; red, hardiness and valor; blue, vigilance, perseverance, and justices. Hope and liberty is our creed. Grant our leaders the intellectual and spiritual ability to encourage, sustain and inspire the populace of our cherished and treasured country, the U.S.A."

Holocaust survivor Laszlo Berkowits of Temple Rodef Shalom in Falls Church, Virginia, 1988: "Our hearts are filled with thanksgiving on this day dedicated to honor the Stars and Stripes, the flag of our beloved country. This flag has been, ever since its creation, a symbol of hope for the oppressed, a banner of liberty for the enslaved yearning to be free. To this very day this precious symbol of free men and women stirs the hearts of our countrymen to deeds of valor and sacrifice as it did for the generations who came before us. For it is the banner of freedom, the proud flag of the liberators. Wherever it is raised and unfurled, it heralds the sacred message: 'Proclaim liberty throughout the land to all the inhabitants thereof.'" Sponsor Rep. Frank Wolf (R-VA): "Rabbi Berkowits says that when he was liberated by the 82d Airborne, the first thing that he saw was the American flag, and that is what is especially meaningful, that the rabbi is giving the prayer here today on Flag Day."

And Richard Marcovitz, 1984: "America is a miracle. The determination of human beings to live as free people. For two centuries this miracle has endured; 207 years ago today, the Stars and Stripes, our flag was accepted as the symbol of this land. In the language of our Biblical patriarchs, the word for 'banner' and the word for 'miracle'—'nays'—are one and the same. May the miracle that is America, as symbolized by that star emblazoned banner, ever serve as a beacon for all peoples who long for freedom."

(On June 30, 1898, at the height of the Spanish-American War, Rabbi Jacob Voorsanger of Temple Emmanuel in San Francisco opened the Senate by praying that the "flag under which we live, that for which our fathers fought, may forever be the sacred emblem of liberty until time shall be no more.")

A star emblazoned banner, sure. But how about something more practical in the household that Americans treasure—like a cool TV?

Balkany in the Senate on November 7, 1991: "The American dream is projected on a wide screen in technicolor."

Wide-screen projection? Yes, that's America, too.

SECTION IX

Diversity: Including the Christians

36: Rabbis Borrow from Christians

Rabbis in Congress pray to a predominantly Christian audience legislating for a predominantly Christian nation. That has begat, from time to time, words and references you would not normally hear in a synagogue. The ultimate case of the performer's maxim, "Know your audience."

Saints, for instance. Opening the House on December 1, 1941, less than a week before Pearl Harbor, Rabbi Julius Mark of Nashville's Vine Street Temple quoted St. Francis of Assisi:

> In a time when the dark forces of tyranny and oppression compass us about, we pray, O God, that Thou mayest so fortify our spirits that we may find wisdom, courage, and decision in the heroic utterance of St. Francis of Assisi, one of Thy most inspired sons:

> "Lord, make me an instrument of Thy peace;
> Where there is hatred, let me sow love;
> Where there is injury, pardon;
> Where there is doubt, faith;
> Where there is despair, hope;
> Where there is darkness, light;
> Where there is sadness, joy . . ."

Using a formula attributed by some to St. Ignatius and others to St. Augustine, Michael Barenbaum of Temple Rodef-Shalom, San Rafael,

California, opened the House on July 23, 1987: "It is written: Pray as if everything depended on God. Act as if everything depended on you!"

Jesus has made cameo appearances in rabbi prayers. In the Senate on February 24, 1961, Morris Gordon of Maryland's Greenbelt Jewish Center began: "I should like to quote the prayer for our country which is recited in the synagogue every Sabbath. Some of the words will be in the language in which Jesus prayed, in which the Bible was written, in which the Jewish people pray to this day—in Hebrew."

A Jesus mention again on October 14, 1993, in the House via Pittsburgh Rabbi Alvin Berkun: "May we be inspired by one of the greatest of Jewish sages, a contemporary of Jesus. Rabbi Hillel, who said, 'Love peace and pursue peace.'"

And praying in the House a year after World War II ended—April 29, 1946—Washington Hebrew Congregation's Norman Gerstenfeld alluded to crucifixion. "Guide us in this hour so that we do not fail the hope of the morrow for which the bleeding torso of a crucified humanity now prays," he said.

There was even a communion reference from Theodore Levy. "As our Nation's Senatorial representatives let us attempt to reach just a little higher from where we are to where we ought to be," the Syracuse rabbi said on March 8, 1984. "Some among us may call it communion while others call it prayer and yet we all know it means the same thing—aspiration."

In the Senate on March 25, 1994, Tzvi Porath extended "our best wishes to all those who are preparing to celebrate the religious festivals, Passover and Easter, that occur during this period."

The Lord's Prayer, which Jesus taught to his disciples and can be found in the Gospels of Matthew and Luke, made an appearance in a rabbi's prayer. Here's how Edward Browne opened the House on December 13, 1917: "Father, who art in Heaven, hallowed is Thy name . . ." Browne closed: "Thine is the kingdom, and the power." Tribute to a divine King is not your typical Jewish summation.

After Rabbi David Philipson offered a Jewish prayer in the Senate on February 2, 1904, chaplain Edward Hale followed by reciting the Christian Lord's Prayer. The Washington, DC, *Evening Star* reported, "The opening prayer was unique today in the fact that it was taken part in by both the chaplain and the visiting rabbi. It has occasionally occurred before that the prayer has been offered by a rabbi." Because Hale both preceded and followed Philipson with his own prayerful offering, the *Washington Times* noted on February 7, 1904, it was the first time the Senate "had ever listened to three prayers on the same day." (The *Times* said Philipson's prayer "was full of deep, patriotic feeling, and his closing paragraph of unusual beauty.")[55]

It happened again the very next time a rabbi opened Congress. Abram Simon of Washington Hebrew Congregation prayed in the House on January 16, 1905. When he concluded, as the *Congressional Record* reported, "The Chaplain thereupon said the Lord's Prayer."

The Lord's prayer replaced a rabbi's prayer in the Senate in 1956 because of emergency. What was the emergency? Traffic. Who offered the prayer in place of the rabbi? Vice President Richard Nixon. Here's the report carried in the July 21, 1956, *Southeast Missourian:*

> Members of the Senate established a precedent in Washington, DC, when, in the absence of their chaplain, they opened their daily session by reciting the Lord's prayer in unison. Veteran legislators said it was the first time the Senate had taken such a step. Dr. Frederich B. Harris, the Senate chaplain, was out of the city. He had arranged for Rabbi Norman Gerstenfeld of Washington Hebrew Congregation to serve as guest chaplain, but the rabbi was held up in a traffic jam and arrived four minutes late. Vice president Nixon delayed the opening of the session for two minutes, awaiting the rabbi, and then led the member present in the prayer.

But don't feel too bad for Gerstenfeld and his commuting woes, likely quaint by today's DC traffic standards. He pulled off five guest prayers in Congress, all in the Senate, presumably arriving on time for each.

It wouldn't be the only time DC road conditions prevented a chaplain from opening the Senate in prayer. Forty years later, from January 6-8, 1996, the East Coast was crippled by a snowstorm. On January 8, Republican Virginia Sen. John Warner was able to make it into work. "In the absence of the Chaplain, it is my privilege to read the opening prayer," he began the proceedings. "We close by thanking the Lord through this most unusual weather storm." Apparently, the weather doesn't prevent the mailman. But it can stop a chaplain. (Nowadays, a spare prayer is kept at the podium, in case a chaplain unexpectedly can't make it and someone else needs to fill the role.)

---

55 Not a bad chaplain for Philipson to share the limelight with. In addition to being a literary master and historian, Hale was grand-nephew of Revolutionary War hero Nathan Hale, who was executed by the British for espionage.

Two rabbis who gave prayers were unusual in their own Christianity-colored biographies.

Herbert Opalek of Brooklyn's Yeshiva Bais Isaac Zvi gave the House prayer on March 2, 1978 ("As this day's session commences, grant these legislators herein assembled the wisdom to act in accordance with Your wishes.") Rep. Leo Zeferetti (D-NY) remarked: "Although still young, Rabbi Opalek has served the Jewish and general community at large as spiritual leader and university professor." In fact, according to Opalek's April 10, 2011, obituary in the *Merced Sun-Star*, "He was ordained as an Orthodox rabbi at 18." He also "converted to Christianity late in life" as a Messianic Jew. The obit reports Rev. Opalek converted this way: "He had flown into Boston . . . but his luggage never made it. . . . Opening a drawer in the night-stand, he found a Gideon Bible. He opened it to a chapter in John. 'On that night and in that room, for the very first time in my life, I encountered the Holy Spirit and allowed God to permeate my being.'"

Those travel woes again. Sometimes you end up not just changing lanes, but changing religions, too.

Another Messianic Jew later opened Congress in prayer. This time, though, he was already a Jesus-believer. George Holland of Beit Hallel Messianic Synagogue in Wilmington, North Carolina, opened the Senate on June 20, 1995. He was sponsored by Sen. Lauch Faircloth (R-NC). Unlike traditional Judaism, Beit Hallel "acknowledge[s] Yeshua (Jesus) as the promised Messiah who lived, died and was resurrected as our King and High Priest." Holland said in his prayer: "For it is in the name of the King of all kings that we pray."

It might have been unintentional, but noteworthy, that later in 1995 a prayer was delivered by the founder of Jews for Judaism, an organization created for "inoculating the Jewish community against the threat of deceptive Christian missionary and destructive cult groups." Jerusalem-based Orthodox rabbi Motty Berger opened the House on December 5: "In a sorely troubled world, filled with all too much hatred, violence, and human misery, we pray to You, dear God, for divine guidance."

Just over 20 years later, on May 18, 2016, the House guest chaplain was Rev. Patricia Venegas of Without Spot or Wrinkle Ministries in La Verne, California. The Congregation calls itself "Judeo-Christian . . . restoring the Church back to her Hebrew roots . . . we serve a Hebrew Lord, who had Hebrew disciples."

Messianic Jews can make politics, well, messy for the White House. Campaigning in Michigan two days after the murder of 11 Jews in a Pittsburgh synagogue, Vice President Mike Pence shared a stage with a Messianic Jew, "Rabbi" Loren Jacobs. "God of Abraham, God of Isaac, God of Jacob," Jacobs prayed on October 29, 2018 in Grand Rapids. "God and Father of my Lord and Savior Yeshua, Jesus the Messiah, and my God and Father, too." Pence had to explain that he didn't invite Jacobs to the rally. Forty years earlier, Jews for Jesus bedeviled the Carter administration. Because of criticism in the Jewish community, in June 1978 Jimmy Carter's sister Ruth Carter Stapleton dropped out as keynote speaker at a conference of B'nai Yeshua. That's Hebrew for "sons of Jesus."[56]

As for showing up at work during Christmastime, that's a task frequently for Jews. The House held a pro forma session on December 26, 2019. Start time: 9 am ET. Who was around to pray? Rabbi Arnold Resnicoff. He opened with three holidays: "Almighty God, we pray, reflect, meditate in different ways, and during these holy days—Christmas, Hanukkah, Kwanzaa, more—some sing different songs, reflecting the beauty, diversity, of communities, cultures, faiths that make our nation rich." It was the second mention ever by a guest rabbi of Hanukkah (joining Yakov Pollak from Young Israel of Jackson Heights in the House on December 12, 1963). Resnicoff wore a festive tie with dreidels. And made the first rabbinical mentions for both Christmas and Kwanzaa.

37: Christians Borrow from Jews

"Give heed, O nations afar: The Lord appointed me before I was born."

—Isaiah 49:1

"You sent Your prophet Isaiah to Your people when they were in need of hope and vision. May Isaiah's prophetic words guide us still."
—The Rev. Patrick Conroy, House Chaplain,
February 27, 2017

Advocating American independence and battling the British monarchy in 1776, Thomas Paine in his pamphlet *Common Sense* rallied the troops by leaning heavily on Jewish tradition:

---

56 "Evangelical Group Stirs Controversy," *New York Times*, June 10, 1978.

> . . . the will of the Almighty, as declared by Gideon and the prophet Samuel, expressly disapproves of government by kings. . . . The children of Israel being oppressed by the Midianites, Gideon marched against them with a small army, and victory thro' the divine interposition decided in his favour. The Jews, elate with success, and attributing it to the generalship of Gideon, proposed making him a king. . . The thing displeased Samuel when they said, give us a King to judge us.

Thus instructed, if not inspired, by a Jewish prophet (although one might hope inspiration did play a role), Americans defeated the British king and created their own government. By the people, for the people—and no monarchy.

Two hundred and thirty-five years later, a British Lord came to the American people's legislature to offer the opening prayer. And he was a child of Israel.

Welcoming Lord Jonathan Sacks to the Senate on November 2, 2011, Sen. Joe Lieberman (I-CT) cited an old advertising slogan, "'You don't have to be Jewish to love Levy's Jewish Rye.' Well, you don't have to be Jewish to benefit from Rabbi Sacks' writing."

Take that a step further: You don't have to be Jewish to benefit from Jewish-themed prayers in the House and Senate. And from the mouths of non-Jews there are abundant thoughts inspired by Jewish teachings. When the House on June 30, 1922, debated a resolution "favoring the establishment in Palestine of a national home for the Jewish people," Rep. Walter Chandler (R-NY) pointed out: "When the Chaplain offers prayer at each day's opening of this House, he invokes upon its Members the benedictions of a Hebrew God and the intercessions of a Hebrew Savior."

An example from six years earlier. The March 14, 1916, Senate guest chaplain was Edwin Dubose Mouzon of Dallas. The Methodist bishop began: "Almighty God, God of Abraham and of Isaac and of Jacob, God and Father of our Lord Jesus Christ."

And even more Jewish inspiration for a Christian prayer four years before that. House guest chaplain Royal Simonds, pastor of Trinity Methodist Episcopal in Knoxville, on March 9, 1912: "We remember the patriotism of the old Jewish nation and how Jerusalem was so dear to them, and how Palestine became the Holy Land because they lived holy lives upon that soil." That message was delivered 36 years before Zionists created the new Jewish nation.

Decades later, Christian chaplains still invoke Jewish tradition and even the Hebrew God for their invocations.

Rev. Edgar Cordell Powers of Baltimore began his April 27, 1970, guest House prayer this way: "Almighty and ever-living God, like Moses at the burning bush, we stand today on holy ground." Not sure if, upon hearing that, any Congressman took off his or her shoes. Nor how many folks today would compare Congress to holy ground.

On October 13, 1999, Senate chaplain Lloyd John Ogilvie offered a prayer "taken from the Jewish Book of Service, Daily Prayers":

> We gratefully acknowledge that You are the eternal one, our God, and the God of our fathers evermore; the Rock of our life and the Shield of our salvation. You are He who exists to all ages. We will therefore render thanks unto You and declare Your praise for our lives, which are delivered into Your hands, and for our souls, which are confided in Your care; for Your goodness, which is displayed to us daily; for Your wonders and Your bounty, which are at all times given unto us. You are the most gracious, for Your mercies never fail. Evermore do we hope in You, O Lord our God. Amen.

He repeated that Jewish prayer on April 15, 2002: "As we celebrate Jewish Heritage Week, we pray for the Jewish people and for the crisis in the Middle East."

Ogilvie returned to Jewish tradition the next month, on May 23:

> Dear God, You have ordained that there is one decision we must make every day. It is the most crucial decision in the midst of all the other decisions we will be called to make. We hear Elijah's challenge, "Choose for yourselves this day whom you will serve."—Joshua 24:15b.

The *Book of Joshua* immediately follows the five books of Moses comprising the Torah. Joshua, who led the Israelites after Moses' death, was recognized a year later. Here's Chaplain Daniel Coughlin opening the House on June 9, 2003: "After Moses, Your servant, died, Lord, You spoke again to Joshua and You speak to Your people even today. 'I will be with you, as I was with Moses. I will not leave you, nor forsake you.'"

In an April 9, 2002, prayer, Coughlin went even earlier in Jewish history to cite Abraham. "Lord God of Passover and Christ's Paschal Mystery, grant peace to the Israeli and Palestinian peoples," he said. "Deepen faith in You at this moment in history; that Your justice and peace will bless the land that all those of Abrahamic faith call holy." And on October 28, 2003, he included Muslims in the Abrahamic tent: "Over the weekend, Jews of this country again kept holy the Sabbath, Christians celebrated their discipleship in Jesus, and Muslims began the great fast and spiritual renewal of Ramadan. We rejoice in oneness of Abrahamic faith as it finds living expression in our time across this country."

Coughlin has cited another notable—and far more contemporary—Abraham. Making a cameo appearance as Senate guest chaplain on January 21, 2003, he said, "Yesterday's holiday brought to mind the wise words of Rabbi Abraham Heschel: 'Martin Luther King Jr. is a voice, a vision and a way. I call upon every Jew to hearken to his voice, to share his vision, to follow in his way. The whole future of America will depend on the impact and influence of Dr. King.'"[57]

Coughlin cited Passover in April 2002. So did his successor as House chaplain 18 years later. In the spring of 2020, Father Patrick Conroy gave a series of prayers focused on the coronavirus pandemic. His April 10, 2020, prayer coincided with Passover. He combined both themes. "Passover, when millions of Americans celebrate the liberation of the chosen people from slavery," Conroy said. "Passover, when millions of Americans experince the lack of freedom—to gather with family, to celebrate the passages of life together."

Another Jewish holiday meriting mentions by Christian chaplains: Purim. Esther, the Purim story's heroine, is a central character in those prayers.

Here's Coughlin again, opening the House on February 26, 2002, drawing on the Jewish tradition for post-9/11 terror attacks inspiration:

> . . . we are mindful of our Jewish brothers and sisters as they "gather together with joy and happiness" for the feast of Purim. The ancient prayer of Esther echoes in our prayer because of the circumstances surrounding our Nation now: "Lord, our King, You alone are God. Help us. At times we feel alone and have no help but You. As children we learned from the people of this land and our founders that You, O Lord, chose us from among all peoples, and that You would fulfill all Your promises to them. Be mindful of us, O Lord, and manifest Yourself in this time of distress and

---

57 Heschel marched with King in Selma in 1965. At the 1984 Democratic National Convention in San Francisco, Jesse Jackson told the delegates: "We are bound by Dr. Martin Luther King Jr. and Rabbi Abraham Heschel, crying out from their graves for us to reach common ground."

give us courage. King of gods and ruler of every power, put in our mouths persuasive words. O God, more powerful than all, hear the voice of Your people in need. Save us from the power of the wicked and deliver us from all our fears."

Bravo for Queen Esther—she scored mentions in both chambers of Congress that day. Chaplain Ogilvie included her in his Senate prayer, too:

Today we join with Jews throughout the world in the joyous celebration of Purim. We thank You for the inspiring memory of Queen Esther who, in the fifth century B.C., threw caution to the wind and interceded with her husband, the King of Persia, to save the exiled Jewish people from persecution. The words of Mordecai to her sound in our souls: ". . . You have come to the kingdom for such a time as this."—Esther 4:14.

Close Ogilvie listeners might have recalled similar—actually, identical—thoughts from him a year earlier in the Senate. On March 9, 2001, Esther had been throwing caution to the wind as well:

We join with Jews throughout the world in the joyous celebration of Purim. We thank You for the inspiring memory of Queen Esther who, in the fifth century B.C., threw caution to the wind and interceded with her husband, the King of Persia, to save the exiled Jewish people from persecution. The words of her uncle, Mordecai, sound in our souls: "You have come to the kingdom for such a time as this."—Esther 4:14.

And if you missed Esther throwing caution to the wind in 2001, perhaps you heard Ogilvie opening the Senate on March 20, 2000:

This week we join with Jews throughout the world in the joyous celebration of Purim. We thank You for the inspiring memory of Queen Esther who, in the fifth century B.C., threw caution to the wind and interceded with her husband, the King of Persia, to save the exiled Jewish people from persecution. The words of her uncle Mordecai sound in our souls: "You have come to the kingdom for such a time as this."—Esther 4:14.

Might as well include Ogilvie opening the Senate on March 2, 1999: "inspiring memory of Queen Esther who, in the fifth century B.C., threw caution to the wind and interceded with her husband, the King of Persia. . . ." And March 11, 1998: "Queen Esther who, in the fifth century B.C., threw caution to the wind. . . ." Quite a streak for Esther throwing caution to the wind in the Senate to close the '90s and open the new century.[58]

Another holiday: Hanukkah. Here's Ogilvie December 18, 1995:

> Today, we join in the celebration of Hanukkah, the Feast of Dedication. We join with our Jewish Senators, the Jewish people throughout our land, and the State of Israel. We remember 165 B.C. and the victory of the Maccabees over tyrant Antiochus Epiphanes and his troops who had occupied Jerusalem, desecrated the temple, and sought to destroy forever the Hebrew religion. We celebrate the Maccabean victory that enabled the Jews to rededicate the temple and once again to worship You freely.

He offered a similar Hanukkah prayer in December 2001.

Rev. Dan Cummins, who has given multiple prayers in Congress, was guest chaplain on December 17, 2018. "This season of Hanukkah and Christmas may we never forget: 'Little is much when God is in it.' A little oil in the Temple Menorah should not have lasted 8 days, but it did," he told the House. "A widow's small jars of oil and flour should not have lasted almost 3 years, but they did. They did because You, Father, were in it, in the Menorah, in the jars."

The October 11, 2019, House guest chaplain was Rev. Alisa Lasater Wailoo of the United Methodist Church in Washington, DC. Her prayer coincided with the Jewish High Holiday season. "We remember Yom Kippur, the Day of Atonement, at-one-ment, where our Jewish siblings spend 25 hours fasting from quick satisfaction and allowing You to reveal the falsities we all feast upon," Wailoo said. "Following their wisdom, let us do the same."

Christian chaplains have given the prophet Micah multiple mentions. Richard Halverson on June 15, 1994, urged Senators "to take seriously the word of the prophet Micah. Grant them the wisdom, the determination, and the courage to do justly, love mercy, and walk humbly before the Almighty."

---

58   Other Jewish women fill the Coughlin prayerbook. He suggested on May 23, 2006: "With the words about Judith from the Hebrew scriptures, let us pray for each of the women who serve in our military forces... 'Enemies have threatened us and set fire to our land. The young they have killed, and they have left us widows and orphans. 'Yet the Lord has fought back with a woman's hand.'" But the Book of Judith comes with an asterisk: it is not included in Jewish texts. It is considered a parable, historical fiction.

Halverson was referencing Micah 6:8. Just like he did in his September 6, 1989, prayer. It's a verse that's seen a lot of use in the legislative branch. None more prominent than opening new sessions of Congress.

The 99th Congress of the United States convened on January 3, 1985. House chaplain James Ford's prayer in that initial session ended, "May we, in all we do, seek justice, love mercy, and every walk humbly with you." Ten years later Republicans took control of the House. When Ford opened the first GOP-majority Congress in 40 years—on January 4, 1995, for the 104th Congress—he concluded, "As the prophet Micah has said, 'And what does the Lord require of you but to do justice, to love mercy, and to walk humbly with your God.'"

Ford returned to Micah two weeks later, on January 19: "You have created each of us in Your image and we earnestly pray that by Your grace we will reflect that image as we do justice, love mercy, and ever walk humbly with You." Ford again on July 14, 1998: "May our shared heritage remind us that in all things we should do justice, love mercy and ever walk humbly with You." [59]

Not just new Houses, Micah has welcomed new Senates, too. When the 112th Congress convened on January 5, 2011, Chaplain Barry Black opened, "Give our Senators the wisdom to exert their best efforts for the security of this land we love. In the words of the prophet Micah, may they do justly, love mercy, and walk humbly with You. Join them in heart, mind, and soul to build a better world."

Like Ford did in the House, Black includes Micah in his prayers:

- February 13, 2012: "Inspire our Senators to be true servants of Your will. In these challenging times, give them the wisdom to labor for justice, to love mercy, and to walk humbly with You."
- April 14, 2016: "Bless our lawmakers. . . . Keep them so dedicated to Your purposes that they will do justly, love mercy, and walk humbly with You."
- July 12, 2016: "Keep us, O God, so dedicated to you and your purposes, that we may do justly, love mercy, and walk humbly with You."

---

59   Ford walked without Micah when he opened the 103rd Congress on January 5, 1993. Instead, he chose a different guide from the Old Testament: the Priestly Benediction, first seen in Numbers 6:23. "The Lord bless us and keep us," he prayed. "The Lord make His face shine upon us and be gracious unto us. The Lord lift up his countenance upon us and give us peace."

A Seventh-day Adventist, Black urged Senators to "walk humbly" at least 20 times between 2004 and 2016. And May 1, 2019: "Thank You for lawmakers who strive to do justly, love mercy, and walk humbly with You." (Black is no stranger to other parts of the Hebrew Bible. On May 9, 2019, he dipped into Psalms 19:14: "Lord, give to all who labor in this Chamber the wisdom, humility, and competence sufficient for this day. May the words of their mouths and the meditations of their hearts be acceptable to You.") House chaplain Patrick Conroy also has included Micah repeatedly.

The Senate hears from Micah 6:8 during particularly trying times. On June 4, 1987, Halverson began his prayer by quoting Micah 6:8. He immediately followed with, "With heavy hearts we pray for all involved in the Iran-Contra hearings. You know the mixed feelings of the members of the select committee, their counsel, those being questioned, the press and media—as well as the audience and TV viewers. You know, Father, this is not an enjoyable experience for anybody."

Neither was it an enjoyable experience twelve years later when the Senate voted to remove Federal District Judge Walter Nixon from the bench by finding him guilty on two articles of impeachment. On that day, November 3, Halverson returned to Micah 6:8, followed by, "Once again the Senators bear the onerous responsibility of standing alone to pronounce the word, guilty—not guilty."

And this combination of Micah and practical Senate business in one Ogilvie prayer on April 29, 1998:

> Your Commandments are in force as much now as when You gave them to Moses. You require us to do justly, love mercy, and walk humbly with You. . . . Today we thank you for Eileen R. Connor, the Supervisor of Expert Transcribers from the Office of Official Reporters of Debates. Tomorrow will be the last day for Eileen after 25 years of dedicated service to the Senate.

House Chaplain Bernard Braskamp began his March 4, 1958, prayer with Micah 6:8, adding that God has "endowed us with a capacity to achieve and accomplish that which is good for ourselves and all mankind." Even zippy pro forma meetings get the Micah treatment. Opening a House session on May 15, 2017, that lasted all of two minutes, Father Conroy still made time to urge congressmen meeting with constituents "to do justice, love with mercy, and walk humbly with You." Speed walking, no doubt.

Christian guest chaplains, too, walk humbly with Micah. Pastor Eddie Bevill of Florida's Parkridge Church offered the June 7, 2018, House prayer:

"Your word in Micah 6:8 is a great reminder: 'He has told you, O man, what is good; and what does the Lord require of you but to do justice, and to love kindness, and to walk humbly with your God?'"

Dr. Wilmina Rowland, the first female guest chaplain in the Senate, ended her July 8, 1971, prayer this way: "For those who serve in this place, we pray that they may go through today's work with faithfulness, strive to do justly, to love mercy, and to walk humbly with you." Exactly three years later, July 8, 1974—the day the U.S. Supreme Court heard arguments on releasing the Watergate tapes—Rev. Edward Elson offered the Senate prayer: "Thou dost answer In Thy Word that we are to 'do justly, to love mercy, and to walk humbly with thy God.'"

More Micah. Rev. Sanford Lonsinger of the Third Presbyterian Church in Newark on April 26, 1956, in the House: "Thou wilt incline the hearts of our citizens to cultivate a spirit of subordination and obedience to government. Dispose us all to do justly, to love mercy, and to walk humbly with God." Rev. Patricia Lyons of Christ Church in Washington, DC, in the House on July 1, 2016: "Inspire us with wisdom and courage to face the complexity and immediacy of your call to ask justly, to love mercy, and to walk humbly." Guest chaplain Steve Berger, pastor of Grace Chapel in Leiper's Fork, Tennessee, opened the Senate on June 9, 2016, by invoking Micah—and several other historic Jewish figures. He prayed "that we would be united in doing what is good in Your sight, and what You require of us, to do justly, to love mercy, and to walk humbly with our God. Father, may our leaders and our Nation also walk in the faith of Abraham, the integrity of Moses, the wisdom of Solomon, the courage of the Prophets, and the self-sacrificing love and compassion of Jesus." And Rev. Asriel McLain, Little Union Baptist Church, Shreveport, Louisiana, closed his July 10, 2019, House prayer: "May Members of this House heed the words of the eighth century prophet Micah when he says that You require us to love justice, do mercy, and walk humbly with our God."

Micah even shows up in presidential inaugural addresses. William McKinley 1897: "Our faith teaches that there is no safer reliance than upon the God of our fathers, who has so singularly favored the American people in every national trial, and who will not forsake us so long as we obey His commandments and walk humbly in His footsteps." Warren Harding 1921: "I have taken the solemn oath of office on that passage of Holy Writ wherein it is asked: 'What doth the Lord require of thee but to do justly, and to love mercy, and to walk humbly with thy God?'" Harding used the same

Bible used by George Washington, belonging to St. John's Masonic Lodge No. 1. It was open to Micah 6:8.

And here's President Jimmy Carter, a Southern Baptist deacon who taught a Sunday school class when he ran for president, at the beginning of his 1977 inaugural address:

> Here before me is the Bible used in the inauguration of our first President, in 1789, and I have just taken the oath of office on the Bible my mother gave me a few years ago, opened to a timeless admonition from the ancient prophet Micah: "He hath showed thee, O man, what is good; and what doth the Lord require of thee, but to do justly, and to love mercy, and to walk humbly with thy God." (Micah 6:8)

He never got to be inaugurated but Adlai Stevenson did conclude his July 26, 1952, speech accepting the Democratic nomination for president with Micah: "In this staggering task that you have assigned me, I shall always try 'to do justly, to love mercy, and to walk humbly with my God.'"

Rabbi Harold Kushner opened Ronald Reagan's June 11, 2004, funeral reading from the Book of Isaiah (40:28). Supreme Court Justice Sandra Day O'Connor, the next speaker at the National Cathedral, said, "The only way to provide for our posterity is to follow the counsel of Micah, to do justly, to love mercy, to walk humbly with our God."

Esther, Micah . . . and Isaiah. Already the most-frequently mentioned prophets by rabbi guest chaplains, Isaiah—venerated by Judaism, Christianity, and Islam alike—gets ample attention from gentiles in Congress.

The October 13, 2015, House guest chaplain Reverend Meg Saunders of the Anglican Church of North America borrowed from Isaiah 61:1: "From the prophet Isaiah You tell us that You have good news for the poor. You comfort those of us with broken hearts." Gen. Jarl Wahlstrom, international commander of the Salvation Army, was Senate guest chaplain on June 12, 1984. It was only the second time that the head of the Salvation Army opened the Senate in prayer. This Army general shared the anti-war message of Isaiah 2:4: "hasten the coming of the day . . . when the peoples shall beat their swords into plowshares and shall learn war no more. . . . In the name of Jesus Christ Thy Son. Amen."

Senate chaplain Black used Isaiah 2:4 on January 6, 2017: "Lead us to the day when we will see peace among the nations of the Earth, when swords shall be beaten into plowshares."

Just after Barack Obama was elected president, Black invoked a power list of Jewish figures: "Sustain also the President-elect, Barack Obama. Give him the integrity of Joseph, the faith of Moses, and the wisdom of Solomon." (And just after Donald Trump became president, in place of Barry Black the guest chaplain was Rabbi Barry Block. Nearly identical names, just one letter off. And like Black, Block invoked Solomon on January 31, 2017: "Like King Solomon before them, let these Senators lead our nation with wisdom.")

In that November 17, 2008, prayer, Black also cited the Psalms: "O God of new beginnings, as our Nation greets the dawn of fresh opportunities and daunting challenges, inspire the Members of this body to trust Your sovereignty. May they remember the words of the 75th Psalm, declaring that You place leaders in positions of authority."

Almost exactly eight years later, November 15, 2016, Black returned to Psalm 75 for another new president: "We also express gratitude for the limitless possibilities available to President-Elect Donald Trump. May he receive inspiration from Your declaration in Psalms 75:6 and 7 that elevation comes neither from the east, west, south or north, but You are the sovereign judge who puts down one and lifts up another."[60]

Perhaps the most famous Psalm is the 23rd: "The Lord is my shepherd; I shall not want. . ."

Here's how Psalm 23 was interpreted legislatively during the depth of the Great Depression. The *New York Times* headline on March 27, 1932: "Chaplain Reads to House Psalm Referring to Oil." The story:

> When the House assembled today, after passing the one-cent embargo tax on oil yesterday, the chaplain, the Rev. Dr. James Shera Montgomery, recited the twenty-third psalm, which contains the following passage: "Thou preparest a table before me in the presence of mine enemies; Thou anointest my head with oil; my cup runneth over."

---

60 How much do non-Jews like Psalms? Consider these two literary anecdotes. Chaplain Black wrote in *From the Hood to the Hill: A Story of Overcoming* (Thomas Nelson, 2006, page 203): "Each day I read one chapter of Proverbs and five Psalms from the Bible." Then there's the example provided by William F. Buckley's father. In his book *A Torch Kept Lit* (Crown Forum, 2016, page 71), a collection of Buckley eulogies, author James Rosen includes what Buckley wrote about his own dad: "Gravely ill after his first stroke, Father lay seemingly unconscious on his hospital bed at Charlotte, N.C. Mother opened his bible and began to read aloud from the psalms in the Old Testament. Father's voice rang out for the first time in four days: 'Boy, could those Jews write!' And, having paid tribute to good prose, which he always admired, he relapsed immediately into his coma."

Chaplain Ford presumably had the Baal Shem Tov, the mystical rabbi who founded the Hasidic movement, in mind when he opened the House on July 16, 1981: "The following prayer was written in Hebrew by a rabbi of a small village in the Carpathian Mountains composed almost 100 years before the founding of our Nation: Master of the universe, Let there be no good hope that is not a command, Let there be no prayer that does not ask to become a deed, Let there be no promise unless it be kept. . . ." (An obscure prayer, sure. But probably wise to remind politicians to keep promises. It also showed up in, of all places, Alaska. Here's Rabbi Johanna Hershenson of Anchorage Beth Shalom Congregation opening the Alaska State Legislature on February 7, 2003: "Let there be no good hope that is not a command. . . .")

The cornerstone Jewish prayer *Sh'ma*, one of only two prayers which are specifically commanded in the Torah, has been incorporated into Christian prayers.

A remarkable example: the *Sh'ma* was recited by the first African-American guest chaplain in the Senate. In his May 5, 1965, prayer, Minister James Kirkland of Philadelphia's Union Baptist Church said, "'Hear, O Israel; the Lord is our God, the Lord is one.' Grant that this fair land of ours may ever hear Thee, the God of Abraham, Isaac, and Jacob, the God of our Founding Fathers; for in Thee we find . . . the great rock that the weathering agents of communism and secularism cannot erode." Even more, Kirkland recited the *Sh'ma* in Hebrew (evidence without video/audio proof: the Hebrew version is included in the *Congressional Record* account of his prayer, implying the words were spoken. It was just four years after Hebrew letters first appeared in the *Record*.)[61]

Guest chaplain Laudis Lanford of The Methodist Home for Children and Youth in Macon, Georgia, opened his May 1, 2001, House prayer with the *Sh'ma* and some Hebrew as well: "The Lord be with you, and for our Jewish friends, Sh'ma Yisrael Adonai Elohanu, Adonai Echad."

On October 4, 1967, the same day as Erev Rosh Hashanah, the Jewish New Year, House chaplain Edward Latch began his opening prayer with:

Hear, O Israel, the Lord our God is one Lord; and thou Shalt love the Lord they God with all thine heart, and with all thy soul, and with all thy might.— Deuteronomy 6:4, 5. O Lord, our God, and God of our fathers, who hast

---

61 The first African-American guest chaplain in the House was two years earlier: Rev. Harold Perry of Mississippi, July 8, 1963.

been the dwelling place of Thy people in all generations and who in Thy gracious mercy has brought us to the close of another year . . .

Senate Chaplain Halverson, a Presbyterian, did similar on June 15, 1981:

"Hear, O Israel: The Lord our God is one Lord; and you shall love the Lord your God with all your heart, and with all your soul, and with all your might.— Deuteronomy 6:4, 5 *(RSV).*

God of Abraham, Isaac, and Jacob, God of Moses and the prophets, God of Jesus and the Apostles, we are created to worship Thee, to love Thee, to serve Thee."

In the midst of heated debate over health care policy, the Senate met on August 13, 1994—a rare Saturday session. It was the Jewish Sabbath, a day of rest. Halverson spoke in Hebrew and said the *Sh'ma* again:

Baruch Hashem. Blessed be the Name of the Lord. God of Abraham, Isaac, and Israel, on this Sabbath morning give us ears to hear, minds to understand, and wills to obey the foundation of all teaching in the Torah. Hear, O Israel: The Lord our God is one Lord: And thou shalt love the Lord thy God with all thine heart, and with all thy soul, and with all thy might. And these words, which I command thee this day, shall be in thine heart: And thou shalt teach them diligently unto thy children, and shalt talk of them when thou sittest in thine house, and when thou walkest by the way, and when thou liest down, and when thou risest up. And thou shalt bind them for a sign upon thine hand, and they shall be as frontlets between thine eyes. And thou shalt write them upon the posts of thy house, and on thy gates.—Deuteronomy 6:4-9. Baruch Hashem. Blessed be the Name of the Lord. Amen.

Halverson returned to the *Sh'ma* when the new Congress arrived in 1995. Republicans had control of both houses for the first time since 1954. Here's his Senate prayer on January 6, right after the 104th Congress started:

Hear, O Israel: The Lord our God is one Lord: And thou shalt love the Lord thy God with all thine heart, and with all thy soul and with all thy might. And these words, which I command thee this day, shall be in thine heart: And thou shalt teach them diligently unto thy children, and shalt talk of them when thou sittest in thine house, and when thou walkest by the way, and when thou liest down, and when thou risest up.—Deuteronomy 6:4-7. God of Abraham, Isaac, and Jacob, God of our fathers, we pray this morning for our families. Be especially with those who are traumatized by the process of moving to Washington—finding a residence and settling in a new neighborhood—as the typical Senate schedule begins to build. . .

Halverson himself left Congress for retirement two months after that prayer. He died in November 1995.

Two years before Halverson's death, his son, Rev. Richard Halverson Jr., opened the Senate in prayer. The son did what the father had done multiple times: borrow from the Jewish Bible. On March 9, 1993, Halverson Jr. read a whopping nine verses about Abraham, "the prayer of Abraham for the deliverance of his city" (Genesis 18:23-32). He concluded:

> Gracious Lord, God of Abraham, we pray that You will raise up in this land not just ten but tens of thousands who are righteous in Thy sight. We pray for spiritual renewal not only political reform. And we dare make this request by faith, because we are children of Abraham in whom You have blessed all nations on Earth. Through the seed of Jacob, Abraham is the father of the Jew. Through the generations of Ishmael, Abraham is the father of the Moslem. And through the lineage of Jesus, Abraham is the father of the Christian.

Halverson Jr. ended, naturally, "It is in His name—the name of Jesus—that we humbly make this prayer. Amen."

38: Members of Congress Go Jewish

> *"These days in the Senate are filled with crucial issues, sharp differences on solutions, and vital votes on legislation. So we begin this day with the question that you asked King Solomon, 'Ask: What shall I give you?' We empathize with Solomon's response. He asked for an 'understanding heart.'"*
> —Chaplain Lloyd John Ogilvie, May 16, 1997

When Rep. Margaret Heckler (R-MA) sponsored Rabbi Barry Rosen on September 9, 1982, she noted "the Hebrew word 'rabbi' means teacher, and the role of teacher is an important one for any rabbi in his relationship with the members of his congregation." Sponsoring Rabbi Jimmy Kessler of Galveston on April 4, 2001, Rep. Nick Lampson (D-TX) said, "Some of my colleagues may not know this, but the word 'rabbi' in Hebrew means teacher."

Ordained rabbis have taught Judaism to Congress. But so, too, have members of Congress acted as rabbi—teacher and Jewish educator. A few even have tried their tongue at Hebrew, with varying degrees of success.

Abraham Hecht of Brooklyn's Shaare Zion Congregation gave the July 29, 1968, House prayer. Rep. Bertram Podell (D-NY) sponsored him. Podell did something unprecedented—and to this day still not repeated. The Jewish member of Congress quoted from the Torah. In Hebrew. As seen in the *Congressional Record*:

> Our House of Representatives was truly honored on this occasion. Mr. Speaker, I believe the best way to express the spirit of Rabbi Hecht is to quote from the Torah itself:

> כִּי—לֹא בְחַיִל, וְלֹא בְכֹחַ
> אִם-בְּרוּחִי

> Which means "not with thy strength, not with thy sword, but only with My spirit, saith the L-rd." And thus Rabbi Hecht is bringing to his community the great spirit of the Lord In the hearts of all mankind. The world at war could well take heed of the spirit of Rabbi Abraham Hecht.

Members have tried Yiddish, too. Non-Jewish members. Sponsoring Joel Levenson of Congregation B'nai Jacob, Woodbridge, Connecticut, on July 10, 2012, Rep. Rosa DeLauro (D-CT) said, "We are joined by what we call the *mishpucha* up in the gallery this morning." (DeLauro is married to Jewish Democratic pollster Stan Greenberg.) Another Connecticut Democrat spoke of a food familiar to Yiddish speakers. Sponsoring Jeremy Wiederhorn on May 24, 2011, Rep. Jim Himes (D-CT) said, "In addition to his spiritual guidance, he introduced me to *cholent*, which for this Presbyterian was a new experience."

Something about Connecticut congressional representation and Yiddishkeit.

Other instances of non-Jewish legislators embracing and instructing Jewish tradition:

- Giving floor remarks after sponsoring Arnold Mark Belzer on April 20, 1988, Rep. Robert Roe (D-NJ) wore a yarmulke.

- The week after Yechiel Eckstein gave the April 8, 1997, Senate prayer he led a Passover Seder for senators and their spouses. Sponsor Sen. Craig Thomas (R-WY) said: "My wife and I attended last year and, as Methodists, we enjoyed it a great deal. We intend to be there again this year. Rabbi, we thank you for your message and sharing with us some of the feelings of the heritage we share as Jews and Christians."
- Another Seder mention by Rep. Donald Norcross (D-NJ) on June 6, 2018. Sponsoring Aaron Krupnick of Congregation Beth El: "I have been fortunate enough to attend services and seder at Beth El."
- On September 22, 1963, for Rosh Hashanah, Sen. Kenneth Keating (R-NY) taught that "the sound of the shofar echoes as an affirmation of the joy of life but at the same time its strangely sad call reminds man that the coming year requires a serious reexamination of purpose."

We saw elsewhere the popularity of Leviticus 25:10 among rabbi guest chaplains, as well as Rep. Barney Frank's (D-MA) suggestion that members of Congress gravitate toward Leviticus. Here's Rep. Maxine Waters (D-CA) combining both. The April 16, 2008, topic: debt cancellation. "Debt forgiveness is a moral imperative, and it is encouraged by many religious traditions," Waters said. "The Bible instructs the people of ancient Israel to cancel debts periodically through the celebration of a sabbath year every 7 years and a jubilee every 50 years. Leviticus 25:10 says, 'Proclaim liberty throughout the lands and to all the inhabitants thereof. It shall be a jubilee for you.' Let us once again proclaim a jubilee for millions of people in some of the poorest countries in the world."

During an October 12, 2017, hearing on federal housing policy, Rep. Emanuel Cleaver (D-MO)—a United Methodist pastor—included Torah in his questioning. "When Abram left Ur going toward the land of promise," Cleaver said, citing Genesis, "he stopped at a place called Haran. Many theologians call that the halfway house. He stayed there until he could find a better route to get to the Promised Land. Public housing is Haran."

During February 14, 1995, floor debate over emergency funding for natural disaster response, Sen. Robert Byrd (D-WV) gave a lengthy lesson about floods, plagues, famine, and earthquakes described in the Old Testament. A sample: "The first tidal wave of which I can find any record was the tidal wave in the midst of the Red Sea which covered the chariots and the horsemen and all the host of Pharaoh that came into the sea in their attempt to overcome and subdue the Israelites who were being led by Moses, and there remained not so much as one of them."

An Isaiah citation showed up during President Clinton's impeachment. From House Minority Leader Dick Gephardt's statement opening the December 18, 1998, floor debate: "In the book of Isaiah in the Bible it was said 'judgment is turned away backward and justice stands far off.'"

On September 12, 2001, when Congress returned the day after the terrorist attacks in New York and Washington, Rep. Mike Pence (R-IN) quoted from the first chapter of Joshua: "My word to the American people is simply this: be encouraged; do not be terrified. Be strong and courageous, for now, as always, throughout our history, the Lord, your God, will be with you wherever you go." The same biblical reference was heard during Sen. John F. Kennedy's July 15, 1960, speech accepting the Democratic presidential nomination: "My call is to the young in heart, regardless of age--to all who respond to the Scriptural call: 'Be strong and of a good courage; be not afraid, neither be thou dismayed.'" And President Franklin Roosevelt borrowed from Joshua in 1934—on Christmas Eve: "Let us make the spirit of Christmas of 1934 that of courage and unity. It is the way to greater happiness and wellbeing. That is, I believe, an important part of what the Maker of Christmas would have it mean. In this sense, the Scriptures admonish us to be strong and of good courage, to fear not, to dwell together in Unity." But don't worry: the first chapter of the Jewish book Joshua isn't just for gentiles. Here's Israeli Prime Minister Ehud Olmert addressing a Joint Meeting of the U.S. Congress on May 24, 2006: "The Bible tells us that, as Joshua stood on the verge of the promised land, he was given one exhortation: 'Chazak v'ematz'; 'Be strong and of good courage.'"

During the Ulysses Grant presidency, Sen. Charles Sumner (R-MA) cited Kings 21:1–3 in opposing annexation of Santo Domingo. He began his December 21, 1870, floor speech: "Naboth the Jezreelite had a vineyard hard by the palace of Ahab king of Samaria. And Ahab spake unto Naboth, saying, 'Give me thy vineyard, that I may have it for a garden of herbs, because it is near unto my house; and I will give thee for it a better vineyard than it; or I will give thee the worth of it in money.' And Naboth said to Ahab, 'The Lord forbid it me, that I should give the inheritance of my fathers unto you.'" Sumner then pivoted and thundered: "The resolution before the Senate commits Congress to a dance of blood. It is a new step in a measure of violence." Grant biographer Ron Chernow wrote that "for sheer histrionics and gratuitous insults," Sumner's *Naboth's Vineyard* speech "was one of the most vitriolic speeches in Senate annals."[62]

On far less acrimonious holy ground, sponsoring a rabbi is a most convenient way to bring forth the inner clergyman lurking inside many a member of Congress.

Rep. Joshua Eilberg (D-PA) noted this about Harold Romirowsky on March 13, 1969: "By ancient Jewish tradition, a rabbi is considered blessed if one of his students follows his example and seeks a career in the rabbinate. Not one, but five of the rabbi's former students were so inspired by his example that they are now studying for the rabbinate."

After Solomon Schiff prayed on June 18, 2009, Rep. Ileana Ros-Lehtinen (R-FL) said, "The spirit of optimism and determination that Rabbi Schiff possesses can be seen in this week's Torah portion. After returning from the Land of Israel, Caleb reports to the Jewish people that 'we should surely go up and inherit the land; for we are certainly able.'"

And sponsoring Peter Hyman on July 30, 2008, Rep. Joe Sestak (D-PA) embraced another ancient rabbinical text:

> There is a midrash, one of the many parables, that embellish upon the Torah. In this particular midrash, there is a man from the land of Israel, a businessman, who was in another country, and when he was there, he was accused of being a spy. He was then told by the judge that he would be executed. He asked for 30 days to go back to the land of Israel and while there finish up his business and come back. The judge initially laughed, but he turned to him and said, "My friend will sit in a jail for me, and if I'm not back, he will be executed." The judge had to see this, and so the man went into jail. And the gentleman went back to the land of Israel and he finished his business. And he would have made it back in time, except there was a storm at sea. And when he finally arrived there, the man, his friend, was about to be hung, executed. And he yelled out as he came closer, "It is I who am to be executed, not him." But his friend said, "No, you're too late; it is to be me." They caused such confusion and commotion that the two men were brought before the king who had to see this, and after listening to their stories, he said, "I will forgive you and pardon you on one condition, that I become your third friend."

---

62   Ron Chernow, *Grant*, Penguin Books, 2017, page 713.

Rep. Mike Quigley (D-IL) showed appreciation not just to a member of the clergy or the Lord, but something much more practical when he addressed the House on April 30, 2015. Sponsoring Michael Siegel, Quigley said his leadership "the synagogue has grown and truly fulfilled its commitment to the entire community of Israel—*klal yisrael*—and healing the word—*tikkun olam*. I am grateful for my punctuation and pronunciation keys. I am also grateful that my constituents can be part of a such an inspiring community—*kehila*."

(When Rep. Jacky Rosen (D-NV) introduced Las Vegas Rabbi Sanford Akselrad on March 29, 2017, she smoothly said "he has shared in the sorrows and joys, from the *simchas* and *shivas*." The future senator had a pronounced advantage in her pronunciation: she's Jewish and previously served as her synagogue's president.)

Not a member of Congress, but still an expert on religious teaching: Senate chaplain Richard Halverson. On May 2, 1994, he offered a story adding to the words inscribed on the chamber's walls: "In God We Trust." Halverson said, "We recall quite a different message which appeared on the wall of another nation in the palace of Belshazzar, king of the chaldeans. We recall that all the king's wisemen—the astrologers, the chaldeans, and soothsayers—could not read the writing nor make known the interpretation thereof. And that it remained for the great Hebrew prophet, Daniel, to reveal its meaning: 'Mene': God hath numbered thy kingdom and finished it. 'Tekel': Thou art weighed in the balances and art found wanting. 'Peres': Thy kingdom is divided and given to the Medes and Persians."

A month later, Halverson, took his knack for citing Judaica in an edgy, even notorious direction. Here's his June 23, 1994, prayer:

> How are the mighty fallen—II. Samuel 1:25. Eternal God, as David joined the nation, Israel, in mourning the fall of King Saul, so our Nation has been traumatized by the fall of a great hero. We pray for O. J. Simpson. . . . Our hearts go out to him in his profound loss.

Samuel. David. Saul. O. J.

"Last week, the U.S. Senate prayed for O. J. Simpson," Sen. Patty Murray (D-WA) reacted. "Our Chaplain led us in prayer for this fallen hero, accused of a crime so horrible it defies description. We heard from the Book of Samuel: 'How are the mighty fallen.' Mr. President, it seems we talk more and more often of fallen heroes, but we sometimes forget who they fall on.

So, Mr. President, this week I would like to suggest that all our colleagues reflect for a moment about the real victims in this case. . . . Remember the victims and let us remember to pray for our children."

Nearly a full year later, Halverson's Simpson prayer still reverberated in the Senate. On June 14, 1995, Sen. Patrick Leahy (D-VT) noted Halverson "gave a long, long prayer here shortly after the arrest of O. J. Simpson, saying we worried about poor O. J. Simpson's state of being, and prayed for him, and hoped he'd be OK, and all that. Some of us suggested maybe there ought to be some prayers for the two people who were also murdered. I do not mean in any way to suggest who committed the crime. But I recall suggesting that maybe if we are going to have the chaplains interject themselves that much into public debate, they ought to be even handed enough to at least pray for those who were dead and not just for somebody who may be a wealthy football star and concerned about the size of his jail cell."

No mention of King Saul from Leahy. But his remarks do show that navigating the tricky waters of policy and current events sometimes can require a chaplain possess the wisdom of King Solomon.

Safer ground lies with Moses. Opening the House on March 16, 2006, Chaplain Daniel Coughlin's entire prayer focused on Moses dealing with his father-in-law. The conclusion: "Moses followed the advice of his father-in-law and did exactly what he said." And House guest chaplain Rev. Alisa Lasater Wailoo on August 10, 2018: "We cry out for all who are home in their districts this month. Refresh their passion to serve, and help them, like Moses, see the burning bushes in their midst."

High Holidays, too, inspire Christian explanation. During the 1970s House Chaplain Edward Latch, a Methodist, offered several Rosh Hashanah greetings to "our Hebrew friends." September 17, 1974: "We lift our hearts unto Thee seeking Thy presence as we with our Hebrew friends enter the sacred festival of Rosh Hashanah." September 5, 1975: "We come before Thee on the eve of Rosh Hashanah to join with our Hebrew friends in entering their new year." October 2, 1978: "Our hearts are filled with gratitude as we join our Hebrew friends in celebrating Rosh Hashanah." (No "Hebrew friends" for Latch's Senate counterpart Rev. Edward Elson on October 11, 1978—Yom Kippur, the holiest Day of Atonement—but he did pray: "Grant us a new beginning. Make us participants in the atonement Thou has opened for all mankind.") And it wasn't just Rosh Hashanah that prompted Chaplain Latch to recognize his Hebrew friends. His April 17, 1973, prayer: "We remember that Thou didst lead the children of Israel from the land of bondage to the life of freedom. In grateful remembrance of that day we join our Hebrew friends in celebrating the joyful festival of the Passover."

A Christian member once paid tribute to a rabbi by describing him as being like a great Christian. Morris Hershman of the Joliet Jewish Congregation opened the House on February 1, 1983. His sponsor was freshman Rep. George O'Brien (R-IL), not yet a month on the job. O'Brien went this route:

> When Rabbi Hershman appears, as he always does, at major community events to open, to conduct, or to close or conclude the affair, as I sit in those audiences I have a curious religious recollection. Some years ago when Latin was in vogue and was the vernacular of the church, when a visiting prelate of great prestige would come to a cathedral or come to a church, he would be greeted by the choir and the choir would usher him in to the moving strains of a hymn called "Ecce Sacerdos Magnus," something akin to "Hail to the Chief;" but the words really mean, "Behold, this good man who in his own day God saw fit to make a great priest." I can think of nothing better as a description of Morris Hershman. "Behold this good man who in his own time God saw fit to make a great priest."

Finally, Ashton Kutcher. Neither a member of Congress nor a Jew. For that matter, not even a minister, but an actor. And a student of Kabbalah. Kutcher testified to the Senate Foreign Relations Committee on February 17, 2017. Concluding his remarks on modern slavery, he attempted Talmudic insight: "I was reminded of a story a friend of mine told me about a rabbi named Hillel, who was asked to explain the Torah while standing on one leg. And he said, 'Love thy neighbor as thyself. Everything else is just commentary.'"

Kutcher mixed up Jesus with Hillel. *The Algemeiner,* though, cut him some slack, awarding points for trying. Kutcher "got the story slightly wrong," the Jewish newspaper ruled on February 19, 2017, "but his sentiment was received in the spirit in which it was clearly intended."

39: "Some of our Boys Died Last Night": Notable Christian Prayers

"A prayer is a request sent to the throne of God. It may be an able request or it may be a crude request, and some of the best prayers have perhaps been the crudest prayers."
—Sen. John Sharp Williams (D-MS), March 17, 1913

"Every Member of this great deliberative body recognizes the need of practicing the habit of prayer as part of clearing mental attitudes and removing petty or puny thinking from the field of performance of congressional duties."
—Rep. Clyde Doyle (D-CA), September 21, 1949

"What we are doing for our neighbors throughout the world in these turbulent times should be an assurance to people everywhere in the world that we are not only a great Nation but that we are a Christian Nation."
—Chief Justice of the United States Earl Warren, Congressional and Presidential Prayer Breakfast, February 5, 1954

"This nation devoutly recognizes the authority and law of Jesus Christ, Savior and Ruler of nations."
—Constitutional amendment proposed in 1961 by future independent presidential candidate Rep. John Anderson (R-IL)

This book is about Jewish guest chaplains. But it is reasonable to note, without risk of shocking the reader, that Judaism is not the predominant religion denomination of guest chaplains, consistent with the reality that this is a mostly Christian nation. [63]

"We are a Christian people," the Senate Judiciary Committee reported on January 19, 1853, "not because the law demands it, not to gain exclusive benefits or to avoid legal disabilities, but from choice and education; and in a land thus universally Christian, what is to be expected, what desired, but that we shall pay due regard to Christianity?" A year later, the House Judiciary Committee made similar assertions. "At the time of the adoption of the Constitution and the amendments, the universal sentiment was that

---

63 A Christian nation by demographics—but not necessarily by practice: An April 25, 2017, Lifeway Research survey found that more than half of Christian Americans have read little or none of the Bible.

Christianity should be encouraged, the Committee reported on March 27, 1854. "In this age there can be no substitute for Christianity. . . . That was the religion of the founders of the republic and they expected it to remain the religion of their descendants." [64]

A century and half later, the Freedom from Religion Foundation calculated religious affiliation of Congress chaplains. Examining the chaplains and guest chaplains from 2000-2015, it found "96.7 percent of all guest chaplains have been Christian, although Christians are 70.6 percent of the U.S. population; 2.7 percent were Jewish, compared to 1.9 percent of the population." [65]

On June 7, 2015, *Roll Call* reported that nearly 18% of the prayers read at the beginning of each House session in the 114th Congress "have referred to Jesus, and all of those prayers have been given by guest chaplains. Of the 29 guest chaplains who have addressed the House in the 114th Congress, 13 of them have made a specific religious reference, all of them to Jesus. All but one of the guest chaplains have been Christian. Guest chaplains are nominated by members of the House, and, given that more than 90 percent of House members are Christian, the probability that a guest chaplain is Christian is high, because members typically invite clergy from their home churches."

Thus, mostly Christian prayers. And lots of Jesus. No wonder the 104th Congress passed a resolution authorizing the use of the Capitol Grounds for the "Washington for Jesus 1996" prayer rally.

And no atheist prayers. The U.S. Court of Appeals for the DC Circuit ruled on April 19, 2019, that the House chaplain could not be ordered to allow a self-described atheist to offer a secular prayer to the House of Representatives. Niels Lesniewski wrote in *Roll Call* that day: "The House chaplain scored a legal victory on Good Friday." (The Third Circuit Court of Appeals ruled in August 2019 that atheists, agnostics and others who don't believe in God can be barred from giving invocations in the Pennsylvania state house. President Donald Trump celebrated that ruling on Twitter.)

Rev. James Wesberry was acting House chaplain in August 1949. "I saw Christ and felt His spirit in the many warm, gracious, sincere expressions the Members of the House made regarding my humble prayers each day," he later said in a sermon at his Morningside Baptist Church in Atlanta. "My

---

64   Glover Shipp, *In God We Trust . . . Or Do We? Our Nation Built on a Christian Foundation*, Resources Publications, 2011, page 81.

65   FFRF website, October 11, 2017.

soul was stirred by the large number of times I heard the Bible quoted in the speeches and discussions on the floor of the House. One day, during the discussion of the bill which had to do with military aid for Europe, I heard the Bible quoted three different times. I told one of my friends how much this impressed me. He later asked me if I heard one of the Congressmen quote all of the Ten Commandments and the song which the angels sang at the birth of Jesus. Yes; I certainly did see Christ in Congress."

All the Jesus talk—does that bother Jewish members? One time after a prayer, a Christian chaplain comforted a Jewish congressman. The *Washington Post* reported on August 3, 1983, that Rep. Ted Weiss (D-NY) praised House chaplain James Ford for seeking him out, "'somewhat chagrined,' after a fundamentalist Christian guest preacher delivered a 'particularly strident prayer." Weiss told the *Post*: "He wanted to reassure me that the guy might be popular at home, in a parochial setting, but that he could not adjust well to another setting."

Rep. William Dickinson (R-AL) seemed to try to offer reassurances as well on March 5, 1984, when he said the opening prayer "is a nondenominational prayer, and the Jewish members and others of other sects do not feel particularly offended, I do not think, and as has been pointed out, especially if a rabbi opens it."

Dickinson said that during extensive debate over constitutional amendment governing prayer in the public schools. Two days later in the *Washington Post*, T. R. Reid reported this gem:

> Toward the end of the marathon, Rep. Marjorie S. Holt (R-Md.) declared that the United States is a Christian nation.
>
> Serving in the speaker's chair then as a favor to the leadership was Rep. Barney Frank (D-Mass.), who is Jewish.
>
> "When I heard that," Frank said afterward, "I thought, well, if this is a Christian nation, how come some poor Jew had to get up at 5:30 in the morning to preside over the House of Representatives?"

And from a January 3, 1995, article in *Christianity Today* on the Senate chaplain:

> Halverson recalls that early in his tenure a few Jewish senators gently reminded him that they felt excluded when he prayed "in the name of Jesus." Not wanting to offend them—but also not wanting to compromise his calling—the chaplain has sometimes closed his prayers in the name of Jesus

and, at other times, in an analogous title like "the Way, the Truth, and the Life." And he has often said to his Jewish friends in the Senate, "You know everything about my faith is Jewish, and my best friend [Jesus] is Jewish."

Elizabeth Holtzman upset Rep. Emanuel Celler by 635 votes to win a 1972 New York Democratic primary. On July 5, 2018, the *New York Times* asked Holtzman "what biases and obstacles she confronted when she arrived in Washington. 'A Southerner in the House approached me and said, "Just because you're Jewish and a woman, don't you worry,"' she answered, leaving her with the impression that there was plenty to worry about."

Here's a different kind of worry for Jewish members: the pop quiz.

Bob Levi was an aide to Rep. Gary Ackerman (D-NY). He sponsored guest chaplain Rabbi Jay Marcus on September 13, 1990. Levi wrote in the *New York Jewish Week* on August 10, 2018, about study groups Marcus conducted for Jewish members in the 1980s. "House Speaker Tip O'Neill got his hands on one of the Jewish texts used by Rabbi Marcus," Levi wrote, "brought it to the Speaker's rostrum in the House Chamber, called one of the House's senior Jewish members to the rostrum, and quietly quizzed the congressman about facts in the text. Failing to give the correct responses, the representative conceded ignorance. Subsequently, the representative demanded that a staff participant in the class provide him with any future study material, so he would not be embarrassed by the Speaker again."

Excavating and compiling information for this book revealed many noteworthy Christian chaplains, prayers and related anecdotes, some hidden in obscurity. A few deserved to be rescued, dusted off and brought down from forgotten history shelves. Even if there's little—perhaps nothing—Jewish about them.

So let's take a look. Starting with famous Christian clergy. And you can't get any more famous than the Pope.

No Pope has even been a guest chaplain. But Pope Francis did address a Joint Meeting of Congress. And just three paragraphs in on September 24, 2015, His Holiness went Jewish:

> Yours is a work which makes me reflect in two ways on the figure of Moses. On the one hand, the patriarch and lawgiver of the people of Israel symbolizes the need of peoples to keep alive their sense of unity by means of just legislation. On the other, the figure of Moses leads us directly to God and thus to the transcendent dignity of the human being. Moses provides us with

a good synthesis of your work: you are asked to protect, by means of the law, the image and likeness fashioned by God on every human face.

Domestic Christian personalities have been part of the Congress mix.

On June 14, 1978, evangelist Oral Roberts addressed the House when it marked the 201st anniversary of Flag Day. Roberts sat at the desk in front of the Speaker's rostrum. Among the honored guests that day: American astronauts, including 29-year-old Dr. Judith Resnick. She became the first Jewish American in space and was among the fatalities when Space Shuttle *Challenger* exploded upon launch eight years later.

Earlier that month another famous evangelist was House guest chaplain. Rev. Jimmy Swaggart on June 2: "Dear Heavenly Father, we have come to You in the name of the Lord Jesus Christ."

Billy Graham was a guest chaplain several times, including June 22, 1960, in the House: "We come to Thee humbly confessing our sense of need of Thee more now than any time in many years. We need Thy wisdom. We pray that Thou wouldst give to this body of men supernatural wisdom in dealing with the problems that they face."

Graham in the House again a quarter-century later, March 19, 1986 (same day as the seventh anniversary of live televised proceedings of the House chamber): "In the midst of our busyness give us the discipline daily to deepen our faith and to seek first in our lives Thy Kingdom and Thy righteousness."

In *The Billy Graham Story*, Rev. Dr. John Charles Pollock notes that after that 1986 House prayer, Graham, "in an unscheduled stop, sat in on the weekly Bible study attended by members from both the House and the Senate." The next month, on April 23, he opened the Senate. According to Pollock, "The assistant secretary of the Senate determined that the prayer should be inscribed on vellum. She gave it to the chaplain, Richard Halverson, a strong supporter of [Graham's] crusade, to hang in his office. Halverson suggested that every senator should have a similar, finely inscribed copy for his office and received many expressions of appreciation when this was done."[66]

In 2015 North Carolina's governor signed legislation that would install Graham's statue in Statuary Hall in the U.S. Capitol upon his death. According to the September 20, 2015, *Charlotte Observer*, Graham would "not be the first religious figure to get a statue in the Capitol. In fact, 12

---

66   Zondervan, 2003, page 235.

states are represented by at least one person who made his or her mark in the world of faith."

Billy Graham's daughter Anne Graham Lotz was a guest chaplain. In the Senate on September 19, 2002, she quoted Jewish biblical figure Daniel: "We come to You as the great and awesome God, one who keeps His covenant of love with generations, with those who love Him and obey Him." Lotz was the last guest chaplain sponsored by Sen. Jesse Helms (R-NC).

The son of Jerry Falwell, Reverend Jonathan Falwell, was House guest chaplain on July 29, 2009. Recognizing him from the Speaker's chair that day was another son of a famous man of the cloth, Rep. Jesse Jackson Jr. (D-IL).

Rep. Jackson's own father did not deliver a Congress prayer. But he was mentioned in one. Senate chaplain Halverson, June 23, 1993: "During the presidential campaign last year, Jesse Jackson reminded us that what is morally wrong cannot be politically right. If we separate morality from politics, we imperil our Nation and threaten self-destruction. Imperial Rome was not defeated by an enemy from without; it was destroyed by moral decay from within. Mighty God, over and over again You warned Your people, Israel, that righteousness is essential to national health."

Famous family connection worked the other way on June 2, 1986. That was the first day of live TV coverage of the U.S. Senate—when C-SPAN2 began. For that historic moment, a guest chaplain opened the proceedings: Rev. Bernard Hawley of the First Presbyterian Church in Salina, Kansas.

Hawley was invited by fellow Kansan and Senate Majority Leader Bob Dole. Which makes sense, politically: take care of the local folks first. Dole said of Hawley: "We are pleased he could take part in a little bit of history this afternoon."

Hawley was linked to celebrity through his son, an astronaut. Dole noted Hawley's "strong ties to America's space program." Hawley had given the invocation at the January 31, 1986, NASA memorial service in Houston for the astronauts who died in the Space Shuttle Challenger explosion. Dole noted that, too. Hawley's son Steve flew five times on the Space Shuttle. Steve Hawley's wife? Another astronaut: Sally Ride, the first American woman in space.

(Steven Hawley and Sally Ride divorced the next year. Sally was in a relationship with a woman, according to her July 23, 2012, *New York Times* obituary).

Hawley's participation that day caught the attention of *Washington Post* TV critic Tom Shales, who wrote on June 3, 1986, about the first day of Senate TV. Shales reported:

> Just after 2 p.m., Strom Thurmond (R-S.C.), the presiding officer, banged the Senate into its first telesession with two whacks of the gavel and the words, "The Senate will come to order." It did. Thurmond muffed the name of the guest chaplain (the Rev. Bernard Hawley), and said he was the father of astronaut Sally Ride, when he is in fact the father-in-law, but otherwise, the day was fairly free of foul-ups, bleeps and blunders, nonlegislatively speaking anyway.

Just before America entered World War II, a different kind of celebrity was guest chaplain—a war hero. Lynn Olson recounts in *Those Angry Days: Roosevelt, Lindbergh, and America's Fight Over World War II, 1939-1941* that the movie "Sergeant York" had its Washington premier in the summer of 1941, "lending [it] the distinct aura of a government-sanctioned film. Troops accompanied York from Union Station to the White House, where Roosevelt told him—and reporters—that he was 'thrilled' with the picture. The morning after its screening, which was attended by members of Congress, military leaders, and other government officials, York was invited to deliver the daily invocation in the Senate."[67]

And just after the Great War, the War to End All Wars, Daniel Couve, chaplain of the 59th Division Infantry, French Army, gave the Senate prayer. On February 1, 1919, he thanked God "for the victory Thou hast given to our allied armies." And Couve asked of God, "Do inspire the President of the United States; do protect the premier of France."

Few wartime prayers can top the one offered the day after the D-Day invasion began. On June 7, 1944, House chaplain James Shea Montgomery began with a message that could easily have been delivered on the Normandy beaches:

> Just a word before we pray. Some of our boys died last night in the crusade for freedom and humanity; some of our boys died last night who had looked through the glimpse of the future and claimed it as their own; some of our boys died last night who dreamed of a happy home and a circle of loved ones; some of our boys died last night in the front row of battle for the country they adored; some of our boys died last night beneath the skies of embattled

---

67   Random House, 2014, page 369.

France; some of our boys died last night for you and me that liberty may not die out of the human breast.

Montgomery added Psalm 46: "God is our refuge and strength, a very present help in trouble." In spotlighting this prayer, the House historian's office website notes that "more than 10,000 Allied soldiers were killed or wounded, including roughly 2,500 U.S. fatalities, during the first 24 hours of Operation Overlord."

Montgomery led the U.S. House in D-Day prayer. Another Montgomery, General Bernard Montgomery, led the British forces in D-Day battle.

Political celebrities, too, have been alongside chaplains. When he was a newly elected Senator from Illinois—and relegated to back-benching, mundane duties such as gaveling in a session—Barack Obama introduced Chaplain Barry Black twice, both times in 2007 (February 1 and June 7). And he introduced (not sponsored) two guest chaplains in 2007: Rev. Dr. Layton Mauze III of Gastonia, North Carolina, on February 15 (five days after he announced his candidacy for president) and Pastor Linda Arey, New Harvest Church, Waynesboro, Virginia on June 22.

On several notable occasions, Christian prayers got wrapped up in news of the day. On June 22, 2016, minority Democrats disrupted House proceedings with a day-long loud, raucous sit-in to demand votes on gun legislation. When the House-operated cameras turned off, the Democrats used social media to broadcast video of the sit-in. The opening session lasted three minutes, enough time to work in the prayer and pledge of allegiance before the majority chair gaveled out the session. The only quiet time during the official session was for the House chaplain's prayer and the pledge of allegiance. Chaplain Patrick Conroy, surely unaware of what the next 25 hours would bring, opened: "Father of mercy, we give You thanks for giving us another day."

A raucous Congress is timeless. Which is why it's easy to imagine this April 5, 1983, opening prayer by Senate chaplain Halverson being repeated today:

> Humpty Dumpty sat on the wall. Humpty Dumpty had a great fall. All the king's horses and all the king's men couldn't put Humpty Dumpty together again. Dear God, in mercy and grace, prevent the Senate from being like Humpty Dumpty. Keep it from being so fractured and fragmented that no one will be able to put it together again.

The *New York Times* printed that prayer on April 12, 1983, calling it "Required Reading."

Halverson's February 26, 1992, prayer seems likewise evergreen:

> Investigative reporting seems epidemic in an election year—its primary objective to defame political candidates. Seeking their own reputation, they destroy another's as they search relentlessly, microscopically for some ancient skeleton in a person's life. Eternal God, help these self-appointed "vacuum-cleaner journalists" to discover how unproductive and divisive their efforts are.

Christian prayers can be heard off the floor and without a chaplain present. A May 15, 2017, House Agriculture Committee hearing opened with a prayer. Chairman Mike Conaway (R-TX) called on Rep. David Scott (D-GA) for the honor. "Dear Heavenly Father, we come before your throne of grace to first of all say thank you," Scott prayed with a bowed head. "We ask a special blessing on our agriculture industry and that your blessings come upon our new Secretary of Agriculture Sonny Perdue." Scott ended: "These and other blessings we ask in your son Christ Jesus name, Amen." The Senate Indian Affairs Committee held a February 25, 2016, roundtable on the Tribal Law and Order Act. A witness opened with a prayer. Native American leader Brian Cladoosby: "As we try to overcome this generational trauma, Lord, may this be one of the tools, one of the avenues that we can use to make our children's generation and the next seven generations better at our homelands. Bless our time together today, bless our conversations. In Jesus' name we pray, Amen."

Jesus appeared during a heated, partisan July 12, 2018, House hearing with FBI Agent Peter Strzok, who was removed from the special counsel's investigation of Russian involvement in the 2016 U.S. elections. "We've heard a lot about ethics, patriotism, and service today. We are all accountable for our actions," Rep. Steve Russell (R-OK) said. "I am mindful of the words of Christ in Luke: You shall know a tree from its fruit. From the abundance of the heart the mouth speaks."

In a private House Republican meeting on May 25, 2016, reported by the *Washington Post*, Georgia Rep. Rick Allen "offered a prayer implying that the 43 Republicans who had supported LGBT rights 'on the floor last night' went against the teachings of the Bible." The *Hill* newspaper reported May 26, 2016, that Allen "launched the GOP's regular policy meeting in the Capitol basement by reading a Bible passage condemning homosexuality and suggesting that supporters of the LGBT provision, which passed the House the night before, were defying Christian tenets."

There was no chaplain in the House on August 5, 2011—yet there was still a prayer. How? Deputy Parliamentarian Thomas Wickham had the honor. No yarmulke or cross—he wore his staff badge. And he appealed to an authority higher than even *Robert's Rules of Order*: "Almighty God, who has given us this good land for our heritage, we humbly beseech Thee that we may always prove ourselves a people mindful of Thy favor and glad to do Thy will. Bless our land with honorable industry, sound learning, and pure manners. Amen."

Christian prayers also instruct us to expect the unexpected. Like unexpected topics.

A prayer for the British royalty, against which Americans once revolted? You bet. The *Montreal Gazette* reported on June 28, 1902, that the House chaplain "prayed for the restoration to health of King Edward": "Hear us when we pray for the King of England. Grant, if in accord with Thy will, that he may be restored to strength to strength to guide and control his people in justice and equity under Thy guidance." On the same day, the Senate chaplain noted President William McKinley's assassination less than a year earlier: "We remember her tears and prayers for us when our great ruler fell. And now we have Christian sympathy and brotherly concern in this, her hour of sorrow. Bless her King and give him a happy issue out of his present sickness."

More royalty. In fact, a prayer for another King, King James. As in, LeBron James. On June 20, 2016, after the Cleveland Cavaliers defeated the Golden State Warriors to win the pro basketball championship, Senate Chaplain Black opened with: "As the final game of the National Basketball Association reminded us of redemption, we place our confidence in You, the Redeemer of humanity."[68] A King, and a Queen. The Queen of Soul. Black's August 20, 2018, Senate prayer: "Lord, we ask You to comfort those who mourn Aretha Franklin's death."

---

68 A different King James in this political threat. Republican Rep. Mo Brooks ran in a 2017 special election for an Alabama Senate seat, losing the primary to Roy Moore. In one campaign ad he urged funding for President Trump's wall on the Mexico border. Brooks looked into the camera and said, "If I have to filibuster on the Senate floor, I'll even read the King James Bible until the wall is funded. And you know what? Washington can benefit from that."

Then there's unexpected choreography. His Holiness the Dalai Lama gave the opening prayer in the Senate on March 6, 2014. When the Buddhist Monk concluded, the Senate went into recess. His Holiness walked from the podium onto the Senate floor. There he stood, next to Majority Leader Harry Reid.

You don't often see the guest chaplain standing among the Senators. There's only one example (based on visual evidence) of that happening with a rabbi. On May 8, 1991, Rabbi Alvin Berkun of Tree of Life Congregation stood next to his sponsor, Sen. Arlen Specter (R-PA).

(Another Buddhist Monk moment with Congress had a different ending. Beside the Dalai Lama, in America the other best-known Buddhist leader is the renowned Vietnamese monk Thich Nhat Hanh. He gave a lecture titled *Leading with Courage and Compassion* at the Library of Congress on September 10, 2003. The target audience was members of Congress. He was introduced by—brace yourself—the late comedian Garry Shandling, who was born Jewish but buried as an ordained Buddhist monk. According to an August 12, 2010, *GQ* profile of Shandling: "The chaplain from the House of Representatives spoke first—'he gave a prayer that was, um, long and dry, to be honest'—so when Shandling arrived at the podium, he got right to the point. 'You're probably wondering why I'm here,' he recalls telling the audience of about 2,000 dignitaries and religious leaders. 'First of all, humor is a wonderful way to deal with our suffering, because if we can laugh at our troubles, we can feel better. Thich Nhat Hanh is a special man who has helped millions with their suffering with incredible technique. But he doesn't know real suffering, because he has not dated as much as I have.'")

How about unexpected sightings of Bible verses? Like on floor charts. On February 26, 2016, Rep. Louis Gohmert showed a chart that displayed 2 Chronicles 7:14.

On July 27, 2017, Rep. Raul Ruiz (D-CA) displayed a chart of a hospitalized child that cited Joshua 1:9 and Romans 8:37-39.

Then there's unexpected windfall—like a boatload of money.

A June 8, 1949, *New York Times* headline "Chaplain Gets $3,750,000 But 3 Zeros Are Nothing." The accompanying *Associated Press* story: "Undoubtedly the highest-paid clergyman in the world, if you take a look at Congressional records, is the Chaplain of the House of Representatives. It says in the official printed Appropriations Committee hearings that his pay is $3,750,000 a year. But it is a typographical error, committee officials hurriedly pointed out today. The salary of the Rev. James Shea Montgomery, the chaplain, is only $3,750 a year."

Real boats were prominent when Rev. Abraham Akaka, pastor emeritus of Kawaiahao Church, Honolulu, Hawaii, was Senate guest chaplain on May 9, 1991. Introduced to the chamber by brother Daniel Akaka (D-HI), Rev. Akaka said: "As our ancient Hawaiian ancestors found new islands of life and order, sailing their brave voyaging canoes even in the face of deadly storms, by making and maintaining connection with their right guiding star, so let it be with our beloved Nation and with all peoples of our planet . . . finding together the best ways for sailing our common canoe surely and safely to our promised new space island. Let our connection with thy light turn MC2 - massive cremation squared, into CM2—creative mutuality squared, that we and all mankind may become one winning crew-sailing our space canoe faithfully with Thee to our New World Order. In the name of Jesus Christ, our Lord-Adonai Elohaynu Adonai Echod-for the Lord our God is one Lord." (Those were his written words. The prayer as spoken— captured on C-SPAN video—differed a bit.)

Another water theme when Rev. Alisa Lasater Wailoo, Capitol Hill United Methodist Church, offered the House prayer on August 29, 2017. She was a guest chaplain the week that Hurricane Harvey devastated Houston. She prayed for "the people of Texas engulfed in a tremendous storm." She asked God to "anchor our hearts in Your truth that speaks only in love . . . until we, like Noah, remember the rainbow, and trust You to lead us together through the storm." (Rabbi Arnold Resnicoff was House guest chaplain four days later, praying to "rescue Harvey's victims.")

Sadly, there has been a chaplain tragedy on a boat. On August 27, 2001, House Chaplain James Ford, a Lutheran pastor who had recently retired from the post, died "aboard his boat at the Gangplank Marina in Washington," according to his September 1, 2001, *Washington Post* obituary. The DC Medical Examiner said that Ford "died of a gunshot wound and that his death was a suicide." He was 70. He had officiated at the wedding for House speaker Newt Gingrich and congressional staffer Callista Bisek. He was, according to the *Washington Post*, the first House chaplain to serve full-time.

But a boat also has brought good luck to a chaplain.

In the nineteenth century Rev. William Henry Milburn was chaplain of the House and the Senate. He was blind (the result of a childhood accident.

The Canadian newspaper *Le Salaberry* offered this June 28, 1900, account of his big career break:

> About 50 years ago a boat carrying over 300 passengers was making its way down the lazy Ohio River. On board the ship were a number of Senators on their way to Washington. A young Methodist minister, 22 years of age, was also a passenger. This young man was totally blind, but quite alive to the card playing and whisky drinking going on on board the boat. One moonlight night he preached a sermon soundly rebuking the Senators for their share in the disgraceful drinking and gambling. They were greatly surprised at his attack, but admired his pluck all the same. They gave him a sum of money and offered him the post of Chaplain of the Senate. In due time he was elected. This young man was the now famous Dr. Milburn, whose sermons are known all over the world.

Despite sermons "known all over the world," the *Jewish Messenger* was underwhelmed by Milburn. "Evidently the chaplain in Congress is bent on making prayers that shall be read and enjoyed by the multitude," the New York Jewish weekly newspaper editorialized on April 9, 1886. "He thinks that with so little legislation allowed to creep through the meshes of politics, some sturdy praying may effect sensation. And for once the chaplain is made a positive quantity in Congress. Eventually he may compose his prayers in pithy paragraphs, so that they readily may be adopted in sections by the House, and added to future party platforms." The broadsheet then leveled this broadside: "Certainly there is a ludicrous side to this sudden and graphic recital before the Deity of the evils that are so intensely typified in Congress."[69]

A narrower, more achievable claim to fame might be the one modern-day House Chaplain Patrick Conroy expressed to the *Catholic News Service*. Conroy told *CNS* on June 2, 2017: "'There's only one thing left that I'd really like to do,' he said, 'to be in a feature-length motion picture. I was a drama guy.' When reminded that there's still time, he answered: 'Oh, I know. Well, heck, I'm on TV, I'm on C-SPAN.'"

---

69   Editorial cited in *Comprehensive Summary of the Press Throughout the World On All Important Current Topcics*, Volume 1, page 13, April-October 1886.

40: Social Media Spreads the Word

"We're kvelling! Senate session opens this morning with prayer from
@HaroldKravitz"
—Tweet from Adath Jeshurun Congregation in Minnetonka,
Minnesota, June 9, 2015

"@USHouse @HouseDemocrats @HouseGOP it is an honor to offer
the opening prayer today. May we all be inspired and open our
hearts as we work for the people."
—Tweet from Rabbi Lawrence Sernovitz, Nafshenu,
Cherry Hill, New Jersey, June 4, 2019

"May the people who work in that House always remember that it
does not belong to them, but to our children who will inherit it."
—Facebook post by Rabbi Steven Abraham,
Beth El Synagogue, Omaha, Nebraska,
House guest chaplain, November 20, 2019

Communications strategy is found in both the Hebrew and Christian Bibles. Jesus embraced word-of-mouth buzz in Matthew 28:19: "Go therefore and make disciples of all nations." In Revelation 14:6 Jesus saw an "angel fly in the midst of heaven, having the everlasting gospel to preach unto them that dwell on the earth." As for the Old Testament, no flying angels for Moses. He went with proven, conventional earthen stone. Moses might have been among the first breaking news reporters when, at Mount Sinai, he was given "the two tables of the testimony, tables of stone, written with the finger of God" (Exodus 31:18). The Ten Commandments, what an enviable scoop. Even better: no embargo.

"Thou shalt set thee up great stones, and plaster them with plaster," Moses instructs the Israelites in Deuteronomy 27:3-4. "Thou shalt write upon them all the words of this law." The law plastered as a huge stone billboard—centuries before the "Hollywood" sign in the Los Angeles hills!

Angels and tablets and stones are credible if ancient forms of communications. Fast forward to present day (skipping past 1455 when Gutenberg invented the movable-type printing press to print the Bible). One current revolutionary communications tool both Jesus and Moses might have utilized: the internet.

Online communications techniques were very much on Senate chaplain Barry Black's mind when he gave a soaring keynote address to the February 2017 National Prayer Breakfast. He told the thousands of religious leaders gathered in the Washington Hilton, "When we pray, we are making our voice—our voices—heard in heaven." But, he noted, "we work at making our voices heard on earth. We march. We lift placards. We're involved in social media. We blog. We've got LinkedIn. And we've got Google and YouTube. And all the ways that we try to make our voices heard on earth."

Black was setting up for a lofty, aspirational teaching: "Far more important than letting our voices be heard on earth is the opportunity to make our voices heard in heaven."

Perhaps. But let's stay grounded on earth. Using Black's practical examples and others like them, consider the ways rabbi prayers in Congress can be heard—and shared—in the modern astral plane of the internet and various transcendent tools of the social digital age.

Wikipedia, for example. Although Black left the online encyclopedia off his listing of new tech platforms, it's a place to find rabbi guest chaplains:

- The Wikipedia entry for Abraham Chill: "In the early 1960s, at the request of his good friend United States Senator John O. Pastore (D.R.I.) he was accorded the honor of opening a session of the United States Senate with a prayer."
- The entry for Sally Priesand: "After her ordination, then member of Congress Bella Abzug arranged for her to deliver the opening prayer at the House of Representatives, making her the first Jewish woman to do so."
- A photo in Wikipedia showing Shmuel Herzfeld "delivering the opening prayer as a guest chaplain at the United State House of Representatives on May 23, 2014."
- Another photo showing Levi Shemtov as Senate guest chaplain on September 17, 1998.
- A C-SPAN picture of Amy Rader delivering the House prayer September 14, 2006, in the Wikipedia article titled "Chaplain of the United States House of Representatives."
- The entry for Lance Sussman: "On March 1, 2001 Sussman gave the opening prayer for a session of the United States House of Representatives."

- And Stuart Weinblatt: "Rabbi Weinblatt has given the opening prayer as a guest chaplain for sessions of the U.S. House of
  Representatives, the United States Senate."

The Sussman and Weinblatt articles link to C-SPAN video of their
prayers, which were created for this book. (Prayers since the beginning of
live television coverage of the House in 1979 and Senate in 1986 can be
found in the C-SPAN Video Library.)

Sussman's prayer also is posted on his Facebook page. He is one of the
earliest rabbi guest chaplains on Facebook. Members of Congress post the
rabbis they sponsor on Facebook, too. An example from Rep. Julia Brownley
(D-CA) on June 18, 2014, with a picture: "It was my great privilege to welcome Rabbi Michael Lotker and his wife Sonia, to the U.S. Capitol today."
Rep. Max Rose (D-NY) posted video of a rabbi on Facebook January 19,
2020: "As we remember the 75th anniversary of the Liberation of Auschwitz
this week, it is my special honor to welcome Rabbi Avraham Hakohen
'Romi' Cohn, a holocaust survivor himself, to the House of Representatives
to deliver today's opening prayer."

Among the earliest rabbi prayers posted on YouTube was from January
22, 2003. It's the first of eight Senate invocations Arnold Resnicoff gave during the first six months that year as that legislative body was in between
permanent chaplains. It was uploaded in February 2010 (five years after
YouTube began) by Resnicoff himself. Other early uses of YouTube include
the prayer offered by Shea Harlig of Chabad of Southern Nevada. Video of
his March 15, 2007, House prayer was posted the same day. Likewise, the
YouTube of Harlig's June 25, 2009, Senate prayer was posted that day. Cheryl
Jacobs was the third female rabbi to offer a Senate prayer. Her February
7, 2008, appearance lives on YouTube. And Maurice Kaprow posted his
September 25, 2008, Senate prayer on YouTube four days after it was delivered. Other videos were uploaded by their congressional sponsors. These
days, video of rabbi prayers in Congress are available on both YouTube and
the C-SPAN Video Library.

Rabbis include their appearances in Congress on LinkedIn (launched
in 2003). Washington Hebrew Congregation's Joui Hessel was guest chaplain on June 4, 2004. Her LinkedIn profile says, "Rabbi Hessel has also
offered the opening prayer at the United States House of Representatives."
Joel Levenson: "Led the opening prayer, July 2012, United States House of
Representatives, the 112th Congress, 2nd Session." Hershel Lutch quickly

added the C-SPAN video and picture of his June 21, 2017, prayer to his LinkedIn page with this message: "Honored to address the US House of Representatives this morning as guest chaplain. The United States is a powerful force for good in the world; it was a privilege to be able to thank the dedicated lawmakers of the Congress who work so tirelessly on all of our behalf."

The LinkedIn profile for Stephen Baars of Aish Hatorah in Bethesda, Maryland, mentions "his training as a stand-up comedian at the Improv in LA" (but not his May 22, 2008, prayer in Congress). He has nearly 10,000 followers on Twitter (as of April 2020), putting him among the guest chaplain rabbis with the largest flocks on Twitter. No wonder his Senate prayer offered insight into the economy of words in the digital age: "There is a Jewish teaching, that a person is granted so many words in this world, and when he or she has used them up, so is his time on this good earth."

As of April 2020, 40 guest chaplain rabbis are on Twitter. (A 41st died in December 2019: Harry Sky, 95, of Temple Beth El in Portland, Maine. He was the earliest rabbi praying in Congress—April 4, 1962 in the Senate— who joined Twitter. One obituary noted: "Sky, who was on Twitter into his 90s, was viewed as a giant in the American rabbi community.") Sally Priesand became the first woman rabbi guest chaplain in 1973 and joined Twitter 40 years later, January 2013 (@rabbisally1).

Laurence Sernovitz tweeted gleefully four times when he was House guest chaplain in 2019, shrewdly tagging both Democrats and Republicans.

Members of Congress use Twitter to get out quick word about rabbis they sponsor. Sen. Al Franken (D-MN) tweeted a picture on June 9, 2015: "Sen. Franken, @Chaplain_Black welcomed Rabbi @HaroldKravitz from MN to give opening prayer at the Senate." Sen. Mark Warner (D-VA) used Twitter to thank Rabbi Israel Zoberman for his December 11, 2014, prayer. Sen. Dan Sullivan (R-AK) tweeted on February 3, 2016: "Glad to see a friend & familiar face: Rabbi Yosef Greenberg of #Alaska offered #Senate opening prayer today."

In the House, Rep. Martha McSally tweeted pictures from her office on May 17, 2017: "Visiting w/Rabbi Thomas Louchheim of Tucson and his family before he led the opening prayer for the House as the Guest Chaplain today." Likewise, Rep. Nita Lowey (D-NY) offered a behind-the-scenes twitter look at Eytan Hammerman's June 11, 2014 House prayer. With a picture of Hammerman and family, she said: "Rabbi Eytan Hammerman, soon joining the Harrison JCC, visited my office after giving opening prayer on

House floor." So, too, Rep. Joaquin Castro (D-TX) with family pictures on twitter January 19, 2018: "This morning, I had the pleasure of introducing Rabbi Mara Nathan to lead the opening prayer on the House Floor today. Rabbi Nathan serves at Temple Beth-El in my hometown of San Antonio. Thank you for your inspirational words this morning."

Rep. Jacky Rosen (D-NV) tweeted floor pictures on March 28, 2017: "Honored to sponsor today's guest chaplain. Rabbi @Sakselrad is a friend, mentor, & spiritual leader who has done so much for NV's community." Rep. Mike Quigley (D-IL) tweeted a picture on April 30, 2015: "Honored to have Rabbi Siegel of Anshe Emet Synagogue as my guest of 114th Congress. He gave beautiful opening prayer." Republican Rep. Robert Dold, also of Illinois, tweeted a YouTube on May 31, 2012, with this message: "This morning Rabbi Aaron Melman of Congregation Beth Shalom in Northbrook delivered the opening prayer for the US House." Rep. Bill Pascrell (D-NJ) tweeted his own YouTube on May 29, 2014: "It was a pleasure to welcome my friend Rabbi Stephen Roth to offer the opening prayer before the House."

And a congressman who sponsored a rabbi from a different state used Twitter to spread the word to his constituents.[70] A June 21, 2017, tweet with pictures from Minnesota Rep. Tom Emmer (R) about a Maryland rabbi: "Today, I recognized my friend Rabbi Hershel Lutch for his incredible work for the Jewish ppl and ppl of all faiths."

Twitter's limit on 280 characters to communicate connects us directly to a legendary Reform rabbi from over a century ago. The connection comes via Rabbi Gary Zola, Senate guest chaplain on May 26, 2005. Zola said, "Let us draw devotional inspiration this morning from the life of Rabbi Isaac Mayer Wise, founder of the Hebrew Union College, who led this Senate in prayer 135 years ago to this very week." A March 31, 1919, *New York Times* story on the 100th anniversary of Wise's birth remembered that prayer as well. It noted Wise "opened the Senate and House of Representatives with prayer, and was complemented by the Chaplain of the Senate, Dr. Newman, for its brevity. Dr. Wise promptly replied: 'One of our sages explained all there is in religion while standing on one foot; why should not I be able to be brief while standing on both?'"

---

70 How unlikely is it for a Senator or Representative to sponsor a rabbi from someplace else? Of the 298 sponsorships which can be identified, 21 (7%) are of a rabbi from a state the member does not represent.

Wise was referring to Babylonian-born Hillel the Elder: developer of the Mishnah, Talmud, and the Golden Rule. And perhaps intellectual forebearer to Twitter?

As the number of online word-of-mouth platforms has grown, so too has their value for spreading the words of rabbis in Congress. Now rabbi prayers routinely include a social media component. Posting guest rabbi prayers on new media platforms is a portion adding to a greater sum of religious education. Jonathan Sacks was a guest chaplain in Congress while serving as Britain's chief rabbi. In an October 31, 2017, feature marking the 500-year anniversary of the Protestant Reformation, the *Washington Post* asked him what he thought needs reforming in the practice of religion in America today. "The reformation the West now needs is to use our technology to spread a love of liberty and the nonnegotiable dignity of the individual, created in God's image," Sacks responded. "We can do this by using words, images and music to communicate a mood of spirituality through brief videos for YouTube and Facebook. We can use the new media to make the study of sacred texts globally accessible. We can use interactive platforms like Facebook Live to allow a potential two billion people to be in dialogue with religious leaders of all kinds. We must use the Web to communicate religion at its best and not as it has been used by ISIS to communicate religion at its most brutal and barbarous."

Sacks' November 2, 2011, Senate prayer is on YouTube. It's on his own channel called "The Chief Rabbi."

Gustav Gottheil was the ninth rabbi guest chaplain—January 16, 1884, in the Senate. The *New York Times* reported on November 21, 1898, a speech he gave marking his 25 years with Temple Emanu-El.[71] Headline: "Dr. Gottheil Says Newspapers Are a Help to Religion." Gottheil: "The press deserves the greatest praise and although reporters now and then play us disagreeable tricks, and credit us with saying things we never thought of, their energies and nevertheless at the disposal of the humblest pulpit." The media "scatter their information from shore to shore," Gottheil said. It "came back from the Far West, where it seemed to create some sensation. This, I think has been the best stimulus to keep the American pulpit happy. It is good for the teacher to know that he is not speaking to the chosen few." These days, the teaching concept is similar even if the underlying media platforms have

---

71 America's largest synagogue, Temple Emanu-El recognizes in its online history "bold departures" in the early days "from Orthodox religious practice . . . the congregation replaced Hebrew with German during service, and eventually English."

evolved. Now, a guest chaplain may offer a prayer in a chamber of Congress in which only a chosen few are present, let alone paying attention. But the video—whether via YouTube or the C-SPAN archives—can be seen by a congregation of thousands, anywhere and anytime.

Adding to Chaplain Black's thoughts on social media from the 2017 National Prayer Breakfast, consider what guest chaplain Rev. Alisa Lasater Wailoo, Capitol Hill United Methodist Church, said in the House on August 29, 2017. She prayed that Jesus "will awaken us to the storms of our own making . . . the floods from the endless news cycle and social media, causing us to miss Your still, small, sacred voice."

Which returns us to National Prayer Breakfast, the one in February 2016. House Speaker Paul Ryan included social media in his remarks. "I have noticed a growing impatience though with prayer in our culture these days," Ryan said. "You see it in the papers, or you see it on Twitter. When people say, 'We are praying for someone or something,' the attitude in some quarters these days, is 'Don't just pray, do something about it.' The thing is, when you are praying, you are doing something about it."

Conclusion

"You make an acquaintance with a book as you do with a person. . . When you have a good book, you really have something of importance."

—Former Israeli head of state Shimon Peres on C-SPAN,
July 4, 1996

"Of making books there is no end." That's how the last chapter ends for a Hebrew Bible book associated with wisdom, Ecclesiastes (12:12).

Abraham Lincoln invoked Ecclesiastes when he delivered his second annual message to Congress on December 1, 1862: "One generation passeth away and another generation cometh, but the earth abideth forever."

Books, generations—and prayers to Congress. They come and go. What legacy do they leave behind?

One broad education benefit of rabbi prayers in Congress: they expose a predominantly non-Jewish audience to Judaism. We've examined what rabbis are saying. But what are Christians thinking when they listen?

Some legislators come to the Senate and House chambers already well-versed in the Jewish tradition. On April 17, 1934, the Senate considered a bill concerning Members of Congress acting as attorneys in matters where the United States has an interest. Sen. Huey Long (D-LA) borrowed from the Hebrew Bible. He also went tabloid. He quoted "a few lines I thought I had forgotten about King Solomon and King David. King Solomon, I believe, had five or six hundred wives, and King David had two or three hundred, and the poem ran something like this:

King David and King Solomon led merry, merry lives,
With many, many concubines, and many, many wives.

But when old age o'ertook them, with its many, many qualms,
King Solomon wrote the Proverbs, and King David wrote the Psalms."

Laughter in the Senate for those catchy rhymes.

Long again cited Solomon the next month during Depression-era floor debate over financial and New Deal programs. On May 4, 1934, he added straight-forward remarks—no sensationalism this time—about the builder of the First Temple in Jerusalem:

> I was about to read from Proverbs, from the words of Solomon, supposed to have been the wisest man who ever lived; and I believe he was. I believe Solomon was the wisest man who ever lived. It is practically the universal opinion of all Christian countries that the wisest man was Solomon. In looking over the situation, with all the wisdom and experience the Creator had given him, he said this: Two things have I required of thee; deny me them not before I die: Remove far from me vanity and lies; give me neither poverty nor riches; feed me with food convenient for me: Lest I be full, and deny thee, and say, Who Is the Lord? or lest I be poor, and steal, and take the name of my God in vain. (Proverbs 30:7–10)

Long also gave a radio address in May 1935 about wealth in America that quoted from Leviticus and Micah.

But other legislators weren't as impressed with Jews.

Consider Rep. John Rankin. The Democrat represented Mississippi's first congressional district from 1921-1953, overlapping for a bit with Huey Long from the neighboring state. During those 32 years Rankin offered these thoughts on the floor of Congress about Jews:

- "If there are any Members of this House who are not familiar with the horrible story of the Katyn Massacre, I trust they will read the article appearing in this month's American Legion Magazine. It will help you to understand the difference between Yiddish communism, and Christian civilization" (1952).

- "This international Sanhedrin up here in New York, the United Nations. . . . The mothers and fathers and the servicemen of this Nation who just fought two wars in the last 30 years do not want that outfit dragging us into a race war in Palestine. I am speaking now for the real Americans . . . we are not going to let this Zionist group, this branch of the Communist movement, drag us into another world war" (1948).

- "Our Yiddish Solicitor General has taken it upon himself to go into the Supreme Court and misrepresent the American people" (1953).
- "Every member of the Politburo around Stalin is either Yiddish or married to one, and that includes Stalin himself" (1953).

Rankin noted "Faker Einstein's joining the Communists in their attacks on America" (1950). He did not care much for Jewish newspaper columnist Walter Winchell, either. Rankin called Winchell "little kike" (1944) and "little slimemongering kike" (1946).

And what to make of the Anti-Defamation League? "Smear bund" and "slimemongers" Rankin called the Jewish hate-fighting organization, with no apparent sense of irony or self-awareness. The ADL's "attacks" on General George Patton during World War II, he said in 1946, "cost the lives of from 10,000 to 60,000 of the finest American soldiers who ever lived."

Delightful. In fact, after Patton was injured in a December 8, 1945, car accident that led to his death shortly before Christmas, Joseph Wilner of the Anti-Defamation League sent him this letter: "In common with all Americans shocked and grieved by your misfortune. Our congregation Adas Israel is offering prayers for your early recovery."

Twenty-six rabbis gave prayers in the House while Rankin was serving there. Apparently the lessons didn't take. If Rankin was worried about being "in bad standing with that bunch of communistic kikes" (1944) he didn't show it.

A fellow Mississippian, Sen. Theodore Bilbo (D), was quite a piece of work, too. A member of the Ku Klux Klan, Bilbo told the Senate on June 27, 1945: "There are 19 States in America which do not prohibit the marriage of Negroes and whites. The District of Columbia is also in that category. Anyone who has no more regard for the integrity of the white race than to encourage, permit, or insist upon intermarriage of the races ought to be liquidated, deported, or put out of business in some way." That day Bilbo also read into the *Congressional Record* "a postcard from an old friend of mine" in Atlanta: "I continuously travel the United States and give my word from close examination that the birds behind all this social race equality stuff are Jews—from that rat Winchell to the most illiterate second-hand man. . . . The sly Jew ingratiates himself with the fool Christian minister."

Bilbo added his own thoughts: "The Negroes, and the Jews in New York, as well as others who are working with them hand in hand—those are the minorities which the politicians fear—are the ones who have been back of this vicious legislation. Therefore, we find the editor of the Washington Post [Eugene Meyer], a Jew, fighting against me, accusing me, and denouncing me and any other man who dares to disagree with him." But Bilbo did allow some wiggle room: "Moses was a Jew, Paul was a Jew, and Peter was a Jew also. They were all Jews. Do not intimate that I am trying to denounce the Jews. Some of the best friends I have in the world are of the Jewish faith."

Obviously, Rankin and Bilbo are outliers. You can never be sure what's in the heart of a member of the House or Senate, but you can read their words in the *Congressional Record* and hear them speak on C-SPAN. Or, these days, follow them on Twitter.

If there was any solace for Jewish-Americans to take about having an anti-Semite serving in Congress, it's that the lawmaker was an equal opportunity offender. Odious remarks about African-Americans during the fledgling civil rights movements, and Japanese-Americans in the immediate aftermath of internment camps, fill Rankin's congressional floor statements.

The Rankin story turned into tragedy. On June 4, 1941, Rankin was complaining in the House that "a little group of our international Jewish brethren are still attempting to harass" America into a war in Europe. Polish-born Rep. Michael Edelstein (D-NY) rose and angrily responded: "Hitler started out by speaking about 'Jewish brethren.' It is becoming the play and the work of those people who want to demagogue to speak about 'Jewish brethren' and 'international bankers.'"

It would be Edelstein's last floor speech. He was dead in five minutes. According to a *New York Times* account, after those remarks Edelstein went into the House lobby. He collapsed from a heart attack. Rep. Samuel Dickstein (D-NY) told the House, "You have seen a Member begin the long journey right on the floor of the House during a debate in which a man sought to protect his people, his integrity, and his Americanism. He died a martyr to a cause. Very few incidents such as we have just seen have occurred. He was a living dynamo a few minutes ago. He is nothing now."

Shortly before that devastating denouement, the day's House session began with a prayer. From a guest chaplain. Methodist Rev. Jacob Payton said, "Deliver us from the sins that beset the soul-the folly of pride and the blindness of bigotry."

Blindness of bigotry. Apparently, Rankin didn't heed Christian prayers, either.

If anything, one can hope that the rabbis who have prayed in Congress show more than a higher level of Jewish achievement in American democracy. They can teach us how to battle ignorance, if not outright hatred, of Judaism. The arsenal? Education.

Addressing the B'nai B'rith convention at the Willard Hotel on May 6, 1935, House Speaker Joseph Byrns (D-TN) said, "Religious prejudice is the worst enemy of democracy because it is always founded on ignorance, which begets suspicion."

A hopeful tone was set in the earliest days when the Senate's seventh rabbi guest chaplain was identified by his academic credentials. Jacob Voorsanger "of San Francisco, Cal., professor of Semitic languages and literature, University of California," reads the June 30, 1898, *Congressional Record*.

Joshua Haberman of Washington Hebrew Congregation, who was guest chaplain seven times from 1970-1997, believed that education—adult Jewish education—is an important way to cope with anti-Semitism. Asked in an interview with the *Washington Jewish Week* what remained with him from growing up in Austria, Haberman said, "The viciousness of anti-Semitism. I was constantly exposed" (December 9, 2015).

The same World War II decade that gave us Rankin also gave us Baeck. Leo Baeck, as we have seen, is important for telling the story of rabbis praying in Congress. A Holocaust survivor, he was the first rabbi guest chaplain to mention Israel in a prayer. When he was released from the Theresienstadt concentration camp near the the end of World War II, he restrained his fellow inmates and victims from violent retribution against their captors. Baeck reportedly told them: "Do not vent your hate, for hatred will not destroy our enemies - it will destroy us first."

(You might recognize a similar sentiment expressed by President Nixon when he told White House staff in his 1974 farewell: "Always remember, others may hate you, but those who hate you don't win unless you hate them, and then you destroy yourself." A rabbinical inspiration, perhaps?)

Among the unlikeliest of legislative bodies you'd hear a Jewish prayer: the German Bundestag. But that's where Shimon Peres recited— in Hebrew—the *Kaddish*, the prayer for mourning the dead. "In memory of, and in honor of, the six million Jews who turned to ashes," Peres told the parliament members on January 27, 2010, International Holocaust Remembrance Day. "My request of you is: Please do everything to bring them to justice. This is not revenge in our eyes. This is an educational lesson. This is an hour of grace for the young generation."

Some members of Congress have considered the opening prayers to be educational opportunities for young Americans. "A grandmother told me the other day, 'Why don't you people just broadcast to every school in America . . . the prayer at the beginning of the House of Representatives on Wednesdays and Thursdays . . . and on Friday, a special day, the prayer at the beginning of the U.S. Senate,'" Rep. Bob Dornan (R-CA), told the House on June 8, 1995. "I would love to see pumped to every school in America rabbis as we have seen here coming invoking the God of Abraham and the code of ethics of Moses."

On May 26, 1941, Rep. Carl Curtis (R-NE) introduced a bill to put the *Congressional Record* in every high school in the country. Among the 25 uses he suggested was this: "Classes in literature might collect and compile the prayers of the Chaplain of the House and of the Senate for their literary value." He ranked that one second.

Also note he emphasized literary value. The ultimate purpose of the American tradition of opening legislative sessions with a prayer is not to advance or proselytize a particular faith or religion. Rather, it is to provide rhetorical means to reflect nonsectarian virtues and values that religion inspires. Benjamin Rush, who signed the Declaration of Independence, suggested that "the only foundation for a useful education in a republic is to be laid in Religion. Without this there can be no virtue, and without virtue there can be no liberty, and liberty is the object and life of all republican governments." Likewise, original chief justice of the U.S. Supreme Court John Jay declared "It is the duty of all wise, free and virtuous governments to countenance and encourage virtue and religion."

Watch Congress on a regular basis and you might sense that members' rhetoric—whether soaring or divisive—is fleeting. A short shelf-life. Much of what Representatives and Senators say is in-the-moment reflection on news of the day. Prayers, however, are in it for the long haul. They're evergreen. No expiration date for these core clergy messages. That rabbi prayers are regularly represented in this legislative experience is a Jewish contribution to American democracy worth learning and appreciating—their ultimate significance.

We began this book with Sen. Robert Byrd's (D-WV) thoughts on congressional prayer. Let's close with him. On March 30, 1988, after Moshe Feller gave one of his many Senate prayers, Byrd said, "I thank the Rabbi for the very timely words of his prayer here at this particular season when it seems that everywhere we look about us all is violence. Sometimes it appears that the world is upside down, so to speak, but prayer and meditation and reflection upon the great old teachings of the Scriptures can give us the strength, the resourcefulness, the courage and the vision to see our way. I thank the Rabbi. I yield the floor."

Which is a good place to yield this story as well. We await what messages the next batch of 613 rabbi prayers opening future sessions of Congress will bring. *L'dor v'dor*, the Hebrew phrase goes, *from generation to generation*. We will be listening. A cornerstone of Judaism is looking to the future. As the bush burned but wasn't consumed, Moses asked God for his name. The response: "I will be what I will be."

On Rosh Hashanah in 2016, my rabbi—Amy Schwartzman of Temple Rodef Shalom, home to 1988 House guest chaplain Laszlo Berkowits—gave a sermon about speech. "Words are so powerful," she said. "In Judaism, speech is a vehicle for holiness. . . . Talking can be a spiritual process." Rabbi Jonathan Sacks, a Senate guest chaplain, received the Irving Kristol Award on October 24, 2017. "At the Burning Bush," Sacks told the American Enterprise Institute, "Moses, the first rabbi of all time, said, 'I am not a man of words,' and then proceeded to speak for the next 40 years.'"

Which does give us hope that maybe, contrary to what Ecclesiastes 1:9 instructs, there *can* be something new under the sun.

Index Of Names

Index of names mentioned in this book.

The 347 bolded names are rabbis who delivered prayers in Congress.

Letter "n" after page numbers refers to the footnote on that page.

"Religion has been a source of unity and strength in America. Our Founders were deeply connected to their faith—from day one. It is fitting that in the first session of the US Senate (in 1789), picking a chaplain to deliver an opening prayer was the first item of business.

Jewish American clergy would not have the honor of delivering an opening prayer in the Senate for another 80 years—in 1870. Now, thanks to Howard Mortman (C-SPAN wasn't around to record sessions of Congress in those early days), we have a comprehensive and fascinating history of the participation of American Rabbis in this important tradition of opening prayers in both chambers of Congress. Howard Mortman tells us not only about the content of the prayers, but also the many remarkable stories behind the men and women who delivered them.

In studying the prayers of Jews who opened our Legislative Branch of Government, we gain valuable insights into the great events, hopes, fears and dreams of a great people in a great country."

— Senator Joseph Lieberman

"This is a fascinating peek at the religious undercurrent of America's history. Combining G-d talk with politics, both topics to be avoided in polite company, Howard Mortman's perusal of the historical presence of the Chaplain's prayer in the Halls of Congress is good fodder for interesting conversations among friends. Most readers will be surprised to learn so much about untold congressional history and internal dynamic."

— Rev. Pat Conroy, S.J., Chaplain,
U.S. House of Representatives

"A masterful work of both scholarship and hope, *When Rabbis Bless Congress* is a must-read for those who study the role of Jews in American civic life and for anyone seeking a deeper understanding of how faith shapes this country. Howard Mortman has given us a meticulously researched and fascinating account of Jewish prayer in one America's most cherished of institutions, the United States Congress."

— Ronald S. Lauder, President, World Jewish Congress

"From the dawn of the Civil War, when the first rabbi delivered a prayer in Congress, until the U.S. Capitol was locked down by a pandemic in 2020, 441 Jewish religious leaders led Congress in prayer. Howard Mortman can tell you how many came from other countries (27); how many were women (14); and how many of the female rabbis wore yarmulkes (half). Moreover, in lyrical prose, with understated humor, and a welcoming teaching style the author explains why it all matters. You don't have to be Jewish to love this gem of a book—or be a C-SPAN junkie. You only have to be interested in the American story. And *When Rabbis Bless Congress* will make you care about it even more."

— Carl M. Cannon, political historian and
Washington Bureau Chief,
RealClearPolitics

"Howard Mortman's masterful work introduces us to the rabbis—and I'm honored to be one of them—who have been honored with the invitation to speak truth to power (Truth with a capital "T") through a prayer in the Capitol, to open a session of Congress. More precisely, these rabbis *speak prayer to power*, offering brief moments of hope, reflection, inspiration, and perspective. They join clergy representing the diverse faith groups of our nation to challenge our leaders to remember that while party tactics might differ, the goal of Congress should be based on shared dreams: a better, stronger, safer, more hopeful, more united America—a more perfect union. Their words are reminders that despite all challenges, 'America has a prayer.'"

— Rabbi Arnold E. Resnicoff, U.S. Navy Chaplain (Retired)

"Perusing the painstaking and thoroughly researched work of Howard Mortman, one gets a sense of history and within it the good fortune of the Jewish people. When walking the halls of the US Capitol complex, any American can explore that which came before us and, with G-d's help, made possible what we have today. And they will better understand how carrying that legacy and protecting it is a vast process which is not easy. Those at the helm of national leadership know they need more than their own power to get the work done.

And so religious leaders are invited to help guide their purpose who, while perhaps not necessarily agreeing on religious matters, do all agree that we are fortunate to have this special opportunity. Within that context, of course, have been Jewish leaders who have brought words of Torah and age-old Jewish tradition to the august Chambers of Congress. I was privileged to be one of them, and the feeling of offering my prayer in such a place was truly special. I always wished that could be shared with the larger public, aside from the Congressional Record. Howard Mortman's excellent work makes that possible."

— Rabbi Levi Shemtov, Executive Vice President of American Friends of Lubavitch (Chabad) and Founder of the Capitol Jewish Forum

"If you jump to the conclusion that a book chronicling the history of Jewish invocational prayers in the U.S. Congress would be of little interest to the general public, you are greatly mistaken. Howard Mortman's extensively researched volume is jam-packed with astonishing facts and enthralling stories. His book is likely to become the final word on this subject. Once you begin to read Mortman's captivating story of Jewish prayers on Capitol Hill you will not want to put it down."

— Dr. Gary P. Zola, Executive Director of The Jacob Rader Marcus Center of the American Jewish Archives and The Edward M. Ackerman Family Distinguished Professor of the American Jewish Experience at Hebrew Union College, Cincinnati

"Howard Mortman's book is a true American treasure. Fascinating from beginning to end, it reminds us of two critical tenets of our unique country. First, our religious roots dig deep into the Jewish faith and traditions. Second, the prayers that have been delivered before the House and Senate are a reaffirmation that our country believes in a higher power to whom we can turn and to whom we must answer for our actions. It is a must read for anyone interested in the rich religious fabric of our nation."

— Honorable James P. Moore, Jr., Founder and CEO of the Washington Institute for Business, Government and Society and author of *One Nation Under God: The History of Prayer in America*

"Prayers at the commencement of each day's proceedings in the two chambers of the United States Congress are an enduring, but not uncontested, tradition in American political culture. In *When Rabbis Bless Congress*, Howard Mortman chronicles the prayers delivered by Jews in the U.S. House of Representatives and Senate and profiles the rabbis who gave them. This encyclopedic examination of a previously untold story in American history, yields keen insights into American public religion, Jews in America, and the delicate and sometimes controversial interplay between religion and civil government in the nation's history. Brimming with details about prayer and the chaplaincy on Capitol Hill and engaging anecdotes about congressional traditions and personalities, this book adds an informative chapter to the history of Congress and religion in American civic life."

— Daniel L. Dreisbach, professor of legal studies, American University, and author of *Reading the Bible with the Founding Fathers*

"Reading *When Rabbis Bless Congress* has made me feel connected to other rabbis around the country across lines of denomination, geography, and theology. Howard Mortman situates the reader within history, scripture, and politics, and does so in a conversational voice that makes you feel like you know him. For the student of prayer, this is a book that will expose you to such a variety of it, with incredible context. For the student of politics and history, this is a book that will walk you through our country's story through the lens of both spirituality and Jewish diversity. Open up this book to satiate your curiosity around this odd juxtaposition of rabbinic blessing and congressional tradition— close it with a deeper understanding of our nation's Jewish history and thought."

— Rabbi Hannah Spiro, Hill Havurah